Excavating the Afterlife

Excavating the Afterlife

THE ARCHAEOLOGY OF EARLY CHINESE RELIGION

Guolong Lai

UNIVERSITY OF WASHINGTON PRESS

Seattle and London

ART HISTORY
PUBLICATION INITIATIVE

This book is made possible by a collaborative grant from the
Andrew W. Mellon Foundation.

Support for this book also was provided by a grant from
the University of Florida through its College of the Arts
Scholarship Enhancement Award Fund.

University of Washington Press
www.washington.edu/uwpress

Cataloging-in-Publication Data is on file with the Library of Congress

ISBN 978-0-295-99449-9

The paper used in this publication is acid-free and meets the minimum
requirements of American National Standard for Information Sciences—
Permanence of Paper for Printed Library Materials, ANSI Z39.48–1984.∞

To my mentors,
Li Ling and Lothar von Falkenhausen,
in gratitude and friendship.

Contents

Acknowledgments

THE SCHOLAR OF MESOPOTAMIA, Leo Oppenheim, famously claimed that a systematic presentation of Mesopotamian religion could not and should not be written. After this disclaimer, however, Oppenheim, and many scholars following him, continued to write about the religious history of that dead civilization. This impossibility is not unique to Mesopotamia. The picture of early Chinese religion that I attempt to present in this book, based on fragmentary archaeological and biased textual evidence, is admittedly an incomplete one. Faced with these enormous but fragmented sources of data, we could just throw up our hands and admit defeat. Nevertheless, along with many scholars before me, I have taken a different approach. I have instead attempted to piece together a picture of early Chinese religious beliefs and practices using the interdisciplinary training I received over the last two decades in art history, archaeology, paleography, phonology, textual criticism, and religious studies. For this training, I would like to express my deepest gratitude to my teachers: the late He Linyi, Gao Ming, the late Wang Wenjin, Li Ling, and Lothar von Falkenhausen. Without their guidance and assistance along the way, this book would not be possible.

This book has benefited over the past ten years from the feedback of many of my friends and colleagues. In particular, I am grateful to Lothar, Alain Thote, Yuri Pines, Thomas Lawton, Don Harper, Tony Barbieri-Low, Amy McNair, Bill Boltz, Bob Eno, Suzanne Cahill, Marianne Bujard, the late Donald McCollum, David Schaberg, Miao Zhe, Zhang Hanmo, Miranda Brown, Jeff Richey, Mario Poceski, Lori Wong, Michelle Wang, Cai Liang, Robin McNeal, and Deborah Del Gais, each of whom has read all or portions of this manuscript or its various incarnations. I also thank Jenny So, Ed Shaughnessy, Wu Hung, Mark Lewis, Marc Kalinowski, Haun Saussy, Benjamin Elman, Barbara Zeitler, Susan Downey, Hui-shu Lee, Gregory Schopen, Bill Baxter, Axel Schuessler, Robert Harrist, Chen Wei, Hsing I-tian, Shih Shou-chien, Hsieh Ming-liang, Chen Pao-chen, Wang Ming-ke, Chen Kwang-tzuu, Liu Shu-fen, and Tsai Che-mao, who listened to my presentations, answered my inquiries, or gave me suggestions and encouragement.

It is my pleasure to acknowledge the many institutions that assisted me in bringing this book to fruition. These include the Smithsonian Institution, through its Library Travel Grant in the Freer and Sackler Galleries of Art, in Washington, DC; Columbia University, through its Andrew W. Mellon Foundation postdoctoral fellowship at the Society of Fellows in the Humanities; Stanford University, through its postdoctoral fellowship at the Center for East Asian Studies; the University of Florida, through its College of Fine Arts Scholarship Enhancement Fund; and the Andrew W. Mellon Foundation, through its Art History Publication Initiative Fund.

I would like to thank the anonymous readers commissioned by the University of Washington Press for their critical input and positive feedback during the review process. I express my gratitude to my editors, Lorri Hagman, Jacqueline S. Volin, and Tim Zimmermann, at the University of Washington Press for their professional assistance. Lorri annotated a printout of the manuscript as she read it on her bus commute and gave me invaluable suggestions. I also thank Chris Crochetière of BW&A Books and my copy editor, Penelope Cray, for their fine job. I thank Zhang Changping, Zhang Chunlong, Jia Hanqing, Feng Shi, and Elinor Pearlstein for their assistance in obtaining permissions for the images reproduced in this book. Professor Qianshen Bai, fellow Chinese art historian and renowned calligrapher, kindly produced the calligraphic rendering of this book's subject on page xiv.

I offer my heartfelt appreciation to my friends and family, especially Miao Zhe, Hanmo, Sam Gilbert, Dou Lei, Yen Shih-hsuan, Yen Shou-chih, my sister Guowen, and my son Tony and my wife I-fen, for their moral support, encouragement, and understanding in the long and lonely process of writing a book.

The first long journey I took was across the Pacific Ocean, from Beijing to Los Angeles, almost two decades ago. That journey began one afternoon at Professor Li Ling's apartment in Jimenli, Beijing. We were chatting and the phone rang. Professor Li went to answer it. It was a long conversation. When he came back, he explained that his friend Lothar von Falkenhausen had just taken a teaching position at UCLA and would be accepting graduate students. Throughout the subsequent intellectual journeys, I have benefited from their erudition, kindness, and generosity. I dedicate this book to both of them.

Chronology of Early Chinese Dynasties

Late Neolithic period	ca. 5000–ca. 2000 BCE
Xia dynasty (legendary)	ca. 2000–ca. 1600 BCE
Shang dynasty	ca. 1600–ca. 1046 BCE
Western Zhou dynasty	ca. 1046–771 BCE
Eastern Zhou dynasty	
Spring and Autumn period	771–ca. 453 BCE
Warring States period	ca. 453–221 BCE
Qin dynasty	221–206 BCE
Han dynasty	
Western Han	206 BCE–9 CE
Xin dynasty	9–23 CE
Eastern Han	25–220 CE

Excavating the Afterlife

楚地宗教的考古學研究

Calligraphic rendering of this book's subject, "archaeological research on the religion of Chu," composed for the author by art historian and calligrapher Qianshen Bai.

Introduction

It is hardly revolutionary to suggest that, had the academic study of religions started quite literally on the ground, it would have been confronted with very different problems. . . . This Archaeology of Religions would have been primarily occupied with three broad subjects of study then: religious constructions and architectures, inscriptions, and art historical remains.

—GREGORY SCHOPEN

THIS BOOK EXPLORES changes in religious beliefs and ritual practices in early China by focusing on groups of well-preserved tombs excavated in southern China. Dating from the fifth to the first century BCE, these tombs are not only the place where the early Chinese buried their dead but also the space onto which they projected a range of imaginings, fears, and concerns that arose in connection with the life and death of their kin, friends, and foes, people known and unknown. As such, death is not the end of one's life but entering a new relationship with both the dead and the living. The tomb is a bridge, a way station on the journey to the afterlife, and a physical manifestation of established conceptions of the afterworld. Consequently, the tomb is both the physical space where religious ritual and sacrifice took place and the imagined space in which people's beliefs about the invisible spiritual world unfolded.

This book examines the dialectical relationship between sociopolitical change and mortuary religion from an archaeological perspective. It shows that new attitudes toward the dead, resulting from the social trauma of violent political struggle and warfare, changed the ways early Chinese dealt with their dead, promoted new methods of communicating with the dead and the gods, and engendered fresh conceptions of this world and the hereafter. Each chapter analyzes a different aspect of the burial practices of the Warring States (ca. 453–221 BCE),[1] Qin (221–206 BCE), and early Han (206 BCE–9 CE) periods in relation to the historical contexts of religious transformations in early China. The rich archaeological discoveries made in recent decades, which include both artifacts and texts, enable us to develop more satisfactory and more nuanced interpretations of early Chinese religion than were possible when scholars depended heavily on the classical written sources that have been transmitted over the past two thousand years.

To survey the ground we will cover and the materials we will encounter, let us begin with two examples of recent archaeological excavations in China.

AT THE END OF DECEMBER 2002, after three months of intensive excavation at the Jiuliandun site in Zaoyang City, Hubei, Chinese archaeologists reached the bottom of two underground tombs (fig. I.1). Resembling inverted pyramids, these tombs were typical of the elite burials in the state of Chu (?–223 BCE) during the Warring States period. The pit in Tomb 1 measures 38.1 meters long, 34.8 meters wide, and 12.8 meters deep at the mouth; the pit in Tomb 2, 34.7 meters long, 32 meters wide, and 11.6 meters deep.[2] The four slopes of each pit were cut into fourteen steps, focusing movement downward to the bottom of the tomb, where rectangular wooden encasements (*guo*), enclosing the lacquered inner coffins (*guan*) and assorted grave goods, were buried (fig. I.2). Leading to the bottom of the pit, an access ramp (more than thirty meters long) cut through the eastern side. To the west of the inverted pyramidal pits were two rectangular horse-and-chariot burials respectively containing thirty-three chariots and seventy-two horses and seven chariots and sixteen horses. Originally, a hemispheric clay mound covered the top of each pyramidal pit, but this domelike layer had eroded over the last 2,300 years, leaving only a small hill several meters in height at the time of the excavation.[3]

These mounds formed the first in a series of nine tumuli extending over three kilometers in a south-north direction. The local name of the site, Jiuliandun, meaning "nine linked mounds," derived from this topography. Four kilometers east of the Jiuliandun cemetery, archaeologists discovered an Eastern Zhou period (771–249 BCE) urban settlement of about 90,000 square meters.[4] Although further archaeological work is needed to establish the exact relationship between the settlement and the cemetery, it is likely that the elite from that community were buried at Jiuliandun, as was the case with most early Chinese cemeteries set into hillocks on the outskirts of cities.

Legend has it that buried beneath one of these nine tumuli was the gold head of a local lord surnamed Zhao, who, during his lifetime, had served as a loyal, honest, and upright advisor to the king of Chu.[5] It is told that the Chu king fell under the influence of corrupt and jealous ministers who slandered Lord Zhao. The king then captured, tortured, and beheaded him. Soon after the execution, the king discovered the truth of the matter. Full of regret, he ordered a lavish burial for Lord Zhao. However, since his rivals had already destroyed Lord Zhao's head, the king

Fig. I.1. Aerial view of the two Warring States Chu elite tombs (Tomb 1, the husband's, on the right; Tomb 2, the wife's, on the left) at Jiuliandun, Zaoyang City, Hubei. Hubei Provincial Institute of Cultural Relics and Archaeology.

Fig. I.2. Bottom of the burial pit of Tomb 2 at Jiuliandun, Zaoyang City, Hubei. Warring States period. Hubei Provincial Institute of Cultural Relics and Archaeology.

commissioned a substitute head to be made of gold and buried it with the corpse. To deceive tomb robbers, the king decreed that nine similar tumuli were to be constructed; this is said to be the origin of the nine linked mounds. After surveying the area, modern archaeologists concluded that the nine linked mounds constituted a cemetery for the Chu elite. In 1992, the Hubei provincial government designated this area a protected, provincial-level historic site.[6] In September 2002, in a rescue operation prior to construction work, the Chinese State Administration for Cultural Heritage approved the local government's request that these two tombs be excavated, to avoid damage during the construction of a highway in the area.

With narratives mingling myth with fact, fantasy with reality, archaeological discoveries have become media spectacles in contemporary China. The Jiuliandun excavation was nationally televised, especially the moments when the encasements and coffins were opened. Tomb 1 had been looted long before the excavation. A tomb robber's tunnel penetrated the wooden encasement vertically, but, fortunately, most of the grave goods were undisturbed (Plate 1). Tomb 2, however, remained intact. When the wooden covers were removed, a pond of clear water appeared, as is often the case in well-preserved, waterlogged southern tombs. Lacquered vessels with carbonized chestnuts and jujubes (some of the foods buried in tombs) floated in the

Fig. I.3. The waterlogged wooden encasement with four side compartments and a central one (where the coffin is located) in Tomb 2 at Jiuliandun, Zaoyang City, Hubei. Warring States period. Hubei Provincial Institute of Cultural Relics and Archaeology.

Fig. I.4. Lacquered wooden bird with deer antlers on top of tiger-shaped figure, excavated from Tomb 1 at Jiuliandun, Zaoyang City, Hubei (M1: W226). H. 109.6 cm, W. 47.6 cm. Warring States period. Hubei Provincial Institute of Cultural Relics and Archaeology.

water (Plate 2). In both tombs, the wooden encasement was divided into five compartments: a center compartment flanked by four side compartments (fig. I.3). The coffins were located in the center compartment, while the four side compartments contained not only bronze ritual vessels (Plate 3), musical instruments, lacquerware (Plate 4), and other quotidian utensils such as a bronze lamp (fig. I.5) but also religious and ritual objects such as the magic wooden figurine wearing a black wig and red cinnabar lipstick (Plate 5), the so-called tomb guardian figure, and the wooden sculpture of a bird with outstretched wings and deer antlers standing on top of a tiger (fig. I.4). Altogether, 4,067 sets of burial goods were recovered in Tomb 1 and 1,066 in Tomb 2.[7] Although the aforementioned gold head was not found, both coffins contained skeletal remains of the tomb occupants: a male of fifty to sixty years (Tomb 1) and a female of forty-five to fifty-five years (Tomb 2). Based on this and other data, archaeologists have suggested that the tumuli covered the joint burial of a husband and wife of the Chu aristocracy, datable to ca. 300 BCE.

The Jiuliandun tombs, with their domed mounds, deep vertical pits, and well-preserved and abundant grave goods, are representative of Chu elite burials. We await the publication of the official archaeological report for a full analysis of the Jiuliandun finds, but similar examples of elite tombs have been excavated in the last four decades. An estimated ten thousand Chu tombs have been scientifically exca-

Fig. I.5. Bronze lamp excavated from Tomb 1 at Jiuliandun, Zaoyang City, Hubei (M1: W286). H. 24.85 cm. Warring States period. Hubei Provincial Institute of Cultural Relics and Archaeology.

vated.[8] Among them are a great number of well-furnished Chu tombs in an unusually fine preservation condition for this period. These tombs were constructed and sealed using unusual methods as well as materials: a tightly constructed wooden encasement, made of huge logs of hard wood, buried deep and surrounded by a thick layer of black charcoal followed by several layers of refined viscous greenish-white clay (*baigaoni* or *qinggaoni*).[9] The clay layers functioned as a sealant and, after the disintegrating foodstuffs consumed the limited oxygen supply, created an oxygen-free, temperature-constant environment in which organic materials, such as wood, bamboo, silk,[10] and even human bodies, could be preserved. This is true in the cases of the ancient corpses from Tomb 1 at Guojiagang (the Warring States period) in Jingmen City, Hubei, Tomb 1 at Mawangdui (the second century BCE) in Changsha City, Hunan, and Tomb 168 at Fenghuangshan (the Western Han dynasty) in Jiangling County, Hubei (fig. I.6).[11]

In less than three hundred years, however, these vertical pit-style tombs were gradually supplanted by horizontal chamber-style burials. Popular first among the

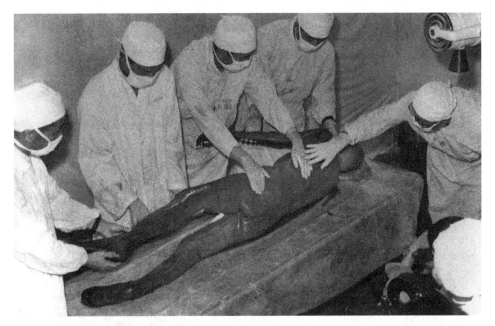

Fig. I.6. Doctors examining the well-preserved corpse excavated from Tomb 168 at Fenghuang-shan in Jiangling County, Hubei. Western Han dynasty.

kings and marquises of the late Warring States period and the early empires, the horizontal chamber-style tombs were soon used by the lower social strata as well. By the late Western Han dynasty, the horizontal chamber-style tomb had become the dominant burial structure in early China. In different geographic locations in China, these burials took different material forms. Accordingly, different terms are used in archaeological literature—including wooden chambered coffin tombs, earthen cave tombs, hollow brick tombs, cliff tombs, brick chamber-style tombs, stone chamber-style tombs, rock-cut cave tombs, mural tombs, and relief tombs—but in this book, I refer to them collectively as "horizontal chamber-style tombs."[12] While the tombs varied in their use of the local features and materials—wood, stone, and brick—available in different regions of China, they all shared the same architectural design of horizontality and accessibility; that is, one could walk into the horizontal burial chamber through an access passage.

The second example of archaeological excavation, a rock-cut tomb at Beidong-shan in Xuzhou City, Jiangsu, is among the earliest horizontal chamber-style tombs in early China. The tomb was discovered in 1954 when a local farmer, herding cattle, accidentally stepped into a tomb robber's tunnel that led to the elaborate, mazelike subterranean burial chambers (fig. I.7). Chinese archaeologists excavated this tomb in 1986, and the official excavation report was published in 2003.[13]

Cut out of the foothill, the tomb consisted of a long passage and a series of small niches and burial chambers arranged in an axial plan totaling 77.65 meters in length with an attached auxiliary section of eleven rooms on the east side (fig. I.8). The

Fig. I.7. Entrance to the rock-cut tomb at Beidongshan in Xuzhou City, Jiangsu, one of the earliest horizontal chamber-style tombs in early China.

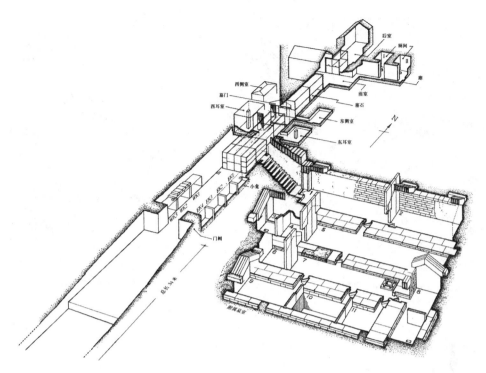

后室 顺间
II
西侧室 槽
墓门 前室
西耳室 塞石
东侧室 N
东耳室
小龛
门阙

Fig. I.8. Rock-cut tomb at Beidongshan in Xuzhou City, Jiangsu, probably belonged to the first king of the Chu kingdom, Liu Jiao (r. 201–179 BCE), of the Western Han dynasty.

stone walls and the ceilings of the burial chambers were plastered and then painted with an undercoat of brown lacquer and an overcoat of red cinnabar lacquer. As a security measure, three rows of huge stopping stones, ranging from seven to three tons, blocked the passageway to the coffin chambers and the two privy chambers in the rear section of the tomb. Small niches cut into the passageway walls featured painted clay figurines and other grave goods (fig. I.9). A staircase in the middle section of the passage leads down to the auxiliary section, about 2.98 meters lower than the main part of the tomb. Its eleven rooms, constructed of dressed stones, include an armory, a privy, a performance hall for music and dance, kitchens, a courtyard with a water well in the northeast corner, and storage areas for vessels, firewood, and ice (see fig. I.8).[14] This tomb probably belonged to the first king of the Chu kingdom of the Western Han dynasty, Liu Jiao (r. 201–179 BCE).[15] During the Western Han period, there was a local kingdom also named Chu, which was mainly centered on its capital, Pengcheng, present-day Xuzhou City, Jiangsu, in the eastern part of the former Warring States Chu territory. Since 1972, sixteen such subterranean rock-cut princely tombs have been discovered or excavated, all located in the mountains near the modern city of Xuzhou. Along with the local kingdom of Changsha, the Chu kingdom represented the Han image of southern Chu culture.[16]

To date, more than twenty thousand Han tombs have been excavated.[17] Horizon-

Fig. I.9. Painted clay figurines in one of the niches on the long passageway in Beidongshan in Xuzhou City, Jiangsu. Western Han dynasty.

tally laid out, the Han tombs were in general more spacious and accessible than the vertical pit-style tombs. Han tomb construction featured new physical as well as religious and magical mechanisms, such as spirit seats, a formalized sacrificial space, tomb guardian figures, and charms, curses, stopping stones for securing and protecting the tomb.[18] The burial contents of horizontal Han tombs, however, were not as well preserved as those of the Chu tombs of the Warring States period. Still, over the last forty years, Chinese archaeologists have recovered a large quantity of grave goods from Han tombs, such as bronze vessels, jade ornaments, wooden sculptures, ceramic figurines, and lacquerware. Some are similar to those recovered from the Chu tombs; some are very different. These burial objects make up the majority of what we now call "early Chinese art," which is exhibited in museums all over the world.

The ancient Chu and Han tombs were in a way the "storage space" of modern museums before archaeologists excavated and brought these art objects into the museum collections. A curious modern museumgoer might wonder: Why were these art objects buried in tombs? Who made them and for what purposes? What can they tell us about the dead, who were provided with all of these objects, and about the bereaved, who provided them? How should we explain these archaeological data? Why did burial practices change over time? What do these changes tell us about the people and the periods in which they lived? These questions are particularly important because most surviving art objects from early China, as with other early civilizations, come from graves, which are the sites of multifaceted religious activities. This book seeks to define the nature of these religious activities and provide a synthetic account of the changing religious beliefs and ritual practices beginning with the Warring States period and extending through to the Qin and Han periods.

A WATERSHED IN CHINESE HISTORY, the Warring States period was a time of political transformation. The old feudal structure of the Shang (ca. 1600–ca. 1046 BCE) and Western Zhou (ca. 1046–771 BCE) dynasties was giving way to the unified bureaucratic empires of the Qin and Han. As the name suggests, this was a time of unprecedented social upheaval and political chaos.[19] The ultimate contest for unification was fought between the states of Qin (ca. 800–221 BCE) and Chu, which originally were two peripheral states, considered in traditional Chinese historiography to be "uncivilized" and outside the "Chinese" (*huaxia*) cultural sphere. In reality, however, long before the Qin unification of China in 221 BCE, both Qin and Chu had already adopted many Chinese (that is, Zhou) social, political, and religious institutions, respectively unified the northwest and the south, and become multiethnic quasiempires.[20]

Religion, even mortuary religion—the religious beliefs and ritual practices associated with death and the dead—played an important role in the creation of these empires. The political changes began during the Spring and Autumn period (771–ca. 453 BCE), the heyday of aristocratic rule, when the heads of the major noble lineages throughout the Chinese world firmly appropriated power in all of its forms: economic, political, social, and religious. Intra- and interlineage struggles were dominant themes in the *Zuo Commentary* (Zuozhuan) and the *Narratives of the States* (Guoyu), two major historical sources for this period.[21] During the three turbulent centuries before the Qin unification, a few powerful states increasingly dominated the political stage. Consequently, smaller polities and weaker states had to rely on shrewd diplomacy to survive the military conflicts that characterized this era, a time in which, as Confucius (ca. 551–ca. 479 BCE) claimed, "the rites were in disarray, and music had collapsed." To strengthen their military, economic, and moral power, various states launched political and social reforms, established specialized industries, and made innovations in arts and crafts. By the fourth century BCE, aristocratic lineages in most states had declined, although those in Chu were arguably stronger than those in the other states.[22] Another extreme case of social restructuring was the western state of Qin, which abolished its hereditary aristocracy, restructured its society, ranked the entire populace according to a merit-based hierarchy of twenty ranks,[23] and established the rule of law with draconian punishments. The early empires of Qin and Han followed almost all of these practices.[24]

Accompanying the decline of the old aristocracy was the rise of the educated gentleman, knight, or scholar-official (*shi*) class that had once occupied the bottom rung of the ranked aristocracy but had now risen to become ministers, officials, political and military advisors, ritual specialists, and intellectuals.[25] At the same time, the commoner class—peasants, artisans, merchants, and conscripted soldiers—entered political life. Although local cultural differences remained, interstate communication—in the form of military conflicts or peaceful trade and political alliances—contributed to the emergence of common cultural traditions.[26] Drawing upon the institutional legacy of the Spring and Autumn period, this transitional Warring States period produced long-lasting social, political, military, economic, cultural, and religious traditions "without which no idea of a unified empire could have been implemented."[27]

In the realm of religious art, several notable and enduring innovations transpired: (1) new burial practices associated with the horizontal chamber-style tombs within which rituals associated with the cult of the dead took place; (2) new funerary customs, such as the pervasive use of spirit artifacts (*mingqi*) to mark the severance of ties between the dead and the living; (3) wider use of anthropomorphic and hybrid images and written texts to communicate with the spirit world; (4) formation of the underworld bureaucracy; and (5) newly evolved conceptions of cosmology, empire, and the afterlife, the last being defined as a journey to a cosmic destination.

FOLLOWING NEW TRENDS in the archaeology of religions,[28] the chapters herein make use of a combination of archaeological, paleographical, and art historical evidence. Earlier discussions of early Chinese religion often built their theoretical frameworks entirely on transmitted texts or simply took scattered bits and pieces of archaeological materials and inserted them into such frameworks. These transmitted texts, written by "small, literate, almost exclusively male and certainly atypical professionalized subgroups,"[29] had been selected, transmitted, and emended by different hands according to various agendas over the centuries. The French sinologists Marcel Granet (1884–1940) and Henri Maspero (1882–1945), for example, constructed a framework that viewed early Chinese religion in terms of social class and distinguished between the "peasant religion" of rural villagers and the "feudal religion" of urban nobles. Granet posited an imperial or "official religion" that grew out of the "Confucian religion" of the educated class of Warring States society and was later adopted by the empires.[30] Maspero also noted the close relationship between the rise of "the great writers and philosophers" and the establishment of the empires.[31] Granet and Maspero did not live to see the great archaeological discoveries in the second half of the twentieth century that challenged their theories, but much scholarship after them has continued their preoccupation with transmitted texts. These texts are often philosophical and political in content. They are seldom religious. In fact, before the great archaeological discoveries of the 1970s, our information about early Chinese mortuary religion in traditional sources consisted largely of piecemeal quotations and scattered references, the religious nature of which was often glossed over by layers of later commentary and rationalistic interpretation.

The nature of early Chinese religion before the rise of religious Daoism and the introduction of Buddhism during the Eastern Han dynasty (25–220 CE) is not clearly articulated in transmitted texts.[32] Although we know that religion played a vital role in forging large coalitions of states, in settling lineage vendettas, and in structuring the social and political order,[33] and although we understand that writing played an important role in early Chinese religious and ritual activities, very few specifically religious records have been preserved.

As Donald Harper has pointed out, the field of early Chinese religion was dominated by scholars trained and engaged in the study of the philosophical traditions,[34] the result being that this topic was often reduced to the discussion of Confucianism, so-called philosophical Daoism, and other philosophies.[35] In this scholarly tradition, the religious dimensions of the Warring States transition were largely overlooked. In their efforts to distill a worldview from a few selected passages, some scholars made much of anecdotal accounts in the *Analects* (Lunyu) that suggest Confucius eschewed any interest in the spiritual realm or "strange things."[36] This text-centered approach began with seventeenth- and eighteenth-century European missionaries, who saw Confucians as rationalists skeptical of the existence of supernatural religious beings, and lasted until the late 1960s and early 1970s, when newly discovered archaeological materials, such as the silk banner painting from Mawangdui, finally drew scholars' attention to the mortuary religion of ancient China.[37]

Consequently, the Warring States transition was treated as one of many stages in the linear development from a superstitious and rigid "dark age"—as exemplified by the "irrational" divination customs and shamanism of the Shang and Zhou dynasties—to the Weberian rational, humanistic, realistic, secular world of the early empires. This textual approach, together with the Western paradigm of philosophical development adopted by influential scholars including Hu Shi (1891–1962), Guo Moruo (1892–1978), Feng Youlan (1895–1990), Herrlee G. Creel (1905–94), and Frederick W. Mote (1922–2005),[38] downplayed the religious elements in early Chinese culture and perpetuated a centuries-old elite prejudice against popular religion.[39] Although some scholars later changed their positions, this general trend endures today.[40] The grand narrative of "humanistic enlightenment" in the Warring States transition is not limited to philosophy and religious studies; similar arguments also persist in the related fields of archaeology, history, literature, and art history.

In addition, Marxist analysis, especially in mainland China, has contributed to an inadequate understanding of the role of religion in the social transformations that took place during the Warring States period. The eminent Chinese historian Yang Kuan's (1914–2005) *History of the Warring States* (Zhanguo shi) paints a lively picture of agricultural, economic, social, political, and intellectual changes during the Warring States period[41] while adhering strictly to the Marxist framework of social structure and historical development. Yang proceeds systematically from economic foundations to political superstructure to cultural epiphenomena. Although his Marxist analyses are useful for relating social, political, and economic developments to religious transformation during the Warring States period, religion it-self has no place in his discussion. This approach prevails in many recent Chinese publications. A recently published book, for example, contains only a brief section on "religion, ritual costumes, and social life" that features minimal, eclectic, and unsystematic discussions.[42]

Recent developments in religious studies and cognitive archaeology in the West, however, advocate taking a new archaeological approach to religious traditions. Through the study of religious beliefs and ritual practices as manifested in ma-terial culture, this approach emphasizes the need to go beyond canonical and sa-cred texts.[43] Scholars of Christianity, Judaism, and Islam, in which scriptures and sacred texts dominated all else, were the first to use this approach, and more schol-ars have begun applying this new approach to other fields.[44] In theory, texts pro-vide only one, albeit important, mode of expression for religious beliefs and prac-tices, even in scripture-based traditions. Other nonlinguistic modes of reflection also serve as "symbolic vehicles for the full load of human experience."[45] Scholars have argued that the linear and logocentric structure of the literary text has failed to capture the wide range of human experience and distorted the historical pic-ture. The textualization of all symbolic actions has reduced cognitive processes to linguistic prescriptions and created layers of bias associated with the agency and materiality of writing. With the development of sociocultural anthropology in the West, including Lévi-Strauss's structural anthropology and the symbolic anthropol-ogy of the 1960s and 1970s, many scholars rejected cultural expression's dependence on language. For example, in many societies outside the Western cultural context, traditional crafts such as canoe building, pottery making, basket weaving, house construction, and musical performance were dominant forms of cultural and eco-nomic practice, creating meaning and becoming part of the cosmological processes thought to sustain the existence of the universe.[46]

Sympathetic to these theoretic perspectives, my approach is aligned most closely with that of Buddhologist Gregory Schopen, who criticizes the modern Western assumption that studying Indian Buddhism means to study its texts; he proposes instead that archaeological evidence should be granted priority. He prefers the "ar-chaeology of religion" to the text-based "history of religion." Considering words and deeds as different modes of cultural expression possessing different values for the historical understanding of religions, Schopen suggests that religious structures, inscriptions, and artworks be considered the three main subjects of the archaeology of religion.[47] The bias of particular texts hinders the proper and full understand-ing of religion and its functions in society. Through his analysis of archaeological and epigraphic materials, Schopen has painted a picture of Indian monastic religion other than that prescribed in the Buddhist canon.[48] Scholars in other fields also dis-tinguish between religious doctrine and religion-as-cultural-and-material-system. The historian Patrick J. Geary draws on archaeological sources for the religious and cultural history of the European Middle Ages,[49] and the archaeologist William G.

Dever uses excavated materials as primary sources for his study of folk religion in ancient Israel.[50] Similarly, archaeologists and art historians advocate the use of material culture to study the changing worldview and religious rituals of early China.[51] From these models, it is clear that, in many fields, evidence for the study of religion is increasingly drawn from a broad and promising collection of archaeological sources.

Reading works of art or objects, however, is as challenging as reading texts, and perhaps more so. On the one hand, works of art serve as an independent source of cultural and religious meaning. In their spatial and iconographic contexts, artworks are neither "illustration nor evidence that validates a particular interpretation of a theological or cultural argument. Rather, works of art are in their own right a mode of human expression that generates theological interpretation and reflection, and that reveals its cultural and theological milieu."[52] On the other hand, mining works of art for cultural and religious meaning is risky. As Robert Bagley has warned, "the statement that objects are material manifestations of belief systems implausibly makes visual forms wholly dependent on beliefs without suggesting any mechanism for translating beliefs into visual form."[53] Besides the mechanical device of translation, two other devices are essential for the productive interpretation of works of art. The first is the intermediate cultural conceptions, which connect these works of art to a belief system. The second is the cultural context in which the works of art were created and used.[54] Drawing on the discussions of Jacques Maquet, who distinguishes objects as instruments from objects as signs,[55] I emphasize the importance of cultural context in interpreting the meaning and function of works of art. Maquet argues that the meanings of objects he calls instruments are obvious because their functions transcend culture. But the meanings of objects that Maquet calls signs are culturally determined and therefore more difficult to ascertain. The meaning of a sign is not inherent in the object itself but resides in the object's relationships as assigned by cultural consensus. Maquet further distinguishes five ways to read objects: "as instruments, as symbols, as images, as indictors, and as referents (they are ranked here from the less culture-specific interpretation to the one entirely dependent on a particular culture). In other words, written sources for historians and interviews for anthropologists become increasingly significant when we move from instruments to referents."[56] Here, texts, especially contemporaneous texts, are employed to investigate the cultural consensus about the meaning and function of a sign. In Bagley's terms, this is iconology with the benefit of texts.[57]

Consequently, texts and inscriptions must be utilized in the archaeology of early Chinese religion. Religious texts excavated from early Chinese burials include inventory lists of grave goods buried in the tombs, records of divination, sacrifice, exorcisms conducted on behalf of the tomb occupants, and official memorials addressed to the bureaucracy of the underworld.[58] Only through careful analysis of the available textual and archaeological data can we begin to understand the religious beliefs and practices of the past.[59] Therefore, this book approaches early Chinese religion from a more inclusive perspective, examining burial architecture, religious texts, and art historical remains excavated from early Chinese tombs.

Burial Archaeology and Archaeological Interpretation

Throughout Chinese history, ancient tombs have been opened for various reasons. For some, the purpose was political revenge, and for others, it was personal enrichment through the acquisition of valuable burial goods. An example of the former is found in the story of Wu Zixu (?–484 BCE), a young nobleman who fled the state of Chu to avoid political persecution and eventually returned as a general of the neighboring state of Wu, leading his army to conquer the Chu capital. In a final act of revenge, he opened the Chu king's tomb and lashed the king's corpse three hundred times.[60] In early Chinese debates over frugal versus lavish burials, those supporting frugal burials warned that elaborate burials would only become the targets of tomb robbers and thereby disturb the peaceful afterlife of the departed ancestors. As Sima Qian (ca. 145–ca. 85 BCE) reports, tomb robbery was a profitable business during the Han dynasty.[61] Looters often targeted ancient Chinese burials marked by prominent tumuli or other structures.

Although Chu ritual bronzes were discovered accidentally as early as the Song dynasty (960–1279), our earliest knowledge of Chu burials came from tomb robberies that took place during the first half of the twentieth century.[62] In 1923, a group of bronze artifacts was unearthed in Shou County, Anhui, where the last Chu capital (known as Shouchun in Warring States records) was established in 241 BCE after Qin military pressure forced the Chu court to relocate several times. Between 1933 and 1938, at Lisangudui near Shou County, local warlords opened a royal Chu tomb and discovered more than one thousand bronze objects, including seventy inscribed pieces, now scattered in various public and private collections in and outside of China. In the 1930s and 1940s, tomb robbers looted many Chu burials near Changsha City, Hunan,[63] another geographic locus of the state of Chu in southern China, including the renowned Chu silk manuscript (Plate 6) from a Warring States–period tomb at Zidanku (formerly Tomb 1, now Tomb 365) near Changsha, now housed in the Sackler Gallery of Art in Washington, DC,[64] and the famous silk paintings at Chenjiadashan (also in Changsha City).[65]

Although modern scientific archaeology was introduced in China in the 1920s, the 1950s marked the beginning of extensive excavations that now include tens of thousands of ancient Chinese tombs.[66] Owing to variations in burial customs and geographic conditions, the state of preservation of ancient tombs is uneven. In general, in northern and central China, conditions for preservation are not as good as in the south and northwest. In the northwest, the dry desert climate is beneficial for the conservation of organic materials. In southern China, many burial sites from the Warring States and early Han are well preserved because of the regional geography and burial customs as described in the Jiuliandun tombs above. As a result, evidence from a substantial number of well-preserved Warring States and early Han tombs located in southern China has greatly enhanced the archaeological records of these important periods.

The term *Chu* in this study refers to the territory historically occupied by the state of Chu during the Warring States period and the Chu kingdom in the Western Han dynasty, in present-day Hubei, Hunan, Henan, Anhui, Jiangsu, and adjacent areas (Map 1).[67] Between these two periods, the Qin Empire reigned over this region for another fifteen years (221–207 BCE). However, before the Qin unification of China in 221 BCE, the major parts of the Chu territory had been under Qin control for over a half century. We include Qin tombs of these periods in our discussion.[68] In addition, it is important to consider early Chinese tombs at all levels of society when archaeological materials are available, as changes in burial customs and religious beliefs were not limited to a particular social group. Current archaeological reports and scholarly literature divide Chu tombs into five or more ranks ranging from high aristocracy to commoners and the poor[69] and Han tombs into four ranks: imperial tombs, the tombs of local kings and marquises, officials' tombs, and tombs of commoners and convicts.[70] Of the Han tombs, we discuss not only the princely tombs of the kingdoms of Changsha and Chu but also tombs from other regions, such as the Mancheng tombs and the commoners' burials at Shaogou in Luoyang City, Henan. In the unified and bureaucratic Han Empire, differences in mortuary practice are mostly class-based rather than regional.[71]

The Jiuliandun and Beidongshan tombs described above provide only two examples of the spectacular archaeological discoveries of the last forty years. In southern China, the hot and humid climate and vertical pit-style tomb, with its enveloping sticky clay layers, effectively preserved many deeply buried tombs. Archaeologists estimate that more than 70 percent of the ten thousand tombs excavated in China are located in this region. Many archaeological reports and studies feature Chu region tombs.[72] A few studies focus on individual Chu and Han tombs or different categories of tomb objects.[73] In a recent synthesis, while discussing selected Chu and Han tombs, Wu Hung intended to "[make] interpretation methods the direct subject of consideration."[74] His book covers three conceptual aspects—spatiality, materiality, and temporality—of Chinese funerary art from the Neolithic period down to the Ming (1368–1644) and Qing (1644–1911) dynasties, even to the modern era. In his own words, Wu's study focuses on the "art and architectural tradition we call Chinese tombs" and aims "to uncover some basic creative impulses underlying the development of an art and architectural tradition over several thousand years."[75] In so doing, he essentially homogenized the complexity of historical changes and flattened the regional diversity of Chinese funerary beliefs and ritual practices, thus rendering funerary art and ritual not as people's responses to ever-changing historical conditions but as conceptual expressions of the "fundamental logic of traditional Chinese tombs." However, a regional study that places this well-defined

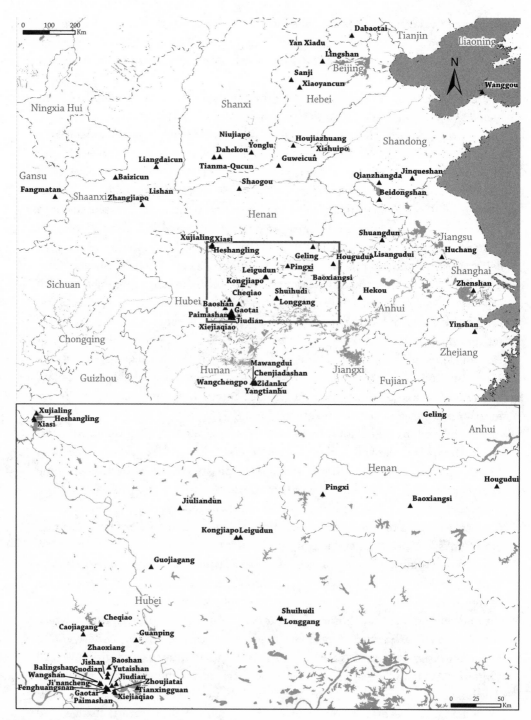

Map 1. Major archaeological sites discussed

group of archaeological data in its historical context is still lacking. I hope this book will fill the gap.

The study of artifacts and burial customs in the former Chu territory has a history of dramatically changing interpretations. In the first half of the twentieth century, when tomb robbers initially unearthed Chu tombs, bronzes, and manuscripts, scholars were not yet able to date the artifacts correctly or decipher their inscriptions. Since that time, the discovery of numerous Chu tombs and manuscripts and the unprecedented speed with which these materials have been published have spurred new studies that focus on establishing chronologies, deciphering graphs, and understanding the philosophical ideas of the Warring States period.[76]

Any assertion about changes in early Chinese religion must, however, be tempered by an awareness of the limitations of our extant archaeological and textual sources. Given the nature of archaeological preservation, which in most cases is accidental, and excavation, any interpretation of archaeological data always must be tentative and cautious. There are two basic questions to ask at the outset.

First, can we make generalizations about Chu mortuary religion based on well-preserved, richly furnished Chu tombs? These tombs, which are exceptional in their state of preservation rather than in their contents, certainly provide insight into Chu mortuary religion. Archaeologists build interpretations largely based on patterns they recognize in archaeological data, and we find similar or recurrent patterns in these tombs. Although the size of the tomb and the quantity of grave goods varied according to the tomb occupant's social rank, the tombs shared a basic burial structure, similar categories of grave goods, and similar individual objects.[77] In addition, not all the well-preserved tombs are elite burials. Archaeologists found a variety of burials in southern China, ranging from richly furnished ones, such as Tomb 1 at Leigudun, the burial of Marquis Yi of the state of Zeng, to relatively small tombs, such as Tomb 56 at Jiudian or Tomb 11 at Shuihudi, each belonging to a ritual specialist or a local official. As a sociological study of the archaeological data shows, during this period the separation between the higher and lower elites became more distinct, and the latter merged with the commoner class.[78] Thus, a relatively large body of the lower elite and commoners shared similar social and political positions as well as religious beliefs. During this period, however, a clear dichotomy between the religious system of the higher elite and that of the rest of the population had yet to develop, contrary to what Granet has argued. The differences in their treatments of death and burials were mainly matters of scale and the quantity and quality of grave goods. Thus, Chu mortuary religion was not a class-based religion, but a religion largely shared by the elite and commoners: all those who could afford to and were entitled to build a tomb for themselves and their relatives to express and follow the religious beliefs and ritual practices of their times.

Second, is the Chu mortuary religion discussed in this book representative of early Chinese religion?[79] I must answer this question with a tentative yes. I hesitate because archaeological data on early Chinese mortuary practices are unevenly distributed. We know less about the details of the religious beliefs and mortuary practices in other regions. To balance the random character of the evidence, this study not only takes a comparative approach, depending on the availability of the archaeological data, but also considers mortuary practices of the Qin and other parts of early China.[80] Several studies of the archaeological data have outlined the different contours of the eastern (including Qi, Chu, Yan, Zhao, Han, and Wei) and western (including Qin) states in the Warring States period.[81] Radical changes took place in the western state of Qin, probably through the agency of the centralized government, while in the eastern states change happened gradually and frequently through struggles among the social forces within each state.[82] For example, the mortuary practice of human sacrifice accompanying burial was widespread in Qin throughout the Spring and Autumn and early Warring States periods but became rare after the middle Warring States period. Scholars have suggested that the sociopolitical reforms initiated by Shang Yang (d. 338 BCE) may have ended this cruel practice. In the eastern states, the changes were slower and more gradual. There were sporadic cases of human sacrifice in Chu, Zeng, and Jin tombs during the Spring and Autumn and early Warring States periods. After the middle of the Warring States period, human sacrifice continued in Jin burials, but in Chu burials, wooden human figurines began to replace actual human sacrifice. The state of Qi in eastern China practiced human sacrifice throughout the Warring States period and sometimes combined it with burying wooden or ceramic figurines.[83] Therefore, we can study not only the similarities and differences among the practices of the eastern states but also the commonalities and distinctions between Chu practices and those of other regions. With more regional studies, such as this book offers, our picture of the changes and continuities in the cultural development of early China should become clearer. In addition, "Chu" in the phrase "Chu mortuary religion" is used as a spatial and temporal designation for the region in southern China of the Warring States, Qin, and early Han periods, not as an adjective to characterize the ethnic group or the contents of the religious beliefs and mortuary practices.[84]

Although transmitted texts and modern scholarly assumptions tell us that regional cultural variations must have existed in early China, there is a growing consensus that in the Warring States period many regional cultural features, previously considered unique to a particular region, were in fact local manifestations of wider trends of social, political, and religious development.

Of course, as in modern China, regional cultural differences existed in early China, such as those between the Qin in the northwest and the Chu in the south,[85] but the Warring States period is famous for the emergence of common cultural traditions through various types of cultural contact.[86] For example, as Liu Lexian shows, a comparison of the almanacs excavated from Chu and Qin burials indicates that while their techniques for determining lucky and unlucky times differed, the underlying principles were similar.[87] Studies have shown that what were once considered regional differences in early Chinese ritual music appear to be only variations on a single music system based on that of the royal Zhou court during the Eastern Zhou period (771–249 BCE).[88] Different languages and writing styles of the Warring States period more clearly manifest this theme.[89] Although different dialects or local languages undoubtedly existed in early China, the paleographic data clearly demonstrate that the vast majority of written materials, even those from the state of Chu, are in the "elegant standard speech" (*yayan*) of Old Chinese.[90] The same is true of weights and measures and many other cultural institutions of the time. In all of these cases, it is obvious that local lords, ritual specialists, and intellectuals promoted and emphasized regional differences rhetorically to fulfill their own political, religious, or other purposes. As Gideon Shelach and Yuri Pines show, the Warring States rulers used local cultural traits to forge ethnic identity among the mass conscripted peasant-soldiers in order to mobilize, manipulate, and control their military forces. [91] Some of these perceived differences were not real cultural divergences, in nature or in origin. Certainly we cannot assume that this commonality of nature and origin was the case in mortuary religion, and we still need to study different approaches to and treatments of the dead in regions other than Chu. Current evidence, however, suggests that Chu and its adjacent areas in southern China—at times viewed as barbaric, exotic, decadent, and peripheral—were in fact quite influential and important in the formation of mainstream early Chinese conceptions of religion, cosmology, and the afterlife.

Religion, Cosmology, the Afterlife, and the Early Empire

Religion, a complex social phenomenon, is difficult to subsume under a single definition.[92] Here, the term is understood in the sense Peter L. Berger delineates: "Religion is the human enterprise by which a sacred cosmos is established."[93] In this functional view, religion is a system of cultural symbols created and manipulated by humankind (often through rituals) to construct and maintain social reality. In other words, religion and its associated rituals make an invisible world visible, tangible, and thinkable, thereby serving as an instrument for dealing with extrahuman powers in response to the social reality.

The period of the late Warring States and early empires was a time of intense speculation in cosmology and of great advances in both geographic knowledge of China and the surrounding world and religious imagination of the afterworld. Anecdotes in the *Zuo Commentary* and other excavated manuscripts indicate that the imagination about the world of the dead inspired various numinous experiences, both dreadful and fascinating. In the binary constructions to which Warring States ritualists were prone, the world of the dead was set both opposite and parallel to the world of the living, as was the case in many other ancient civilizations.[94] In maintaining the ritual order of this world, as I argue in this book, the purpose of burying "spirit artifacts" in Warring States tombs was to demarcate the boundary between this world and the next.

On the other hand, in the early Chinese context, the constructed cosmos and the associated rituals for maintaining this cosmos were not always as opposed to the secular world, as we might expect. This led some early scholars to characterize Chinese religion as essentially "secular" or as having a this-world orientation.[95] This attitude originates at least in part in the abovementioned bias of text-centered scholarship on Chinese religion, which substitutes later Confucian rationalistic interpretations for the whole range of early Chinese religious beliefs and practices. But partly this is because the religious nature of these creations is socially and culturally determined.[96] Although religion concerns relationships and communications between human and extrahuman beings, in the final analysis religion centers on relationships among human beings. This is true of the creation of the underworld bureaucracy, a unique feature of Chinese religion. Not only does it mirror the development of the Chinese imperial bureaucracy in its early stages, but it also serves as a metaphor projecting a conscious, deliberate construction of religious imagination based on ideas, symbols, values, or structures of the time.

This view of religion as a cultural system enables us to include in our analysis of early Chinese beliefs a broad range of religious experiences that are outside of organized religion, systematic theology, dogma, or canonical scripture. In addition, religion permits us to perceive the mechanism of world building through symbolic means. Religion and cosmology were inextricably intertwined before the development of the specialized academic disciplines of religious studies and cosmology. By drawing upon previous scholarship,[97] my study proposes to restore the connection between religion and cosmology. Here, cosmology is understood according to the anthropologist Stanley Tambiah's definition: "frameworks of concepts and relations which treat the universe or cosmos as an ordered system, describing it in terms of space, time, matter, and motion, and peopling it with gods, humans, animals, spirits, demons and the like."[98] Cosmology had an intricate relationship with social, political, and ritual order in early China. Between the Shang dynasty and the Han dynasty, there was a shift from four quarters (*sifang*) cosmology to five agents (*wuxing*) cosmology, and this cosmological transformation was closely associated with the unification of the early Chinese empire.[99] And as scholars have pointed out, as in other early cosmologies, the early Chinese conceptions of the universe centered on the question of abodes of the dead.[100] More specifically, this cosmological transformation had a direct impact on physical and mental constructions of the postmortem environment: the tomb and the religious conception of the afterlife as a journey. As a funerary monument, the early Chinese tomb is not only the repository for the body of the deceased but also a site of funerary rituals, the cult of the dead, and an expression of individual and collective concerns about death and the afterlife.

Among the previous studies on early China is the extreme position held by Frederick W. Mote, whose *Intellectual Foundations of China* was once influential and is still used as a textbook in U.S. and Chinese college introductory courses on China.[101] He wrongly claimed that, before the introduction of Buddhism, there was "no such thing as an 'other world' in ancient Chinese thought at all. . . . There was no heaven or hell, no creator God, and no expected end of the universe once it had emerged from primeval chaos. All was natural, and within Nature."[102] Using this problematic hypothesis as his starting point, Mote explained that because the Chinese people had no creation myth, no god, and no ultimate cause, life and death were integral parts of a natural process.[103] Mote recognized the existence of religious deities in Chinese society but thought that they were just "the vulgarized versions of this rather philosophical conception."[104]

Archaeological discoveries over the past four decades, however, have rendered such preconceptions untenable, and many scholars have already argued convincingly against this position.[105] It is now clear that indigenous Chinese conceptions of the afterlife and other religious beliefs, as well as the related institutions that grew around them, existed long before the introduction of Buddhism to China. Scholars have used various archaeological materials to demonstrate the existence of pre-Buddhist religious concepts and to reassess the nature and functions of religion in ancient China. These materials include funerary texts that feature land contracts and grave-securing writs,[106] art historical remains such as the Mawangdui silk banner paintings,[107] and tomb structure and furnishings.[108] Using both archaeological and paleographical data excavated in Chu, Qin, and early Han tombs, this book marks a further step in the archaeological studies on early Chinese religion.

1

The Dead Who Would Not Be Ancestors

Their bodies may have died, but their souls are living:
Heroes among the shades their valiant souls will be.

—ATTRIBUTED TO QU YUAN, "HYMN TO THE FALLEN"

IN RECENT DECADES, large caches of bamboo manuscripts dating to the Warring States period have been excavated from Chu elite tombs in southern China. A subset of these texts records divinations, sacrifices, and exorcisms performed on behalf of the tomb occupants (figs. 1.1a and 1.1b). This subset is particularly important for the archaeology of early Chinese religion, as it constitutes a category of text, firsthand religious documents, that scholars had not encountered before. Buried with the dead, such documents left virtually no trace in the vast corpus of classical texts from antiquity that, through repeated copying, has been transmitted to us. The excavation and deciphering of these religious texts, which "have been actually known or read at a given place at a given time, or have governed or shaped the kind of religious behavior that had left traces on the ground,"[1] open a new window on the religious pantheon of the Warring States period.[2]

Scattered references to spirits and mythical figures appear in other types of texts, but their religious nature was glossed over by later textual systematization and layers of traditional commentary.[3] These newly excavated manuscripts, however, reference a spectrum of deities that were consulted regarding the tomb occupant's ultimate fate. The religious connotations of these statements are unambiguous. The language is formulaic, recording the type and quantity of the offerings and the specific gods or spirits to whom these sacrifices and exorcisms were made. After a divination had identified the cause of the calamity, sacrifices and exorcisms were offered to a pantheon of spirits in hopes that the illness would be cured or the misfortune averted.

At first glance, these divination records appear similar to the oracle-bone in-

(a)

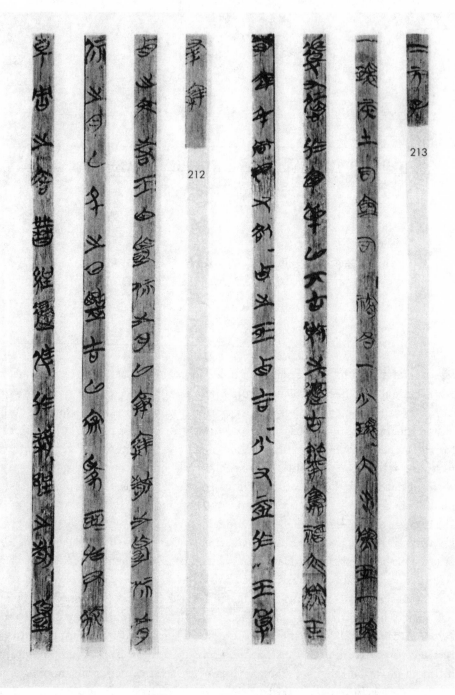

213

212

Figs. 1.1a and b. Divinatory and sacrificial records excavated from Tomb 2 at Baoshan, Jingmen City, Hubei; Strips 212–215. Ca. 316 BCE. Warring States period. Hubei Provincial Museum.

(b)

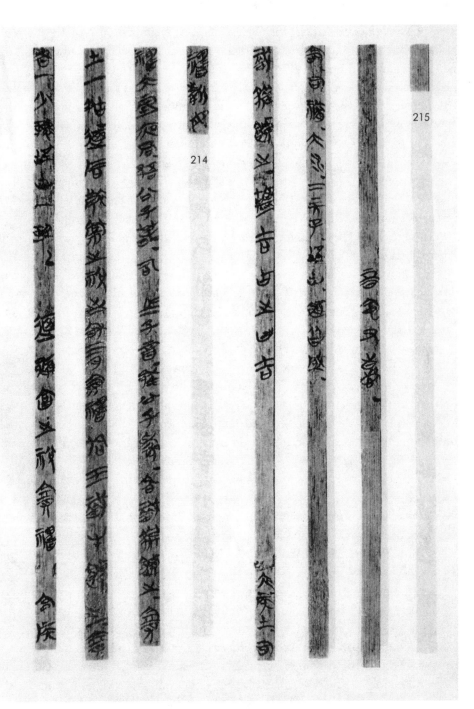

214

215

scriptions of the late Shang dynasty (ca. 1200 BCE) carved onto turtle shells and animal bones about a millennium earlier. In fact, scholars have noted that the language, structure, formats, and ritual actions are similar to those of the older records.[4] A closer look reveals, however, that the type of religious agents has shifted from ancestors to a group of spirits that did not appear in previous enumerations of the Shang and Western Zhou pantheons. This new group of spirits, which evolved over the Eastern Zhou period, consists of individuals who died without posterity (*juewuhouzhe* 絕無後者), who perished violently (*qiangsi* 強死), and who were slain with weapons (*bingsi* 兵死). This class of spirits, who could not become part of the ancestral lineage because of their violent death or lack of progeny, challenged the religious system passed down from the Shang and Western Zhou dynasties.

This account of the decline in the religious potency of ancestors coincides with the collapse of the Zhou ritual system and the diminishing importance of ancestors in general, which is apparent from inscriptions cast on ritual bronze vessels of the Spring and Autumn period.[5] These inscriptions note that many more bronze vessels were made for the owner's use than for sacrifice to one's ancestors, as was the case with earlier vessels. Moreover, the earlier Shang and Western Zhou religious systems were centered on ancestor cults.[6] The dead were often depersonalized and collectively regarded as primarily benevolent ancestors.[7] Eastern Zhou accounts, however, often describe the dead as having strong personalities and suffering premature deaths, which prevent them from becoming benevolent ancestors. While ancestral sacrifices continued, the ritual propitiation of this new category of the dead—unquiet ghosts or victims of violent death who were regarded individually rather than collectively—took center stage in Warring States religious life.

Starting in the Spring and Autumn period, the various lineages gradually became embroiled in political struggles. These struggles would provide the context for the need to pacify the vengeful ghosts. The victors in these political battles attempted to erase their enemies from social memory by excluding them from their ancestor cults, confiscating their sacrificial bronze vessels, denying them proper burial rites, and expelling them from lineage cemeteries.[8]

To counter these actions, the conquered parties or their sympathizers engaged with emerging historical accounts of conflict, crime, and revenge to articulate a vision of the afterlife in which the spirits of the deceased could become ghosts and wander among the living. The circumstances surrounding these individuals' deaths prevented them from becoming venerable ancestors; instead, these dead were believed to haunt and threaten the living. The new religious system provided ritual methods for placating these unquiet spirits, who sought revenge on the victors.

The increasing size of armies and the scale of combat during the Warring States period yielded an attendant increase in atrocities in military conflicts and violence in Chinese society, both of which triggered a dramatic change in attitudes toward death and the dead.[9] While anecdotal accounts from earlier periods refer to the elite's fear of those who died violent deaths in political struggles, such fear soon expanded to include the war dead, such as the battlefield heroes described in the "Hymn to the Fallen" (Guoshang) in the epigraph to this chapter. During the subsequent Warring States, Qin, and Han periods, the ancestral dead were considered frightening and ambivalent, especially during the liminal stage before they transformed completely into ancestors.

Research on attitudes toward death and the dead holds an important place in anthropological and Western historical studies.[10] The French historians Philippe Ariès (1914–84) and Michel Vovelle (b. 1933), considered the leading scholars in this field,[11] along with various historians of the ancient, medieval, early modern, and modern periods,[12] have generally agreed not only that conceptions of death have changed over time but also that changes in attitudes toward death reflect social and political changes. The modern scholarly consensus holds that if an objective picture of a society's attitudes toward death is to be reached, subjective individual testimonies in art, literature, diaries, wills, personal memoirs, and other writings must be balanced by available demographic data on mortality and birth rates. Such statistics are rarely available for ancient civilizations; as a result, scholars examining this topic need to be creative and balanced in their use of evidence.[13]

The evidence on changes in conceptions of death in early China is strong. A comparison of the religious practices of the Shang period with those of the Warring States period reveals a significant, qualitative change in attitudes toward the dead: a new, previously undocumented category of unquiet ghosts appears in the religious pantheon.[14] These vengeful ghosts became a dominant spiritual force in Eastern Zhou and later religious life. This novel category of the dead initially included only aristocrats who suffered violent deaths during political struggles but subsequently grew to encompass conscripted commoners who died in war and other members of the general population. The emergence of this new category of the dead, along with religious practices for dealing with it, had an enormous impact on early Chinese mortuary religion and funerary practice.[15]

Religious Texts from Chu Tombs

To glimpse how early Chinese conceptions of the dead changed, we turn to a cache of bamboo manuscripts recovered from a tomb in southern China. These manuscripts reveal that the religious pantheon of the Warring States period differed significantly from that of the earlier Shang and Western Zhou dynasties. In this later era, the most efficacious members of the pantheon were individuals who had died violent deaths. Fear and anxiety among the living about the harm such spirits could bring led these figures to be incorporated into the Warring States ritual system.

Seven Warring States–period Chu tombs have yielded divination records; the best preserved are those from Tomb 2 at Baoshan. Excavated in 1986, this tomb is located in Jingmen City, Hubei, sixteen kilometers north of the fourth-century BCE Chu capital in present-day Ji'nancheng in Jiangling County, Hubei.[16] It is one of numerous elite cemeteries scattered throughout the area surrounding the ancient capital. Altogether, five Chu tombs have been excavated (Tombs 1, 2, 4, 5, and 6). With the exception of Tomb 2, the burials had all been looted long ago. Even in Tomb 2, grave robbers had managed to dig a tunnel as far as a point directly above the wooden encasement, fortunately stopping just before and leaving the tomb undisturbed. Archaeologists unearthed a total of 448 thin, long, and narrow bamboo pieces (used for writing, see figs. 1.1a and 1.1b), of which 278 were inscribed. Of these, 196 strips are legal documents, 28 strips are burial-goods inventories, and 54 strips (Strips 197–250) concern divinations, sacrifices, or exorcisms. In addition, 1 bamboo rod and 1 strip are funeral-gift lists.

According to these manuscripts, the tomb occupant, Shao Tuo, Chief Minister of the Left (Zuoyin) at the Chu court, divined for three years about his official activities and personal health, until his death in the spring of 316 BCE.[17] The records of his divinations, which indicate that he died of a heart-related illness, contain twenty-six reports dating from 318 to 316 BCE. Each report opens with a date, the diviner's name, the method of divination (by turtle shell or yarrow stalk), the concern or "charge," the prognostication, and the ritual proposals (sacrifice or exorcism) directed to specific superhuman powers. Often Shao called upon multiple diviners to divine for the same concern. Each divination concludes with the same stock phrase: "For this reason a prayer is directed to the spirit [who is the cause of the calamity]" (Yi qi gu shui zhi 以其故說之).[18] Prescribed ritual actions, including exorcism (gongjie 攻解, gongchu 攻除), sacrifices, and the promise of sacrificial offerings, follow this declaration.[19]

Chu sacrificial records note three basic types of sacrifices (dao 禱). The first, initial sacrifice (yidao 弌禱), is directed toward Shao Tuo's direct ancestors (a total of five generations) and his mother.[20] The second, promissory sacrifice (yudao 與禱), is a pledge to make offerings to specific superhuman powers if the participant's prayers are answered. The third, requital sacrifice (saidao 賽禱), is the sacrifice of thanksgiving, the delivery of the offerings promised to the specific superhuman power when the participant's prayers have been answered.[21]

In Shao Tuo's three years of divinations, sacrifices, and exorcisms, the early offerings usually went to his direct ancestors—King Zhao of Chu (r. 515–489 BCE), the Lord of Pingye (named Ziliang, Shao Tuo's great-great-grandfather),[22] the Lord of Wu (named Zichun, Shao Tuo's great grandfather), Marshal Ziyin (Shao Tuo's grandfather), the Lord of Cai (named Zijia, Shao Tuo's father), and Shao Tuo's mother—and to the three mythic royal ancestors of the state of Chu (san Chuxian, i.e., Laotong, Zhurong, and Yuxiong).[23] Also included was a group of nature deities, such as the Grand One (Taiyi, also named Tai or Shi Tai),[24] the Lord of Earth (Houtu), the Controller of Lifespan (Siming), the Controller of Misfortune (Sihuo), the Grand Water (Dashui), the Two Children of Heaven (Ertianzi),[25] the Five Mountains (Wushan),[26] and sacred Mount Wei (Weishan).[27]

Despite continuous pledges, sacrifices, and prayers, Shao Tuo's illness apparently took an unexpected turn for the worse. The records reveal that sacrifices were made at this point to members of the pantheon that cannot be traced back to earlier Shang or Western Zhou sources. The record for the first month (*xingyi*) of 316 BCE can serve as a case in point. Five diviners were called, and each of them, using either the turtle-shell or yarrow-stick method, conducted divinations concerning two sets of charges. The first was the yearly consultation for Shao Tuo's official business: "In his coming and going in the service of the king, from this first month till first month of the next year, may it be that all through this period he not undergo any harm" (Strips 226–35). The initial predictions were auspicious, noting only "some small worries." But the ritual proposals for sacrifice and exorcism on this occasion were unusual, to say the least. Instead of the usual recipients of Shao's sacrifices, such as his ancestors, the royal ancestors, and the nature deities, other individuals were named: his deceased brothers Shao Liang, Shao Cheng, and the Lord of Xian-luo. The records tell us nothing about these relatives, only that each of them died without posterity.

The second charge, concerning Shao Tuo's failing health, continues this shift in attention toward these ghosts. One record reads, "Heart and abdomen are affected, he is unable to breathe and has no appetite for food, there has been no improvement for a long time, may it be that his health improves rapidly and there be no calamity" (Strips 236–48). The initial predictions state that, though the oracle indicated auspicious signs for the long term, the illness was difficult and recovery would be slow. The recipients of the proposed sacrifices include almost all the spirits of the Chu religious pantheon: the nature deities; the royal ancestors, including the three royal ancestors of the Chu and the Chu kings (Jingwang) from Xiongli to King Wu (r. 740–690 BCE); Shao Tuo's direct ancestors; his uncle Dongling Lianxiao (named Zifa),[28] who, the records indicate, had died violently (*shang*); the earth god (*she*); the shaman (*wu*?); and the high hill and the low hill at Zhu.[29]

The exorcism that followed also targeted some of the new spirits, who had rarely appeared in earlier enumerations of the religious pantheon: the celestial deity Sui, the fecundity god (*zu* or *mingzu*),[30] those who were slain with weapons, the spirit of At-the-Water (Shuishang),[31] those who drowned (*niren*), the sun and the moon, and the blameless dead (*bugu*).[32] The noteworthy additions to these lists are those who died unusual or violent deaths. Note also that while nature deities were to receive sacrifices, vengeful ghosts were exorcized.

The last record of divination, conducted twenty days later, reflects changes that occurred in the religious pantheon during the Warring States period. Despite all of these efforts, Shao Tuo was evidently dying, and in a last act of desperation, the charge pleaded for him to be spared: "The illness presents intumescences, he cannot breathe; may it still be possible that he not die." The initial prognostication indicated, "He will not die, but there are calamities stemming from those who died without posterity and signs of calamities appearing on the wooden stand for the fecundity god (*jian mu wei* 渐木位)."[33] The suggested ritual remedies were a pledge sacrifice directed toward those who died without posterity and an exorcism directed toward the fecundity god. Here again, in a final effort to rescue the dying Shao Tuo, the sacrifices and exorcisms were directed *not* to ancestral spirits or nature deities but to those who had died without posterity and to the fecundity god. These divinations indicate not only that the Chu people believed each deity had different powers and jurisdictions but also that religious efficacy had shifted to a group of unquiet ghosts and the fecundity god. According to a burial-goods inventory excavated from his tomb, Shao Tuo died shortly thereafter, and his funeral took place forty-eight days after the last divination.

Changes in the Warring States Pantheon

Taken together, the Baoshan divinations and the sacrifices and exorcisms they prescribed shed light on the composition of the religious pantheon of the Warring States Chu elite. In Shao Tuo's case, the divination records suggest that the pantheon included the following members (the designations 1 through 5 are for purposes of categorization only and are not hierarchical; categories for the Warring States pantheon are subsequently referred to as W1, W2, etc.):

W1. His direct ancestors: King Zhao (r. 515–489 BCE), the Lord of Pingye (Ziliang), the Lord of Wu (Zichun), Marshal Ziyin, the Lord of Cai (Zijia), and Shao Tuo's mother; these are the five generations of Shao Tuo's recent ancestors;

W2. Royal ancestors of the Chu state: the three royal ancestors (Laotong, Zhurong, and Yuxiong) and the Chu kings from Xiongli to King Wu;

W3. Nature deities: such as the Grand One, the Lord of Earth, the Controller of Lifespan, the Controller of Misfortune, the Grand Water, the Two Children of Heaven, the Five Mountains, Mount Wei; the sun and the moon; the five household deities (*wusi*), including the gods of the door (*hu*), the stove (*zao*), the chamber (*shi*), the gate (*men*), and travel (*xing*); and the four directional deities, such as the south (*nanfang*);

W4. Individuals who died violent deaths or without posterity: Shao Tuo's uncle Dongling Lianxiao (Zifa) and his brothers Shao Liang, Shao Cheng, and the Lord of Xianluo; and

W5. Those slain with weapons, the spirit of At-the-Water, those who drowned, the blameless dead, and others.

From other Chu divinatory and sacrificial records from the Warring States period, we learn that the new religious pantheon was not only individualized but also hierarchical: people of different social ranks sacrificed to pantheons of different scales. The pantheons differ mainly in terms of the lineage ancestors, royal ancestors, and terrestrial deities addressed. For example, the occupant of Tomb 1 at Wangshan, Dao Gu (d. ca. 331 BCE), a descendant of King Dao of Chu, held the same rank as Shao Tuo and also sacrificed only to his direct lineage ancestors. In contrast, the occupant of Tomb 1001 at Geling, the Lord of Pingye (Cheng, d. ca. 377 BCE) and the son of Ziliang (Shao Tuo's great-great-grandfather), was able to sacrifice to many more ancestors and Chu kings and with greater frequency than was Shao Tuo.[34] This is probably because the Lord of Pingye (Cheng) was of a higher social rank than was Shao Tuo. In addition, he was the head of the Zhao (trunk) lineage, whereas Shao Tuo belonged to a branch of that lineage. Moreover, not all members of the Chu elite sacrificed to royal ancestors. For example, Tomb 1 at Tianxingguan, in Jiangling County, Hubei, the burial place of Pan Sheng (d. ca. 350 BCE), the Lord of Diyang, contains no records of sacrifices to royal Chu ancestors. He offered sacrifices to Pan clan's ancestors (Panxian) rather than to the ancestors of the Chu royal lineage.[35]

In their entirety, and despite important structural continuities with the Shang period, the Chu religious records reveal stunning changes in the composition of the religious pantheon. For example, scholars have divided the Shang religious pantheon into the following categories according to the ritual treatments they received (again, the designations 1 to 6 are for purposes of categorization only and are not hierarchical; categories for this Shang pantheon are subsequently referred to as S1, S2, etc.):[36]

S1. Pre-dynasty kings of the Shang people;

S2. Shang dynastic ancestors, starting with Da Yi (also called Tang, the founder of the Shang dynasty);

S3. Heir-producing ancestral consorts;

S4. Former lords: human spirits outside the Shang lineage core, such as Yi Yin;

S5. Nature deities, such as river gods, mountain gods, the sun, and the earth; and

S6. Di, the supreme god and the highest celestial power.[37]

Scholars have stressed the distinction between core lineage ancestors (S1, S2, and S3), on the one hand, and other spiritual powers (S4, S5, and S6), on the other. The latter had no direct kinship relationship with the Shang core lineage.[38] The core lineage ancestors, the direct ancestors of the Shang rulers, were their closest allies in the spiritual world; they were seen as immediate supporters and protectors of the Shang kings and their people. In contrast, the supreme god was an abstract figure to the people of the Shang and Western Zhou dynasties. Although this deity received basic, regular sacrifices, its interaction with the living was often mediated through the royal ancestors.

The spirits outside the core lineage in the Shang pantheon include the ancestors of others (S4), nature deities (S5), and the supreme god (S6). The latter two, categories S5 and S6, represent a universal set of celestial and terrestrial deities to which the Shang royal lineage sacrificed to expand their social and territorial bases and enhance their claims to political legitimacy. As far as category S4 is concerned, opinions differ as to whether the Shang actually sacrificed to the ancestors of others.[39] Although scholars agree that the Shang and Western Zhou kings generally restricted their sacrifices to their own ancestors, this restriction was intended to maintain the Shang king's monopoly on political power. The political and religious functions of the ancestor cults rest in the claim that one's ancestors are stronger, smarter, and more powerful than the ancestors of others, and enjoy a special audience with the supreme god in the spiritual realm. It also insists that only the ruling king, "I, the one person" (*Yu yi ren* 余一人), as the direct descendant, can communicate with his ancestors, who will intercede for him in front of the supreme god in Heaven and protect him on earth. As an important literary and historical source for the Spring and Autumn period, the *Zuo Commentary*, for example, includes statements such as "The spirits of the dead do not enjoy the sacrifices of those who are not of their kindred, and . . . people only sacrifice to those who were of the same ancestry as themselves."[40] The *Analects* features a similar comment: "To offer sacrifice to the spirit of an ancestor that is not one's own is obsequious."[41] In other words, ancestor cults in the Shang and Western Zhou dynasties were exclusive. While instances of extralineal sacrifice can be found in Shang and Western Zhou oracle-bone inscriptions, as a rule, the main objects of the ancestral cult were direct ancestors.[42] This exclusivity was a way for the ruling class to maintain its political power and legitimacy. At the same time, however, the Shang royal house did sacrifice to human spirits outside the Shang lineage core, such as Yi Yin, to widen its political authority over its ethnically diverse state.[43] Although the Shang rulers prohibited others from accessing their sources of religious and political power, they did sacrifice to other people's ancestors in a bid to gain wider political support.[44] In other words, for the purpose of religious and political control, the Shang ruling house could sacrifice to other people's ancestors, but other people could not sacrifice to the Shang royal ancestors.[45]

This important distinction between the core lineage ancestors and the other spirits survived into the Warring States period. In the Warring States pantheon the core lineage ancestors are the W1 group, which in Shao Tuo's case are his five generations of direct ancestors and his mother; the special ritual treatment that they received is the initial sacrifice. The other spirits outside the core lineage, although differing in content and scale from the Shang categories, include the royal ancestors of Chu (W2; the Shang equivalent is S4) and the nature deities (W3; the Shang equivalents are S5 and S6). Because the Zhao lineage to which Shao Tuo belonged was not the Chu royal lineage, the only royal ancestor to whom Shao Tuo could sacrifice was King Zhao, the founding ancestor of the Zhao lineage of the early Chu kings. Other royal ancestors included the heads of the other elite Chu lineages. Their relations with Shao Tuo resemble those between Shang kings and the former lords in the Shang pantheon.

While the Chu religious pantheon may have inherited the structure of the Shang pantheon, the contents of these categories are somewhat different. For example, scholars generally agree that in the oracle-bone inscriptions of the Shang pantheon

Di or Shangdi (High God) was the supreme god,[46] whereas in the Chu and Western Han pantheon the Grand One was the supreme god.[47] But the relationship between the two supreme gods is not one of complete substitution; instead, these parallel deities existed simultaneously in different religious frameworks for a long period.[48] Religious efficacy, however, shifted from Di to the Grand One because the latter became the focus of intensive religious cults in the Warring States and Western Han periods. The origin of the supreme Grand One remains a mystery. The cosmogonic text known as "The Grand One Generates Water" (Taiyi sheng shui), excavated from Tomb 1 at Guodian in Jingmen City, Hubei (dated ca. 300 BCE), mentions a numinous entity named Taiyi, but the relationship between this Grand One (also called Dao in late Warring States philosophical texts) and the Grand One that appears in the divinatory and sacrificial records is still unclear.[49] Unlike monotheistic religions, where there is only one supreme god, the early Chinese religion has multiple high gods, each functioning in its own sphere of influence. The religious rituals and sacrificial offerings that these spiritual entities received from human beings express their power.

The expansion of the pledge ritual in the Warring States period also distinguishes Chu from Shang treatment of individual members of the religious pantheon.[50] The pledge ritual was a type of bargaining typical in Chinese religious practice: a certain number of offerings were pledged to the spirits and later, when the prayers were answered and the wishes granted, the requital (i.e., thanksgiving) sacrifice would be made to those spirits who had been efficacious in granting the requests.[51] Based on extant evidence, while in the late Shang period such pledges were apparently directed primarily at the core lineage ancestors, in the Warring States period they were made to almost all members of the religious pantheon.[52] This expansion corroborates Gilbert L. Mattos's observation that the bronze inscriptions of the Spring and Autumn period reflect a decline in belief in the religious efficacy of ancestors.[53] It further demonstrates the elite's belief in the Warring States period that religious efficacy of other spirits exceeded that of the core lineage ancestors.

In divination records of the Warring States period, we also find new spirits (W4 and W5) who did not appear in the Shang religious pantheon. Newcomers include those who died violent deaths, drowned, died without posterity, or were slain with weapons, and the blameless dead. There are also significant differences between groups W4 and W5. In Shao Tuo's case, the former (W4) are his relatives: his uncle and his brothers who died without posterity. Other Chu records suggest that three generations of victims of violent death received sacrifices.[54] The relatives who died violently were not members of the core lineage so they did not receive the regular ancestral sacrifice. Instead, both promissory and requital sacrifices were offered to these spirits. The latter group (W5) included individuals slain with weapons, the spirit of At-the-Water, the drowned, and the blameless dead. These individuals were not relatives, and in most cases they were grouped with nature spirits as targets of exorcism rather than sacrifice. We can regard this group of the dead (W5) who would

The Dead Who Would Not Be Ancestors

not become ancestors as complete "strangers," or, to use Arthur P. Wolf's famous classification of the pantheon in late imperial China, "ghosts."[55]

Why were those who died violently or without posterity incapable of becoming ancestors? Why did the people of the Warring States treat members of this group of the dead so differently from other deceased individuals? In the case of those who died young or without posterity, the answer is clear enough: they had no descendants to offer sacrifices to them. In early China, as in many other ancient civilizations, ancestors and descendants represented two sides of the same coin; the existence of each depended on the other. The continued life and well-being of ancestors relied on regular sacrifice by descendants. If there were no descendants, there were certainly no ancestors. The reason for excluding from the ancestral order those who died violent deaths but did have descendants is less obvious. How did the early Chinese conceive of violent death? To answer this question, we must trace the emergence of new notions of violent death in the Spring and Autumn period.

Violent Deaths and Ghost Narratives

One of the earliest textual references to "violent death" is found in the *Zuo Commentary*, in an entry under 617 BCE in the *Annals*: "The Chu polity put to death its minister Yishen." The *Zuo Commentary* provides more details about this story. Yishen, also known as Zixi, once the marshal (Sima) of the Chu army, was from the Dou lineage in the state of Chu. In earlier years, a shaman predicted that King Cheng of Chu (r. 671–626 BCE), Chief Minister Ziyu, and Marshal Zixi would all "die violent deaths." Indeed, as the story unfolded, King Cheng was forced to hang himself when the palace was under siege by his own son, the future King Mu.[56] Ziyu, also known as Dechen, from the Cheng lineage of the state of Chu, was forced to commit suicide after his defeat by the northern alliance led by Jin in a famous battle at Chengpu in 632 BCE.[57] Zixi, who narrowly escaped suicide after the battle of Chengpu, was executed after his attempt to assassinate King Mu.[58] As is often the case in the *Zuo Commentary*, the prophecy turned out to be correct.

Stories such as these abound in the *Zuo Commentary*. Scholars have noted more than thirty-six instances of subordinate officials assassinating their rulers.[59] These stories reflect the reality of internal and external conflicts between both states and lineages during the Spring and Autumn period. In the 259-year interval it covers, the *Zuo Commentary* records more than five hundred military conflicts among states and more than one hundred civil wars within states. Indeed, the roots of many transformations of Chinese society during the Warring States period can be traced back to the Spring and Autumn period, when the concept of violent death as bad death was first articulated over and against preexisting ideals of good death, which found expression in commemorative bronze inscriptions. To the elite, a good death meant that one lived out his or her allocated lifespan and died at an old age in the comfort of one's home. This notion of a good death is certainly a cultural ideal rather than a reality, but the ideal became particularly appealing in this period of social and political turmoil.

Although fear of the dead is arguably instinctual, the dread of individuals who died a violent death reflected an early Chinese cultural predisposition. Linguistically, one of the Chinese words for fear (*wei* 畏) was a cognate of the word for ghost (*gui* 鬼).[60] In Spring-and-Autumn-period literature, the graph *gui* specifically connoted "ghost."[61] In the matrix of intralineal struggles in the Spring and Autumn period, personal fears and expectations concerning death were encoded as ghost narratives. In general, ghost stories address unfinished business between the dead and the living. The dissatisfied departed return to haunt the living, and in this regard, ghost stories of the Spring and Autumn period are not exceptional. Ghost narratives in the *Zuo Commentary* and other early texts probably originated in diverse contexts and had various political implications. Japanese scholar Ogata Nobuo's study of the forty cases of violent death in the *Zuo Commentary* reveals that these cases occurred in the context of intense conflicts between polities or political struggles between lineages.[62]

Early Chinese ghost narratives did not emerge from a vacuum but drew on prior religious notions of justice, good or evil spirits, and good or bad omens. For example, in Shang oracle-bone inscriptions, the graph *gui*, when used as an adjective, often denoted inauspicious subjects such as bad dreams (*guimeng* 鬼夢), inauspicious days (*guiri* 鬼日), and neighboring polities that took an adversarial stance toward the Shang (*guifang* 鬼方).[63] Despite this term's long history, only in the Spring and Autumn period did it come to encompass the fear of unquiet ghosts. This ghost story from the *Zuo Commentary* provides a representative example:[64]

> The Lord of Jin dreamed of a huge vengeful ghost (*li* 厲), with disheveled hair hanging to the ground. It beat its chest, leapt up and down, and said, "For you to slay my descendants was unjust. I have already obtained the approval of the God (Di) for my request." It smashed the main gate of the palace, advanced to the gate of the Lord's chamber, and entered. Terrified, the Lord withdrew into the inner chamber, but the ghost smashed that door too. The Lord then awoke and summoned the shaman of Mulberry Fields, who described a situation that corresponded exactly to the content of the Lord's dream. "What is it about?" asked the Lord. "You will not live to taste the grain of the new harvest," the shaman replied.

Like *gui*, the term *li* denotes "vengeful ghost," "evil spirit," or "baleful demon" in early Chinese texts, denotations probably derived from its meaning "cruel," "ugly," or "wicked."[65] As the story continued, the Lord of Jin became seriously ill, so ill that the doctor sent by the Lord of Qin could not save him. Before the Lord of Jin's death, he had the shaman who predicted his demise executed, but still he could not escape his fate. He "accidentally" fell into the privy and died.[66]

This short story embodies the basic structure and characteristics of ghost narratives in the *Zuo Commentary*. First, such ghost stories often start with one protagonist doing something to cause another's sudden death. The ghost of the deceased or of his or her ancestors then returns to take revenge. In the above story, the Lord of Jin was haunted because two years earlier, in 583 BCE, he killed two of his ministers, Zhao Kuo and Zhao Tong.[67] The vengeful ghost that the Lord of Jin dreamed about was an ancestral spirit of the Zhao lineage, who returned to take revenge. Second, as in this case, the evil spirit in ghost narratives often appears in dreams or possesses human beings or animals. Here the interaction between the avenging ghost and the Lord of Jin in the dream is vividly described. Third, there is a higher level of authority at play in ghost narratives. The supreme god, it is often proclaimed, approves the ghost's action. In other words, the supreme god has jurisdiction over both protagonists, the living and the dead, and eventually the wrongdoer is rightfully punished for his unjust act. The ghost of the Zhao ancestor spoke of the supreme god's approval of his avenging the unjust treatment of his lineage. Another ghost story in the *Zuo Commentary* uses the same phrase, "I have already obtained the approval of the God for my request," to justify Qin's attack on the Jin polity.[68]

In political struggles, the victors often denied the losers the proper rites of burial as a form of punishment. This tactic is apparent in the *Zuo Commentary* and other early literature. For example, in 573 BCE, Lord Li of Jin was assassinated by his ministers and buried outside the eastern gate of the city of Yi, as opposed to being interred appropriately in the royal cemetery of Jiang.[69] The *Zuo Commentary* entry for 544 BCE similarly states, "In the second month on the *guimao* day, the Qi people buried Lord Zhuang in the northern suburbs." By way of explanation, the later commentator Du Yu (222–85) noted, "Those slain with weapons cannot be buried in the lineage cemetery." Elsewhere the *Zuo Commentary* notes that, when the minister Cui Zhu assassinated Lord Zhuang, the scribe and his brother insisted on recording, "Cui Zhu assassinated his lord." After winning the political struggle, Cui Zhu set up Lord Zhuang's half-brother as a puppet ruler. "Cui Zhu placed the coffin of Lord Zhuang in the northern suburbs," the scribe wrote, "and on the *dinghai* day he buried it in the village of Shisun." The village of Shisun is not the location of the royal cemetery. The scribe added a description of the funeral that clearly did not befit the exalted rank of the deceased: "There were [only] four plumes to the carriage; travelers were not warned to stay out of the way, and there were [but] seven inferior carriages in the funeral procession, without any men at arms."[70] In both cases, Lord Li of Jin and Lord Zhuang of Qi were punished after their deaths by being buried outside the lineage cemetery and without the funerary rites befitting their status.

A set of recently published Chu manuscripts in the Shanghai Museum provides additional evidence of the practice of denying the dead proper rites of burial as a punishment. The manuscript collection contains two texts, virtually identical to each other, titled "The Burial of Zijia of Zheng" (Zheng Zijia sang) by the modern editor.[71] The manuscripts relate the death of Zijia, minister of the state of Zheng. When Zijia's death was reported to King Zhuang (?–591 BCE) of Chu, King Zhuang told his ministers that since Zijia had previously murdered his own lord, he should not "now preserve his [i.e., Zijia's] grace and honor and take those with him to the underworld." "If the supreme god and the spirits become angry about this," King Zhuang asks, "what could I do in response?" Using this event as an excuse, the Chu king decides to besiege the Zheng capital for three months. The people of Zheng finally proposed to "bury Zijia in a wooden coffin three inches thick, bundled in coarse ropes, and, without carrying it [the coffin] through the middle gate, bury him at the foot of the city wall." The Chu king is satisfied with the proposal of a meager funeral for Zijia as a posthumous punishment.[72]

The *Zuo Commentary* also relates that those who died violent deaths could likewise, as a punishment, not be buried in the lineage cemeteries.[73] A regulation in the *Rites of Zhou* (Zhouli) states, "Those who were slain with weapons should not be buried in the lineage cemetery."[74] Although later commentators proposed various interpretations of this instruction, modern scholars have pointed out that the connotations of the phrase "those who were slain with weapons" are different in the Eastern Zhou period.[75] In the Spring and Autumn period, the phrase refers specifically to those who died violently in lineage struggles and were punished by burial outside the lineage cemetery. In the Warring States period, however, the phrase refers to the war dead in general. Utilizing archaeological materials, Japanese scholar Suetsugu Nobuyuki has suggested, in contrast, that this practice did not begin until the Spring and Autumn period. In Shang and Western Zhou dynasties, the war dead, some of whose heads were severed by their enemies in combat following the custom of cutting off heads (*guo*) seen in oracle-bone inscriptions, were in fact buried within lineage cemeteries.[76] Starting in the Spring and Autumn period, however, victors of lineage struggles tried to eliminate the social memory of their opponents. As a result, those killed violently were excluded from the lineage cemetery, on the assumption that this would prevent them from reuniting with their ancestors in the afterlife. Because they had suffered a bad death and were buried outside the lineage cemetery, they would be left alone, hungry, and forgotten. Because the victors wished to erase the victims of violent deaths from social memory for political reasons, these dead could not be permitted to become ancestors.

Spring-and-Autumn-period bronze inscriptions also reflect this practice of erasing one's enemies from social memory. A number of ritual bronzes dated to the late Western Zhou and the Spring and Autumn periods had their cast bronze inscriptions, especially the owner's names, excised. For example, among the three tombs of the late Spring and Autumn period at the Yuan (also Wei) lineage cemetery at Xiasi in Xichuan County, Henan, Tomb 1 contains a set of nine bells and two *sheng*-tripods, on which the name of the original owner was intentionally chiseled out. The same tomb contains six bronze vessels bearing the original owner's name, Peng, two dowry vessels bearing the name Meng Teng Ji (elder daughter of the Ji clan from the polity of Teng), and one *li*-tripod bearing the name Jiang Shu X (X, the junior [daughter] of the polity of Jiang).[77] Tomb 2 has two *li*-tripods (figs. 1.2a and 1.2b) and one *jian*-basin with the original owner's name removed, a set of seven *sheng*-tripods with long, ornate inscriptions naming Prince Wu (Wangzi Wu) on the bodies and Peng on the lids (figs. 1.3a and 1.3b), two dagger-axes of Prince Wu, twenty-six bells and two dagger-axes made for Wangsun Gao, and an additional seventeen bronze vessels bearing the name Peng.[78] Tomb 3 contains four bronze vessels with the original owner's name removed, six inscribed with the name Peng, and two dowry vessels bearing the name Wei Zhong Ji Dan (the second-born Dan from the Ji clan [married into] the Yuan [i.e., Wei] lineage).[79] Bronze inscriptions bearing the owner's name are important evidence of the identity of the tomb occupant. But how can we determine the identity of the occupant when multiple identities are inscribed on objects in a tomb? Why did those bronze vessels have their owners' names removed?

Although scholarly debates surround these questions, contextual evidence weighs in to help us determine the identity of the tomb occupants.[80] Scholars generally agree that the cemetery at Xiasi in Xichuan belongs to the Yuan lineage of the Chu aristocracy. As Li Ling has convincingly argued, the occupant of Tomb 2 is Peng, and the other two tombs belong to his two wives.[81] All three tombs contain bronzes made for him; it was a common practice to bury a husband's ritual bronze vessels in his wife's tomb as her social standing directly correlated with his. The two wives' tombs contain dowry vessels made by their own natal families. All three tombs contain bronzes with the original owner's name removed, and Peng's tomb contains ritual vessels made for Prince Wu and Wangsun Gao. Both Prince Wu and Peng appear in the *Zuo Commentary*. Prince Wu (d. 552 BCE) was the Chief Minister (Lingyin) of Chu, while Peng was the Grand Marshal (Da Sima).[82] The *Zuo Commentary* does not specify how Prince Wu died, but records indicate that after the death of Wu, King Kang of Chu (r. 559–545 BCE) wanted Peng to be the Chief Minister. Peng was advised against taking that position because of fierce internal conflicts, and so declined it. King Kang, in conflict with the next chief minister, killed him at court. The king then offered the position to Peng again, and Peng accepted. Peng died in 548 BCE. Although we do not know the details of Chu court politics, from the archaeological evidence we can infer that Peng had received bronzes from the estate of the previous chief minister, whose family had probably fallen out of favor in the course of factional strife at court.[83]

In the tombs of Peng's wives, the original owner's name was scraped off, while in Peng's tomb the set of bronze tripods bore Prince Wu's name on the bodies with Peng's name added on the lids. The erasure of the original owner's name was a traditional practice directed to eliminating the memory of the disgraced opponent, whereas Peng's retention of his defeated enemy's name while claiming ownership of the objects ostentatiously displays his victory.[84] Such display amounts to a punishment more severe than forgetting because punishing the memory, *damnatio memoriae* in Latin, prolongs the disgrace.[85] Similar to the regulation that "those who were slain with weapons should not be buried in the lineage cemetery," the victor's display proclaims the losers' elimination and punishment.

Yet the victors do not always write the historical accounts. In Chinese tradition,

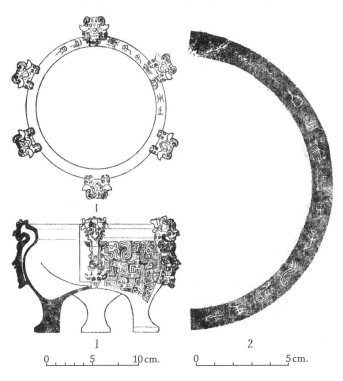

Figs. 1.2a and b. Bronze *li*-tripod and inscription on the rim, excavated from Tomb 2 at Xiasi, Xichuan County, Henan (M2: 59). H. 12.6 cm. Late Spring and Autumn period. The name of the original vessel owner at the beginning of the inscription was intentionally erased. Henan Provincial Museum.

1

0   5   10 cm.

2

0   5 cm.

王子午鼎

佣之遲（遲）鶣，
唯正月初吉丁
亥，王子午擇
其吉金，自
乍（作）鏐
彝鑄（鑄）鼎，用
享以
孝于我皇祖文
考，用祈眉壽，
畣畀敥尾畏
畏（忌）
趩趩敬厥盟
祀，永
受其福余不畏
不羌（差）于政德，
愄（淑）于威義（儀），
誾誾（簡簡）
闌闌（簡簡），
獸獸（優優），
命（令）尹子庚，
之所亟（極），
殷民
萬年無
諆（期），子孫
是制

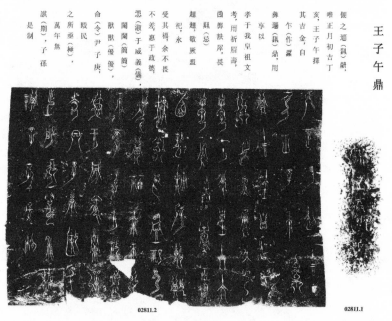

02811.2   02811.1

Fig. 1.3a. (*top*) Bronze tripod with lid, excavated from Tomb 2 at Xiasi, Xichuan County, Henan. H. 34 cm. Henan Provincial Museum.

Fig. 1.3b. (*bottom*) Inscriptions on the bronze tripod (left, modern transcription above) and on lid (right), attributed respectively to the Chu Prince and Prime Minster Wu (aka Zi Geng, fl. mid-sixth century BCE) and his successor Peng (d. 548 BCE), excavated from Tomb 2 at Xiasi, Xichuan County, Henan. Henan Provincial Museum.

in fact, history has had an integral relationship to ghost stories.[86] Episodes of unquiet ghosts were inserted into serious historical accounts, such as dynastic histories, to show that evil deeds were punished and that justice eventually prevailed. This moralizing function of history can be traced back to the *Zuo Commentary* and the *Narratives of the States*.[87]

Furthermore, ghost stories as "paradigm[s] of a forgotten and potentially disruptive past" retrieve repressed memory.[88] Using both anthropological field investigation and psychoanalysis, anthropologist Stephan Feuchtwang argues that ghost stories are "stories of unbidden retrieval of memory, covering loss that is taboo, too shameful, and too repressed to be told."[89] This insightful analysis applies to ghost stories in the *Zuo Commentary* and in many other Chinese texts. Although the ghost stories in the *Zuo Commentary* had probably been told and retold, and thus were several degrees removed from their original context of political struggle, the narratives retained their basic structure as repressed memories of the defeated.

To the victors of political struggles and to society at large, vengeful ghosts are "hostile," "evil," and "fearful." Yet to their kin, sympathizers, and believers, such ghosts possessed spiritual and religious power. Studies on deity cults in imperial China also show that the traditional demarcation of boundaries between "evil" and "good" and among gods, ghosts, and ancestors were fluid and indeterminate.[90] Such fluidity and indeterminacy begin in the Spring and Autumn period and appear in classical literature such as the *Zuo Commentary*.

The ghost narratives of the Spring and Autumn period are largely political tools that defeated noblemen and their sympathizers used to fight back and to demand reconciliation with the dominant political powers of the day. The stories promoted the belief that the slain would return as vengeful ghosts to haunt their enemies by telling their side of the story. The slain also became powerful spirits and later were often venerated in local and popular Chinese religious cults.

Concepts of the Soul and the Rise of the Afterlife

Although earlier ideas about life after death likely abounded, a clearly articulated, written, and collective version of the afterlife emerged against the background of the lineage struggles in the Spring and Autumn period. This version appears in a ghost tale from the *Zuo Commentary* that had a tremendous impact on subsequent ideas about the afterlife in early China.

According to the ghost story, the nobleman Boyou, also known as Liang Xiao (from the Liang lineage) of the state of Zheng, was murdered by his rivals in an internal political struggle.[91] The murdered nobleman then returned as a vengeful ghost (*li*) to kill his surviving opponents on appointed days:[92]

> The people of Zheng frightened one another about Boyou, saying, "Boyou is here!" at which they would all run off, without knowing where they were going. In the second

month of the year [536 BCE] when the punishment documents were cast, one man dreamt that Boyou walked by him in armor and said, "On the *renzi* day I will kill Dai, and next year, on the *renyin* day, I will kill Duan." When Zidai died on a *renzi* day, the terror of the people increased. That year [535 BCE] during the month that the states of Qi and Yan made peace, Gongsun Duan died on a *renyin* day, and the people became still more frightened, until in the following month Zichan appointed Gongsun Xie [Gongsun Duan's son] and Liangzhi [Boyou's son] as successors to their fathers to soothe the people, after which their terrors ceased. When Zidashu asked his reason for making these arrangements, Zichan replied, "When a ghost has a place to return, it does not become an evil spirit. I have made such a place for the ghost."[93]

The terror that Boyou's ghost engendered and the events that followed prompted the eminent statesman Zichan to make a famous speech in which he explained the existence of ghosts in terms of *hun* and *po* dualism. According to the story, when Zichan went to Jin, someone asked him why it was possible for Boyou to become a ghost (*gui*). Zichan replied:

> In the transformation of human life the first stage is called *po* 魄. After this has been produced, its *yang* is called *hun* 魂. Through the use of material substances the quintessential essence is multiplied, and the *hunpo* become strong, and thus the quintessential vigor grows and reaches the level of spirit illumination. When an ordinary man or woman dies a violent death, his or her *hunpo* are still able to possess (*pingyi* 憑依) someone in the form of a malevolent ghost (*yinli* 淫厲). This is all the more so in the case of Liangxiao [i.e., Boyou], a descendant of our former ruler Mu Gong, the grandson of Ziliang, and the son of Zi'er, who were ministers of our state and belonged to a family that had held the handle of government for three generations![94]

Here Zichan articulates an elite view of the afterlife: if someone, especially a member of the nobility, suffers a violent death, then his or her *hunpo* could become an avenging ghost. Zichan applies the contemporary understanding of the concepts of the *hun* and *po* to the discourse on the emergence of the vengeful ghosts.

Much ink has been spilled over this passage and the concepts of *hun* and *po* in early China. These concepts evolved over time, but scholars have often tried to infer their essential meanings by mixing different layers of later commentaries and abstracting nuanced interpretations from divergent textual contexts. To avoid these pitfalls, I focus on the early meanings of the terms in this passage.

In the passage above, Zichan refers to the transformation (*hua*) of a human being: A person starts with *po*, and after this has been produced, *hun* comes. Through the consumption of material substances, the *hunpo* become an entity with quintessential vigor that can grow and reach the point of spiritual illumination. This description of the formation of human beings resembles the narrative of the stages of formation of the human fetus found in a medical text, "The Treatise on Generation of the Fetus" (Taichanshu), excavated from Tomb 3 at Mawangdui (before 168 BCE): "Thus when human beings are engendered . . . in the first month it [the fetus] is called 'flowing into the form.' Food and drink must be the finest. . . . In the second month it first becomes lard (gao 膏). . . . In the third month it first becomes suet (zhi 脂), and has the appearance of a gourd."[95] Similarly, in the "Quintessential Spirit" chapter of the *Master of Huainan* (Huainanzi), we find a passage that refers to the first stages of the gestation as lard and suet, which usually are white substances. According to these records, the early phases are characterized by a white embryonic substance.

Edward Schafer, on the other hand, translates this passage as follows: "At birth a man begins to form a *po*, and after birth of the *po* his *yang* is called *hun*."[96] Yang Bojun and other scholars, based on later Han literature, locate this transformation of the *hun* and the *po* at the point of a person's death rather than his or her birth.[97] In light of the descriptions in "The Treatise on Generation of the Fetus" and the *Master of Huainan*, however, human transformation probably more rightly begins with the fetus, rather than with, as Schafer asserts, birth, or as Yang and others assert, at death. It is possible that the white substance (*po*) in Zichan's speech refers to these early stages of the human fetus, rather than, as scholars have suggested, the abstract brightness of the waxing moon.[98] *Po* is the material base or the starting point of human beings. The translation of *po* as "soul" or even "bodily soul" misses the point. Admittedly, Zichan's stages of development are simpler and rougher than those found in the Mawangdui medical texts, the *Master of Huainan*, and other early Chinese medical texts. But the power of his argument lies in its synthesis of the discourse on avenging ghosts and the newly emerging theories of *hun* and *po*.[99]

With these concepts of *po* and *hun*, Zichan articulated a version of the afterlife in which the ghosts of those who died violent deaths did not become ancestors but instead haunted the living. As a result, these ghosts needed to be fed, sacrificed to, pacified, and remembered. In addition, a wandering ghost could imperil the living, and so it was necessary to give it a place, separate from the living: "When a ghost has a place to return, it does not become an evil spirit."[100] In addition to the vivid description of the terror in the *Zuo Commentary* episode, the text suggests that one could pacify an unquiet ghost by securing a "place" for it. Here the "place" is provided through the transmission of the father's official position to the son, thus enabling him to offer sacrifices to his deceased father. Similar stories of vengeful ghosts in the *Zuo Commentary* and other early texts likewise point to the belief that the living could pacify and segregate the avenging dead through sacrifices intended to secure a place (such as a tomb) for them.[101]

Most students of early Chinese religion have argued, following Anna Seidel, that the Chinese cult of the dead and the conception of the afterlife did not fully evolve until the Han dynasty.[102] Chu mortuary data from the Warring States period, however, shows that the popular conception of the afterlife was fully developed by this time. In the Boyou story, we see this development beginning in the Spring and Autumn period. To be sure, conceptions of the afterlife underwent significant changes during the Han. The idea of a "transcendent paradise," such as the realm of the Queen Mother of the West, likely dates to the mid–Western Han, but this transcendent paradise should not be confused with conceptions of the afterlife or a destination for the spirit's journey.[103] In fact, one destination for departed souls in the Warring States period was Mount Buzhou, thought to be located in a northwestern section of the universe.[104] The descriptions in various texts of the different destinations for departed souls testify to the cultural diversity of early China. The transition from the Warring States period to that of the early empires united these competing conceptions of the afterlife and their associated religious practices.

Shifts in Attitudes toward the Dead

The foregoing discussion focuses on avenging ghosts in the context of political struggles and on the rise of the afterlife during the Spring and Autumn and early Warring States periods. The need to pacify baleful ghosts and victims of violent death during this period of political disruption transformed the traditional ritual structure of ancestor cults and introduced new perspectives on the dead in the Warring States period and that of the early empires.

The religious notions of violent death, the fear of unquiet ghosts, and the cult of the dead persisted through the Eastern Zhou period, but their connotations and applications changed along with social developments. For example, the concept of the dead slain with weapons, which had previously referred only to those elite killed by their opponents in intralineal struggle or warfare, came in the Warring States period to include conscripted commoners, soldiers, and generals—war dead, such as those described in the "Hymn to the Fallen," who sacrificed their lives for the state. Chinese archaeologists have discovered at least two sites that testify to the increased intensity and atrocity of war during the Warring States period.

Discovered at Xishuipo, Puyang County, Henan, the first site houses the mass graves of the dead from a brutal battle.[105] Archaeologists found more than thirty orderly burial pits arrayed in twelve rows, four of which have an east-west orientation and eight of which have a north-south orientation. Each pit contains at least eighteen male skeletons, aged twenty to twenty-five, and varying numbers of severed heads (fig. 1.4). Many of the human bones bear cuts by knives or arrowheads. It is evident that all had been slain with weapons and had suffered violent deaths. Altogether, more than five hundred individuals were buried in these pits. This site is near the famous battlefield of Chengpu, where the northern alliance led by Jin defeated the Chu army led by Chief Minister Ziyu and Marshal Zixi in 632 BCE. In the absence of chronologically specific grave goods, archaeologists are not able to make a definitive identification of this site. Just two and a half kilometers from this site is another famous battlefield by the name of Tie, where in 493 BCE the Jin army

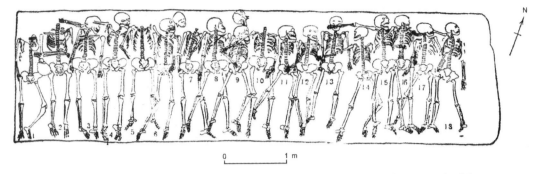

Fig. 1.4. Burial Pit 175 at Xishuipo, Puyang County, Henan. Mass grave, possibly for war dead from the Battle of Chengpu in 632 BCE.

defeated the Zheng army.[106] The mass graves probably contain the war dead from one of these famous battles.

The battles of the Warring States period were far more intense than those of the Spring and Autumn period. During the two and a half centuries of the Warring States period, wars, as the period's name suggests, were the norm rather than the exception, and the scale of warfare drastically increased.[107] The "Annals of the Six States" (Liuguo nianbiao), a chapter in the *Records of the Grand Historian*, chronicles 186 large-scale wars among the states during this period. Compared to the previous Spring and Autumn period, the scale and intensity of wars were significantly greater, while their frequency was reduced (the *Zuo Commentary* records 483 military conflicts of the Spring and Autumn period, an average of two wars per year).

The second archaeological battlefield, discovered at Gaoping in Shanxi, testifies to the intensity of war in the Warring States period. There, in 260 BCE, the Qin army led by General Bai Qi (d. 257 BCE) killed or buried alive 400,000 soldiers of the state of Zhao. This military campaign proved a turning point in the Warring States period; from this time onward, the state of Qin was destined to conquer all other states and thereby unify China. Starting in 262 BCE, the campaign lasted for more than two years. According to the *Records of the Grand Historian* account, the Qin besieged the Zhao army at Changping (present-day Gaoping County in Shanxi), and 400,000 Zhao soldiers surrendered. Fearing that the Zhao troops might revolt, General Bai Qi ordered that the Zhao soldiers be massacred: "Counting earlier and later actions, he took prisoner or cut off the heads of 450,000 men, leaving the people of Zhao trembling with fear."[108] Although these numbers may not be exact, the extreme cruelty of wars during the Warring States period is beyond doubt.

Scholars and local people alike have recognized this famous battlefield throughout Chinese history.[109] Mass graves lie scattered all over the valley of the Dan River, a small tributary of the Yellow River. In 1995, archaeologists excavated a pit about 9.4 meters long, 2.7 meters wide, and 0.7–0.9 meters deep at Yonglu in Gaoping County, Shanxi. They unearthed the skeletal remains of more than 130 soldiers, at least one-third of which had been approximately thirty years old at the time of death. The piled bones, severed heads, and fractured skulls confirmed that the soldiers buried there had suffered violent deaths (figs. 1.5a and 1.5b).[110]

The large numbers of war dead from the increasing intensity of war became a social and religious problem during the Warring States period. The famous "Hymn to the Fallen" from the south is considered "one of the most beautiful laments for fallen soldiers in any language."[111] This poem offers a poetic eulogy to warriors who died on a battlefield after fierce fighting. The title of the poem refers to those who died prematurely, cut down in their prime in service to the state. Scholars generally agree that this poem is a liturgical hymn used in state sacrifices to the war dead.[112] The nameless war dead, often buried in mass graves, make up a special category of the dead. The state assumed responsibility for conducting proper rituals to pacify their unquiet ghosts. This contributed to the development of public sacrifice, especially sacrifices to evil ghosts and the nameless war dead, as part of the state religion in the imperial era.[113]

The high mortality rate during the Warring States period reflected increasing violence in society and the dramatic changes in warfare that took place between the fifth and fourth centuries BCE. Chariot warfare led by aristocrats was replaced by battles between large-scale infantry armies. Peasants and other commoners were conscripted to serve in the military.[114] Advanced weaponry and other military technology produced more casualties and higher mortality rates on the battlegrounds. These mortality rates gradually altered people's general attitudes toward death and the dead.

Scholars agree that dramatic changes in demography and mortality rates are among the most important factors throughout human history in people's perspectives on death and the dead. The transition from the Warring States period to that of the early empires is a case in point. Based on anecdotal accounts in historical sources, historians estimate that between the middle Warring States period and the early Han dynasty the population decreased by almost half.[115] This extraordinary demographic shift coupled with the high mortality rate dramatically affected people's perspectives on death and the dead during the Warring States, Qin, and Han periods.

Perceptions among the living of ghosts and calamities are symptoms of the troubled age. Anthropologists and ethnographers have studied the universality of the fear of death and the dead across societies, as well as forms of death pollution—the social disorder, ritual unclearness, physical decay, and psychological chaos caused by the death of a member of the community—and the varieties of funerary rites meant to avoid or overcome such fear and contagion.[116] Attitudes toward death and the dead are not individual but part of the collective mentality of an age, conditioned by the social and political reality of the times, which includes individuals' perspectives not only on their own deaths but also on the deaths of others.[117]

Additionally, death rituals allow the bereaved to celebrate the life of the departed

Figs. 1.5a and b. Mass graves at Yonglu, Gaoping County, Shanxi, where the army of the state of Zhou was besieged and massacred by the Qin, 262–260 BCE.

and to negotiate power and prestige among the living. As a rite of passage, death entails a ritual process that is best understood in a particular cultural context.[118] It is not just the end of an individual's life but the beginning of a new relationship between the living and the dead. Moreover, the mourners, through their symbolic actions, can control and create the death status of the departed individual.[119]

Tomb 2 at Baoshan provides a useful illustration of the change in perspective on death at the individual level. As Chief Minister of the Left of the state of Chu, Shao Tuo (d. 316 BCE) was anxious about his official activities and his interaction with the Chu king. He divined about his "coming and going in the service of the king," and once, when he was ill, he asked almost all the celestial, terrestrial, and human spirits in the Chu religious pantheon, including his recent ancestors and the unquiet ghosts both inside and outside his family, for their help. Of them, the most efficacious spirits were the vengeful ghosts, whether Shao Tuo's relatives or not. In the last divination before his death, he asked, "May it still be possible that [I] not die," and the divinations indicated that the calamities were coming from those who had died without posterity and from the fecundity god who managed life and death.

The documents excavated from Shao Tuo's tomb do not specify whether he had any descendants, but his death arguably was a bad one: he died in agony and in fear of mortality, pleading with the avenging spirits to prevent his death. We know few details about the funerary rites used in Shao Tuo's case, but from the funerary documents and grave goods buried in his tomb, we can surmise that he was well equipped to start his next stage of existence in the afterlife.[120]

Shao Tuo's tomb was structured like the Jiuliandun tombs: fourteen step-ledges descend on all four sides and a sloping ramp on the east side leads to the burial encasement at the bottom of the pit. The encasement is divided into four side compartments surrounding a central compartment where the three nested coffins are located. Underneath the wooden encasement is a small "waist pit" (yaokeng), in which a goat (as was the case in Tomb 2 at Jiuliandun) was buried. The waist pit is a standard feature of earlier Shang and Zhou burial customs. Archaeologists have so named it because it is located in the middle of the pit, just under the waist of the tomb occupant. There is no consensus regarding its meaning, but it is likely an expression of religious beliefs.[121] Some speculate that dogs or goats in the waist pit functioned as guides, leading the deceased to the land of the dead.[122] Only a few elite Chu tombs have this feature, and its disappearance in the transition from the Warring States period to the early Han probably marked changes in related religious ideas.[123]

The four compartments of Shao Tuo's tomb contained 1,935 artifacts and 448 bamboo strips, 278 of which are inscribed. The artifacts include a large number of bronze, lacquer, and ceramic sacrificial vessels, weapons, chariot fittings, and personal belongings. The texts include legal and administrative documents and lists of grave goods. Like the religious pantheon discussed above, grave goods in Warring States elite tombs are categorically similar to those in Shang and Western Zhou elite burials, but the prevalence of spirit artifacts and luxury objects among the personal belongings in Warring States elite tombs distinguish this later burial tradition from earlier ones. The changes in grave furnishings of Warring States tombs reflect new attitudes toward the dead. The religious significance of other grave goods will be discussed in chapter 5; below, we focus on the purpose and meaning in Warring States burials of burying spirit artifacts as a tie-breaking ritual.

Redefining the Relations between the Dead and the Living

As its name suggests, a tie-breaking ritual severs the bond, or tie, between the living and the deceased and is performed to break the old life pattern.[124] According to French anthropologist Arnold van Gennep, death is but one of a series of ritual passages through the life cycle.[125] The tie-breaking ritual simultaneously emphasizes the mourner's separation from the dead and integration with the living. The purpose of this ritual is twofold: it facilitates the psychological transition of the bereaved and ensures that the soul of the deceased makes its proper transition from earthly life to its new life in the land of the dead. Tie-breaking acts include the ceremonial "killing" of objects at funerals, the disposal of the belongings of the dead, the placement of a taboo on the name of the deceased, and the bereaved's temporary or permanent changing of residence.[126] But in Warring States China, providing proper grave furnishing became an important part of the tie-breaking ritual.

Earlier Shang and Western Zhou aristocratic traditions continued, as the preoccupation with burying symbols of social status such as chariots and sets of bronze vessels makes clear. However, new categories of grave goods and new compositions of artifacts belonging to the old categories constantly emerged. An examination of the medium-size tombs excavated at Zhaojiahu in Dangyang County and at Jiudian and Yutaishan in Jiangling County, all in Hubei, reveals that new categories of grave goods, in particular personal belongings, household utensils, and food provisions, came to accompany the traditional sets of ritual vessels.[127] These new artifacts include weapons, utensils for dress (combs, mirrors, and belt hooks), musical instruments for personal entertainment (*se* zithers), utensils for eating and drinking, bamboo mats, pillows, and fans. It is not coincidental that most of the new categories of personal belongings and household utensils are listed under the heading "travel paraphernalia" (*xingqi*) in the grave-goods inventories buried in Tomb 2 at Baoshan.

Although low-quality or miniature imitations of ritual vessels made of clay, lead, and other materials appeared in Shang and Western Zhou, and even Neolithic, tombs, the self-conscious systematic use of spirit artifacts in funerary rites was characteristic of Warring States religious phenomena.[128] The use of the spirit artifacts may have inspired Warring States philosophers to discuss their religious significance. The term *spirit artifact* is loaded with various meanings in contemporary scholarly literature.[129] When modern scholars began to use this term in the early twentieth century, it referred only to ceramic sculptures of human figures (*yong*), animals, and daily utensils employed in mortuary settings after the Warring States period. The term later was extended to cover all funerary objects made for tomb furnishing.[130] Extensive Warring States philosophical reflections on the religious phenomenon of burying spirit artifacts in tombs afford a rare case wherein archaeological and transmitted textual materials corroborate each other.

Compared to its modern usage, in Warring States ritual and philosophical texts the term refers to a broader range of materials but defines more narrowly their intended functions. Spirit artifacts marked the difference between this world and the other world, between life and death, and between the material and the spiritual. These artifacts were made "unfinished," or "secondary" and "inferior" to everyday utensils in terms of their materiality, size, and craftsmanship. The concept of a spirit artifact was "not determined by medium or form, but was based on ritual function and symbolism."[131] This concept apparently was widespread among intellectuals of the Warring States period. For example, the Confucian philosopher Xunzi, in his "Discourse on Ritual" (Lilun), defines a spirit artifact as something that "resembles real objects but cannot be used."[132] Here, the quality of the spirit artifacts, like the attitude toward the dead, is a paradox: the objects are familiar but different. Objects of this sort belong to what anthropologists identify as a "tie-breaking ritual."[133]

All over the world, from prehistoric times onward, when there is less status competition, we find cheap and miniature objects manufactured in clay used as offerings to gods and the dead.[134] But there are other religious or moral reasons for gods and spirits to accept humble substitutes for expensive gifts. It is said that the recipients cared only about the intention, or the "heart," of the givers, not the cost of the gifts.[135] This type of morality is discussed in the historical and philosophical literature of the Warring States period.[136] Archaeological evidence indicates that spirit artifacts were first widely used in Qin tombs early in the Spring and Autumn period but became more prevalent in the late Spring and Autumn and early Warring States periods.[137] At almost the same time, a lively debate regarding whether "the dead have knowledge" began in some philosophical circles.[138] The debates transpired primarily between Confucian advocates of lavish mortuary rites and Mohist advocates of frugality.[139]

Archaeological records also show that in burial practice bronze and ceramic vessels were mixed together to form a set of grave objects.[140] Not only spirit and ritual vessels but also luxury nonritual objects, such as lacquered vessels, exotic jewelry, and personal ornaments, were buried in tombs. These objects form a sharp contrast to the spirit artifacts in terms of artistic quality. In the Baoshan tomb, besides the bronze ritual vessels, the music instruments, the ceramic storage jars, and other daily utensils, the most exquisite and valuable objects are lacquered vessels such as a set of lacquered cups with a leather bag (item 4), a double bird-shaped drinking cup (item 189), a pair of spouted cups with dragon and phoenix motifs (items 25 and 31), and a painted lacquered box with a pictorial decoration (item 432).

As Paul Rosenblatt and others have pointed out, tie-breaking rituals, which are a common response to death in many cultures, take many different forms.[141] In the Chinese context, the tie-breaking ritual included the burial of spirit artifacts and the interment of new and old personal belongings. One entry (Strip 15) in a grave-goods inventory excavated at Yangtianhu in Changsha City, Hunan, describes "one new shoe, one old shoe."[142] In the inventory from Tomb 3 at Mawangdui, old personal belongings are listed as being buried in the tomb.[143] This tradition of burying new and old personal belongings survived in later mortuary practice.

Burying spirit artifacts and personal belongings helped the bereaved reduce and eventually sever their ties with the dead while maintaining the connection between the world of the living and the world of the dead. The rituals were also designed to help both the bereaved and the deceased negotiate the gradual transition from life to death.

THIS CHAPTER SETS THE STAGE for subsequent arguments by documenting changes in conceptions of death and the dead during the Warring States period. Why did the early Chinese come to perceive the dead primarily as a threat?[144] Early Chinese texts such as the *Zuo Commentary* and the *Narratives of the States* record a political culture of violent death and an emerging literary genre of ghost narratives as well as new concepts of the afterlife. Within the context of political struggle among the lineages and states, the winners tried to eliminate the social memory of their opponents by denying them a ritually appropriate burial in the lineage cemetery and by engaging in other associated forms of ancestor cults. These dead—who suffered violent deaths, died young, or died without posterity—belonged to the cultural category of "bad death" and would not become ancestors. Instead, because they could not receive sacrifices from their descendants, they turned into hungry ghosts. The ghost narratives of the Eastern Zhou period, circulated among conservative educated elites, articulated new concepts of the afterlife and of the soul.

During the Warring States period, mass conscription brought a large number of the war dead into the religious realm. The view of the dead as a threat spread and eventually fostered an ambivalent attitude toward ancestors. As the Warring States pantheon in the Baoshan records shows, previously undocumented vengeful ghosts came to be regarded as more potent than other spirits. The material and textual remains recovered from Chu tombs disclose profound, but often overlooked, changes in cultural perspectives on the dead that evolved during the Eastern Zhou period. Finally, the prevalent ritual of burying spirit artifacts in tombs suggests that these changing perspectives, which earlier concerned only those who had died violent deaths, now encompassed almost all the dead, including ancestors. This conception of the dead as threatening prompted significant changes in the funerary rituals and burial practices in the Warring States period and that of the early empires.

2

The Transformation of Burial Space

There is no architecture without action, no architecture without events,
no architecture without program.

—BERNARD TSCHUMI

THE PERIOD BETWEEN the Warring States era and the early Han dynasty marks a transition in Chinese mortuary practice and burial ideology during which horizontal chamber-style tombs gradually supplanted vertical pit tombs as the dominant form of burial structure.[1] What factors caused this transformation is an age-old question in the study of Chinese tombs. Certainly, the historical process was multifaceted and took place in fits and starts over a broad area. Scholars have focused primarily on formal aspects of the tomb, such as precedents of the horizontal orientation in the catacombs, the uses of different construction materials (stone, brick, wood, etc.), the expansion of storage pits to contain more burial goods, and the evolution of burial types.[2] Others attempted to explain it in ideological and religious terms.[3] Building on previous scholarship, this chapter presents three direct driving forces behind this transformation.[4] The first is the shift in burial ideology from the hiding of the corpse in the Shang and Western Zhou periods to its luxurious public display in the Warring States period and the early empires. The second is the pragmatic demand for burying a husband and wife together in a single burial space, a demand that reflects fundamental social changes in early China from a lineage-based structure to a more family-based structure.[5] For example, while the husband and wife recovered at Jiuliandun were buried side by side in two vertical pit-style tombs, after the middle Western Han period, they likely would have been buried in the same chamber in a horizontal tomb. This practice started among members of the middle and lower levels of Western Han society and gradually spread to the upper level of society as well. Indeed, even some princely and imperial tombs adopted this practice of joint burial in the same chamber.[6] To inter the second coffin the tomb must be reopened, and the horizontal chamber-style tombs not only made this easier but also enabled people to construct and decorate tombs for a longer period than did the vertical pit-style tombs.

The third direct driving force behind the spatial transformation was the new conception of the dead as baleful and potentially threatening ghosts that needed to be pacified and segregated. The mortuary transformation was closely linked to the establishment of sacrificial spaces inside tombs—a new feature of the horizontal chamber-style tombs[7]—which reflected changes in the status of the dead and the sacrificial rituals associated with them. Formalizing the longer mourning period (up to three years) in the Han period meant prolonging the deceased's liminal period, which starts at death and ends after the spirit tablet is enshrined.[8] The horizontal chamber-style tombs created a home-like tame environment that afforded mourners the ability not only to walk into the tomb and perform funerary rites within it, close to the bodies of the deceased, but also to use rituals more efficiently to separate the dead from the living and manage the pollution and contagion caused by death. As the liminal space for the recently departed, the tomb became the locus for the cult of the dead, aimed at helping the deceased transform from potentially dangerous ghosts into benevolent ancestors.

Methodologically, archaeologists and social anthropologists have long recognized that space may be used as a means of categorizing the world and classifying human experience.[9] Changes in the symbolic use of mortuary space can help us to understand the social transformations that were underway. In addition, theoretical developments in the studies of ritual through the lens of performance-as-spectacle and through its architectural settings shed new light on early Chinese alterations in tomb structure.[10] Particularly, the analysis here is influenced by the architectural theorist Bernard Tschumi's concept of architecture as event-places, that is, as a combination of spaces, events, and movement.[11] This is definitely the case for the horizontal chamber-style tombs in early China. Concern for the efficacy of the ritual and for the well-being of the departed ancestors compelled the early Chinese to create a sacrificial space within the tomb. This interpretive strategy combines both the material aspects of tomb structure and furnishings and the nonmaterial aspects of funerary rites. The structure of a tomb not only provides the space for burial ceremonies but also is an integral part of the mortuary rites. Tombs and their contents essentially reflect a funerary ritual process.

The Vertical Pit-Style Burial and Its Ideology

The dominant form of burial in early China was inhumation in a vertical pit. The philosophical debates of the Warring States period considered not only human nature and the organization of government but also funerals and mourning.[12] Nearly all thinkers of this period voiced opinions about how the dead should be buried and mourned, variously advocating moderate, frugal, or elaborate burials.[13]

Archaeologically, burial in vertical pits can be traced back to the fifth millennium BCE at Neolithic sites. These earliest burials consisted of a small ditch just big enough to contain a body and a few funerary objects such as tools and ceramic vessels. As social complexity increased, burials became more elaborate. As early as the Majiayao culture (ca. 4000–ca. 2250 BCE), many tombs, like those at Liuwan in Ledu County, Qinghai, contained a wooden coffin along with ritual pottery vessels.[14] The early development of burial structure culminated in the late Shang royal tombs at Anyang, where large vertical shafts with one, two, or four ramps led to a burial pit. The large excavated tomb at Houjiazhuang, Tomb 1002, consists of a rectangular pit with four ramps in the shape of a gigantic cross (fig. 2.1). At the bottom of the fifteen-meter-deep pit is a wooden encasement containing a lacquered wooden coffin and grave goods. Because this tomb was repeatedly plundered before its excavation in 1935, we do not know how richly the grave was furnished. The sheer size of the tomb, however, indicates the high rank of its occupant. On the other hand, the smaller, undisturbed tomb at Anyang, that of Fu Hao (or Fu Zi), consort of Wu Ding, yielded more than six thousand cowries and nearly two thousand bronze objects (together weighing more than 1,625 kg), as well as jade, stone, bones, ivory, clay, and shells. This is a simple rectangular pit lacking even a ramp. It is just eight meters deep and about twenty-two square meters at bottom. In contrast, Tomb 1217 at Houjiazhuang measures 330 square meters. Burial grounds of average noble tombs

Fig. 2.1. Aerial view of the royal tomb (M1002) of the Shang dynasty at Houjiazhuang, Anyang City, Henan. Collection of the Institute of History and Philology, Academia Sinica, Taiwan.

ranged from about ten to twenty square meters, whereas the size of a commoner's burial was sometimes less than two square meters. Other features of the Shang tombs include the extensive use of human and animal sacrifice and a small waist pit.

Burials of the Western Zhou dynasty and the Spring and Autumn period continued the basic Shang forms with a few innovations, such as the use of "piles of stone and heaps of charcoal" to surround the wooden encasement, keeping off moisture and fortifying the grave (figs. 2.2a and 2.2b). Archaeological evidence suggests that starting from at least the ninth century BCE strict sumptuary rules restricted the use of ritual vessels and chariots. Although the scale of these burials is much smaller than that of the Shang royal tombs, excavated elite burials in vassal states such as Yan (in Beijing), Jin (in Shanxi), Guo, Ying, Wei (all in Henan), Lu (in Shandong), and Yu (in Shaanxi) indicate that the Shang tradition of vertical pit-style tombs continued in the Zhou cultural sphere during the subsequent Spring and Autumn period. Following the Spring and Autumn period, the Zhou vassal states in the Central Plains as well as peripheral polities such as the Qin and Chu adopted in varying degrees the Shang-Zhou burial tradition. These rival states accepted the Shang-Zhou burial tradition but added their own regional innovations.[15]

The religious ideology underlying the vertical pit style was the hiding (*cang* 藏) of the corpse. This is evident linguistically in that the word *zang* 葬, "to bury," was a cognate of the word *cang*, "to hide."[16] In the Eastern Zhou period, the Qi nobleman Guo Zigao explained this concept further: "Burying means hiding away; and that hiding of the body is from a wish that people should not see it. Hence the clothes are sufficient to adorn the body; a coffin encloses the clothes, an encasement encloses the coffin, and earth encloses the encasement. And shall we go further and raise a mound over the grave and plant it with trees?"[17] This definition of burial as the process of hiding the corpse also occurs in other early Chinese texts such as *Master Lü's Spring and Autumn Annals* (Lüshi chunqiu, third century BCE).[18] Certainly, it is possible that these are Warring States and Han rationalizations of contemporary burial practices.[19] Nevertheless, it is significant that people of the time understood not only that one reason for burial was to conceal the corpse but also that a proper burial of the physical remains ensured the well-being of the deceased in the afterlife.

The spirits of the dead were eventually transformed into venerable ancestors, but their bodies needed to be hidden and securely interred. Early Chinese texts describe incidents of death pollution and explicitly place taboos on the handling of the bones and flesh of the dead. Magical ritual performances to exorcise evil influences were also developed. As a practical ritual manual dating to the Warring States period, the *Protocols of Ceremonies* (Yili) prescribes that during the funerary rites, clothes, quilts, and tents were utilized to cover the corpse in order to hide it from view.[20] When approaching the corpse (and the coffin) during funerary rites, people were advised to take precautionary exorcising measures to avoid death pollution.[21] Although early Chinese did not preserve corpses as systematically as the ancient Egyptians,[22] they

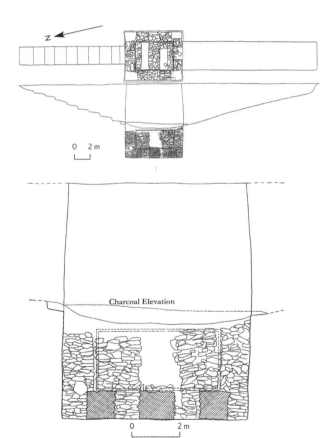

Fig. 2.2a. Aerial view of the Western Zhou elite tomb in the cemetery of the state of Jin at Tianma-Qucun site in Quwo County, Shanxi.

Fig. 2.2b. Line drawing of the Western Zhou elite tomb in the cemetery of the state of Jin at Tianma-Qucun site in Quwo County, Shanxi.

Charcoal Elevation

0   2 m

0   2 m

did make an effort to keep the physical body intact and understood this as important for ensuring the well-being of the deceased's soul.[23]

This is the religious background for the stories of Wu Zixu, a hero of the Spring and Autumn period, who fulfilled his vendetta against the King of Chu by exhuming the king's corpse and lashing it three hundred times.[24] Anecdotes about the Han imperial court struggles among consorts and concubines describe the mutilation of their rivals' corpses as a magic measure to impair the spiritual power of the enemy,[25] a practice similar to the punishments of the dead in the political struggles among the lineages of the Spring and Autumn period.

Shifts in Ancestral Sacrifice in the Afterlife

Not only were corpses properly concealed, but grave goods were also interred with the dead to keep the spirits content in the afterlife. In Shang or Western Zhou elite tombs, bronze ritual vessels were typically grave goods accompanying the deceased in the other world. For the early Chinese elite, the bronze ritual vessels were the "inalienable possessions."[26] This understanding is evident in the ubiquitous formula found at the end of bronze inscriptions, a practice that began during the mid-Western Zhou: "May sons and grandsons eternally use this [vessel] for sacrifice." Sets of bronze sacrificial vessels symbolized one's rank and status. But why were they, if precious and inalienable, buried in tombs? What ideology supported this practice of burying ritual vessels in tombs? The Japanese scholar Hayashi Minao (1925–2006) raised this paradoxical issue in early Chinese burial practice: If these treasured bronze vessels were buried in the tomb, then how could the sons and grandsons of the deceased use them and treasure them forever? What were the functions of these ritual vessels in tombs?

Hayashi believed that the bronze vessels buried in tombs were for the deceased to continue sacrificing to their ancestors in the afterlife, and that the sons and grandsons would eventually join the ancestors in the lineage cemetery in the afterlife. Bronze inscriptions and anecdotes in the *Zuo Commentary* suggest that at that time family members of different generations were understood to meet again after death,[27] and thus they could use and treasure the bronze heirlooms eternally, just as they had done in life in their lineage temples.[28] This chain of ancestral sacrifice—the living to their deceased ancestors and the deceased ancestors to their ancestors in the afterlife—explains the mechanism of early Chinese ancestor cults.

This insight has tremendous implications for understanding early Chinese mortuary religion. It shows that, despite having themselves joined the ranks of the ancestors, the dead have to continue sacrificing to their own ancestors in order to maintain their social status. For the early Chinese elite, sacrifice to their ancestors was an essential part of everyday life. As indicated in the five ritual cycles practiced during the late Shang dynasty, the communication between them was on daily, weekly, monthly, and yearly bases.[29] Ancestral spirits reciprocated by playing an important role in maintaining the social and political well-being of their descendants. Typically, one's social and political position was determined by how many generations of ancestors one was entitled to sacrifice to and how many bronze ritual vessels one was permitted to use in the ancestral sacrifice.[30]

In the Shang and Western Zhou periods, ancestor cult worship was not just a private or personal religious practice; instead, it was a symbolic act, a political competition among powerful clans and lineages to provide their own ancestors with the "richest" and "best" offerings. In this process of political strife, ritual bronze vessels played a vital role. The display of bronzes in ancestral temples as well as in funerals was a sign of political power and religious devotion. The control of copper, tin, and other natural and social resources was converted into political authority through the mechanism of ancestor cults.[31] Thus, ritual bronze vessels previously used for everyday eating and drinking, especially the cooking and serving cauldron (ding), became symbols of political power in early China.

Therefore, the use of real and prestigious bronze ritual vessels for sacrifice as grave goods expressed the seriousness of the worshipers' commitment to the spirits. As H. G. Creel has pointed out, "The Shang people buried with their honoured dead objects in such quantity and of such quality as must have in some measure impoverished the living, especially when we consider that bronze was almost certainly scarce. They did not, of course, consider these things wasted. The help of ancestors on the battlefield was considered far more valuable than the possession of a few extra weapons."[32] The bronze sacrificial vessels solidified the chain of ancestral sacrifice in the afterlife and connected the living with the dead.

In an imaginary, unspecified location in the afterlife, the ancestors continued the luxurious life they had enjoyed while living and retained all of their former social relations. This elite view of their continued and privileged existence after death manifested in the cosmology and the abode of the dead in the Shang and Western Zhou dynasties. We have no strong evidence for the exact place to which the ancestral spirits would go; early literature speaks only vaguely and abstractly about the departed ancestors residing somewhere underground or climbing up and coming down (shangxia) and ascending to and descending (zhijiang) from the "court/place of the god" (diting, disuo, or dizhipi).[33] An inscribed bronze tripod excavated from a late Spring-and-Autumn-period tomb (Tomb 439) at Luoyang City, Henan, speaks of the tomb occupant, posthumously named Ai Cheng Shu, who continued to serve his former lord in the underground (xiatu).[34] Another set of bronze vessels, including inscribed ding and fou, excavated in a Spring-and-Autumn-period tomb in Xiangyang City, Hubei, were made by the grandson of Lord Zang of Zheng for his deceased parents, who were "moving to the underworld" (xi yu xiadu).[35] This underworld of the dead, it seems, was not yet as gloomy and perilous as "the Dark Capital [of the dead]" described in the "Summons of the Soul" (Zhaohun) chapter of Songs of the South (Chuci).

In the Shang and Western Zhou burial ideology, although the ancestors' physical remains were "hidden" underground, their spirits could roam freely up and down. The cross-shaped burial structure of the Shang elite symbolized the center of the tomb, the center of the kingdom, and the center of the universe in Shang cosmology.[36] Probably from this center, the ancestral spirits could ascend and descend. The *Book of Poetry* (Shijing) and paleographical data envision the afterlife of the ancestors as one in which they can freely travel between the heavenly and earthly realms and be "in the entourage of High God" (*zai Di zuoyou*), and "oversee (their descendants) from above" (*yan zai shang*). As a result, these ancestors brought blessings and protection to their descendants below (*yi zai xia*).[37] The deceased ancestors became new "bureaucrats" in the Shang political system who received "salaries" in the form of sacrifices for their jobs as intercessors between the king and the High God.[38]

In Shang-Western Zhou religious practice, the ancestral spirits played an important role in maintaining the political legitimacy of the royal house and the social status of their descendants. Not only the Shang and Western Zhou royal houses and their allies but also other states, such as Qin and Chu, adopted this political ideology of ancestor cults. From very early in the Spring and Autumn period, the royal houses of Qin and Chu identified with the Zhou royal house, thereby forging a political connection with the royal Zhou and wholeheartedly adopting the Zhou political ideology as well as its burial tradition.[39] In this burial tradition, the mortuary space was constructed to reflect the sociopolitical status of the deceased, reflected in both the size of the tomb and the number of funerary objects.

Texts from the Warring States period preserve the idea of a location wherefrom the deceased continue to conduct ancestral sacrifice in the afterlife. The grave goods inventory excavated from Tomb 2 at Baoshan refers to a dining hall or sacrificial chamber (*shishi*),[40] under which heading bronze ritual vessels and foods were listed. Most scholars have assumed that this refers to the eastern compartment of the Baoshan tomb because some objects listed under this heading were discovered there. But the eastern compartment, like most Warring States burial compartments, is rather small and cramped; therefore, it could not have been used as a real space for conducting ancestral sacrifice.[41] Instead, it is my contention that the term refers to an imaginary place, just like the place of the god, in the afterlife—a place where the tomb occupant's sacrifice to his or her ancestors took place. This is a case of the strong conceptual continuity between the Shang and Western Zhou and the Warring States period. The term used to refer to a dining hall or sacrificial chamber was, as I will show later, also the name for the stone shrine near the burial sites in the Eastern Han dynasty.[42] In this case, an imagined place in the afterlife is materialized in architectural form (according to Wu Hung, in a process of "architecturalization").[43]

As status indicators, ritual bronzes were still present in elite graves during the Warring States period. However, they occupied increasingly less important positions in the grave goods.[44] In fact, the most valuable objects in the Warring States, Qin, and early Han tombs were no longer the bronze ritual vessels, for which ceramic imitations were gradually substituted, but the newly added luxury objects, including personal adornments and utensils made of gold and silver, precious beads and jewels, expensive silk clothes, and lacquered vessels of high quality. For example, the ritual bronze vessels found in Tomb 2 at Baoshan were conventional and plain and neither inscribed nor elaborately decorated. They are in fact bronze spirit artifacts with many cast defects. The most significant objects were found inside a lacquered cosmetic box excavated from the northern compartment (Item 432; about 27.8 cm in diameter, 10.8 cm in height). A band of narrative, figurative painting occupies the upper register of the box. Inside, archaeologists found two bronze mirrors, one square and one round, a pair of clamshells, two bone hairpins, a silk cosmetic applicator, and two small wood pieces of unknown function. These changes in the grave goods indicate that, although the sacrificial chain continued, it had gradually weakened and the emphasis had shifted from ancestor cults in the afterlife to the cult of the recently deceased ancestors. The sacrificial vessels and foods reappeared in Han burials at a later time but for entirely different purposes (these were sacrificial offerings to the dead, rather than to the ancestors of the dead).

The Warring States Innovations

The horizontal chamber-style tombs, as a new architectural form, marked a dramatic change in the concept and function of the burial.[45] The alteration of the physical space significantly changed the relationship between the dead and the living, which in turn had an enduring impact on later developments in Chinese burial practice. Not only did tomb chambers grow large enough to accommodate visitors, as well as mortuary ceremonies, but the grave also developed into a structure with multiple openings appropriate for the interment of couples and other family members.[46]

Although burial practices began to change in the Spring and Autumn period, the rate of these changes intensified in the Warring States period and continued in the Qin and Han dynasties. The burial practices in the state of Chu, which had already adopted the standard set by the Shang and Western Zhou tradition, with vertical pit-style tombs and the associated burial ideology, began to innovate and to assimilate eclectic elements from various sources. As regional contact among states and cultural spheres increased, cultural conflicts and contradictions appeared, followed by adaptation and acculturation. Amid this seemingly chaotic period of change, some general trends and logics in the development and the transformation of the burial space can be discerned. Many experimental changes aimed at issues related to the developing burial ideology and the redefined relationship between the living and the dead originated in Chu and its adjacent areas. Some of these changes had lasting universal effects, and some had only temporary or regional impacts. In these endeavors, however, we begin to see the logic behind the spatial developments and to sense the concerns and possible motives for the transformation of burial architecture in early China.

The spatial transformation of burial architecture in early China has been characterized as the transference of religious activities "from temple to tomb."[47] According to this theory, during the Shang and Zhou dynasties, temple and tomb coexisted as twin centers of ancestor cults. In the Eastern Zhou period, however, the balance began to shift to the tomb. This culminated in the Eastern Han Emperor Ming's (r. 58–75 CE) abolition of temple sacrifice; as a result, the cemetery became the sole center for ancestor cults.

This interpretation, however, has met with serious criticism.[48] Because we have less archaeological data for the home than for the tomb, we know less about the religious activities that took place in domestic households and temples. The almanacs excavated from Warring States, Qin, and Han tombs mention "sacrificial chambers" (*jishi* in Jiudian Strip 49, *cishi* in Shuihudi rishu A, Strip 18 back 5),[49] which referred to the places in ordinary households where descendants sacrificed to their ancestors. Nevertheless, the religious functions of the temple were not completely replaced by those of the tomb, even in the Han dynasty. Temple-tomb dualism did not entirely disappear, and, at other levels of early Chinese society, both types of sacrifice remained.

Moreover, even at the imperial level, not all temples and temple sacrifices were abolished. As late as the Western Han dynasty, imperial ancestral temples were established not only in the capital Chang'an but also in local kingdoms and provinces (similar to "the royal household cult," in the Qin legal documents)[50] for the purpose of establishing religious authority and orthodoxy in the newly established empire.[51] Furthermore, following the practice of the First Emperor of Qin, who considered himself a deity and established for himself the Temple of Pivot (Jimiao), the Han emperors began to establish their own temples devoted to the cult of themselves, during their lifetimes. Emperor Ming specified in his will that a separate imperial temple for him be abolished; however, his spirit tablet (*zhu*) is housed in the temple of the founding emperor Guang Wu (5 BCE–57 CE) (Shizumiao) in Luoyang, a practice more or less followed by later generations of Eastern Han emperors.[52] In addition to the High Temple (Gaomiao) housing the spirit tablets of the Western Han emperors in Chang'an, at least two imperial temples held regular sacrifices through the Eastern Han dynasty. Although, after Emperor Ming's reform, imperial temples, specifically, the chamber of rest (*qin* 寝), were relocated to an area near the tombs, the religious importance of the temple increased rather than declined.[53] Eventually, at the end of the Eastern Han dynasty, the dualism between temple and tomb was revived.[54]

The factors that caused the spatial transformation of burial architecture in early China are certainly complex. Besides religious and ritual reasons, there are pragmatic aspects relating to architectural construction. For example, in the vertical pit-style burial tradition, while the coffins, grave goods, and other burial apparatus could be prepared a long time before the burial, the excavation of the vertical pit was a one-time event, and the duration of the excavation corresponded to the scale of the tomb. In horizontal chamber-style tombs, on the other hand, many ready-made materials, such as bricks, stone slabs, and wooden planks, were used, and the tombs have a more complicated, decidedly architectural form, including developed interior spaces with doors and windows, a drainage system, and security measures. Artisans were able to spend more time on the construction and decoration of these tombs. The more grandiose the tomb construction, the more time it took to build it.

Another pragmatic consideration was the accessibility of the tomb space. In horizontal chamber-style tombs, people can, at least theoretically, repetitively open and enter the tomb chamber without damaging the structure, a feature that is almost impossible to achieve in the vertical pit-style tombs. In the vertical pit-style tombs, once the pit is excavated, the encasement is constructed, and the coffins and grave goods are lowered vertically into the encasement. The encasement is then sealed with a heavy lid made of planks, the pit is refilled with layers of charcoal and clay, and the mound is built on top. If the need to reopen the tomb were to arise, doing so would be rather inconvenient, although not impossible; the horizontal chamber-style tomb construction eliminates this problem.

Scholars have also suggested external influences for the shift in construction style. For example, some suggest that the horizontal chamber-style tomb developed as the result of outside influences, especially the catacomb from the northwestern state of Qin.[55] This burial style, characterized by a vertical pit with a lateral burial cave at the bottom, was indigenous to northwest China. In central China, it first appeared in Western Zhou–period cemeteries, in Fufeng County, Shaanxi, and in Zhangjiapo near Xi'an City, and then mysteriously disappeared, only to reappear several centuries later in the middle Warring States period in Qin territory (present-day Shaanxi).[56] Nevertheless, as other scholars have pointed out, the structure and burial ideology of the catacomb are aligned with those of the vertical pit-style tomb.[57] As a regional burial style influenced mainly by the local cave dwellings in the loess plains of Shaanxi, then, the catacombs are unlikely to be the antecedent of the horizontal chamber-style tomb.

As I show below, the archaeological evidence suggests that the inspiration for the transition to the horizontal multicompartmented chamber-style tomb may have come from the Chu and adjacent regions in the south.[58] Certainly northern and southern influences were not mutually exclusive, and acculturation did not develop in a strictly linear fashion. Moreover, the Warring States period was a time when multiple cultural elements converged to create the basis for a unified empire. Nevertheless, some prominent southern contributions likely transformed burial space in early China.

BURIAL MOUNDS "AS TALL AS MOUNTAINS"

In the Warring States period, grandiose burial mounds were erected as ostentatious displays of power and wealth. This development in burial construction accompanied rapid developments in urban planning and palatial architecture, brought about by technological advances in the Warring States period. Writing in the late third century BCE, the authors of *Master Lü's Spring and Autumn Annals* declared that the contemporary burial mounds were "made as tall as mountains, and the trees planted on them are like forests." Architectural features, such as towers and courtyards, chambers, halls, and stairways, "make the burial resemble a city" and "make a spectacle for the world to see and are a means by which to display one's wealth."[59]

Scholars have different views on when and how this practice of erecting burial mounds started. Confucius reportedly stated, "I have heard that the ancients made graves, and raised no mound over them," and other similar passages in early texts have led some scholars to conclude that burial mounds appeared only in the late Spring and Autumn period.[60] But other scholars posit that Shang elite tombs already had mounds and ritual structures built on top of them.[61] Because most ancient mounds eroded away over time, it is difficult to determine whether they ever existed. Recent archaeological discoveries in the Shang elite cemetery at Qianzhangda in Tengzhou City, Shandong, have shown that, indeed, there were ritual structures above the tombs, but it seems there were no mounds.[62]

Some of the earliest burial mounds appeared in the cultural interaction zone in the Huai River valley in southeast China. The earliest mound, dating to the early Spring and Autumn period, is at Huang Jun Meng's and his wife's tombs at Baoxiangsi in Guangshan in southern Henan. The mound, reaching about seven to eight meters in height, covered the tombs, which consisted of two connected pits, each containing a wooden encasement and a coffin.[63] In addition, archaeologists excavated another tomb, Huang Ji Tuofu's tomb, 165 meters away that had a mound about 10 meters high.[64] Scholars have suggested that this was the cemetery of the small polity of Huang, which the state of Chu annexed in 648 BCE.[65] Probably belonging to the Pan clan,[66] another tomb (Tomb 5) discovered at Pingxi in Xinyang City, Henan, also featured a mound; we do not know its exact height, because local farmers removed some of the clay to manufacture bricks before the excavation.[67] Archaeologists also excavated an early Spring-and-Autumn-period tomb at Hekou in Shucheng County, Anhui, which local people reported had had a mound about two meters high. But the layers of pounded earth before excavation were only about 0.25 meters high.[68] It seems that this region of the Huai River valley is where the burial mounds first became popular in the early Spring and Autumn period.[69]

The best-preserved mounded tomb of the Spring and Autumn period is Tomb 1 at Hougudui in Gushi County, Henan. It is a single-occupant burial with a cone-shaped mound seven meters in height and fifty-five meters in diameter. The mound was made of pounded earth and was constructed layer by layer, each layer being about forty to fifty centimeters thick.[70] The tomb is in the vertical pit style with one ramp entering the pit from the east. At the bottom of the pit is a large encasement with the coffin of the tomb occupant at the center, surrounded by six companions in death (*xunren*) within the encasement and an additional eleven surrounding the encasement. Skeletal analyses indicate that the tomb occupant was a woman about thirty years old, and among the companions in death, all of whom had their own coffins and simpler burial goods, twelve were female of about the same age or younger, and five were adult males. Among the rich grave goods of bronzes, lacquerware, jades, and ceramics are proto-porcelain cups, indicating a close cultural tie with the southeast, where such glazed and high-fired ceramics originated.[71]

Not only the burial goods but also the burial structure of these tombs linked southern Henan with southeast China. From the early Shang period, mounded burials (*tudunmu*) were indigenous to the Lower Yangzi area in southeast China, in present-day Jiangsu, Anhui, and Zhejiang. These mounded burials differ from the Shang–Western Zhou vertical pit-style tombs in that there usually was no pit. Instead, stones were piled to prepare the burial ground where the body and grave goods would be placed. The grave was then covered with layers of pebbles and earth to form a mound.[72] After the middle Spring and Autumn period, stone-lined cists or wooden encasements and coffins gradually replaced this southeastern burial tradition, which began to incorporate the structural elements of the vertical pit-style tomb, especially of Chu tombs. It is in such settings, where local traditions weakened and outside influences dramatically increased, that innovations occurred. For instance, the late Spring-and-Autumn-period tomb at Zhenshan in Suzhou City, Jiangsu, is situated on the peak of the highest rocky hill. The burial pit is cut into the bedrock and a mound about 8.3 meters (from the bottom of the pit to the summit of the mound) was constructed on top of it. The tomb is the largest of a series of burials on top of the hill, where the royal cemetery of the state of Wu was located. Scholars have identified many "Chu" cultural elements in these burials.[73] However, these cultural influences were not unidirectional. A heavy traffic of goods and, possibly, of ideas took place in the cultural interaction zone among the Zhou in the Central Plains, the Chu and adjacent polities in the south, and the Wu, the Yue, and many other polities in southeast China.

In the Chu region, before the Warring States period, burial mounds were rare, if used at all. During the Warring States period, however, almost all the tombs of occupants from above the middle elite stratum feature burial mounds and tomb access ramps. Moreover, the higher the social rank of the tomb occupant, the larger the scale of the mound, and often the richer the contents of the tomb. Archaeologists have divided the more than eight hundred burial mounds discovered in the suburbs of the Warring States–period Chu capital of Ji'nancheng at Jiangling County, Hubei, into four categories according to the diameter of the mounds (A: 100–80 m; B: 80–50 m; C: 50–30 m; D: 30–10 m).[74] In the Paimashan cemeteries in the south, of the seventeen mounded tombs, one is an A tomb, one is a B tomb, and fifteen are C tombs. In the Yutaishan cemeteries in the east, of the 103 mounded tombs, 5 are C tombs and 98 are D tombs. In the Jishan cemeteries (eleven km to the north), of the 134 mounded tombs, 1 is a B tomb, 20 are C tombs, and 113 are D tombs. In the Balingshan cemeteries (four km to the west), of the 274 mounded tombs, 1 is an A tomb, 9 are B tombs, 64 are C tombs, and 189 are D tombs. In the latter cemeteries, the largest mound is about 96 meters in diameter and 14 meters in height; the smallest is about 16 meters in diameter and 3 meters in height. These numbers suggest that there were strict sumptuary regulations governing the size of the burial mounds, although we do not know exactly what those regulations were.[75] In addition, the layout of the cemeteries appears to have some regularity. Commoners' tombs (without burial mounds) were located within a distance of five kilometers around the city (especially to the south and the east), while the elite were buried far from the urban center to the north and the west.

Starting with the late Spring and Autumn period, almost all the major powerful states built their rulers' tombs on the outskirts of their capital and covered them with high pyramidal mounds. Archaeologists have studied these necropolises at Xintian, the last capital of the state of Jin (present-day Houma City in Shanxi);[76] at Handan City, Hebei (the state of Zhao);[77] at Guweicun in Hui County, Henan (the state of Wei);[78] at Yan Xiadu in Yi County, Hebei (the state of Yan);[79] at Xinzheng County, Henan (the state of Han);[80] at Linzi District, Zibo City, Shandong, the capital of Qi;[81] and at Sanji in Pingshan County, Hebei (the state of Zhongshan).[82]

However, some characteristics of the Chu burial mounds differ from those in the north within the Zhou cultural sphere. First, in appearance as well as in function, the Chu burial mounds are closer to the mounded burials in the Lower Yangzi area. They marked the tomb occupant's social status, rather than serving, as in other parts of the Zhou cultural sphere, as the foundation for the grand multistoried buildings erected on top of them. The never-finished necropolis of King Cuo's mausoleum of the state of Zhongshan at Sanji in Pingshan County, Hebei, is one typical example from the north.

Second, in the state of Chu, not only the rulers (the highest elite) but also the high and middle levels of the Chu elite could have a burial mound, albeit of a different scale, while in other parts of the Zhou cultural sphere, the gap between the higher and lower elites was more dramatic. The contrast between the rulers and the ordinary members of the Warring States elite reflected the growing power of increasingly despotic rulers and the decline of the traditional lineage-based elite.

THE HIGH CULTURE OF LUXURIOUS PUBLIC DISPLAY

Among the important forces driving the spatial transformation of burial architecture in early China were the changes in burial ideology. For the noble and powerful of the Warring States period, the occasion of death was no longer one of burying ("hiding") the dead body; rather, it became another opportunity to engage in increasingly intense status competition. If "burying" truly meant "hiding away," why, as Guo Zigao asked, did people raise high mounds and plant trees to identify the burial? Such mounds contradicted the traditional burial ideology of the Shang and Western Zhou dynasties. Burial mounds were considered fashionable and extravagant in the Warring States period, but the authors of *Master Lü's Spring and Autumn Annals* denounced the practice as improper.[83]

Despite official regulation and some philosophers' and statesmen's advocacy of moderate and frugal burials, however, the obsession with extravagance and spectacle persisted. In the Warring States period and early empires, luxurious objects were added to the grave goods, including articles for personal adornment, such as silk clothes, high-quality lacquered vessels, gems, and beads. Burial practices engaged a new aesthetic that valued ostentatious public display and featured new styles of ornaments for grave goods.[84] This "high culture" of luxurious public display, according to Warring States philosophers such as Xunzi (ca. 312–230 BCE), gratified the human desire for pleasure and material goods, reinforced the authority of the ruler and the solidity of an orderly society, and created a stable hierarchy by which goods were distributed and people rewarded according to a ritual norm of sumptuary rules. These philosophical texts and traditional historical accounts as well as modern archaeology testify to the lavish public display that characterized funerary practices in early China.[85]

In many regards, the design of the Chu inverted-pyramidal pit, with its four stepped slopes and a ramp leading to the burial encasement, establishes the burial site as the focal point of funeral rites. A photo of the Baoshan excavation (see fig. 2.7) shows a group of local men, women, and children standing at the four edges of the pit, watching the archaeologists bring the burial goods one by one from the tomb compartment. This image suggests how the burial structure may have not only facilitated public viewing but also created an aura of mystery around that experience of participation by keeping the onlookers at a certain distance. Based on this photo, one cannot help but imagine how spectacular Shao Tuo's funeral must have appeared to the participants and onlookers standing at those very spots more than two thousand years ago. Besides their practical function in preventing a landslide, the number of steps in a tomb also corresponds roughly to the scale of the tomb and the social status of the tomb occupant. The higher the tomb occupant's social rank, the deeper the burial pit, the longer the ramp, and the higher the number of steps, although there is no fixed number of steps for each rank.[86] Tomb 2 at Baoshan has fourteen steps, as do Tombs 1 and 2 at Jiuliandun, while Tomb 1 at Tianxingguan has fifteen steps, the most numerous discovered so far.[87]

"IN DEATH YOU SHALL SHARE MY GRAVE"

In early China, the great shift in basic social organization was from the lineage of the Spring and Autumn period to the household of the Warring States period and the early empires.[88] The spatial organization of early Chinese burial practice also reflects this shift. The popularity of joint burials of husbands and wives in the same tomb space increased, the sentiment of which is expressed in the old poem: "In death you shall share my grave."[89] Even in lineage cemeteries, the tendency was for husbands and wives to be buried in the same tomb space.[90] In the vertical pit-style tomb, husbands and wives were often buried side by side, in two separate pits. The earliest known case of a joint burial of a husband and wife in different pits was found in the Yu lineage cemeteries of the middle Western Zhou period in the southern suburbs of Baoji City, Shaanxi.[91] This burial practice continued into the Spring and Autumn period, as seen in the Yuan lineage cemeteries in Xiasi, Heshangling, and Xujialing in Xichuan County, Henan; the Warring States period, as seen in the Jiuliandun tombs (Tombs 1 and 2); and even the early Han dynasty, as seen in the Mawangdui tombs (Tombs 1 and 2).

In some regions, burial customs began to change as early as the Spring and Autumn period. One of the earliest joint burials of a husband and wife in the same pit is probably Huang Jun Meng's and his wife's tombs at Baoxiangsi in Guangshan County, Henan. This joint burial in the same pit was a rare occurrence in vertical pit-style tombs because of the great difficulty of reopening the pit for the second interment.[92] In such joint burials, either the first coffin would have been stored or buried temporarily somewhere else while awaiting the demise of the partner, or the same pit would have been opened again. It is more common in vertical pit-style burials for the joint grave to consist of two pits laid side by side and covered by a single mound.

According to the bronze inscriptions on the ritual vessels found in the tombs, the northern encasement belonged to a lord of the local state of Huang, whereas the southern one belonged to a noble woman in her forties who in the inscriptions identified herself as the wife of the lord of Huang and a daughter of the Ji clan. She had the surname (i.e., the clan name) of the Zhou royal house, and the furnishings of her tomb were much richer than those of her husband. It is possible that the couple was buried under the same mound, because the wife, who had a high political status as a royal daughter, was treated specially.

The practice of burying a couple in vertical pit tombs continued during the Western Han dynasty in southeast China (present-day Jiangsu), but it generally died out once the horizontal chamber-style tomb had become popular.[93] From the middle Western Han dynasty onward, with the exception of imperial tombs, the joint burial of a husband and wife in a horizontal chamber-style tomb was popular among the middle and lower levels of Han society.[94] In any case, a growing trend toward joint burials propelled the transition from vertical pit-style tombs to horizontal chamber-style tombs.

THE TOMB AS AN UNDERGROUND HOUSE

In the Shang and Western Zhou vertical-pit-style burial tradition, the tomb was simply a space for "hiding" the corpse. Some scholars have suggested that the cross-shaped structure of Shang royal tombs may have been intended to invoke the Shang conception of the cosmos,[95] but these are still vague ideas. In the late Western Zhou period, the coffin began to be associated symbolically with the residential structure for the deceased. Archaeologists have discovered strings of small bronze fish in Western Zhou–period tombs at Zhangjiapo near Xi'an City, Shaanxi. This archaeological feature was convincingly linked to the coffin decoration described in early ritual texts, and a direct connection can be established between these decorations and those found on houses. The bronze fish were originally hung on the pall, which assumed the form of a textile tent from which the ornaments were suspended along

Fig. 2.3. The burial at Yinshan in Shaoxing City, Zhejiang, fifth century BCE, one of the earliest instances of a tomb conceived as an underground house.

the eaves or gutters.[96] Motifs such as suspended fish and birds and grass were often painted on houses in ancient China.[97] In the middle Spring and Autumn period and even in some middle Warring-States-period tombs, small bronze fish were used to decorate the coffin.[98]

Although the idea, as idealized in received texts, that tombs resemble an underground house or palace is well established, scholars have different opinions about where and when this idea first materialized archaeologically. Some scholars think it was in the Central Plains in the middle of the Western Han, while others think it was in the Warring-States Chu tombs.[99] A closer look at the archaeological evidence, however, suggests that these innovations came from many different sources and from culturally peripheral and politically weak regions (from the standpoint of the Central Plains).

Such was the case for one of the earliest discovered tombs that resembled an underground house or private domicile. The burial at Yinshan in Shaoxing City, Zhejiang, probably the tomb of a fifth-century BCE ruler of Yue, is located at the top of a small hill surrounded by rectangular moats.[100] A rammed-earth mound surmounts a rectangular burial pit, and a fifty-four-meter-long ramp leads to a log house of sophisticated construction (fig. 2.3).[101] This is not the usual rectangular box-shaped encasement common in the Shang–Western Zhou tradition but an inhabitable underground house shaped like a huge triangular prism and made of more than 170 wooden logs. The structure is about 5.5 meters high, and its base is 33.4 meters long and 5 meters wide. The interior space is divided into three sections: the ante-

Fig. 2.4. Aerial view of the tomb of Marquis Yi of Zeng at Leigudun, Suizhou City, Hubei, just before it was opened in spring 1978. Hubei Provincial Museum.

chamber; the main chamber, which contains the coffin, made of two halves of a log, 6 meters in length and 1.12 meters in diameter; and the rear chamber. Although the tomb was repeatedly robbed, eighteen jade mat weights, including two still resting on a fragmented bamboo mat, were discovered in the main chamber near the coffin; an additional jade weight was found in a tomb robber's tunnel. The division of the interior space into chambers indicates that this structure was regarded as a house.

THE TOMB AS AN UNDERGROUND PALACE

The idea of the tomb as an underground palace derives from the tomb-as-house idea. The tomb of Marquis Yi of Zeng, for example, is extremely large, probably because of his rank as the ruler of the, albeit politically weak, polity of Zeng (fig. 2.4). The division of the interior space simulates the organization of a domestic dwelling (fig. 2.5). The burials conducted in the small state of Zeng, which was politically affiliated with the state of Chu, had some distinct features.[102] Owing to natural erosion and human destruction, we cannot tell whether there was a mound above the burial. However, as at Yinshan, the tomb is situated on top of a small hill. The irregularly

Fig. 2.5. Aerial view of opened tomb of Marquis Yi of the state of Zeng at Leigudun, Suizhou City, Hubei. Warring States period, ca. 433 BCE. The division of the interior space simulates the organization of a domestic dwelling. Coffins for thirteen female attendants are scattered about the western compartment. Hubei Provincial Museum.

The Transformation of Burial Space

shaped structure, with four interconnected large compartments made of catalpa logs, resembles the four main components of a palace compound.[103] The eastern compartment, where the marquis's inner and outer coffins (Plate 7) were located and his eight female companions in death (*xunren*) were buried, could be likened to a ruler's private quarters, just as the central compartment, where the famous bronze chimes and bells and ritual vessels were discovered, could be considered his ceremonial court. The northern compartment, where weaponry, shields, armor, and horse and chariot fittings were stored, could be considered his armory; and the western compartment, in which an additional thirteen coffins containing the bodies of maids were buried, could be his harem. Near the marquis's coffin, four identical bronze mat weights, bamboo mats, offering tables, lacquered vessels, and so forth were discovered. We cannot pinpoint the exact functions of these objects, but their purpose as ritual implements suggests that they were probably related to sacrificial activities of some sort within the burial space.

Similar to Marquis Yi's and the Yinshan tombs, many Chu burials of the Warring States period featured multiple wooden compartments around the coffin in which were placed different types of grave goods. This is in contrast to the Shang and Western Zhou tradition, wherein different types of grave goods were grouped together and placed in various locations in the space between the coffins and the encasement. This increasing compartmentalization of the burial space is an important feature of the Warring-States Chu burials. One, often central, compartment was reserved for the coffin, and other spaces were designated for various grave goods. Because the size of the tomb and the quantity of the grave goods were generally related to the sociopolitical status of the tomb occupant, the more spacious the burial encasements, the higher the social rank of the deceased.

The interior of Marquis Yi's tomb was designed as a continuous space, which was thought to increase the mobility of the soul. More than three meters in height, the encasements are large enough to walk through, although no ramps lead in or out, just small openings at the base of the interior walls symbolizing doorways or windows. Furthermore, the marquis's and some of the women's coffins are painted with doors or windows, indicating that the souls could move within the confines of the tomb space.[104] Many elite Chu tombs have similar structural details, either actual or painted on the panels that divided the interior.[105] These real and imagined passageways suggest the autonomous existence of the soul in the tomb.[106]

THE TOMB AS CHARIOT

The tomb symbolized not only a house but also a chariot. The shape of a fifth-century BCE tomb (Tomb 10) at Wanggou in Changdao County, Shandong, resembles a four-wheeled chariot: each side has two wheel-like structures, and the burial encasement represents the carriage (fig. 2.6).[107] The multiple conceptions of tomb construction in the Warring States period are also reflected in the *Xunzi* (third century BCE) and other early Chinese texts.[108] These texts often make analogies between the tumulus,

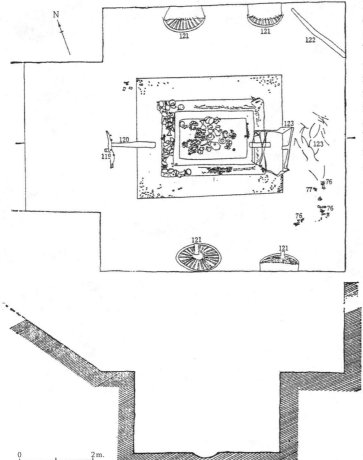

Fig. 2.6. Fifth-century BCE tomb (Tomb 10) at Wanggou, Changdao County, Shandong, in the shape of a four-wheeled chariot, with two wheels on each side, and the burial encasement representing the carriage.

the coffins and encasements, the pall decoration, and the burial construction, on the one hand, and the house, the carriage of a chariot, the decorations of a tent, and the enclosing structure of a house, on the other. All of these architectural forms—houses, tombs, coffins, chariots, and tents—are simultaneously the bases and the products of religious imagination rooted in the cosmological notions of Heaven and Earth.[109] Likewise, the tomb, with its large, round aboveground tumulus and square underground burial pit, imitated the basic cosmological model of a round Heaven and a square Earth. As such, the structure of tombs imitated the structure of the cosmos.[110]

THE TOMB AS A WAY STATION

The idea of the tomb as an inhabitable domestic space should not be overstated. It was but one of many ideas circulating in the Warring States period. In some Warring-States Chu burials, such as Tomb 2 at Baoshan (figs. 2.7 and 2.8), the ways

Fig. 2.7. Aerial view of Tomb 2 of Chu elite Shao Tuo (d. ca. 316 BCE), excavated at Baoshan, Jingmen City, Hubei. Local people standing at the four edges of the pit watch the archaeologists bring the burial goods out of the tomb compartments.

the tomb space was divided and the grave goods were stored suggest that it was not an inhabitable space. It is simply too cramped to be suitable for residential use. Rather, the Baoshan materials point to another important innovation of the Warring States period: the tomb conceived as a way station, a liminal place from which the soul would journey to a cosmic destination. First, the inner coffin at the center of the burial space is a rectangular wooden box that is 184 centimeters long, 46 centimeters wide, and 46 centimeters high (Plate 8). Unlike the inner coffin in Tomb 1 at Leigudun (see Plate 7), it has no window or door painted on its surface. Instead, it is covered with a polychrome decoration of seventy-two serpentine dragons and an equal number of mythical birds, which may have a protective and apotropaic function.[111] This decoration seems to indicate that the coffin was a container or storage for the corpse rather than its residence. Second, the inventory list excavated at the tomb divides the grave goods into several categories, and one category is explicitly designated as travel gear for the deceased to use in its spirit journey in the afterlife. Therefore, contrary to what many scholars have argued, the tomb was neither the deceased's sole destination, nor its happy home, nor the jail that would permanently imprison its spirit.[112]

Furthermore, while the tomb symbolized a domestic structure, it did not directly

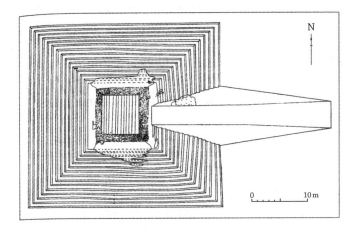

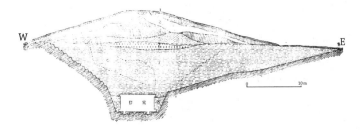

Fig. 2.8. Plan and section of Tomb 2 at Baoshan, Jingmen City, Hubei.
Warring States period, ca. fourth century BCE.

replicate a house. Rather, the tomb was meant to provide a tame, familiar, comfortable space for the deceased. The distinction between wild space and tame space was an important component of the conception of the afterlife in early China.[113] During funerary rituals, old garments, recognizable objects, and personal belongings were used as tokens of familiarity in constructing a place of safety, comfort, and delight. The tomb simulated the old abode and served as a quiet and restful home for the departed soul.

THE TOMB AS MICROCOSM

The tomb was metaphorically constructed as a house, a palace, a chariot, a city, and ultimately a cosmos.[114] The cross-shaped royal tombs of the late Shang period may be a precedent, but it was not until after the Spring and Autumn period that tombs were built as an alternative world, which aligned with strengthening ideology of the afterlife as parallel to the living world and increasingly elaborated in the latter's image. Some have suggested that several elements of burial construction—the presence of models, the homelike "catacomb," ceramic human figurines in the Qin tombs—indicate that the tomb was conceived of as a microcosm.[115]

Recent discoveries of Tomb 1 at Shuangdun near Bangbu City, Anhui, and Tomb

1 at Bianzhuang in Fengyang County, Anhui, further indicate the importance of the Huai River valley to burial innovation.[116] According to the inscriptions on bronzes that were excavated, the tomb occupants were two rulers of a small polity named Zhongli in the late Spring and Autumn period. The Shuangdun tomb has one of the earliest domelike mounds, sixty meters in diameter and nine meters high. Many features of this tomb lead scholars to think that it took as its model the configuration of the cosmos. For example, the mound and the circular burial pit were filled with clays of five colors: yellow, greenish grey, black, red, and white. The black and white clays were not locally available and must have been imported from somewhere else for this special purpose. The exact meaning of this is not clear, but a little later, in the Warring States and Han periods, the five colors figured among the elements in the five-agents cosmology.[117] Under the burial mound is a huge ring-shaped white-clay layer about twenty to thirty centimeters thick. Like a huge disc, the white clay ring could symbolize the round Heaven in traditional Chinese cosmology. The burial pit is circular (fourteen meters in diameter), but inside is a cross-shaped burial ground on which twelve pits, three on each side, are arrayed, with companions in death and grave goods in them. The ruler of the Zhongli polity was buried at the center of the cross (fig. 2.9). The top of the Bianzhuang tomb was damaged long before the excavation, so we do not know whether there was a burial mound, but the layout of the burial pits is similar to that of the Shuangdun tomb (fig. 2.10).

In southern China, the concept of a round Heaven and a square Earth, well documented in the Warring States period, was reflected in tomb structure.[118] Warring States burials featured a huge, rammed-earth hemispherical mound built atop a deep square pit. When first introduced in the late Spring and Autumn period, this tumulus form was limited to the graves of local rulers, but starting in the middle Warring States period, such mounds spread to the burials of lower-ranking individuals in southern China. The form also became popular in the Han dynasty.

The idea of a tomb as a cosmological model appears in a famous passage in *Records of the Grand Historian*, wherein Sima Qian describes the mausoleum of the First Emperor of Qin (r. 221–210 BCE) at Lishan near Xi'an City as containing "[r]eplicas of palaces, scenic towers, and the hundred officials, as well as rare utensils and wonderful objects . . . brought to fill up the tomb. . . . *Above were representations of all the heavenly bodies, below, the features of the earth* [my emphasis]."[119] In many respects, the tomb of the First Emperor of Qin combined the diverse burial trends of the Warring States period on an unprecedented scale.[120] The tomb has a huge, four-sided, truncated, pyramidal mound made of rammed earth. It now stands fifty-two meters high, but it was originally much higher. To the east of the mound, an underground army of life-size terra-cotta soldiers was discovered in 1974. The high concentration of mercury in the soil near the site corroborated the account in the *Records of the Grand Historian* that "mercury was used to fashion imitations of the hundred rivers, the Yellow River and the Yangzi, and the seas."[121]

The desire to separate the dead from the living may have served as one motivation

Fig. 2.9. Inside the circular burial pit at Tomb 1 at Shuangdun in Bangbu City, Anhui, the cross-shaped burial ground on which companions in death and grave goods were buried in twelve pits. The ruler of the Zhongli polity was buried at the center of the cross. Late Spring and Autumn period.

Fig. 2.10. Layout of the burial pit in Tomb 1 at Bianzhuang in Fengyang County, Anhui. Late Spring and Autumn period.

for fashioning the tomb as a microcosm. By the Warring States period the relationship between the dead and the living had changed drastically. Whereas the dead had once been regarded as benevolent supernatural helpers, they were now considered potentially harmful spirits. Presenting the tomb as a microcosm was meant "to separate [the dead] from the living and to secure them with a universe of their own."[122] This universe had two related functions: First, it controlled and protected the dead so that they would not wander around the world and harm the living. This led to the bureaucratization of the afterlife and explains the installation of clay figurines with outstretched arms in the access ramps leading to the Mawangdui tombs, as well as other horizontal chamber-style tombs near Changsha. The outstretched arms were believed to prevent evil influences from entering the tomb. Second, the universe served as a tame domestic environment that would protect the postmortem existence of the deceased. Thus, the burial chamber was filled with figurines, objects used in daily life (including lamps), and exotic luxury items intended to guard and entertain the tomb occupant.[123]

The Appearance of the Horizontal Chamber-Style Tomb

The idea of the tomb as an inhabitable microcosm served as an important stage in the transition from the vertical pit-style tomb to the horizontal chamber-style tomb. The changes in burial ideology triggered a shift in the emphasis of ancestral sacrifice from the cult of benevolent ancestors to the cult of potentially malevolent recent dead. The latter cult required a sacrificial space within the tomb, and this requirement in turn transformed early Chinese burial practice.[124] What materialized in the early Han dynasty, however, was the physical fashioning of a sacrificial space from the abstract notion of a "sacrificial chamber" put forward on the Baoshan inventory list. Actual sacrificial spaces within tombs first appeared in elite burials but gradually spread to the lower social strata. The earliest horizontal chamber-style tomb appeared in the stave-walled[125] tombs (ticou) that started at the end of the Warring States period and flourished in the Western Han, particularly among the high elite of local kings and marquises.

The term ticou 題湊, meaning "gathered heads," referred in early Chinese texts to a luxurious mortuary practice.[126] We have epigraphic evidence for the practice of stave-walled tombs in the Warring States period. Engraved on a bronze plate of 48 x 94 centimeters, a construction plan (fig. 2.11) for the tombs and sacrificial halls of the Warring States–period King Cuo (d. ca. 310 BCE) of Zhongshan and his consorts was discovered at Sanji in Pingshan County, Hebei.[127] Although the funerary necropolis was never completed and several planned tombs were not finished, the construction plan specifies their details. The inscriptions in the two squares on both ends of the five squares in the middle of the plate state, "The hall for the royal lady (furen) measures one hundred and fifty chi square [1 chi is about 22 cm]. The sizes of her inner and middle coffins accord with those of Queen Ai. The length of

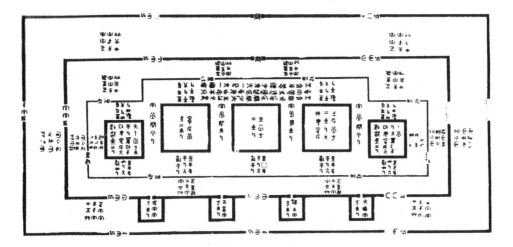

Fig. 2.11. Line drawing of a bronze plate inlaid with the construction plan of King Cuo's mausoleum in the kingdom of Zhongshan, discovered at Sanji in Pingshan County, Hebei. L. 94 cm, W. 48 cm. Warring States period.

the *ticou* is three *chi*."[128] Because these two tombs were never built and King Cuo's burial pit was robbed, we do not know the exact format of this stave wall, but from Han dynasty literature and later commentaries, we know that stave-walled tombs constituted a barrier composed of stacks of timbers or stones surrounding the wooden encasement.[129] The burial pit of King Cuo's tomb was cut vertically into the bedrock of the mountain, after which the four walls were built of piled stones and charcoal was deposited around the wooden encasement. Thus King Cuo's is a typical Zhou elite burial with "piles of stone and heaps of charcoal," as was common in northern China.[130] King Cuo's burial, along with such Warring States royal burials as the state of Wei at Guweicun in Hui County, Henan,[131] and the royal mausoleum of the state of Zhao in Handan City, Hebei, is unusual in its aboveground pyramidal tumulus with an associated sacrificial structure on top. Although it differs structurally from the southern burials, with their deep vertical pits and hemispherical mounds on top, the burial ideology of luxurious public display is the same.

To date, Chinese archaeologists have discovered over twenty stave-walled tombs from the Western Han period. The early ones, such as Zhang Er's tomb at Xiaoyan village in Shijiazhuang City, Hebei, dated to 202 BCE,[132] are similar to King Cuo's Warring States–period mausoleum. In both cases, the main burial is in the tradition of the vertical pit but includes some of the features of the horizontal chamber style. The same is true of the famous Mawangdui tombs, although they had no stave-walled structure and adhered to the basic vertical pit-style burial structure with multiple compartments (fig. 2.12). These transitional examples are important for our understanding of the spatial changes in early Chinese burial practices.

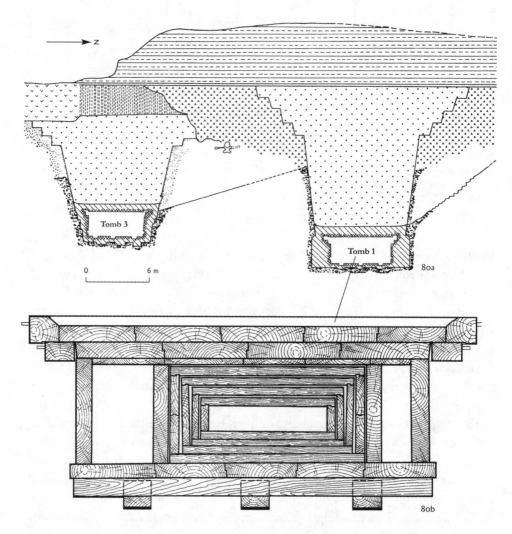

Fig. 2.12. Cross section of Tombs 1 and 3 (upper), and cross section of the inner and outer coffins of Tomb 1 (below) at Mawangdui, Changsha City, Hunan. Early Western Han period.

Fig. 2.13. Wooden encasement and four side compartments in Tomb 1 at Mawangdui, Changsha City, Hunan. Early Western Han period.

The burial space of Tomb 1 at Mawangdui was divided into five compartments: one in the middle, in which four nested coffins were located, and four additional spaces surrounding it, one on each side (fig. 2.13).[133] According to the inventory list buried in the tomb, the central compartment was "the middle of the encasement" (*guozhong* 槨中); the northern compartment, "the head of the encasement (i.e., the coffin case)" (*guoshou* 槨首); the southern compartment, "the foot of the encasement" (*guozu* 槨足); and the eastern compartment, "the left of the encasement" (*guozuo* 槨左).[134] The layout of the compartments conformed to the orientation of the corpse, aligned north to south, head to foot, in the innermost coffin. In other words, "the head of the encasement" (the northern compartment) is close to the head of the corpse, and "the foot of the encasement" is close to the feet. Therefore, the names of the compartments reflected the perspective of the deceased.

The compartmentalization of burial space also reflected the two stages of funerary ritual clearly distinguished in early Chinese ritual texts: the disposal of the dead

Fig. 2.14. Tomb guardian figure on the east side of the passage leading to Tomb 2 at Mawang-dui, Changsha City, Hunan. Early Western Han period. The deer antlers on the head have been removed.

body (i.e., the "rites of disposal") and the broader activities of mourning and celebration performed by the living (i.e., the "funerary rites").[135] The enshrouding and enclosure of the corpse in the coffin, according to the *Protocols of Ceremonies*, was a private act, hidden from public view and conducted in the residence of the deceased. The funerary rites, including the procession to the burial site, the public announcement of the funerary gifts, and the interment of grave goods, were for public display. Even funerary gift giving was divided between offerings to the dead (*zeng* 贈) and gifts to the bereaved (*fu* 賻).[136]

However, the Mawangdui tombs did incorporate important new design features that appeared in other early Han elite burials. For example, tomb guardian figures, with deer antlers on the head and two extended arms (fig. 2.14), were placed in the two niches on the walls of the access ramp leading to the burial chamber in both Tombs 2 and 3.[137] In Tombs 1 and 3, of the four side compartments, the largest and the most spacious is the northern compartment, which in Tomb 1 measures about 296 centimeters wide, 92 centimeters long, and 144 centimeters deep (fig. 2.15). It had silk curtains hung on the walls and a bamboo mat on the floor (fig. 2.16). The west end contained a spirit seat framed by a painted lacquered screen (figs. 2.17a and 2.17b), a mat, a cushion, and other personal belongings such as a pair of silk shoes, a cane, two toilet boxes, lacquered dishes and cups and other utensils filled with food,

Fig. 2.15. Northern compartment in Mawangdui Tomb 1 where the framed spirit seat is located. Early Western Han period.

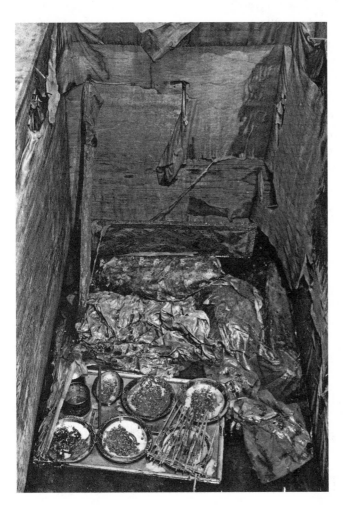

Fig. 2.16. View of the western half of the northern compartment of the encasement with burial goods, at the moment of discovery. Tomb 1 at Mawangdui, Changsha City, Hunan. Early Western Han period.

Figs. 2.17a and b. Painted wooden screen (front and back) used to frame the spirit seat, excavated from Tomb 1 at Mawangdui, Changsha City, Hunan. Early Western Han period. Lacquer on wood, H. 62 cm, L. 58 cm, W. 72 cm. Hunan Provincial Museum.

all designed to indicate the presence of the dead (fig. 2.16).[138] This space resembled a stage set for feeding the departed soul while entertaining it with music and dance. The presence of the tomb guardian and the spirit seat and the configuration of the northern compartment are the defining features of the horizontal chamber-style tomb (see below).

The next development, which marks the most important transition from the vertical pit style to the horizontal chamber style, appears in Tomb 1 at Xiangbizui and the so-called Yuyang queen's tomb, both in Changsha City, Hunan. Dated to 157 or 128 BCE, the Xiangbizui tomb shares some features with vertical pit-style tombs.[139] As in the Mawangdui tombs, this vertical pit had one stamped-earth access ramp leading to the burial ground surface. Near the east end of the ramp stood a pair of tomb guardian figures (indicated by two small squares in the diagram in fig. 2.18). In this case, the end of the ramp was at the same level as the burial chambers. Similarly, in the Yuyang queen's tomb, at Wangchengpo near Changsha City, dated to between 168 BCE and 150 BCE, the burial chamber and the access ramp are in a spatial continuum (fig. 2.19). Based on the archaeological features, archaeologists have postulated that the funerary rites took place within the burial chamber before the doors of the burial chamber were closed and that the two tomb guardians with deer antlers and extended arms were placed at the tomb-level entrance of the access ramp.[140]

The structure of the Xiangbizui tomb and the Yuyang queen's tomb had many new features.[141] First, a wall of stacked timbers buttressed the wooden chamber from the outside. Second, the compartments that appeared in earlier stave-walled tombs were replaced by two concentric corridors (*huilang* 回廊).[142] Third, in the Xiangbi- zui tomb, the length between the tomb-level entrance of the access ramp and the ground surface of the burial chamber is much shorter, and in the Yuyang queen's tomb, the burial chamber and the tomb-level entrance of the access ramp are spa- tially continuous. In Tomb 3 at Mawangdui, for example, the length between the

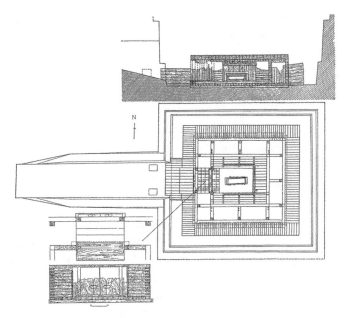

Fig. 2.18. Plan of Tomb 1 at Xiangbizui, Changsha City, Hunan.
Ca. second century BCE.

Fig. 2.19. Stave-walled tomb of the Yuyang queen, the Kingdom of Changsha, excavated at
Wangchengpo, Changsha City, Hunan. Early Western Han period.

tomb-level entrance of the access ramp and the ground surface of the burial chamber is 3.1 meters, while at Xiangbizui it is only 0.58 meters. This small gap is paved in logs, thus forming a corridor that leads to the double door of the encasement; wooden boards frame and protect both sides of the corridor. As Chinese archaeologists have observed, this spatial continuum is a defining feature of the horizontal chamber-style tomb in that it allows one to walk into the tomb chamber via the access ramp. Fourth, both the Xiangbizui tomb and the Yuyang queen's tomb had two tomb guardian figures with deer antlers, extending their arms to block the passage in the access ramps, to function as magic protective mechanisms to safeguard the burial chambers (fig. 2.20).

In the Xiangbizui tomb, the doors leading into the tomb are about 3 meters tall and 1.38 meters wide; no longer merely symbolic, these are functional gateways to the inside of the tomb and, from there, to the outside world. The coffin chamber, which sheltered the three nested coffins, was open on the side facing the passageway. A visitor could easily walk into the interior of the burial chambers through a chain of connected structures: the access ramp, a functional double-door opening to the outside, a transitional space, and a second set of double doors to the coffin chamber, the final destination. The transitional space of the tomb thus expanded into a sacrificial space where rituals took place and vessels and offerings were displayed.[143] This spatial arrangement significantly departs from that of the stave-walled tombs. The occupant of the Xiangbizui tomb was probably the king of the local kingdom of

Fig. 2.20. Tomb guardian figures in the passage leading to the tomb of the Yuyang queen, the Kingdom of Changsha, excavated at Wangchengpo, Changsha City, Hunan. H. 88 cm. Early Western Han period. The deer antlers on the top of the heads have been removed.

Changsha, which the Western Han dynasty (206 BCE–9 CE) established in 202 BCE in the former territory of Warring-States Chu and which the usurper Wang Mang (ca. 45 BCE–23 CE) abolished in 9 CE.

In both the Xiangbizui tomb and the Yuyang queen's tomb, the burial space is arranged not from the perspective of the deceased lying at the center of the tomb but from the perspective of a visitor, with an access ramp leading to the interior of the tomb and the corridors surrounding the central coffin chamber. It is also possible that these design features were meant to create a familiar (i.e., tame) space that could ease the dead's transition from the world of the living to that of the afterlife.[144] Scholars have convincingly argued that these new structural changes originated in the Chu elite tombs in the south and then spread to other parts of the Han empire.[145] The use of greenish-white oily clay to seal the burial chambers, characteristic of the southern Chu tombs, continued not only in southern horizontal tombs but also in some northern tombs, such as the Western Han princely tombs at Dabaotai near Beijing.[146]

PIANFANG AS "THE CHAMBER OF PEACE"

This strong southern connection in the burial architecture is supported in recently discovered Chu bamboo manuscripts. In Han literature, this type of tomb construction is called *huangchang ticou*, or "yellow battens aligned together," after the bright color of freshly cut cypress or other timbers. Both historical records and archaeological data show that this burial practice was reserved for members of the Han imperial family. Nevertheless, in several cases such a burial was also granted as an imperial favor to high officials. For example, Emperor Xuan (91–49 BCE) granted the famous military general Huo Guang (ca. 130–68 BCE) a full imperial funerary treatment with "a jade suit (*yuyi*), a set of catalpa coffins (*zigong*), *pianfang* 便房, and a stave wall of the yellow cores of cypress."[147] Much ink has been spilled on the terms that appear in this description. With the help of archaeological materials, we now better understand the structure and function of the jade suits, the catalpa coffins, and the stave walls; only the term *pianfang* remains a puzzle.

Based on the description of Huo Guang's burial, scholars agree that *pianfang* must refer to a structure located between the catalpa coffins and the stave wall, but they disagree on the form and function of this structure. Some also suggest that *pian* 便 in *pianfang* refers to the certain type of *pian* 楩 wood used in burial construction, while others variously suggest that the term refers to the front chamber, the side chambers near the coffins, the U-shaped corridor, the coffin chamber, the entire burial chamber, and so on.[148]

Newly published Chu manuscripts collected at Qinghua University shed new light on this debate.[149] A middle Warring States–period bamboo manuscript that modern scholars named "the residence of Chu" (Chuju) and that narrates both the genealogy and migration of Chu kings and the origins of some ritual and religious activities mentions a term *pianshi* 楩室. From this context, it is clear that the term refs to a structure in which the Chu king performed certain sacrifices, in other words, to a sacrificial hall.[150] This meaning is consistent with the claim that *pianfang* refers to the entire burial chamber as a place to pacify and offer sacrifice to the deceased, where the spirit seat of the dead is often located. Here *pian* means in the adjectival form "quiet," "comfortable," and "peaceful," and in the verbal form "to pacify" and so on. This meaning also applies to the terms for "palace of peace" (*piandian*) and "spirit seat" (*pianzuo*) in Han literature.[151] This linguistic connection between *pianfang* in Han imperial burial construction and *pianshi* in the Chu manuscript is significant. It strongly suggests that some of the standard Han imperial funerary nomenclature, as in the case of other religious practices, such as the cult of Taiyi (see chapter 3), may be of Chu origin.

THE ESTABLISHMENT OF THE SACRIFICIAL SPACE WITHIN THE TOMB

The movement of the sacrificial space to within the tomb itself is the main distinguishing feature of the horizontal chamber-style tombs.[152] As we have seen in the princely tomb at Beidongshan in Xuzhou City, Jiangsu, this innovation began in elite burials in southern China. Although the main features of the Mawangdui tombs reflect the vertical pit style, the northern compartment, with its spirit seat, sacrificial foods, and wooden figurines of musicians and dancers, certainly points to an early attempt at establishing a sacrificial space within the tomb. Both contemporaneous with the Beidongshan tomb, the Mawangdui and the Xiangbizui tombs enable us to see the process of the structural development from vertical pit-style tomb to horizontal chamber-style tomb—that is, the burial space develops from a self-contained compartmentalized storage space to an open, accessible sacrificial space. The renaming of this wooden encasement as *pianfang* or *pianguo*[153] marked its transformation in function from a space for storing grave goods to a place for offering sacrifice to pacify the potentially dangerous deceased. The main function of the chamber of peace is to offer sacrifice to the deceased. This separation of the sacrificial space from the coffin chamber is an important step in the development of the horizontal chamber-style tomb.[154]

This early form of the horizontal chamber-style tomb with sacrificial space soon spread to other parts of the Western Han empire. Renowned examples include the Western Han princely tombs at Dabaotai (Tomb 1, dated to 45 BCE; Tomb 2, late Western Han dynasty) near Beijing (fig. 2.21). In comparison with the Xiangbizui tomb, the sacrificial space in Tomb 1 at Dabaotai is considerably larger: the coffin chamber (the upper half of the central rectangle) has been pushed farther back into the interior, leaving a wider antechamber for ritual activities in front of the coffin. A tiger-shaped mat weight was discovered in the antechamber of Tomb 2 at Dabaotai, suggesting that these weights were used to mark a spirit seat for the dead.

In addition, the sacrificial space was established not only in the wooden chamber-style tomb but also in the other major type of princely burial: the rock-cut or rock-piled tomb. Popular in the eastern part of the Han empire (present-day Hebei, Shan-

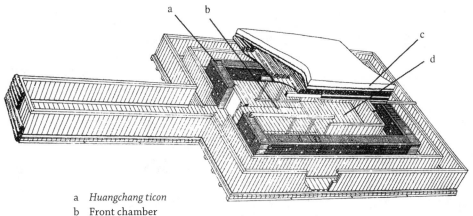

a   *Huangchang ticon*
b   Front chamber
c   White clay and charcoal layers
d   Rear chamber

Fig. 2.21. Cross section view of the stave-walled tomb of Liu Jian, king of Guangyang (d. 44 BCE) at Dabaotai near Beijing.

dong, Henan, and Jiangsu), these rock-cut tombs were often located at the foot or the middle of a mountain and cut horizontally into the mountain to create tunnels and caves. The tomb usually has an axial plan, with the access ramp, tomb-sealing devices (such as heavy stop-stones), double doors, sacrificial space, coffin chamber, and corridors aligned along the horizontal axis, and secondary chambers for storage, stable, kitchen, bath, toilet, and for many other purposes situated off axis. Some rock-cut tombs are constructed like an underground maze. Among these, the most important space is certainly the sacrificial space. Scholars have rightly insisted that there must also be chambers of peace in rock-cut tombs,[155] but the definition and the location of this space remains to be determined.

Take, for example, the twin burials of Liu Sheng (d. 113 BCE, Tomb 1, fig. 2.22) and his consort Dou Wan (Tomb 2) at Lingshan near Mancheng County, Hebei. A younger half-brother of the mighty Emperor Wu (156–87 BCE), Liu Sheng was the king of the state of Zhongshan, and these burials are famed for their jade burial suits.[156] The tombs were carved out of the rocky mountain. The tomb access ramp, or tunnel, leading to the interior was originally blocked by iron barriers poured on location when the tomb was sealed. Each tomb has two long, narrow side rooms: one a stable for horses and chariots, the other a storehouse containing wine and food. The coffin chambers, built as stone houses with gabled roofs that resembled the inner sections of a domestic residence, housed the coffins of the prince and his consort. Both bodies were shrouded in jade suits stitched with gold thread. A small side room adjoining the coffin chamber of each tomb resembled a bath.

It has been suggested that the coffin chamber in the back is the sacrificial space (*pianfang*), but the archaeological evidence suggests that the antechamber in Liu

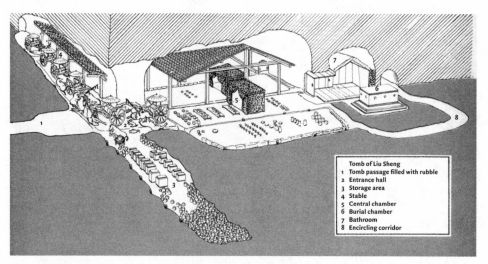

Fig. 2.22. Cutaway view showing a tentative reconstruction of Liu Sheng's tomb at the time of burial. Western Han dynasty. After *The Great Bronze Age of China*, fig. 112.

Sheng's tomb is where sacrifices were offered to both Liu Sheng and Dou Wan. The antechambers and the side rooms in both tombs were fitted with tile-roofed structures, which further recalled a palatial setting. The center for ritual activities was, however, the antechamber in Liu Sheng's tomb (Tomb 1), where two textile tents, various food vessels, drinking vessels, lacquerware, exquisite lamps, incense burners, and other ritual and everyday vessels and instruments were neatly placed (fig. 2.23). Although the coffin chamber in Tomb 2 is located off the horizontal axis, the antechamber remains the focus of the ritual activities performed before the tomb was sealed. A set of four leopard-shaped mat weights inlaid with precious stones, gold, and silver were discovered in the antechamber. Like many mat weights discovered in Han and later tombs, these demarcated the sacred boundaries of the spirit seat,[157] which is associated with bronze ritual vessels for eating and drinking.

Scholars have noted that two textile tents represent two spirit seats—both located in the antechamber of Tomb 1; Tomb 2 has none—and that both Liu Sheng and his consort Dou Wan must have received sacrifices in this shared sacrificial space.[158] According to historical accounts, Liu Sheng died in 113 BCE, but Dou Wan, from the powerful Dou family (the natal family of Liu Sheng's grandmother), was buried several years later, an estimation based on the dating of excavated objects from the tomb.[159] Although we do not know exactly the length of this interval, it is conceivable that the entrance to Liu Sheng's tomb was either left unsealed or reopened after the death of Dou Wan, so that her spirit seat could be set up there. We do know that the stone double door leading to Liu Sheng's coffin chamber could be sealed only once because there is a mechanism built into the floor such that once the doors were closed they could not be reopened. However, the entrance to the antechamber, the sacrificial space, could be reopened when necessary. Han historical accounts also

Fig. 2.23. Archaeologists clearing the sacrificial space in the antechamber of Liu Sheng's tomb at Mancheng County, Hebei. Western Han dynasty.

suggest that the antechamber was accessed more than once; among these are accounts of people living near the tomb during the mourning period and of a man named Zhao Xuan who, in order to carry out his mourning rites in the burial access ramp, left his father's tomb unsealed for more than twenty years.[160]

Converging Performance and Place

The *Book of Rites* (Liji) specifies that a deceased Son of Heaven be coffined seven days after his death and interred seven months after, but where was the coffin located in the interim?[161] In traditional funerary rites, as prescribed in the *Protocols of Ceremonies*, this period between the coffining and the interring is called *bin* 殯, a word derived etymologically from *bin* 賓, or "guest." From this point onward, the deceased is treated as a guest and no longer as the master of the household, and the coffin containing the corpse is placed at the guest's position in a ceremonial hall of the house.

This protocol marks a turning point in funerary rituals. As a rite of passage, the funerary ritual consists of several gradual transitions whereby the deceased transforms from a living person to a corpse, from the host of the house to a spirit-guest, and from a potentially harmful ghost to a benevolent ancestor. In the *Book of Rites*, Confucius's disciple Zi You described the funerary ritual process in terms of the spatial movement of the corpse:

Rice and precious shell are put into the mouth of the corpse under the window [i.e., in the southwest corner of the idealized chamber]. The corpse is washed and dressed inside the chamber door. Then the corpse is wrapped with more clothes and put into the coffin at the top of the host's steps. The coffin is laid at the guest's position [i.e., at the top of the west steps] for a period. Then the deceased bids farewell to the ancestors in the courtyard [of the ancestral temple]; and finally the coffin is buried at the grave.[162]

Furthermore, the burial and the ensuing lengthy period of mourning, sacrifice for associating the tablet, and two sacrifices for good fortune are concluded with the final "sacrifice of repose" (*yuji*) to mark the end of the funeral process; the deceased person is then assumed to have transformed into a benevolent ancestor. The *Protocols of Ceremonies* and the *Book of Rites* prescribed these funerary rites, associated with the vertical pit-style burial tradition.

It has been suggested that the chamber of rest (*qin*) is probably where the corpse was housed during this liminal stage.[163] Recall that in Emperor Ming's ritual reform, the chamber of rest was the first ritual structure to be relocated to the burial site. After the coffin was interred and the mourning period ended, the chamber of rest near the tomb became the place where later generations could sacrifice to their ancestors; only in this sense did the chamber of rest share the same function as the ancestral temple. Apparently, in the Eastern Han dynasty, because of the changes in house structure and the new attitude toward death, the *bin* rite was no longer performed in everyday domestic settings, which could produce "offence to any scruples of sanctity or interruption of daily life." Rather, the *bin* rite was moved to the burial site, a special ritualized space. By relocating the chamber of rest to the burial site, people sought to avoid death pollution and to continue to sacrifice to the deceased emperor—a way of assisting the dead during their transformation in the afterlife.

The difference between the traditional account of the burial ritual provided in the *Book of Rites* and the Eastern Han practice is clear: the *Book of Rites* prescribes a potential temporal gap between the closing of the tomb and the end of the mourning period, especially when this mourning period is lengthy. During this period, the departed person, who is still in his or her liminal stage, had no formalized place to receive sacrificial offerings because of his or her in-between status. In the Eastern Han practice, however, the dead could receive sacrifice in the chamber of rest before the end of the mourning period. In this way, the bereaved by means of sacrifice could assist the dead in their transformation. This may well have motivated Emperor Ming's ritual reform.

This situation certainly characterized the imperial level during the Eastern Han dynasty. But what about the funerary rites of the horizontal chamber style at other levels of Han society?[164] Given the relatively poor preservation condition in the horizontal chamber-style burials and the paucity of available religious texts, we do not know much about the funerary rites. But archaeological materials show that among

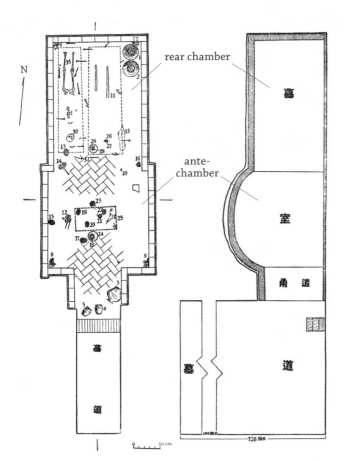

rear chamber

ante-
chamber

N

墓

室

甬 道

道

墓

墓

道

50 cm.

726 厘米

Fig. 2.24. Plan and cross
section of Tomb 1026 at
Shaogou in Luoyang City,
Henan. Late Western Han
dynasty.

the burials of the middle and lower levels of society, it had become customary by the late Western Han dynasty to set up sacrificial space inside the horizontal tombs. This space often housed a set of lacquerware including cups, a low table (*an*), plates, spoons, and sacrificial meats. For example, Tomb 1026 at Shaogou in Luoyang City, Henan, consists of an antechamber (1.74 meters long, 1.88 meters wide, and 1.76 meters high) and a rear chamber (2.36 meters long, 1.64 meters wide, and 1.390 meters high) where the two coffins were located (fig. 2.24). In the middle of the antechamber is a lacquered table with four lacquered cups with two attached ear-like hands on the top and several nearby. On the east end of the table are animal bones, and on the west end is a complete set of chicken bones.[165] These artifacts suggest that funerary ritual activities took place in the antechamber before the tomb was sealed. The archaeological report rightly states that such funerary ritual performance within the tomb propelled production of sacrificial space in the horizontal chamber-style tomb,[166] such as in the Western Han princely tombs discussed earlier.

Recent archaeological evidence shows that the underground sacrificial space, often considered a closed, private space for the dead, could be public space too. Not only could the bereaved hold the final funerary rite inside the burial chamber but

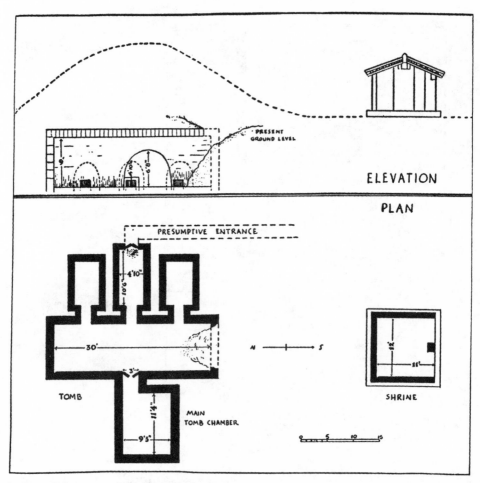

Fig. 2.25. Plan and cross section of Zhu Wei's tomb and offering shrine (*citang*), Jiaxiang County, Shandong. Eastern Han dynasty. After Fairbank, "A Structural Key to Han Mural Art," fig. 16.

the public could also visit the tomb. Two inscriptions in a second-century CE brick tomb at Baizicun in Xunyi County, Shaanxi, written on either side of the access ramp leading to the tomb chamber, state: "All viewers must take off shoes before entering" and "Those who wish to view must take off shoes before entering."[167] An ancient custom, removing shoes before entering a room was the proper social etiquette for meeting senior or high officials. Thus, removing shoes before entering the tomb was a sign of respect for the tomb occupant.[168] For a certain period during the funeral rites, at least in the Eastern Han dynasty, the tomb was not completely a private space; the public also had the opportunity to view the pictorial decoration and pay tribute to the deceased. As exquisite as it is, the Mawangdui silk painting, once buried in the innermost coffin after the funeral procession, would no longer be visible; the pictorial decoration on horizontal chamber-style tombs, however, could be viewed by the public before the tomb was sealed. This change extended the process of assisting the recently deceased in their postmortem transformation, which appears to be the function of the silk paintings and other imagery. This accessibility of the sacrificial space is the fundamental difference between vertical pit-style tombs and horizontal chamber-style tombs.

In the Han dynasty, funerary shrines, monumental towers, and stone steles were common near burial sites. Funerary shrines were referred to as sacrificial halls (*citang*) or dining halls (*shitang*) in some Eastern Han shrine inscriptions,[169] denoting these as places where descendants continued to offer food to their ancestors. As scholars have pointed out, many Han funerary shrines have two halls (*tang*)—one serving as the sacrificial space in front of the coffin chamber and the other as the aboveground shrine near the burial site.[170] Instead of seeing the latter as the effect of the relocation of religious activities from temple to tomb,[171] we could see these aboveground shrines as spatial extensions of the underground sacrificial space devoted to the cult of the dead, as shown in the case of the "Zhu Wei" shrine at Jiaxiang County, Shandong (fig. 2.25).[172] After subterranean burial chambers were sealed, sacrificial rituals continued in the shrines above. Accordingly, the chain of ancestral sacrifice continued, but the focus had shifted, as it had in many other aspects of the funerary rites, from the nexus between the dead and their ancestors to that between the living and the dead.

THE TRANSFORMATION OF BURIAL SPACE from vertical pit-style tombs to horizontal chamber-style tombs was closely related to the changing ideology around burial, the practical need to bury a husband and wife in the same burial chamber, and the changing religious status of the deceased ancestors. The change in mortuary architecture reflected a new conception of the postmortem residence of the spirit and the manner in which the living and the dead interacted during the prolonged mourning period. The change accommodated sequential tomb occupancy, which paralleled an apparent redirection of interest away from the greater lineage and toward the nuclear family among the elite as well as the commoner classes.

The establishment of sacrificial spaces inside tombs also reflected changes in the status of the dead and the sacrificial rituals associated with them. This spatial transformation represents the materialization of an "abstract" sacrificial space in the imagination of the afterlife as a "concrete" one within tombs and was the result of the transference of religious efficacy from benevolent ancestors, in the Shang and Western Zhou dynasties, to the potentially harmful dead, in the Warring States period and the early empires. This move owes much to the new awareness of the frightening potential of individual ghosts and reflects the bereaved's increasing efforts to pacify the deceased by converging the funerary ritual performance and the tomb. This process started with the establishment of sacrificial space within the tomb and culminated in the Eastern Han dynasty with the construction of the aboveground shrine near the tomb.

Plate 1. Bronze ritual vessels in the eastern compartment during the excavation of Tomb 1 at Jiuliandun, Zaoyang City, Hubei. Warring States period. Hubei Provincial Institute of Cultural Relics and Archaeology.

Plate 2. A group of wooden lacquer vessels in the waterlogged southern compartment during the excavation of Tomb 2 at Jiuliandun, Zaoyang City, Hubei. Warring States period. Hubei Provincial Institute of Cultural Relics and Archaeology.

Plate 3. Square bronze wine vessel excavated from Tomb 1 at Jiuliandun, Zaoyang City, Hubei (M1: E157). H. 79.8 cm. Warring States period. Hubei Provincial Institute of Cultural Relics and Archaeology.

Plate 4. Square lacquered, wooden wine vessel excavated from Tomb 2 at Jiuliandun, Zaoyang City, Hubei (M2: E37). H. 79.2 cm. Warring States period. Hubei Provincial Institute of Cultural Relics and Archaeology.

Plate 5. Painted wooden figurine, with a long braided wig and red cinnabar lipstick, excavated from Tomb 2 at Jiuliandun, Zaoyang City, Hubei (M2: N384). H. 69.5 cm. Warring States period. Hubei Provincial Institute of Cultural Relics and Archaeology.

Plate 6. Chu silk manuscript excavated by tomb robbers from Tomb 365 at Zidanku, Changsha City, Hunan. L. 38.5 cm, W. 47 cm, ink on silk. Warring States period. The Arthur M. Sackler Foundation, courtesy of the Arthur M. Sackler Gallery, Smithsonian Institution, MLS2028.

Plate 7. Lacquered inner coffin and bronze framed outer coffin, excavated from Tomb 1 at Leigudun, Suizhou City, Hubei. The two archaeologists standing nearby are Shu Zhimei (1934–2007, right) and Chen Zhongxing (1939–, left), the former directors of the Hubei Provincial Museum. Outer coffin H. 2.19 m, L. 3.20 m, W. 2.10 m; weight 7,000 kg. Inner coffin H. 1.32 m, L. 2.50 m, W. 1.27 m. Warring States period. Hubei Provincial Museum.

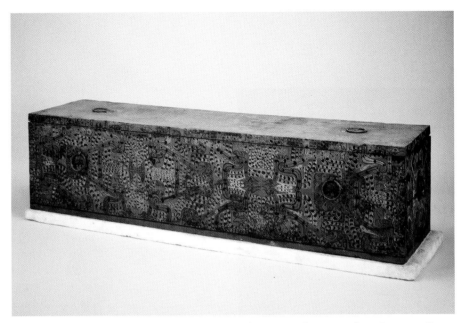

Plate 8. Painted, lacquered inner coffin, excavated from Tomb 2 at Baoshan, Jingmen City, Hubei. H. 46 cm, L. 184 cm, W. 46 cm. Ca. 316 BCE. Warring States period. Hubei Provincial Museum.

Plate 9. Terra-cotta human figurines, excavated from Ash Pit 358, Trenches A14, A16 at Xiaotun, Anyang City, Henan. Tallest 16.4 cm. Yinxu period, Shang dynasty. Collection of the Institute of History and Philology, Academia Sinica, Taiwan.

Plate 11. Early example of the fecundity god figure with a single phallic pole, excavated from Tomb 4 at Zhaoxiang, Dangyang County, Hubei (M4: 32). H. 60 cm. Middle Spring and Autumn period. Hubei Yichang Museum.

Plate 10. Bronze kneeling figurine, with inscription on the body identifying it as the chief of the Huai barbarian, an enemy captured by the army of the state of Jin. H. 17.2 cm. Western Zhou dynasty. Private collection.

Plate 12. Fecundity god figure. Wood, pigment, and refurbished deer antler. H. 57.5 cm, W. 27.5 cm, D. 30.8 cm. Warring States period. Middle Yangtze River valley. Gift of Thomas Colville in honor of Curator Dr. Jenny So. S2000.125a-l. The Arthur M. Sackler Gallery, Smithsonian Institution.

Plate 13. Fecundity god figure excavated from Tomb 18 at Yutaishan, Jingzhou City, Hubei. Wood, pigment, and refurbished deer antlers. H. 55.2 cm. Warring States period. Hubei Provincial Institute of Cultural Relics and Archaeology.

Plate 14. Silk diagram of "Taiyi Incantation," excavated from Tomb 3 at Mawangdui, Changsha City, Hunan. L. 43.5 cm, W. 45 cm. Ink and pigments on silk. Ca. 168 BCE. Early Western Han dynasty. Hunan Provincial Museum.

3

The Presence of the Invisible

All art is "image-making" and all image-making is
rooted in the creation of substitutes.

—ERNST H. GOMBRICH

The striving for resemblance marks our attempts to make
the absent present and the dead alive.

—DAVID FREEDBERG

SWEEPING TRANSFORMATIONS in attitude toward images of the invisible powers—pictorial representations of the dead and gods—occurred in early Chinese art during the Warring States period. The ambivalent attitude toward the dead that characterized this period prompted the living to strive to identify, control, and assist the dead through the magic power of image-making. This effort to capture the dead in pictorial form inspired a strong tendency toward anthropomorphic and hybrid representations of gods and spirits, a tendency that has been called "affecting presence" or "the power of images."[1] Out of this wish "to make the absent present and the dead alive," anthropomorphic representations of the dead and gods came to figure prominently in early Chinese art.[2]

The Sympathetic Magic of the Human Figure

The human figure was not a prominent theme, and verisimilitude generally not privileged, in early Chinese art.[3] Although small, highly schematized anthropomorphic images or fragments of such objects have been excavated from Neolithic and early Bronze Age sites, their contexts are often unclear and generally do not provide enough information to allow us to elucidate their meanings and functions.[4]

A notable exception is a group of anthropomorphic sculptures discovered at a

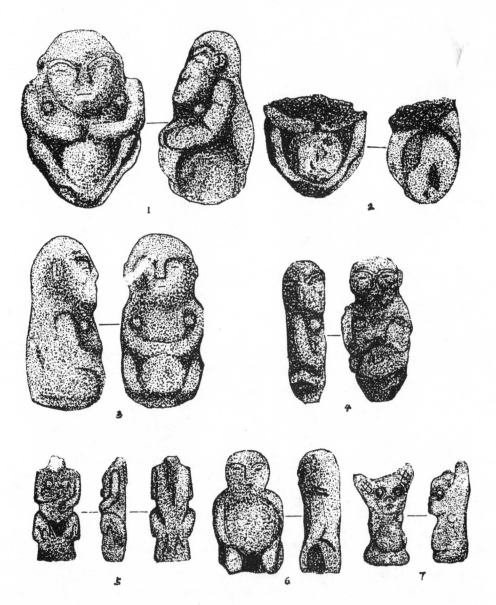

Fig. 3.1. Drawings of a group of stone female figurines from Houtaizi, Luanping County, Hebei. Ca. 5000 BCE.

Neolithic site at Houtaizi in Luanping County, Hebei (fig. 3.1).[5] Dated to 4500–4000 BCE, the group consists of seven stone sculptures, some of which are badly damaged and fragmented. These sculptures, which depict the different stages of a woman giving birth to a child, range from thirty-four centimeters in height to as little as seven-and-a-half centimeters. The first, and the largest, is a frontal image of a big-bellied woman in a squatting pose with both of her hands placed on top of her belly. The fifth depicts the woman's legs wide open in a later stage of labor. In this sequence, the woman's belly becomes smaller and eventually flat, and the seventh

Fig. 3.2. Terra-cotta head of a female figurine, excavated at Niuheliang site, Lingyuan County, Liaoning. Clay. H. 22.5 cm. Hongshan Culture, fourth millennium BCE.

and last sculpture is of an alert newborn with open eyes and two raised arms.[6] These stone figurines are not statues of a so-called Venus or goddess, as some scholars have suggested,[7] but rather instruments of "the sympathetic magic of the human figure" (*renxing fangshu*).[8] According to this belief, the sculptures served to help women during the process of labor.

Stone, or more often clay, sculptures of pregnant women have also been discovered at the Neolithic Hongshan Culture site of Dongshanzui in Kazuo County, Liaoning. Those are small and fragmentary, while the so-called goddesses discovered at Niuheliang, Lingyuan County, Liaoning (fig. 3.2) are large clay statues, often life-size. They are broken probably because, as ethnographic evidence suggests, when the process did not go smoothly, these images often became the target of grievances.[9] More than ten groups of such female images have been discovered in northeast China and Inner Mongolia.[10] There seems to have been a regional cultural tradition in which female figurines were used as fertility symbols or ritual devices for image magic. Although these Neolithic images may not have any direct historical relevance to later Shang and Zhou practice, they suggest that concepts such as image magic may have existed in some regional cultures in ancient China.[11]

During the Shang and Western Zhou periods, zoomorphic motifs were vividly depicted. In contrast, the human figure, still rare, occupied a secondary and subordinate role and was either transformed into a partially hybrid form or metamorphosed completely into the shape of an animal. The rarity of human figurines in early China has been explained in terms of the dominant shamanistic institution in Shang society.[12] According to this theory, human figures or faces were sometimes incorporated into animal designs, as with the famous bronze *you*-container in the Sumitomo collection in Kyoto, where a human, probably a shaman, was placed under the mouth of a crouching tiger and embracing the fearsome beast.[13] Whether most human figures in Shang elite art can be interpreted as shamans remains unclear. Scholars still debate the extent to which shamanism as a belief system dominated Shang society.[14]

Anthropomorphic representations of gods and ancestors are limited. In the Shang religious pantheon, deities like the supreme god were sometimes conceptualized anthropomorphically as beings in possession of will and intention. They could command (*ling*) rain and wind, send down blessings as well as misfortunes, and approve or disapprove of human actions, as revealed in divination records excavated from Anyang City, Henan. But these Shang gods, far from being represented anthropomorphically, were not depicted at all. Often they were not the direct recipients of sacrificial offerings; instead, the ancestral spirits were the intermediaries between the human and the spiritual worlds.

In communal sacrificial rituals, living impersonators (*shi*) represented the ancestors, but more often the ancestors were represented "depersonalized," in the form of abstract wooden or stone tablets.[15] Ancestors were considered collective entities in Shang religion, to be enlivened only by the memories of their descendants, as opposed to being given a physical form. For example, after their death, they were given posthumous temple names (*miaohao*) consisting of one of the ten heavenly stems (*tiangan*), and those ancestors with the same heavenly stem were sacrificed to collectively.[16] The absence of anthropomorphic images in early Chinese art is largely reflective of the religious conception of the ancestors and the practice of impersonators in ancestor cults.[17] As in many other early civilizations, representation and its place in religious conception were inextricably connected in ancient China.[18]

The use of impersonators in religious ceremonies can be traced back at least to the Shang dynasty. Traditional writings such as the *Book of Poetry*, *Protocols of Ceremonies*, and *Book of Rites* include accounts of a living person serving as an impersonator and hosting the spirit of a deceased ancestor during the sacrificial rites. The impersonator's movements, accompanied by ritual music, structured the sacrifice. These ritual texts explain how to select an impersonator by divination, how to salute the person selected, how to act during the ceremonies, and so forth. Several poems in the *Book of Poetry*, such as the "Chuci" (Ode no. 209), describe the ritual process for the ancestor cult.[19] Archaeologists found stone tablets inscribed with ancestral posthumous temple names in Shang tombs (fig. 3.3).[20] Similar tablets, though lacking inscriptions, were discovered at the famed tomb of Fu Hao at Anyang City, Henan. The practice of using nonrepresentational wooden or stone tablets to stand

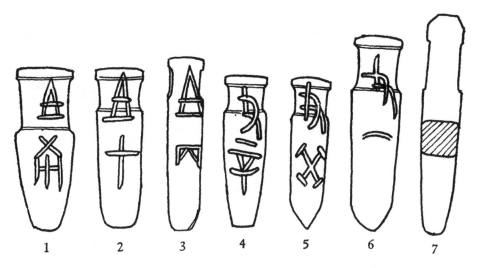

Fig. 3.3. Jade tablets inscribed with ancestral names, excavated from a tomb at Hougang, Yinxu, in Anyang City, Henan. Shang dynasty.

in for an ancestor was extended to nature deities in the Warring States period; a set of wooden tablets on which the names of the five household gods were inscribed was excavated from Tomb 2 at Baoshan (fig. 3.4).

The currently available documentation offers no direct proof of the existence of an "image taboo" on divine and ancestral images in early China.[21] Nevertheless, it seems that people in the Shang and Western Zhou avoided material representations of the divine or the ancestral. As some scholars suggest, the general absence of the human figure in early elite art "seems to have been based on culturally distinctive choices concerning what was important or appropriate to represent."[22] And in ancient China, gods, ancestors, kings, and other elite figures were seen as too important to be represented in material form.

When human figures do appear, they represent people who held minor or negative positions in society. Far from being kings and gods, they are primarily "other," the marginalized and unprivileged subordinates or enemies and outsiders around whom the identity of the civilized "we" coalesced.[23] The avoidance of portraying gods and kings in elite art, the use of impersonators and abstract tablets to represent ancestors, and the tendency of most depictions to present the social other suggest that images, particularly of the human figure, had certain magical functions. In addition, depictions of the human figure may have been associated with a kind of black magic, in which the maker would gain control over the subject. This may explain why human figures are rare in early Chinese art.

Image-making can be seen as a form of social control, just as assigning a name has magical significance. In early China, an image was produced primarily for its "magical power" to enact social or psychological control; this function stands in

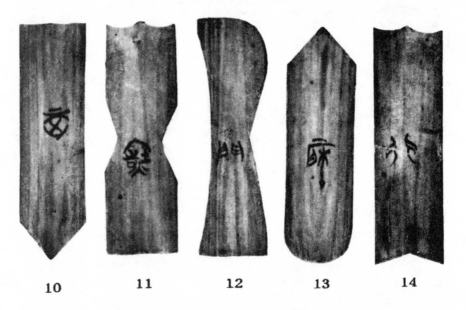

Fig. 3.4. Wooden Tablets of the Five Household Deities (Hall, Stove, Gate, Door, Travel), discovered in Tomb 2 (Item Nos. 415-2 to 415-6.), dated to 316 BCE, at Baoshan, Jingmen City, Hubei. In this picture from the original archaeological report the first tablet on the left is placed upside-down.

sharp contrast to the role of images in biblical traditions, where the making of an image itself constitutes an act of worship.[24] In Jewish, Christian, and Islamic art, both icon worshippers and iconoclasts established their doctrines on the basis of this notion of image-making. For example, in Christianity, the subject matter of the image is often divine, invisible power.[25]

In contrast, the social status of the figure depicted in early Chinese art was often very low: the subjects were often naked, crippled, and toiling, or criminals and enemy captives. As scholars have demonstrated, other than a small number of monsters, hybrid creatures, and androgynous and fertility figurines (probably for use in ritual and magic), the major categories of representation include the heads and images of barbarian chiefs, prisoners, slaves, and servants. For instance, two clay figurines excavated from the Shang royal cemetery near Anyang City, Henan, and now housed in the Academia Sinica, Taiwan, are dressed in long gowns and have their hands tied and necks bound, indicating that they were prisoners (Plate 9). Bronze ritual vessels in the late Western Zhou and early Spring and Autumn periods were often supported by small human figures rather than cast feet or rings. The bronze *he* excavated from Tomb 31 at the Tianma-Qucun site at Quwo County, Shanxi, is only one of numerous examples. A bronze kneeling figure with his hands tied behind his back is clearly identified as a prisoner; according to the inscription on his body, this is an image of the captured chief of the Huai "barbarians," who fought against the state of Jin (Plate 10).[26] The rim of the plaque on top of his head is uneven, suggesting that his head had been broken and that this figure originally served as a stand for a vessel or a lamp. This is confirmed by the recent discovery of a bronze lamp excavated from a Western Zhou tomb (Tomb 1017) at Dahekou, Yicheng County, Shanxi, in the form of a similar kneeling figure with a big bronze basin on his head.[27]

In the Shang and Zhou dynasties, there is no evidence of a cult of images of the type that existed in the biblical and other traditions.[28] Instead, the rendering of the human figure in early Chinese art had magical power, which in turn translated into a form of social control. Representing someone or something in material form was in some sense seen as controlling the subject itself.[29]

The Ambivalent Attitude toward Verisimilitude

Verisimilitude was not often privileged in early Chinese art, and early Chinese attitudes toward it were ambivalent. On the one hand, it is said that Confucius denounced tomb figurines because their lifelike appearance implied human sacrifice.[30] In another anecdote in the *Han Feizi*, a painter reportedly said that it was easier to draw a ghost or a demon than a dog or a horse, because horses and dogs were everywhere to be seen and everyone was familiar with their appearance, whereas ghosts and demons were products of the imagination. Thus, the painter could draw them in whatever way he liked.[31]

On the other hand, verisimilitude was deemphasized. When the human figure was depicted, depending on who was represented, verisimilitude was deemed neither necessary nor even desirable.[32] This ambivalent attitude toward verisimilitude concurs with the avoidance of human depiction in early Chinese art. At the root of both the ambivalence and the avoidance was the place in the social hierarchy of the subject depicted. At one end of this hierarchy were gods and ancestors, whose high status required that they not be materialized in any tangible form; their presence was communicated through abstract association and the magic spiritual power they possessed. At the other end of this spectrum are the socially marginalized—slaves, enemies, and people of low social status, those subjects of the "image magic" in the Shang and Western Zhou periods.

The rise of the tomb figurine in the Western Zhou and the Spring and Autumn periods was indeed an extension of the earlier practice of "image magic."[33] The tomb figurines of servants, guards, and musicians represent those who accompanied and served the dead in the afterlife. These figurines were substitutes for human sacrifices, particularly for "companions in death." Here "substitute" means a representation intended to serve a purpose, to "fulfill certain demands of the organism."[34] The "organism" in this case was the early Chinese conception of the afterlife, in which the privileged dead needed and demanded the same or better service from their underlings. The companions in death were relatives, consorts, officials, retainers, and servants—people who had close relationships with the dead and higher social

Fig. 3.5. Aerial view of Tomb 502 with four human figurines at the four corners of the secondary ledge, excavated at Liangdaicun, Hancheng City, Shaanxi. Late Western Zhou period.

Fig. 3.6. Drawings of one of the four human figurines excavated from Tomb 502 at Liangdaicun, Hancheng City, Shaanxi. Late Western Zhou period.

status than the slaves and prisoners depicted earlier. Often they received a full funerary ritual with their own coffin and grave goods.

The early literature suggests that these companions, demonstrating their loyalty, vowed to die with their masters, who were often kings. Certainly many were probably forced to do so. One story in the *Zuo Commentary* (Lord Zhao 13th year, 529 BCE) tells of King Ling of Chu, who committed suicide in exile while hiding in Shen Hai's home. To express his loyalty, Shen Hai forced his two daughters to be the king's companions in death.[35]

Recent archaeological evidence suggests that the practice of using tomb figurines can be traced back much earlier, at least to the middle Western Zhou period. In Tomb 1 at Dahekou in Yicheng County, Shanxi, archaeologists discovered a pair of wooden figurines, each over one meter tall and standing on top of a wooden turtle. Their extended hands seemed to hold something, and in front of them were buried lacquerwares and wooden objects.[36] In another Western Zhou elite tomb, Tomb 502 at Liangdaicun in Hancheng City, Shaanxi, archaeologists discovered four wooden figurines, each standing at one of the four corners of the second-level ledges before reaching the burial pit (fig. 3.5).[37] Two of them, each about one meter tall, had two arms tenoned into their bodies and two hands grasped in a circle. The excavators concluded they were charioteers because horses and chariots were buried nearby. The other two, about sixty centimeters tall, also had arms tenoned into their bodies and their hands extended, seeming to hold something (fig. 3.6).

Most of the wooden figurines buried in tombs were substitutes for companions in death. This fact is apparent in another set of tomb figurines of the late Spring and Autumn period, discovered in Tomb 7 at Niujiapo in Changzi County, Shanxi (fig. 3.7).[38] The vertical pit-style tomb, whose occupant was an elite adult woman, had a wooden encasement, an outer coffin, and an elaborately painted inner coffin, and the furnishings included bronze ritual vessels, jades, wooden and lacquered objects, and pottery vessels. Three burials of companions in death were placed on the west and south sides of the inner chamber, with their own coffins and bronze and jade ornaments. More significant, on the east and north sides of the outer coffin were two pairs of wooden figurines, lying head-to-toe. Together the three human victims and the wooden figures surrounded the tomb owner in protection, as was common practice in sacrificial burials in early China.[39] The substitutes are each about sixty-seven centimeters high, painted entirely in black lacquer, and once had movable arms. Their red-painted robes are folded from left to right and held in place with a belt hook, and their faces, originally molded in clay and attached to the flat wooden base, had disintegrated by the time the tomb was opened (fig. 3.8). It is extraordinary that such elegant wooden figurines took the place of human victims. Their clay-molded faces and movable arms are particularly noteworthy and suggest their designers were "striving for resemblance." Although we do not know why these three people were sacrificed while the other four were represented by wooden figurines, the four

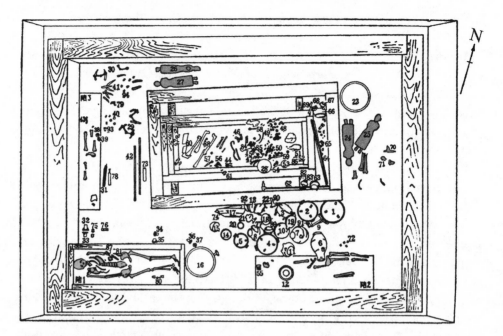

Fig. 3.7. Plan of Tomb 7 at Niujiapo in Changzi County, Shanxi. Late Spring and Autumn period.

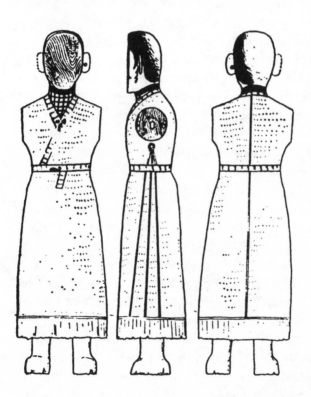

Fig. 3.8. Drawing of one of the wooden human figurines excavated from Tomb 7 at Niujiapo in Changzi County, Shanxi. Wood with black lacquer. H. 67 cm. Late Spring and Autumn period.

figurines probably represented four actual humans. Verisimilitude, it seems, was a concern.

While the use of tomb figurines did not end human sacrifice in early Chinese mortuary practice, the rising popularity of tomb figurines did coincide with a decline in human sacrifice.[40] The coexistence of human victims and wooden figurines, as in Tomb 7 at Niujiapo, has led some scholars to question the substitutive function of tomb figurines.[41] Certainly, in its early stage of practice, the substitution probably involved a one-to-one replacement of human victims with figurines. Nevertheless, in later stages, the substitutions may have shifted away from the simple logic of one-to-one correspondence, and the figurines may have represented a category of people. In other words, they played a role in the construction of the image of the afterlife. The use of tomb figurines enabled lower-status individuals, who previously would have been neither entitled to nor able to afford this degree of mortuary treatment, to imitate their betters. In the Chu region, for example, tomb figurines began to appear in the early Warring States period.[42] In the middle Warring States period, about half of Chu elite tombs contained figurines, and by the end of the Warring States period, almost all elite and commoner tombs contained figurines.[43]

Other factors, such as local traditions, the status of the deceased, and new religious or philosophical ideas also influenced the use of human sacrifice in different regions. Western Zhou elite burials were already distinct from those of the Shang in their infrequent use of human sacrifice.[44] Moreover, contemporary criticisms of the practice, as voiced in *Mencius* ("Liang Huiwang xia" chapter), the *Book of Rites* ("Tan Gong xia" chapter), and the *Book of Poetry* ("Huangniao," Qinfeng, ode no. 131), reflect the social unease with the high elite's practice of sacrificing human beings. Although isolated examples of human victims appear even in late imperial times, the emergence of tomb figurines more broadly coincided with the decline in human sacrifice during the Eastern Zhou period.[45] The substitution of tomb figurines for actual human beings was integral to the development of spirit artifacts and the new religious practices discussed in chapter 2, which may have promoted the dissemination and wider consumption of tomb figurines during the Warring States, Qin, and Han periods. At some point in the development of these figurines, they came to be depersonalized, representing types or roles associated with companions in death rather than the individuals who were to be companions in death.[46] Tomb figurines were substitute companions in death but were not intended to be real presences. In other words, the figurines had forms but no souls. These were representations without presence.

At this stage of development in the representation of the human figure, it is significant that the subjects were mostly attendants, guardians, musicians, dancers, and servants. Examples of these types are found among the tomb figurines in Tomb 2 at Baoshan (fig. 3.9). Of the twelve figurines excavated from that burial, ten were created from one block of wood (about fifty-five cm high) without articulation of the legs; these figurines were located in pairs along the four sides of the tomb. Ex-

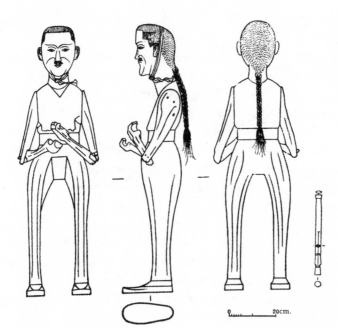

Fig. 3.9. Drawing of three views of a wooden figurine excavated from Tomb 2 at Baoshan, Jingmen City, Hubei. Warring States period. Fourth century BCE.

cept for the second pair in the eastern compartment, each figurine carried a wooden sword about thirty-two centimeters long. Their faces were painted white and their facial features carved out or painted, they had long hair, painted black and hung down their backs, and they wore round caps. All were dressed in fine clothing. Each figure originally had two outstretched arms, presumably positioned to hold their swords.

The third pair of figurines in the eastern compartment was twice the size of the ten legless figurines (about 112 cm high). Their constituent parts—heads, main bodies with lower limbs, hair, ears, and upper limbs—were premanufactured and then assembled. Long, neatly braided wigs were fixed to their heads, their lips were painted red, and they wore black painted shoes. One of them had a band around his neck, which attached to his head. Their two arms were movable, but as in the previous group, they were not actually designed to move; rather, they were positioned to hold wooden swords to emphasize their function as guards.

Tomb figurines were also mentioned in Warring States inventories of grave goods. The Leigudun inventory mentions fifty-seven servants (Strips 212, 213), though only one wooden figurine was found in the tomb.[47] The inventory from Tomb 2 at Wangshan describes nine spirit servants (*wangtong*),[48] all wearing colorful yellow, red, or purple silk clothing (Strip 49).[49] Sixteen wooden figurines were excavated from this burial.[50] The inventory from Tomb 2 at Changtaiguan in Xinyang City, Henan, records eight "spirit servants" (*mingtong*, Strip 28), and ten were excavated from that grave.[51] In all of these cases, the human figurines were designed to accompany the deceased master into the underworld and to serve him there.

Chapter Three

Eastern Zhou–period tombs feature yet another category of small figurine that may have functioned differently from those described above. These are also substitutes, but instead of replacing companions in death, they represent the enemies or relatives of the deceased. In Tomb 1 at Changtaiguan, four wooden figurines were discovered at the four corners of the rear compartment along with a lacquered wooden sculpture of the so-called tomb guardian figure. One of the four figurines has a bamboo needle piercing its chest.[52] Another, sitting on his knees in the right rear compartment, has a bamboo needle piercing the back of his head and two earlobes. We do not know the exact meaning of this practice, but it is clear that similar tomb figurines were treated differently, depending on the burial context.

Simple wooden figurines were also found in the famous Tomb 1 at Mawangdui.[53] Thirty-three figurines carved from peach branches with eyes and eyebrows painted in black ink were found on top of the innermost coffin near the silk banner painting (see fig. 3.15, lower left corner). These figurines, ranging in size from eight to twelve centimeters long, were either split in half or left whole (fig. 3.10, the weaved roll in the upper register and the three on either side in the lower register). They are categorically different from the other wooden servants and musicians found in the tomb (figs. 3.11a and 3.11b). Archaeologists have pointed out that this group of wooden figurines had the power to ward off or expel evil spirits.[54] Three other small wooden figurines (about 11–12 cm high) with red and black ink outlining the eyes and eyebrows were lodged between the innermost coffin and the next outer coffin, in the gaps along three of the coffin's sides. Two wore deep-red silk clothing with silk belts at their waists. The last was enveloped in coarse sackcloth with only the head sticking out (see fig. 3.10, the two in the middle of the lower register). These three figurines are of special interest because of their unusual clothing. In ancient China, untrimmed and trimmed sackcloth, roughly and finely processed cloth, and silk cloth were used to make five different types of mourning dress.[55] Accordingly, these three figurines could be the substitutes for the mourners, Lady Dai's relatives of different degrees of closeness. A similar type of wooden figurine, what archaeologists call the "slim wooden figurine" (mupian yong), can be traced back to the late Spring and Autumn or early Warring States period. Examples of these include objects from Tomb 5 at Caojiagang in Dangyang County, Hubei, and from Tomb 635 at Jiudian in Jiangling County, Hubei.[56]

Of these two categories of figurines, the first encompasses a generic group, which emphasized a degree of verisimilitude through the depiction of hair, clothing, painted facial features, and so forth. Even in small jade pendants, the figure's formal features, ornaments, and clothing could be vividly depicted (fig. 3.12). In the second group, in contrast, verisimilitude was deemphasized, and the figurines could be made present only by means of magic. The tomb figurines are essentially miniature in size and inferior in materials, made mostly of clay, wood, or lead, and later of paper.[57] Yet all of these figurines, from the tiny wooden or clay figurines to the extraordinary life-size terra-cotta army of the First Emperor of Qin (fig. 3.13), share some

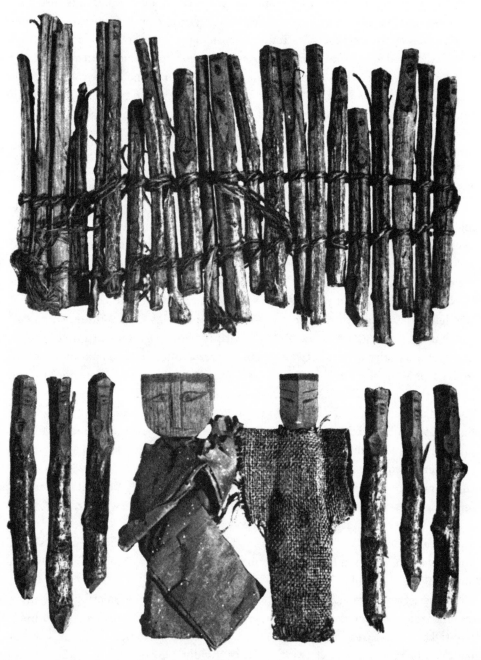

Fig. 3.10. Slim wooden figurines found on top of the innermost coffin in Tomb 1 at Mawangdui, Changsha City, Hunan. Early Western Han dynasty.

Figs. 3.11a and b. Different groups of wooden figurines excavated from Tomb 1 at Mawangdui, Changsha City, Hunan. Early Western Han dynasty.

Fig. 3.12. Pendant in the form of
a female dancer. Jade (nephrite).
H. 8.0 cm, W. 3.5 cm, D. 0.5 cm. Warring States period. The Freer Gallery
of Art, Washington, DC, Purchase
F1938.16.

Fig. 3.13. Group of life-size terra-cotta soldiers discovered near the mausoleum of the First
Emperor of Qin near Xi'an City, Shaanxi. Qin dynasty.

elements of magic.[58] Consider the use of real human hair in the Baoshan guardians and the bright, painted red lipstick and real hair in the figurine from Tomb 2 at Jiuliandun (see Plate 5). Formal similarity is not at issue here. In this tradition of image magic, the verisimilitude of the human body is not the major concern. Rather, the body is made present through the power of the magic.

Concerning the Identity of the Dead

The most significant artistic development in early China occurred during the Warring States period, when figure paintings first appeared in Chu elite tombs. Scholars have often attributed this advance to outside influences, such as those from the north and northwest or from the south or southeast.[59] True, the Warring States period is characterized by intensive cultural exchange between the central states and the periphery. But without a clear understanding of the internal mechanism by which these external, non-Chinese influences were absorbed, claims of outside influence based on formal similarity cannot be substantiated. Instead, the anthropomorphic representation of the deceased and spirits may be associated with an internal, native mechanism: the bereaved's attempt to identify, control, and assist the deceased during the liminal stage, a period of transformation from potentially dangerous and recently dead to benevolent ancestor.

Although representations of the deceased can be subsumed under the Shang and Western Zhou notion of "image magic," the application of such magic to the realm of the dead represented a new phase in the evolution of this concept. To begin with, the social status of the subject of the image magic had changed. In addition, the attitude toward those being represented had also shifted. Through their anthropomorphic depiction, the deceased elite were now subject to the same control as other groups of the Shang and Western Zhou periods. This transformation arose from the desire on the part of the bereaved to preserve in anthropomorphic form the social identities of the deceased so that they could transition smoothly from this world to the afterlife. Here the deceased were regarded as "other" and were feared, yet their bereaved relatives also desired to care for and express their affection for them. The Chu elite's urge to depict the dead and the gods in anthropomorphic form and to illustrate abstract religious ideas in concrete terms paved the way for figural representations in later Chinese art.[60]

We can see this transition to using images of the deceased in ritual ceremonies, particularly in the liminal soul-calling stage during the Warring States period, in literary sources. In *Songs of the South*, for example, the poems entitled "Summons of the Soul" (Zhaohun) and "The Great Summons" (Dazhao) both mention the use of images (*xiang*) to call back the soul of the deceased in the soul-summoning ritual. The ceremony, which began with warnings that the soul should not wander in the vast and dangerous outside world but should instead come back to its "old abode," continues with more blandishments:

O soul, come back! And enter the gate of the city.

Skilled priests are there who call you, walking backwards to lead you in.

Qin basket-work, silk cords of Qi, and silken banner of Zheng:

All things are there proper for your recall; and with long-drawn,

    Piercing cries they summon the wandering soul.

O soul, come back! Return to your old abode.

All the quarters of the world are full of harm and evil.

Your *image* (*xiang*) is set up in your quiet and reposeful home.[61]

Scholars have interpreted the word *xiang* 像 in the final line of this passage as a reference to the image of the deceased[62] and have suggested that ancestor cults transitioned from using impersonators in rituals in the Spring and Autumn period to using images in the Warring States period.[63] This transition is also reflected in the modification of the word *shi* 尸 from its earlier sense of "impersonator" to a new meaning of "human corpse."[64] Some scholars estimate that the decline of the impersonator occurred around the end of the third century BCE, when Qin unified China;[65] at the same time, the practice of impersonation stopped.[66]

Very few figural paintings on silk survive. But their scarcity speaks to the difficulty of preservation rather than to their historical prevalence. To date, only four silk paintings of the Warring States period have been excavated. Of the two from the region of the metropolitan Chu capital Ji'nancheng, the one from Tomb 1 at Mashan in Jiangling County, Hubei, is the earliest but the badly damaged silk has been folded and is now stuck together. Except for faint traces of a dragon head painted in black ink on white silk, little of its iconographic program can be discerned. The second, which has yet to be published, is a banner featuring phoenix and bird motifs found on top of the coffin in Tomb 5 at Guanping in Jingzhou City, Hubei.[67] The two better-preserved examples were found in the southern territory of the state of Chu in Hunan. One, from Tomb 365 (formerly numbered Tomb 1) at Zidanku in Changsha City, Hunan (see fig. 5.1),[68] was discovered in 1973 when Chinese archaeologists re-excavated the tomb from which the famous Chu silk manuscript was unearthed by tomb robbers in 1942. The second was unearthed at Chenjiadashan near Changsha, also by tomb robbers, in 1949.[69] Although the Chenjiadashan silk painting was said to have been found in a bamboo case,[70] the Zidanku specimen was located between the wooden boards covering the vault and the wooden boards above the coffin.[71] It is 37.5 centimeters long and 28 centimeters wide. A silk ribbon is attached to the middle of a bamboo stick supporting the upper edge of the painting, which suggests that it was hung during the funerary ritual and presumably deposited in the tomb before it was closed. Archaeologists report that similar bamboo sticks have been discovered in many Chu tombs and surmise that the silk paintings originally attached to them had disintegrated. These Chu silk paintings are the immediate precursors of the famous early Western Han silk banner paintings excavated from Tombs 1 and 3 at Mawangdui near Changsha, from Jinqueshan in Linyi City, Shandong, and from several other locations at which other fragments of silk paintings have been unearthed.

These excavated paintings and banners were likely used in funerary ceremonies. Both the early literature and the excavated paintings themselves indicate that, during the Warring States and early Han periods, such images functioned as representations of the dead in the liminal stage. The Chenjiadashan and Zidanku paintings, which depict the deceased in some form of transformation during the spirit journey,[72] served a purpose similar to that of the silk banner paintings from the Mawangdui tombs.[73] Scholars have suggested that these silk paintings are "portraits" of the tomb occupants and served the same function of identifying the deceased during the funerary rites as the name banners (*mingjing*) of the Eastern Han dynasty did, both described in early ritual texts and known from archaeological discoveries in northwest China.[74] Scholars further argue that the Mawangdui banner painting represented the tomb occupant Lady Dai's existence in her "happy home" (i.e., the inner coffin) and that the image functioned to ensure that "her spirit could be 'identified and loved' by the living."[75]

The Mawangdui silk painting and other early figural paintings excavated from Warring States and early Han tombs were more than just "name banners" (fig. 3.14). These early Chinese portraits did not depict their subjects as isolated individuals but instead rendered them in terms of other social relationships.[76] These paintings represent the tomb occupant on a spirit journey in the afterlife and thus possessed the magical power to assist and guide the deceased through the liminal stage to the afterlife.[77]

The whereabouts of the spirit during this liminal stage was a major concern of the early Chinese. The chapter on funerary ritual in the *Protocols of Ceremonies* prescribes that after the corpse was shrouded, a name banner and soul stand (*chong*) were to be made for the deceased because their form was no longer visible. After the placement of the soul stand, foods were offered there to the deceased. Concern for the identity of the dead was tremendous, as the disembodied recent dead were considered to be at their most dangerous. As with naming things, depicting things is also a way to control them. These early Chinese paintings point to the magic function of image-making[78] and represent attempts to control and assist the recent dead in their transformation. For the bereaved, the decision to make a figural painting rather than just inscribe the name of the deceased on a banner stemmed from their ambivalence toward the deceased and their wish to both comfort and control them.

The bereaved's ambivalent attitude toward the recent dead is expressed well in the chapter on the "Obsequies of a Gentleman" (Shi sangli) in the *Protocols of Ceremonies*. Establishing guidelines for the sequence of funeral rites, the "Obsequies of a Gentleman" describes the funerary ritual as a rite of passage consisting of several gradual transitions. The deceased transformed from a living person to a corpse, from the host of the house to a spirit guest, and finally to an ancestor. At the start of this process, after the soul-calling ritual, the name banner for the deceased was prepared. Then

Fig. 3.14. Silk banner excavated from Tomb 1 at Mawangdui, Changsha City, Hunan. Early Western Han dynasty.

the body was washed, dressed, and shrouded, and a soul stand was made. These two objects directly relate to concerns with the identity of the dead. One influential theory, proposed by Wu Hung, about the ritual significance of the name banner posits that the banner symbolized the otherworldly existence of the dead. He writes: "This banner thus symbolized the otherworldly existence of the dead. In his commentary to this passage, Zheng Xuan explained its ritual significance: 'Because a person can no longer be recognized after his death, the living use his banner to identify him and to express their love towards him.' While various other ritual activities were still taking place in the mourning hall, this banner was posted on a bamboo pole in front of the hall. Afterwards, it was removed to cover the spirit-tablet of the dead." [79]

It is clear that the name banner functioned to identify the deceased and show the concern ("love") of the living for the disembodied soul. Nevertheless, the banner, it seems, does not represent the deceased's otherworldly existence, since the deceased had not yet completed his or her transformation and reached the otherworld. In addition, at least during the early Western Han dynasty, the name banner was distinct from the spirit tablet in that it was used only during the liminal stage of transformation.

What Wu Hung calls the "spirit tablet" is in fact the "soul stand." As Zheng Xuan explains: "When a gentleman has just died, and the spirit tablet has not yet been made, use the soul stand to lodge (zhu) his spirit." [80] Later commentators have understood the soul stand to be a wooden pole, against which the soul of the recently deceased could rest (yi or pingyi). Although both functioned to lodge, or as Steele termed it, provide a refuge for the disembodied soul or spirit of the dead, the soul stand and the spirit tablet belonged to two different ritual realms: the soul stand was considered to be "inauspicious" and was used during the liminal stage, whereas the spirit tablet was seen as "auspicious" and was used after the "sacrifice of repose" (yuji), after the dead were successfully transformed into ancestors. [81]

According to Zheng Xuan's commentary, for a gentleman the soul stand was a three-foot-long (chi) wooden pole with a hole on the top, from which two small cauldrons (li) were suspended. The cauldrons contained a rice gruel cooked from the remains of the rice used to fill the mouth of the corpse. It is noteworthy that here raw rice is used to fill the mouth of the dead body whereas cooked rice is used to feed the disembodied soul. This structural parallelism between the binaries of the body and the soul and the raw and the cooked is part of the gradual process of transforming the dead into ancestors. In prescriptions found in the Protocols of Ceremonies, food and other offerings, together with the lamp, were placed in the southwest corner of the main chamber, which is also where the deceased used to sleep. This practice was motivated by the belief that, though the soul had left the body, it continued to wander about the places the deceased had frequented while alive, enjoying the same foods and other offerings.

In Chinese death ritual, as one anthropologist has observed, "offerings of food and other items, including a lit candle for location, serve to structure, to give form to, the soul's existence in the liminal stage."[82] The bronze, ceramic, or wooden lamps in early Chinese tombs had a similar function.[83] The lighting of a lamp was part of these efforts to identify, soothe, and guide the disembodied soul. People believed that after death "the soul [was] in limbo, homeless, wandering, in need of comforting and sustenance, unable to differentiate night and day,"[84] and the world of the dead is described as alienated, gloomy, and dark. In the *Zuo Commentary*, the term *zhunxi* used to refer to the tomb means "long night," according to the third-century commentator Du Yu.[85] Equating death with the long night, the authors of the *Book of Rites* justify burying the dead in the north because that was the region of darkness (*you*), and in the *Songs of the South*, the world of the afterlife is called Dark Capital (*youdu*).[86] In the darkness of the afterlife, as in a pitch-dark night, artificial light was seen as a necessity.[87]

Therefore, all of these devices—the name banner, the soul stand, the food, and the lamps—were used to identify and help the dead in the liminal stage. Because the disembodied soul, like the unquiet ghost, was believed during the liminal stage to have no fixed abode, these provisions were required to make things easier: "The offerings all indicated the ritualized expression of concern for the deceased in this transitional, betwixt-and-between phase; the offerings also indicate that the deceased is represented as akin to a ghost, rather than approximating an ancestor."[88] In early Chinese funerals, after the dying person had stopped breathing and the calling back of the soul had failed, various efforts were made to identify, pacify, blandish, and assist the disembodied soul. After the corpse was shrouded, the name banner was made to assure the identity of the deceased, the wooden soul stand was erected in the courtyard, and foods were offered to the dead soul. Using these means, the bereaved endeavored to direct, succor, and nourish the disembodied soul.

To be sure, the *Book of Rites* is a prescriptive text that may not have matched actual funerary rituals performed in the state of Chu during the Warring States period. But concern for the well-being of the deceased and anxiety over the dead are clear from the ritual actions it recommends. Although there is no mention of the use of images of the dead in the *Protocols of Ceremonies*, archaeological discoveries suggest that images were used in Chu funerary rituals. Admittedly, the *Protocols of Ceremonies* does not explicitly state how to dispose of the name banner. Still, archaeological discoveries suggest that it was deposited in the tomb, as in the Mawangdui tombs (fig. 3.15) and the Chenjiadashan and Zidanku (see fig. 5.1) tombs. After the sacrifice of repose, a spirit tablet was made, while the soul stand was buried elsewhere. In representations of the deceased during the liminal stage the image triumphed over the written word. As such, it testifies to "the power of images"; images with a direct visual appeal are superior to the lure of the written word. In accordance with the Chinese tradition of image magic, the deceased was identified in the figural banner and was compelled to follow this set program of ascendance to its spiritual destination.

Scholars tend to date the origin of the cult image to the Eastern Han dynasty,

Fig. 3.15. Innermost coffin in Tomb 1 at Mawangdui, Changsha City, Hunan, where the silk banner was placed along with a jade *bi*-disc on the top and a group of wooden human figurines on the lower left. Early Western Han dynasty.

when portraits of tomb occupants were directly carved into or painted onto the walls of tombs or family shrines.[89] But in fact, based on the above analysis, the date can now be moved up to at least the late Warring States period. During the liminal stage after death and before burial, the name banner or the image of the dead was also the subject of sacrificial offering. In the latter case, as in the cases of Zidanku and Mawangdui, the figural image was venerated for the spirit of the dead that it represented. This practice eventually evolved into the custom of presenting portraits of tomb occupants in Eastern Han tombs or shrines.[90]

The Evolving Iconography of the Fecundity God

In addition to figural portrayals of the deceased, visual representations of the gods were another significant development of the Warring States period. Here are two prime examples. First, the image of the fecundity god evolved from an abstract phallic symbol (Plate 11) to a hybrid and anthropomorphic figure (see fig. 3.20). It is my contention that the so-called tomb guardian figure, a popular feature of the vertical pit-style Chu tomb in the south, is not in fact a tomb-securing device but a symbol of the fecundity god in early China. Like representations of the dead and the ancestors, the fecundity god developed from an abstract pole to a more concrete and anthropomorphic form, testifying to the manifested power of the human figure. Second, as an outgrowth of the first, representations of gods and spirits assumed a hybrid form with both human and animal features, and in the next section we will explain why.

Perceived often as a unique artistic and religious phenomenon of the state of Chu, the so-called tomb guardian figure commonly consists of three parts: a square wooden (or, more rarely, bronze) base, a long-necked animal head rising out of the center of the base, and one or more pairs of deer antlers on top of the head. However, archaeological evidence shows that this category of object is not unique to the state of Chu or to the Chu cultural sphere as broadly defined. In the early 1950s, in Tomb 1 at Zhaogu in Hui County, Henan, archaeologists excavated painted antlers on top of a heavy lead stand.[91] This cemetery belonged to the polity of Wei. Similar bronze stands have been discovered outside the core of the Chu territory, in Jiangsu, Anhui, Shandong, and Zhejiang.[92] While deer antlers are common in archaeological excavations, wooden stands and sculptures are rare outside the Chu region. This is another case in which the popularity of this category of object in southern China is due to its superior archaeological preservation.

Since the 1930s, when it was first excavated by tomb robbers in Changsha, this enigmatic figurine has been the subject of numerous studies conducted by both novices and seasoned senior scholars of early Chinese art.[93] There are more than twenty different theories about the nature and identity of this mysterious creature, variously described as a mountain god, earth lord, death god, spirit guardian, shaman, tomb guardian, and so forth.[94] As Li Xueqin summarizes it, "[t]hese tomb-guarding

Figs. 3.16a and b. Bronze base of the fecundity god figure with inscription, discovered in Tomb 2 at Heshangling in Xichuan County, Henan. Late Spring and Autumn period / early Warring States period. Henan Provincial Museum.

animals were probably used to guard against evil ghosts, but what they were originally called is not clear."[95] The theory that this figurine represented a deity of some sort and might have functioned as a guardian of the tomb in which it was found derived mainly from its frightful appearance, including its intimidating sharp antlers, bulging eyes, protruding tongue, and beastly zoomorphic or anthropomorphic faces. Thus came its popular name "tomb guardian figure."

In recent years two archaeological discoveries shed new light on this mystic figure. The first is a bronze base with an inscription identifying the object, excavated from Tomb 2 at Heshangling in Xichuan County, Henan, dated to ca. 500 BCE (figs. 3.16a and 3.16b).[96] When excavated, the base was at the center of the tomb, associated with a pair of deer antlers nearby (fig. 3.17; the bronze base is numbered 66).[97] Based on the lacquered fragments, the wooden remains found inside the bronze pole, and the deer antlers, scholars have suggested that there was once a wooden head into which the antlers were inserted; the head was then set on top of the bronze pole; this gives us one of the so-called tomb guardian figures.[98] The bronze inscription reads: "The zushi 且埶 of XX of the middle lineage from Zeng" (see fig. 3.16b). The two characters XX, not yet deciphered, are likely the personal name of the tomb occupant. From other archaeological evidence we know that this is the tomb of a woman from the polity of Zeng who was married out to the Wei family and buried at this location. According to this inscription, the bronze stand with a pair of deer antlers was called zushi, or "the stand of zu."[99]

But what is zushi? The excavators suggest that the zu 且 be read as zu 詛, "to curse" (OCM *tsrah); others read it as zu 祖, "ancestor" (OCM *tsâʔ), or as the name

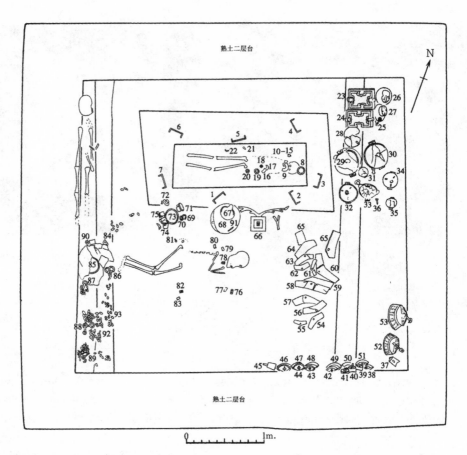

Fig. 3.17. Distribution of the grave goods in Tomb 2 at Heshangling, a female noble-woman's tomb, excavated at the Yuan lineage cemeteries in Xichuan County, Henan. Late Spring and Autumn period. Item 66 is the bronze base shown in Fig. 3.16a.

of a road ritual before a journey,[100] as *Wanqi* 宛奇, the name of a ghost-devouring monster mentioned in Qin daybooks,[101] as the soul stand *chong*,[102] and so forth.[103] Scholars have constructed theories based on unbelievably complicated twists and turns of phonological, philological, or paleographical maneuvers, but the interpretations are, at best, tenuous.

The second discovery constitutes important clues that scholars have previously overlooked. These are the divinatory, sacrificial, and exorcism records excavated from Chu tombs that I have discussed in chapter 1. In these records, there are references to this enigmatic *zushi*. Through philological research and phonological reconstruction, the graph *shi* 埶 in *zushi* could mean "a stand," or "that which is set up, established, erected."[104] References to such a stand in the Tianxingguan records are written as *zuwei. Shi* and *wei* 位 (stand or position; related etymologically to *li* 立, "to stand, to stand up") are interchangeable because of shared semantics.[105] The context of the reference to *zuwei* 禩位 is the ritual remedy of "exorcism targeted at the blameless dead, those who died violent deaths, and *zuwei*." One scholar has suggested that here *zuwei* may refer to some type of stand or tablet for ancestral spirits.[106] This interpretation is, however, not correct. In Chu religious ritual practice, the treatment of ancestral spirits was distinct from the treatment of other spirits. In other words, ancestral spirits were never the targets of exorcisms. This *zushi* or *zuwei* could not have referred to an ancestral spirit. The graph *zu* 且 here in fact means the phallus; *Zushi* or *Zuwei* refers to the fecundity god in Chu religion. Similarly, the deity named *Mingzu* 明禣 (= *Mengzu* 盟禣), which appeared several times in the divinatory, sacrificial, and exorcism records and also in Chu and Qin daybooks.[107]

That the graph *zu* represents and means the phallus is well established. In his famous essay of 1929 on the technical names for ancestor (*zu*) and ancestress (*bi*), Guo Moruo suggested that *zu* in the Shang divination records originally represented the phallus.[108] The following year, apparently without knowing Guo's work, Bernhard Karlgren independently reached the same conclusion.[109] This meaning of the graph *zu* has been almost completely glossed over in transmitted literature. The inscription on the Heshangling bronze base again suggests that it means the phallus. Thus the bronze stand, representing the fecundity deity, was placed in Tomb 2 on behalf of the woman who occupied the grave. It is likely that she used this object in her lifetime.

This emphasis on emic understandings does not rule out the significance of well-structured etic classifications and insightful observations made in this vein.[110] John S. Major, a veteran of Chu religious studies, made one such observation, suggesting that the "antler and tongue" motif (i.e., the "tomb guardian") symbolizes a phallus. He posits that the phallus could be a naturalistic depiction of an erect penis or, in the case of the "antler and tongue," represented by a protruding tongue, horns, or antlers. These apotropaic images represent "demons, or gods, harnessed (coerced?) to provide protection for the master of the tomb."[111]

Typological studies of the more than four hundred examples of so-called tomb guardian figures excavated from Chu tombs support this observation.[112] One of the earliest forms of the figure consists of a single wooden pole with a more articulated head,[113] representing a phallus, erected on top of a square base (see Plate 11); examples of this type date from the middle or late Spring and Autumn period into the early Warring States period. The figure continued to flourish after the middle Warring States period, when fantastic antlers, protruding tongues, bulging eyes, and other animal attributes were added to the pole (Plate 12 and Plate 13, fig. 3.18 and fig. 3.19). In the late Warring States period the fecundity god assumed an anthropomorphic form (fig. 3.20).[114]

In addition, the deer antlers, signifying the ultimate male power, corroborate the phallic image of the fecundity god. Most of these antlers came from a type of Asian deer known as *milu* 麋鹿 in Chinese, or Père David's deer (*Elaphurus davidianus*), currently extinct in the wild but which was native to the subtropics of China.[115] The male deer usually has two pairs of antlers every year. The summer antlers, the

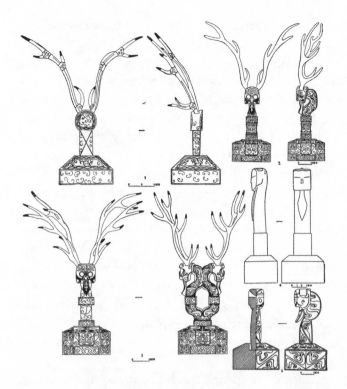

Fig. 3.18. Drawings of different types of the fecundity god figure excavated from the Chu cemeteries at Yutaishan, Jiangling County, Hubei. Warring States period.

Fig. 3.19. Fecundity god figure. Wood with polychrome pigments and lacquer horns. H. 48.9 cm. Warring States period. Gift of Florence M. Schoenborn 1986.1308. Image No. 00037948-01. The Art Institute of Chicago.

Fig. 3.20. Fecundity god figure with human face and protruding tongue. H. 43.7 cm (from base). Wood with deer antlers. Southern China. Warring States period. Asia OA 1950.11.15.1. © Trustees of the British Museum.

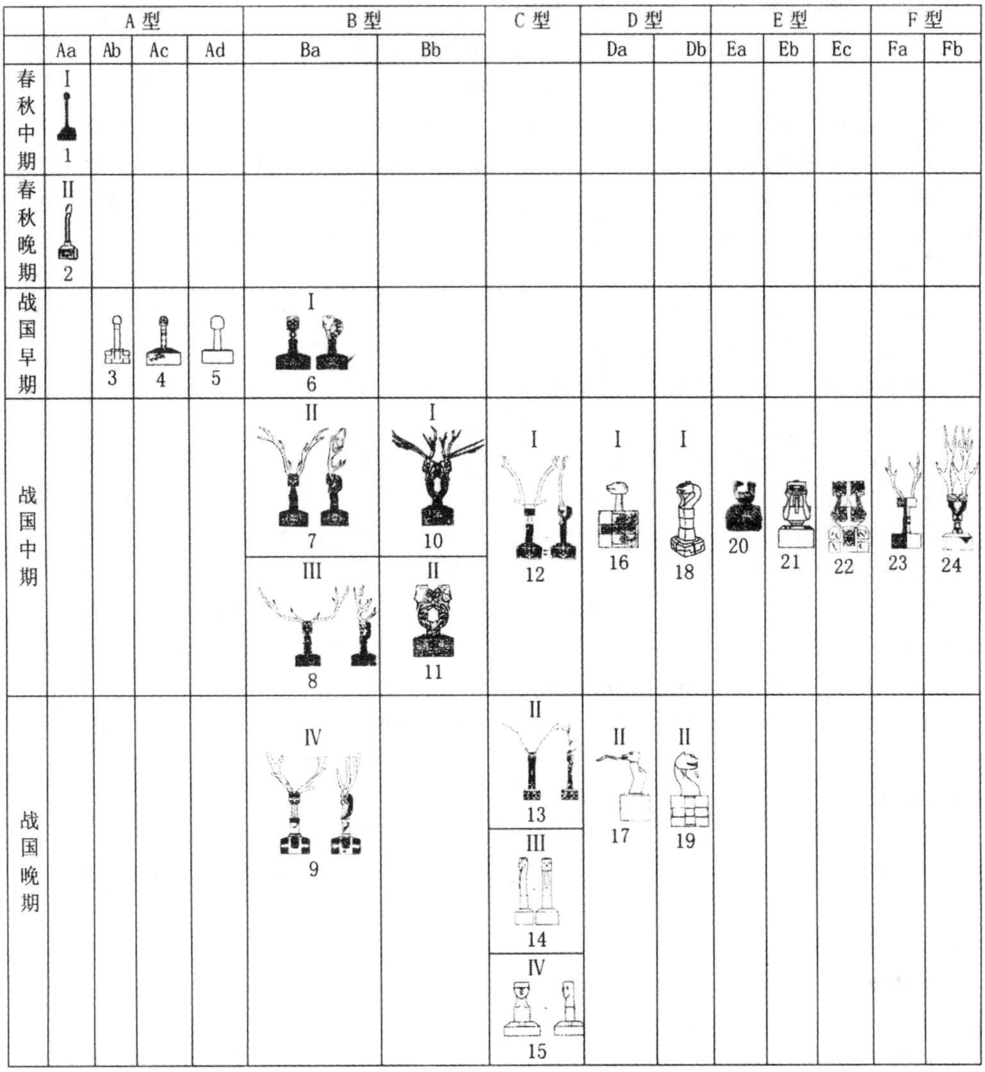

	A 型				B 型			C 型	D 型		E 型			F 型	
	Aa	Ab	Ac	Ad	Ba	Bb			Da	Db	Ea	Eb	Ec	Fa	Fb
春秋中期	I 1														
春秋晚期	II 2														
战国早期		3	4	5	I 6										
战国中期					II 7 / III 8	I 10 / II 11		I 12	I 16	I 18	20	21	22	23	24
战国晚期					IV 9			II 13 / III 14 / IV 15	II 17	II 19					

Fig. 3.21. Typology of the fecundity god figure, after Ding Lan, "Chu shi 'zhenmushou' tezheng zonglun," 100, table 2. The six types (A–E) are listed in vertical columns; the five horizontal rows refer to the middle and late Spring and Autumn periods, the early, middle and late Warring States periods.

larger set and often long, sharp, and branched shortly after the base, are dropped in November after the summer rut. The early Chinese must have concluded from their observations of the dominant male deer that these fantastic antlers were symbols of male power.

Among the more than four hundred samples excavated from Chu elite tombs, most are made of wood and are painted with lacquer (fig. 3.21). Only a few early examples are made of cast bronze, like the one found in Heshangling Tomb 2 (see fig. 3.16a). The early bronze specimens (from the late Spring and Autumn and early

Warring States periods) often came from the tombs of elite women, even though in some cases the sex of the tomb occupants cannot be determined.[116] But we have strong evidence that the occupants of Tomb 2 at Heshangling, and Tomb 1 at Xiasi, Xichuan County, Henan (dated to ca. 548 BCE) are female. Another clear example is from the tomb of the wife of Huang Jun Meng, excavated at Baoxiangsi in Guangshan County, Henan (dated to the mid-seventh century); the inscription explicitly states that the husband made the object for his wife.[117] An even earlier bronze stand excavated from Tomb 17 at Guojiamiao in Zaoyang City, Hubei, dated to the late Western Zhou or early Spring and Autumn period, is probably also from the tomb of an elite woman, the wife of a marquis of the polity of Zeng.[118]

Beginning in the middle or late Spring and Autumn period, wooden stands were added to the tombs of elite males, such as the ones from Tomb 4 at Zhaoxiang and Tomb 5 at Caojiagang in Dangyang County, Hubei (see Plate 11).[119] Based on the available evidence, it seems that the cult of the fecundity god has its origins in burial practices for elite women, usually the wives and consorts of nobles and rulers. This conclusion makes sense: the women were responsible for producing heirs for the lineage, which in turn assured the continuity of the state. Therefore, it seems likely that these fecundity stands were owned by these elite women during their lifetimes and were buried with them after their deaths. Over time, these stands came to be buried with other members of elite society, including men. But why were such fecundity symbols buried with men? What were the functions of the fecundity god in the afterlife?

First, from a broader anthropological perspective, death and fecundity are closely linked in many cultures: "It is a classical anthropological paradox that symbols of rebirth and fertility are frequently found in funerary rituals throughout the world."[120] In their introduction to the edited volume *Death and the Regeneration of Life*, Maurice Bloch and Jonathan P. Parry trace scholarship on the symbiosis of death and fertility to the nineteenth-century Swiss antiquarian and anthropologist Johann Jakob Bachofen (1815–87), who discussed the significance of eggs as symbols of fertility and femininity in some Roman tombs and funerary games.[121] James Frazer's (1854–1941) classic explanation of killing as a rite of fertility and renewal also acknowledges the close relationship between death and regeneration. Anthropologists have discussed various ways in which the symbolism of sexuality and fertility is used in the mortuary rituals of many historical and contemporary cultures.[122]

Second, in early China, specifically, death and fecundity were closely associated with ancestor cults. Ancestors and descendants were mutually dependent. One could not exist without the other. For their own benefit, therefore, the deceased continued to pray to the god of fecundity for the regeneration of their family to save themselves from becoming hungry ghosts. In addition, from the perspective of the living, once the deceased ancestors had become powerful spirits in the otherworld, certainly their blessings, and in this case, their prayers for the prosperity of the lineage, would be more efficacious.

Finally, evidence shows that the fecundity god was in charge not only of fertility but also of the human lifespan. Support for this theory is found in religious documents dated to 79 CE that record offerings of prayers and sacrifices on behalf of a certain woman named Xuning.[123] On one strip, a statement explicitly addresses a spirit to which the family members of the dying Xuning had prayed for favor at the earth altar, from whom one requested sons (*qingzi she* 請子社).[124] The earth altar was apparently dedicated to the fecundity god, and by inference this spirit to whom the family had prayed was also responsible for Xuning's life. The sacrifice to the fecundity god at the end of Shao Tuo's life, as mentioned in chapter 1, is also consistent with this pattern. In a final effort to save him, the ritual remedies included a pledge sacrifice directed at evil ghosts who had died without posterity (*juewuhouzhe*) and exorcisms aimed at the fecundity god (*jianmuwei*).[125] In elite burials, therefore, the fecundity god (*zu*, *mingzu*, *zuwei*, or *zushi*) could function not only as an apotropaic or protective deity but also as a symbol of the regeneration of life.[126] In later Han-dynasty literature, the deity Siming was also in charge of both lifespan and fecundity.[127] And in Chu tomb texts, Siming regularly appears in the Chu pantheon (see chapter 1). As yet, it is not clear whether *mingzu* in the Chu manuscripts is the same as the later Han Siming, or whether the later Han Siming combined the religious functions of both Chu deities *mingzu* and Siming.

Based on this evidence, and on the fact that tomb guardians along with other burial securing devices were invented only for the horizontal chamber-style tomb, I contend that the so-called tomb guardian figure, popular in the Spring and Autumn and Warring States periods, is the representation of the fecundity god in early China. It evolved from a simple phallic symbol to an icon that acquired various animal and human attributes; its iconography developed into an anthropomorphic and zoomorphic hybrid image that harnesses "the power of images."

The Power of Hybrid Images

Another prominent feature of early Chinese visual culture of the period under discussion was the production of imaginary, hybrid creatures that combine zoomorphic and anthropomorphic attributes. By the early Warring States period, the fecundity god was represented in a hybrid form that merged different animal attributes, including fantastic antlers and snake heads. In the late Warring States period, depictions of the god came to incorporate anthropomorphic elements, such as enigmatic faces and protruding tongues. Related examples of anthropomorphized deities and spirits include the guardian figures painted on the surface of the inner coffin from Tomb 1 at Leigudun in Suizhou City, Hubei, and the twelve deities associated with the months at the margins of the famous Chu silk manuscript (removed from the Zidanku tomb near Changsha in 1942, dated to ca. 300 BCE), now housed in the Freer and Sackler Galleries in Washington, DC. Finally, a much debated dagger axe, excavated at Cheqiao in Jingmen City, Hubei, and which dates to the late fourth century BCE, bears an image of a hybrid figure in frontal view identical in type to the preceding examples. The figure, which wears feathered headgear and has a body covered in scales, holds a lizard-like creature in each hand and rests his two feet on the sun and moon.

The late K. C. Chang and David Keightley employ the shamanism theory to explain the proliferation of the hybrid image. They claim that these strange combinations of human and animal forms depict shamans transforming from animal to human form.[128] On the other hand, Michael Loewe suggests that the hybrid imagery stems from the identification of man with animal (as in the practice of totemism), as well as the historicization (i.e., euhemerization) of early myths and gods.[129] In Loewe's view, animal figures were portrayed in anthropomorphic terms. In a recent article Alain Thote has attributed the sudden appearance of hybrid images to the cultural influence of local ethnic populations absorbed into the state of Chu, as well as to influences from the Near or Middle East.[130]

Within the early Chinese context, however, the validity of shamanistic and totemistic explanations and the theories of the historicization of early myths and gods in early China have been seriously questioned in recent decades. We have no proof of the existence of an earlier animal or mythological world that was subsequently transformed into a human or historical account, or vice versa. In addition, although the incised pictorial bronzes that Alain Thote discussed might have been produced locally, we have no proof that the artistic motifs of hybrid images belong to one particular local culture. These images belong to a phenomenon that is not confined to one particular region's visual art but also appears in early Chinese literature such as the *Zuo Commentary* and the *Classics of Mountains and Seas*. "The hybrid images of spirits in the *Classics of Mountains and Seas*," as Mu-chou Poo puts it, "are not the creation of a certain author, but originated from a mental background common to the Warring States."[131]

This "mental background" consists of at least three parts. The first is the changing perspective on the human figure, which became a popular motif in artistic depiction as the bereaved attempted to identify, control, and assist the recent dead while they were in the liminal stage. Although depictions of the human figure in the Warring States period still carry the connotation of magical control over the subject, this attitude appeared less domineering and more sympathetic. As a result, beginning in this period, the human image had a significant impact on early Chinese art. Second, the religious notion of spirit possession (*pingyi*) emerged and spread widely during the Eastern Zhou period.[132] Third and finally, hybrid images are psychologically powerful. A silk diagram excavated from Tomb 3 at Mawangdui (dated to 168 BCE) has been discussed infrequently but is of paramount importance to our understanding of early Chinese visual culture (Plate 14). It provides crucial evidence for why, in early China, gods and demigods were represented in hybrid form. In what follows, we use the Mawangdui silk diagram to illustrate the last two of these developments.[133]

The silk diagram was discovered among other Mawangdui manuscripts in a lacquered box in the eastern compartment of the tomb. Modern scholars have pieced together the diagram, which was drawn in five colors (azure, red, yellow, white, and black) on a sheet of silk about 43.5 centimeters long and 45 centimeters wide, based on traces of color and ink, inscriptions, images, and folding lines. The illustrations are divided into three registers. The top register, which is severely damaged, consists of the head of the central figure flanked by the thunder lord (*leigong*) and the rain master (*yushi*). The central figure's body appears in the middle register, where it rides a yellow-headed black dragon and is flanked on the right by two martial disciples (*wu dizi*) and on the left by Chiyou, the god of warfare, and an unknown spirit (the label beside him is probably lost). The lower register is occupied by the lower section of the black dragon's body, flanked on the right by a yellow dragon and on the left by an azure dragon.

Of the seven figures, the central one is painted red; he wears a zigzag antler on his head, has big round eyes, and is dressed in trousers painted in azure or black. On the left side of his head is a textual fragment starting with the words, "The Grand One is about to travel . . ." Accordingly, some scholars have identified the figure as the Grand One, the supreme celestial deity in the Chu pantheon during the Warring States period. Under his armpit and to the right is the character for earth god (*she*) enclosed in a circle. Other authorities believe that this character is the label for the central figure. The martial disciples, who appear in the central register, have big eyes and outstretched tongues and are shown with strange mountain-shaped caps on their heads. They raise their left arms and hold some type of weapon. On the other side of the central figure, also raising his left arm, is Chiyou, who wears a hat with a horn on top. The enigmatic fellow beside Chiyou has a zigzag antler on his head and looks away oddly. Scholars have assigned the diagram different names based on their various understandings of its parts. For example, Zhou Shirong calls it "the diagram of the earth god" (*sheshen tu*), while Li Ling, focusing on his reading of the labels near the martial disciples and Chiyou, thinks it is a magical "diagram to repel weapons" (*bibing tu*). Referencing the label beside the head of the central figure, Chen Songchang calls it "the diagram of the Grand One who is about to travel" (*Taiyi jiang xing tu*).

All of these studies, however, pay insufficient attention to the relationship between the images and the texts inscribed on the right edge of the diagram. Both these internal clues and external evidence (e.g., the structure of incantation texts) suggest that the text on the right edge needs to be rearranged: the silk fragment bearing the last section is misplaced and should be relocated to the beginning of the text. In addition, this evidence suggests that an incantation text is closely related to the images depicted on the diagram.[134] These images illustrate the farewell ritual during which an incantation is uttered before the supplicant begins a journey. The text on the right edge of the diagram reads: "The Incantation of the Grand One: Today so-and-so is about to [travel] . . . draw the bow. The Great Yu goes first. Red vapors and white vapors dare not to turn toward me. The hundred weapons dare not harm me . . . is called insincere. Use the North Dipper as the right direction. Spit to the left and right. Go straight, do not look back." Similar incantation texts for the farewell ritual have been discovered among Warring States, Qin, and early Han manuscripts.[135] The Taiyi incantation contains all the formulas of a spell: the use of "so-and-so" as a place holder for the name of the traveler; the practice of the Pace of Yu (Yubu), a prescribed indexical magical ritual dance step;[136] the use of spitting as a magical gesture; and the final magical formula of "going straight and not looking back." Although repelling weapons is a significant part of the activity or consequence of this ritual, the overall purpose of the diagram is not merely to repel weapons but to protect the traveler on his or her journey. The diagram therefore is a visual representation of the farewell ritual in which the Taiyi incantation is uttered, and its purpose is to help the traveler visualize the fantastic entourage that will accompany him on the journey.

To date, the most contentious problem in analyzing this diagram has been the identity of the central figure. Was it the Grand One, the Lord of Earth, or the Great Yu? It is my contention that this central figure could be all of these figures and, more importantly, the traveler as well. The figure represents the traveler in the guise of all of these celestial and terrestrial deities. The key religious concept here is "spirit possession."

In the communal ceremonies of ancestor cults in the Shang and Western Zhou dynasties, the ancestral spirits routinely possessed the impersonator (shi), usually a junior member of the lineage, whose physical body was used to act out the role of the ancestor according to a prescribed ritual program. During the Spring and Autumn period, in the ghost stories of the Zuo Commentary and Narratives of the States, an ordinary man or woman who died a violent death could assume the form of a malevolent ghost and possess (pingyi) people. Even natural objects like stones could be possessed by spirits and made to speak.[137] In the Warring States period, the use of the impersonator (shi) and communal ancestor cults declined, but, in what constituted a new development, the notion of "spirit possession" extended to other fields of religious ritual. Through newly devised ritual means, the gods and spirits could be made to possess humans. In other words, humans could have the power of the gods and spirits as a result of self-cultivation or magical ritual action. This is the religious and ritual background to the practice that Michael Puett calls "self-divinization."[138] Here a traveler, following the ritual dance of the Pace of Yu and the magic act of spitting, could invite the Grand One, the Lord of Earth, or the Great Yu to possess him or her and thereby secure protection on the road. These ritual acts were subsequently incorporated into later Daoist texts, which not coincidentally contain the same instructions for the performers.

There are possible connections between the image of the central figure on the Mawangdui diagram and some of the travel paraphernalia described in the inventory list for Tomb 2 at Baoshan. The opening section of the inventory list contains the following itemization: "The paraphernalia used for travel: one *xie* cap with silk strings, one funeral cap, two fox-skin trousers. . . " Notably, the travel paraphernalia does not include chariots, horses, and other obvious travel equipment that one needs on the road, but rather caps, trousers, shoes, towels, combs, pillows, folding beds, lamps, and so forth. Personal belongings, especially items for dress and adornment, filled the compartments of elite burials during the Warring States period.

The *xie* cap is of particular interest. The inventory from Tomb 2 at Wangshan also records two *xie* caps as grave goods (Strip 62). The term *xie* cap also appears in the transmitted literature. A *xie* cap is mentioned in an anecdote in the *Master of Huainan* (Huainanzi), which states that King Wen (?–675 BCE) of Chu liked caps of this design and therefore all the people in Chu wore them.[139] Modern scholars follow the lead of Han dynasty scholars and conclude that it was a cap with a horn on top.[140] Owing to the poor state of the tombs' preservation, the excavators were unable to retrieve such caps from the Baoshan or Wangshan tombs. Yet a horn carved with three intertwined dragons from the Baoshan tomb was discovered in the northern compartment with other items for personal adornment, including a wig, four jade and bone ornaments, and a miniature sculpture of mythical animals in a square bamboo case (Item 431). It is possible that the horn was originally worn on the *xie* cap listed in the inventory. The *xie* (also known as *zhi*) was a mythical animal with one horn and was represented on bronze vessels of the Warring States period[141] and in the form of freestanding sculptures or paintings that appeared on the walls of later Han tombs.[142] The horn may have been part of the *xie* cap (*xieguan*) that Shao Tuo, the occupant of Tomb 2 at Baoshan, was to use in his spirit journey to the afterlife. Although the zigzag antler on the head of the central figure on the Mawangdui diagram is not exactly the same as the single horn of Shao Tuo's travel paraphernalia, both are symbols of apotropaic power (see below). The *xie* cap and the two trousers included among the travel paraphernalia in Shao Tuo's tomb resemble the costume of the central figure on the Mawangdui diagram. In other words, what the Mawangdui silk diagram illustrates is a fully equipped traveler wearing a *xie* cap and two trousers and riding a fantastic dragon.

All the seven gods and demigods on the diagram are hybrid in form. Why were deities and spirits represented in this manner in early Chinese art? This brings us to the third element that characterized the "mental background" of the Warring States period, that is, animation of the hybrid image's psychological power. In a pioneering study of hybrid images (so-called *zhenmushou*), or what he called the "antler and tongue," Alfred Salmony adopted a diffusionist approach, citing the then-popular theory of the "migration of artistic motifs," and argued that the Chinese antler-and-tongue motifs were inspired by India and came from Central Asia. In reviewing Salmony's book, several scholars disagreed with him, pointing out that one should look for humanity's "common substratum" or "common heritage" to explain similarities in art motifs. This "common substratum" or "common heritage" is rooted in the psychological power of the hybrid image.

The Presence of the Invisible

Over a long period, art historians have observed a visual phenomenon known as the "Medusa effect," named after the Medusa head in Western art. These apotropaic images of faces, genitals, and dangerous animals were intended "to disgust, to paralyze the viewer, to trigger the feeling of fear, or to produce a sense of awe."[143] Scholars have further argued that the hybrid drawings on the margins of medieval manuscripts and the grotesques in Renaissance ornament "preserved the 'apotropaic' heritage of animation."[144] Recent developments in studies of art and science, especially in neuroscience, have substantially increased our knowledge of this "common heritage" in our human experience and within the structure of the human brain.[145]

The Mawangdui diagram of the Taiyi incantation points to an important transition in the evolution of Chinese visual culture. Here the main figure is no longer the subject of "image magic" but is instead a traveler, someone with whom the living could identify. This shift away from the magical potency of images to a new kind of representation, in which hybrid images fused anthropomorphic form and zoomorphic attributes, signaled an important change in early Chinese attitudes toward representation during the Warring States and early Han periods.

THE RELIGIOUS WORLD is an invisible virtual realm. Human beings are universally concerned with how to communicate with invisible powers, how to make them present, and how to control them. The technical knowledge of how to induce the presence of the gods and the immortals or the departed ancestors, that is, how to make the invisible present, was very important in early China. After hearing a report on the appearance of the heavenly giants, the First Emperor (259–210 BCE) of Qin purportedly made twelve bronze statues modeled after the giants in hopes that they would return. The Emperor Wudi (156–87 BCE) of the Han dynasty was told to build a chamber painted with images of Heaven, Earth, Taiyi, and all the other gods and place within it sacrificial vessels filled with delicious foods to entice the spirits. In yet another story, the emperor built a high-rise tower and set out dried meat and jujubes, believing that the immortals liked to live in such towers and consume such foods. Early Chinese art theory and practice developed within this context of seeking gods and immortals.

In light of the discussion in this chapter, David Freedberg's theory of response should be substantially revised. His claim that presence depends on a visual recognition of formal likeness is invalid in the context of early Chinese efforts to make present invisible ancestors and gods. In early China, a variety of forms and methods were used to induce the presence of ancestors and gods. Anthropomorphic images form only one means of securing such presence. Certainly, we can see generally that images sometimes triumphed over writing and the dead, during their liminal stage, came to be represented in figural form. But the presence of gods and spirits can also be established through indexical representation. Although the Mawangdui diagram depicts gods in hybrid form, the emphasis is on the indexical ritual representation, as in the Pace of Yu. This ritual dance ensures the possession of the traveler by the gods. Certainly, such presence can be induced by symbolic representation, that is, through language and writing. Such was the case with the abstract wooden spirit tablets of the five domestic gods excavated from Tomb 2 at Baoshan. Gods and spirits could possess human, animal, and even more abstract forms.

Thus, the real presence of the deceased, gods, and spirits could be established through iconic (i.e., Freedberg's emphasis), indexical, and symbolic representation, to use the semiotics of Charles S. Peirce (1839–1914).[146] Iconic representation, that is, the representation of physical likeness, is the most salient of the three and historically has been privileged in Western European art and in later Chinese art. In early China, however, during the Warring States period, the recent dead in the liminal stage were first represented in anthropomorphic form, and gods and demigods were presented in hybrid form with half-human and half-animal attributes.

4

Letters to the Underworld

Writing created a literary double of the actual world, and this invented world became the highest reality.

—MARK EDWARD LEWIS

AS WITH IMAGES, writing as a technology became a means for reshaping the Chinese understanding of the physical and spiritual worlds. The original context in which Chinese writing was invented remains enigmatic. Nevertheless, whether writing was designed for administrative bookkeeping or for ritual and religious purposes,[1] or both, once it was created, it quickly became an important means of communication with invisible gods and spirits. In China, the earliest extant writings are records of divination inscribed on turtle shells and animal scapulas, which were first excavated at Anyang City, Henan, the last capital of the Shang dynasty. The records of divination and sacrifice in the Warring States period are the direct descendants of these oracle-bone inscriptions. Such divinations and sacrifices assumed tangible form in writing, thereby establishing a solid contractual relationship with the gods and spirits. In the case of the "pledge sacrifice" in particular, certain offerings were promised to specific deities.[2] In some instances, however, the scale of the sacrifice was so outrageous that the promise must have been magico-religious rather than a genuine record of an intended offering. In one case, one thousand cows and one thousand people were promised as sacrificial offerings to the ancestral spirits.[3] In Chu records of the Warring States period, the pledges were modest in relation to those made earlier, under the Shang. When a divine favor was requested, the supplicant made an initial deposit, often in the form of jade and silk (both also served as writing materials). Later, a larger thanksgiving bonus, usually in the form of an animal sacrifice (of a cow or a horse or some other creature), was promised to entice the gods or spirits to grant the supplicant's wishes. Such promises were recorded on bamboo, silk, or jade, in part to convey to the supplicant tangible assurance of his pledge to the unseen gods and spirits. In addition, this documentation may have helped to alleviate the supplicant's doubts as to whether the favor would be granted. In the remote past, as in the present, written contracts were used to insure the implementation of an agreement and protect against failure to comply with its terms.

Such sacrificial records were buried in Warring States tombs because they were contracts between the spirits and the living and represented unfinished business between the human and spirit worlds. In two sets of prayer and sacrifice documents, dated to 79 CE, the dying old woman Xuning is said to have brought the contract writs—the prayer and sacrifice records—personally, with the intention of reporting to the Heavenly Sire (Tiangong).[4] Writings of this type are "funerary texts," "scripts that directly concern the burial rite and the postmortem fate of the deceased."[5] Changing conceptions of the dead are evident in the texts that accompanied the dead into the afterlife.

The entombment of texts is a noteworthy feature of elite burial practice during the Warring States, Qin, and Han periods. Yet the texts found in early Chinese tombs, particularly the funerary-object lists (*qiance* or *fengshu*) and the official memorials addressed to the underground bureaucracy (*gaodishu*), were unique genres of texts for the dead. The important role that writing played in communication with the spiritual world was also manifested in the public reading of such inventories and announcements and in the burying of other texts, including philosophical treatises, technical and ritual manuals, and legal and medical compilations. Some of the manuscripts that came from personal libraries and collections were thought to be useful to the deceased in the afterworld. In addition, this body of material included registers that bore the names and gifts of the individuals who attended the deceased's funeral, a sign that death did not sever the relationship between the deceased and his or her personal circle. These texts contributed to the articulation of early Chinese concepts of the afterlife.

The Funerary-Object Lists

Buried with the dead in tombs, the funerary-object lists are bamboo strips or wooden tablets that recorded a catalogue of objects, sometimes with a brief description of their quality and quantity. Of the different types of excavated manuscripts, these are less studied not only because they are often fragmentary and difficult to decipher but also because modern scholars do not understand such lists as an independent genre. Although lists of funerary goods are mentioned in traditional ritual texts, premodern scholars probably were not aware of any surviving examples from early China.[6] Only in the early 1950s did researchers begin to realize that the lists excavated from Warring States tombs were the inventories described in ritual canons.[7] Moreover, with the accumulation of new data, scholars have begun to recognize that lists of grave goods (*qiance*) should be distinguished from lists of funerary gifts or records of donated items (*fengshu*).[8] For example, among the twenty-eight inscribed bamboo strips excavated from Tomb 2 at Baoshan is a bamboo stick whose four sides are inscribed with the following text: "In the year when the grand marshal (da sima) Dao Hua rescued the state of Fu, in the *xiangyue* month, on day *bingxu*, Yu Yin received: a *zheng* chariot . . ." The stick proceeds to describe the elaborately decorated *zheng* chariot; these descriptions match exactly the *zheng* chariot described in Strips 271, 276, 269, and 270. Another strip, Strip 277, which is the same size and in the same format and writing style as the strips recording the chariots and the bronze sacrificial vessels, reads: "Ke Fu received: one bamboo container with leather shield, twenty bronze-tipped arrows . . ." The date on the bamboo stick, *bingxu*, was one day before the date on which Shao Tuo, the occupant of Tomb 2 at Baoshan, was buried. The archaeological reports lump these records together with the lists of grave goods, but, as scholars correctly point out, they differ from the grave-goods lists.[9] These are *fengshu*, the funerary gift list or record of donated items that Shao Tuo's family received during the funeral ceremonies.

Both lists, with their emic explanations about the function, purpose, category, and association of these objects, promise to provide crucial insight into funerary rites and social life in early China. Existing scholarship has largely been devoted to efforts to match the lists with the objects excavated from the tomb,[10] an arduous but important undertaking. But the nature and function of the inventory lists in Warring States and early Han tombs are largely ignored.

Since 1960, about fifty lists of funerary objects have been excavated from tombs dating from the Warring States period to the Western Han period, the majority of which were located in southern China.[11] These lists represent only a fraction of the material remains of a phenomenon that may have been far more widespread. Although the conditions for archaeological preservation are much better in the south than in the north, preservation in general is still the exception rather than the rule. Based on the materials currently available, it seems that the lists were a form of bookkeeping used in funerary sumptuary control and were buried in tombs to serve their magico-religious function as inventories of substitute objects.

The Textual Structure of the Lists

The textual structure of the funerary lists corresponds to that of the funerary ritual. A list of funerary goods often starts with a date, followed by an overarching title, and then by a description and itemization of the categories of grave goods. The list from Tomb 2 at Wangshan begins, "In the year . . . Zhou, the eighth month, [day of] *xin* . . . the register of chariots and artifacts."[12] The Baoshan list opens, "In the year [following that in which] the grand marshal (da sima) Dao Hua rescued the state of Fu[13] (ca. 316 BCE), in the *xiangyue* month, on day *dinghai*, the Chief Minister of the Left was buried." The strip proceeds to describe five elaborately decorated chariots that were used in the funerary procession before enumerating other categories of objects. In the case of Tomb 2 at Baoshan, a clear organizational principle dictated the placement of the list in the tomb: parts of the list were placed in six different locations in the eastern, western, and southern compartments, along with their corresponding artifacts. The Baoshan list can thus be divided into six sections, each of which is identified with one of these physical locations. Moreover, Baoshan Strips 153 and 154 show that when listing items, a general spatial order existed in Chu cultural practice that gave precedence to the south and then proceeded counterclockwise to the west.[14] The order of the Baoshan grave goods and the structure of the list both start from the south and proceed to the east, north, and west. This order is also consistent with the manner in which artifacts and inventories were laid out in the tomb. Not coincidentally, in Warring States cosmology "the way of the earth" (*didao*) moves from the right to the left (i.e., counterclockwise, or *youxuan*), and in funerary rites (*sangli*) precedence is given to the right.

A list could "serve as a guide for future action, a plan."[15] Such is the case with the Mawangdui lists. For example, notes were written on the strips to indicate the locations of particular groups of objects in the compartments: "The object on the left will be buried at the head of the outer coffin," or "the objects on the left will be buried at the left [of the outer coffin]." In addition, one strip among the inventory from Tomb 3 at Mawangdui states, "Sixteen ceramic tripods [are still] lacking and must be bought" (strip 104).[16] Moreover, an example from received texts states that lists were written as plans for organizing the funerary rites.[17]

The Contents of the Lists

In most tombs in which lists of funerary goods were discovered, archaeologists have found that the registers did not record all the burial goods. In other words, the list was not an exhaustive inventory. Only specific categories of grave goods were recorded: ritual vessels for food and wine; musical instruments; chariots and accessories, horse harnesses, flags, and weapons; clothing, household furniture, and foods. Many items are enumerated under headings or subheadings such as "chariots" (*che*) (Leigudun, Tomb 2 at Wangshan, Tomb 2 at Baoshan); "objects" (*qi*) (Tomb 2 at Wangshan) or "burial goods" (*zangqi*) (Tomb 5 at Caojiagang); "the metal objects used in the grand sacrifice" (*dalao zhi jinqi*), "wooden objects" (*muqi*), "the metal objects for use in the sacrificial hall" (*shishi zhi jinqi*), "the foods in the sacrificial hall" (*shishi zhi shi*), "the bamboo cases containing foods in the sacrificial hall" (*shishi suoyi bao gong*), "the objects that are brought together to be used in travel" (*xiangxi zhiqi suoyi xing*) (Tomb 2 at Baoshan); "the instruments of the musicians" (*yueren zhi qi*), "the vessels for the cooks" (*ji chu zhiqi*) (Tomb 1 at Changtaiguan), and so forth.

Among these grave goods, the chariots, ritual vessels, and musical instruments were symbols of the tomb occupant's social status, and the clothing, furniture, and foods were newly introduced categories of grave goods that became popular during the Warring States period. Although we have no material evidence, it is conceivable that before the Warring States period authorities used lists, for example, as a form of bookkeeping to record sumptuary spending.

The List as a Form of Sumptuary Control

The list as a literary form is a well-known administrative tool in the scribal traditions of most ancient civilizations.[18] Lists are suitable for cataloging animals, plants, agricultural products, linguistic signs, and so forth, for the purpose of administrative bookkeeping and basic literacy education. Scholars have argued that the writing system developed out of the use of the list as a form of bookkeeping. In the early stage of cuneiform writing in Mesopotamia, for instance, the earliest types of clay tablets are lists, such as administrative records of bookkeeping and education devices.[19] In ancient Greece and Rome, lists were used in state administration and literacy education. Schoolchildren read, wrote, and memorized not only the alphabet but also a variety of lists. In higher education, an essential part of rhetorical training was the memorization of written lists. The development of an encyclopedic tradition in the Hellenistic period dramatically extended the cultural role of lists.

In early China, too, the list played an important role in administration and education.[20] Although we have only limited material evidence, mainly in the form of imperishable materials, it seems likely that lists were widely used in Shang and Zhou administrative and educational practice.[21] Although we do not know whether such lists were used in economic transactions in China as in the Near East, they appear to have played a major role in the political and religious arena, where they were widely employed. In scheduled royal rituals and sacrifices and in planning such ceremonies, not only the lists of kings and their consorts but also the tables and lists of a permutated cycle of denary stems and duodenary branches were essential. In the oracle-bone records, the lists of kings were embedded in the dedication section of the sacrificial records. Other similar lists appear in the inscriptions on a Shang bronze knife and on the so-called family genealogy carved on a bone.[22] In the Western Zhou dynasty, lists of gifts, the royal genealogy, and clan and family genealogies[23] were embedded in the royal investiture inscriptions cast on commemorative ritual bronzes.[24] Originally, these gifts and genealogies must also have been itemized as lists written on bamboo or other writing materials. Historical annals (such as the *Spring and Autumn* chronicle) were written in the form of lists that enumerated significant dates and events. Lists were also used in administrative practice to record important persons (lists of rulers and genealogies) and objects (lists of gifts and produces) and to support literacy.[25]

Early inscriptions on occasion encompass the tallying of accounts. Among Shang oracle-bone inscriptions, one type, often located at the edges or corners of the bones or shells, notes that so-and-so delivered (*ru* or *na*, literally "to enter") certain quantities of bones or shells. These inscriptions also record the use of bones or shells (*yong* or *chu*, "to use" or "to take out"). Later these terms appear on the Shuihudi Qin bamboo strips, which document *chuqian* and *ruqian, chuhe,* and *ruhe* (Jinbu Lü). Like "credit and debit" in Western bookkeeping terminology, *chu* and *ru, shou* ("to receive"), and *yong* became standard accounting terms.[26] Finally, the Baoshan inventory lists share the same basic features of these administrative lists, utilizing a system of bookkeeping that records dates, names, numbers, and objects. The accuracy required in both administrative and ritual transactions required the spread of literacy in early China. Be it for utilitarian or ceremonial purposes, the goal of literacy was the achievement of a degree of accuracy. The list as a literary form has close ties with bureaucratic practice. As the idealized system in the *Rites of Zhou* demonstrates, the most important function of the bureaucracy is to manage the flow of information and goods.[27] The lists are an essential way to control and manage the flow of goods, including grave goods.[28]

The Public Reading of the Lists

The public display of grave goods and reading of inventory lists during the funeral rites were for the benefit of both the living and the dead. According to the "Obsequies of a Gentleman" chapter in the *Protocols of Ceremonies*, the tomb inventories and gift lists were to be announced publicly. This announcement took place before the funeral procession when all grave goods and funerary gifts were displayed.

> The scribe of the master of mourning asks for permission to read the [list of] funerary gifts. [An assistant] follows [the scribe] with the tallies. They go to the east of the coffin and take their stand abreast of the foremost tie-ropes, with their faces to the west [i.e., toward the coffin]. Then, without any command being issued for the stopping of wailing, the mourners stop one another leaving only the master of mourning and his wife to continue. The lamp is then brought to the right side, and the bearer stands facing South. As the scribe reads the lists of gifts, the tallyman sits and tallies the items. When this is finished, he orders the mourners to resume their wailing. The lamp is extinguished, and they withdraw in the reverse order of their entrance. Then the ruler's scribe stands at the west side, facing east [i.e., toward the coffin]. The mourners are ordered to stop wailing, and the master and his wife are not excepted. The scribe then reads the lists of grave goods. When this is finished, he orders the mourners to resume their wailing. The lamp is then extinguished, and he withdraws.[29]

The scribe of the master of mourning reads the gift lists while the ruler's scribe reads the lists of grave goods. The reading of the contributions and grave goods was performed for the benefit of the deceased, the mourners,[30] the participating guests, and the public in general. The deceased was assured that he or she would be well supplied in the otherworld; the mourners gained prestige in that their deceased relative had received so many gifts; the guests enjoyed the display of royalty and of their

Fig. 4.1. Handwritten copy of the inventory list excavated from a Warring States-period tomb at Yangtianhu in Changsha City, Hunan. At the lower section of some of the strips there are check marks. After Guo Ruoyu, *Zhanguo Chu jian wenzi bian*, 105–6.

generosity. The oral delivery of these lists occupied an important place in this ritual communication, which aimed to connect the spiritual and the human worlds.[31]

The passage from the *Protocols of Ceremonies* cited above allows us to better understand the function of the writing and special marks on Warring States inventories. The Marquis Yi inventories often have thick black dots at the beginning of a list under the name of the gift giver. The color and format of the dots suggest that these notes were made probably by a second hand. At the end of some Yangtianhu inventories, characters like 勾 (*gou*, meaning "checked") and 已 (*yi*, meaning "completed") appear (fig. 4.1).[32] This system of check marks, which later became standard in Han accounting and bookkeeping systems, is the same with the system of accounting that the scribe's assistants used during the ritual reading of the tomb inventories. Both the inventory lists and their public reading are remnants of an earlier sumptuary control mechanism used in the Zhou court, but by the Warring States period these practices had been incorporated into the funeral rites.

In addition, the Warring States funerary lists appeared only in the exalted category of tombs of high aristocrats, suggesting that the lists had previously served as a way to control their funerary expenditures. Among the Warring States tombs with bamboo manuscripts, there is a distinction that scholars often overlook: the tombs that yielded funerary-object lists are categorically different in terms of the tomb occupant's social rank from the tombs that produced almanacs, manuals, and philosophical literature. The former are often the graves of members of high-ranking aristocratic families, whereas the latter often belong to lower-level state functionaries in the local government. Tomb 56 at Jiudian, in which archaeologists discovered daybooks and ritual manuals, is the smallest tomb at that site, and the tomb occupant's social rank was not particularly high.[33] Even Tomb 1 at Guodian, which contained a large cache of philosophical texts, was a relatively small tomb, and thus we can assume that the social rank of the deceased was not very high.

But in the Qin and Han periods, the previous distinction between higher and lower elite tombs containing manuscripts blurred. Although both categories of texts —lists of funerary objects, on the one hand, and everyday manuals, philosophical writings, and related texts, on the other—sometimes appeared in high elite burials, such as Tomb 3 at Mawangdui, whose occupant was the son of the chancellor of the local kingdom of Changsha, by the Qin and Han periods funerary-objects lists appeared mainly in tombs of people of lower social status. The Mawangdui tomb is a notable exception (for greater detail, see below). Yet, at the same time, the contents and nature of the funerary lists also changed in the imperial period. Qin and Han inventory lists contained mainly personal belongings that had no direct relevance to the social standing of the deceased. Particularly after the middle of the Western Han dynasty, the location of the inventory lists also changed, moving from the compartments outside the coffin to the interior of the coffin. Such lists comprised indices of clothing and other personal belongings.

The Magico-Religious Function of the Lists

In the Warring States period, the nature of the practice of burying the lists changed from a bookkeeping device for sumptuary control to a symbolic, magico-religious instrument of substitution. It is significant that not all the objects recorded in the tomb inventory were buried in the grave.[34] Some organic materials in the tomb decomposed; other objects were seized by grave robbers. But in those tombs that remained intact until archaeologists excavated them, objects believed to be made of durable materials were not found. For instance, the lists from the Marquis Yi's tomb at Leigudun recorded elaborate chariots, weapons, and decorations, but only a few of these chariot fittings and other related objects were discovered in the tomb's northern compartment. There is a discrepancy between the grave goods listed and those actually buried.[35] If no inventories had been made, we would never have known about the discrepancy between the goods that were intended for interment and those actually buried.

Scholars have different explanations for these discrepancies between the inventory lists and the actual contents of tombs. Some think that the discrepancy is the result of mere accident. Others suggest that the inconsistency is a function of the nature of the inventory lists: in the process of conducting funeral rites, the public reading of the lists permitted the bereaved family to boast of their social connections by exaggerating the quantity of grave goods interred.[36] Yet ritual classics make it clear that the rite of publicly reading lists of funeral gifts and grave goods was for the benefit of both the deceased and the living. In the "Tan Gong" chapter of the *Book of Rites*, Zeng Zi says about the reading of lists of funerary gifts or of donated items: "It is not an ancient practice; it is a second announcement [to the departed]."[37] Following the traditional commentary, James Legge (1815–97) made an interesting note: "The contributions had been announced by the bier, as if to the departed, and a record of them made. To read this list, as is here supposed, as the procession was about to set forth, was a vain-glorious proceeding, which Zeng Zi thus derided."[38] Legge thus followed the Confucian interpretation of the rite, which criticized many contemporary ritual practices and strategies employed by the rising new elites as "not being ancient" (ancient being the standard or norm), "violating ritual propriety" (*feili*), or "usurping the rites or blasphemy" (*jian*). In this context, however, "vain-gloriousness" is exactly what the ritual performance intended to convey. Pierre Bourdieu's criticism of the structuralist approach to gift exchange makes exactly this point: The ritual exchange of gifts and the reciprocal obligation it forged did not necessarily establish an equal relationship between the two parties in the transaction.[39] Instead, ritualized exchange was "a performative medium for the negotiation of power in relationships."[40]

The ritual act was instrumental in the transition from oral communication to written text. The aim of the ritual proclamation was to connect the human and spiritual worlds.[41] The scholarly discussions of *gao* in the oracle-bone inscriptions have already touched on this issue.[42] There the "reporter" (the subject of the verb *gao*) was the diviner,[43] and *not* the spirit, the shell, or the bone, as has been previously suggested. Yet the sound of the cracking of heated bones and the sound of the oral declaration by the diviner were important parts of the communication between humankind and the spirits, as were other audible phenomena (*shengxiang*) such as music, song, and voice.[44]

The ritual proclamation of the lists suggests that tomb inventories were not just lists of goods that the deceased needed in the afterlife but declarations and affirmations of the relation between the dead and the living. The writing and the reading together fulfilled this function by confirming publicly the quantity of grave goods designated for the deceased. This point can be better explained using speech act theory.[45] From that perspective, the public reading of lists functioned at some level as metonyms for the objects. Archaeological evidence indicates that not all funerary goods were recorded on the inventory lists, and not all listed grave goods were found in the tombs.[46] These symbolic associations between the object and its name did not apply to all funerary goods, but because of the fragmentary nature of the lists and the objects' different preservation conditions, it is difficult at this point to clearly identify all categories that might be the target of such associative action. From the fragmentary evidence, it seems that funerary objects that signify the tomb occupant's social status were often just recorded or only partially buried in the tomb, while customary everyday utensils for burial furnishings were not recorded at all. For example, at Baoshan and in most Warring States Chu tombs, only parts of chariots were buried; the Jiuliandun tombs are exceptional. It seems that the burying of the lists and the tomb furnishings were two separate but related acts. Although in many cases the objects listed matched the objects actually interred, words, images, and artifacts were inextricably connected within the ritual context of the public reading of the lists. Not only were the boundaries between "institutions of the visual" and "institutions of the verbal" blurred, but the basic human experience of space and time also changed, creating the imagined afterlife that the people of the Warring States period desired.

To summarize, by contextualizing the funerary-object lists in the burgeoning bureaucracy of the Warring States and early Han periods (as was the case in the state of Chu), it becomes clear that the list functioned as an administrative practice for controlling the flow of goods. The use of lists in the funerary context, moreover, added religious significance to this mundane practice of bookkeeping. Analysis of the relevant ritual texts shows that the funerary rites included the public display of gifts and grave goods and the public reading of lists before the funeral procession. In funerary ritual, such public display played an important role in the implementation and negotiation of sumptuary rules in Warring States Chu society. The act of publicly announcing the contents of these lists not only informed the participants and spectators of the deceased's social status and of the mourners' generosity but also ultimately commended the living to both the dead and the underworld. In so doing, these acts connected the human world with the spirit world.

Letters Addressed to the Underworld Bureaucracy

The magico-religious nature of the funerary-object lists becomes even more apparent when considered in close association with another genre of tomb text, what modern scholars refer to collectively as documents addressed to the otherworld authorities (*gaodishu*) of the Qin and Han periods. These documents, written in the exact language and format of official Qin and Han administrative or legal documents, concern the personal possessions, legal status, and tax and travel privileges of the tomb occupant. Notably, they were addressed to an envisioned underworld bureaucracy that the deceased would encounter in the afterlife.

The burying of documents addressed to the otherworld authorities in Qin and Han tombs reflected the social reality of the imperial era, in which the imperial bureaucracy closely monitored and supervised the lives of imperial subjects. Three separate but interdependent local institutions were involved: the twenty ranks of merit that defined social status; the household registration system (*mingshu*); and the responsibility group (*shiwu*). In addition, mobility and travel were tightly re-stricted; according to recently excavated texts, numerous legal measures were taken to regulate travel. In death, as in life, therefore, the dead were to be controlled and directed. Death was conceived as a journey, and the dead were equipped with the appropriate travel documents for use in the afterlife.

To date, more than ten official memorials addressed to the underground bureau-cracy have been discovered; most are from tombs in southern China, but several have been found in Han tombs in the northwest. Based on the social status of the tomb occupants, these texts can be divided into three types: those associated with commoners, with kings and marquises, and with convicts.

FUNERARY DOCUMENTS FOR COMMONERS

Funerary travel documents for commoners are the most widespread because they deal with legal matters such as the transmission of personal belongings and burial goods, credentials for household registration, and tax and travel privileges. This group of documents is closely associated with the lists, and sometimes the two doc-ument types were physically joined, as was the case with a wooden board excavated from Tomb 10 at Fenghuangshan in Jiangling County, Hubei.[47] On the recto of the board was a list of funerary objects that continued onto the verso, followed by an additional column of text stating that the tomb occupant, Zhang Yan, reported to the lord of the underworld. The text reads: "In the fourth year [of Emperor Jing] (i.e., 153 BCE), in the intercalary ninth month, on the day *xinhai*, Zhang Yan of Ping Village, ranked *wu dafu* (the ninth rank), [presumes to report] to the lord of the underworld (*dixia zhu*): Yan's clothing and the objects [he uses] to sacrifice (?) all objects have been inspected (?) and are approved. Order the clerk to set to work in accordance with the statutes."[48] The list of funerary objects includes bamboo cases, boxes, furniture, utensils, drinking cups, ceramic vessels, wooden figurines of male and female servants, and foodstuffs and wine. The additional document states that the tomb occupant had reported to the lord of the underworld and that the list of funerary objects had been approved; it then urges the underworld clerk to follow the statutes and proceed accordingly.

The format of this document, although similar to many other everyday admin-istrative documents, is odd in two aspects: its recipient and its voice.[49] First, the document's recipient is the lord of the underworld. In other documents addressed to the underworld, this figure was called the Lord of Earth (*dizhu* or *tuzhu*). The un-derworld bureaucracy apparently had a simple two-tier structure in which the lord of the underworld was in charge of his clerks (*li*) or assistants (*dixia cheng*). Such an arrangement was modeled on Qin and Han local administration rather than on the larger-scale imperial bureaucracy, as is the case in later imperial popular religion.[50]

In addition, the administrative texts and tax documents from the same tomb indicate that Zhang Yan was a powerful official in the local canton (*xiang*).[51] As with all administrators, Qin and Han bureaucrats were conscious of the social hierarchy within their jurisdictions. In this case, Zhang Yan, probably because he was the head of the local jurisdiction, reported directly to the lord of the underworld rather than to an assistant, the more common recipient of documents addressed to the underworld. Second, in this document the tomb occupant Zhang Yan, who was presumably dead and is identified as the deceased on a wooden seal bearing the name "Zhang Yan," as well as in other administrative texts, was delivering the report. In other words, while Zhang Yan was already dead, the document was written in his voice. This document must have been drafted on behalf of Zhang by someone familiar with the jargon and format of administrative documents. These two unusual features suggest that the funerary document was a text with a magico-religious role that manifested during the funerary rites rather than a genuine legal document used in everyday life.

Although other excavated postmortem travel documents were not physically connected with funerary-object lists, they were nevertheless closely associated with them. For example, the text excavated from Tomb 1 at Xiejiaqiao in Jiangling County, Hubei, dated to 183 BCE, was bundled together with the funerary-object list. In Tomb 168 at Fenghuangshan in Jiangling, dated to 167 BCE, the document and the list of grave goods were placed in the same side compartment. In addition, in other cases discussed below, when these documents mentioned funerary objects, those items were recorded separately on wooden boards or bamboo strips as part of a list of funerary objects. Yet another tomb, Tomb 8 (dated to 142 BCE) at Kongjiapo in Suizhou City, Hubei, held no separate inventory list; the text mentioned grave goods, including six slaves, a carriage baldachin, and three horses, that matched perfectly the figurines of human and animals excavated from the tomb.[52]

Similarly, in Tomb 18 at Gaotai in Jiangling, dated to 173 BCE, four wooden boards were bundled together (fig. 4.2). The first was an address label (*fengjian*) with two big characters written on the upper part identifying the receiver's address as "Andu," or "the capital of peace," and a handwritten "seal of the assistant of Jiangling" (*Jiangling cheng yin*), the sender, in the lower section.[53] The text on the second wooden board consisted of the document addressed to the underworld. In it, someone named Qi of the Zhong canton reported that an adult woman named Yan spoke, self-reporting (*ziyan*) that she had taken two male slaves and a female slave and moved to "the capital of peace" (*Andu*); Qi requested that the underworld bureaucrats accept her household and property registration (*mingshu*). Mr. Long, the assistant to the local administrator of Jiangling, "respectfully transmitted" (*jingyi*) the documents to the assistant of the capital of peace. The third wooden board records Yan's household and property registration, which stated her rank, her identity as the widow of a "noble of the interior" (*guannei hou*, nineteenth rank), and the identities of the two male slaves A (*jia*) and B (*yi*) and a female slave by the name of Fang. On the lower half were six written characters: "The family exempted from taxation, no poll tax or labor tax" (*jia fu busuan buyao*; see discussion below). Finally, the fourth wooden board recorded a list of grave goods including

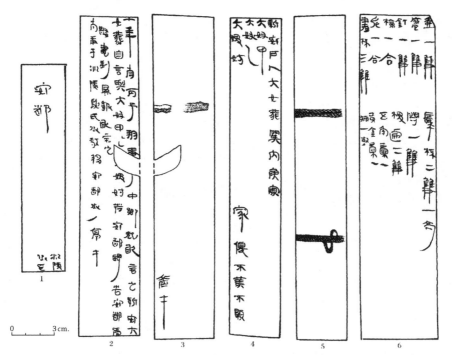

Fig. 4.2. Handwritten copy of the wooden boards, with letter and inventory list addressed to the underworld bureaucracy, excavated from the head compartment in Tomb 18 at Gaotai, Jingzhou City, Hubei. Early Western Han dynasty. 1 is the front of the first board, 2 and 3 are the front and back of the second, 4 and 5 are the front and back of the third, and 6 is the front of the fourth board.

ceramic jars, boxes, lacquered cups, and dried meats, most of which were found during the excavation of the tomb. Although we do not know the identity of this woman, the statement in this document that she is the widow of a "noble of the interior," the second highest rank of the twenty-rank system in the Han dynasty, is doubtful. More likely, her social rank was inflated in this document addressed to the underworld authority. In addition, the use of the variables A (*jia*) and B (*yi*) to refer to the two male slaves indicates that this is a document of magico-religious function, suggesting that this may have been made ready for burial purposes.

These documents, however, all have features similar to those of local administrative or legal documents in which a local official, writing to his counterpart in the underworld bureaucracy, applies the bureaucratic system employed in official Qin and Han administrative or legal documents. The general formulaic presentation opens with a date and the statement that the sender "presumes to report" (*gan gao zhi* or *gan yan zhi*) someone's personal account (*ziyan*) of some events or requests (usually a transference of personal property and household registration). Then the matter is decided, and the local official transmits (*yi*) the documents to his counterparts in another bureaucratic unit, in this case the underworld bureaucracy, to request that they set to work according to the statutes.

Letters to the Underworld

To further illustrate how the legal privileges of this world were transmitted to the next and what those privileges were, let us look at the document excavated from Tomb 1 at Xiejiaqiao.[54] The document, written on three boards, begins:

> In the fifth year [of Empress Lü] (i.e., 183 BCE), in the eleventh month, which began on a day *guimao*, on day *gengwu*, Chen of the western canton presumes to report: The gentleman of the interior Chang, ranked *wu dafu*, reported in person that his mother, adult woman Hui, died. [She took with her] her clothing, burial objects, and her sons and their wives, consorts, and slaves, and horses and cows. Each of the objects and persons was recorded on one strip. [Altogether] 197 strips. The Chang family was exempt from taxation. There are edicts and orders. Report to the assistant of the underworld and set to work. [I] presume to report this.[55]

The second board continues: "In the eleventh month, on day *gengwu*, the assistant of Jiangling Chi transmits [the document] to the assistant of the underworld. [The request is] approved. Order the clerk to set to work. Zang handled [this]."[56] The third and last board states: "The mother of the gentleman of the interior Chang, ranked *wu dafu*, and family belongings (i.e., the accompanying persons mentioned above) shall be exempted from taxation."[57] Besides reporting the transmission of the list of funerary objects and accompanying persons, the document observes that Chang's mother and the family belongings that went down into the afterworld were entitled to the legal privilege of exemption from taxation. The first board is the request; the second board is the official document that transmits the decision, recorded in the third board, to the underworld bureaucracy. Thus, through these funerary texts, the privileges that the rich enjoyed in this life were extended to the afterlife.

FUNERARY DOCUMENTS FOR LOCAL KINGS AND MARQUISES

The second type of document addressed to the underground bureaucracy was prepared for local kings and marquises of the early Western Han. Thus far only a single, and controversial, example, from the famous Tomb 3 at Mawangdui in Changsha City, Hunan, is known. In 2008 Chen Songchang and Michael Friedrich pointed out that the format of the text did not match that of other previously discovered documents addressed to the underground bureaucracy, including those discussed above.[58] Therefore, they suggested that the documents discovered at Mawangdui were not addressed to the underworld authorities but rather served as an everyday administrative and bookkeeping record. Consider the pertinent text:[59] "In the twelfth year [of Emperor Wen] (i.e., 168 BCE), in the second month, which began on a day *yisi*, on day *wuchen*, the household assistant named Fen transferred [it] to the gentleman of the interior in charge of burial: Transmitted a batch of documents listing burial goods. As soon as the documents arrive, check [the goods according to the list], and report fully to the lord in charge of burial."[60] The main point of the debate concerns whether the officials referred to here ("the gentleman of the interior in charge of burial" and "the lord in charge of burial") are fictitious underworld bureaucrats or real entities. According to the *Protocols of Ceremonies*, participants in the funerals of higher-ranking officials could include the ruler and his assistants:[61] "Members of the latter [i.e., the lower nobility] were to be honored by the presence of a representative of the imperial court overseeing the funeral and investing the heir. This ordinance[62] also restricts expenditures at funerals which, together with a desire to control these important ritual events, might have been the original intention."[63]

The public reading of the lists and the presence at the funeral of higher-level officials or even the ruler may have continued into the Han dynasty. Such practices were perhaps part of the social mechanism for sumptuary control. But it is important to note that higher officials were always considered "guests" of the bereaved family and came only to "oversee" the funeral and not to "take charge" of it. The *Protocols of Ceremonies* and other early literature explicitly state that the funeral was managed and presided over by the "master of mourning" (*zhuren* or *sangzhu*), who was often the son or the closest relative of the deceased. Therefore, "the gentleman of the interior in charge of the burial" and "the lord in charge of burial" could not have been the officials sent by higher authorities.

In addition, the gentleman of the interior (*langzhong*) was in the early Western Han dynasty a generic title for the lowest rank of the court attendants, those awaiting appointment or reappointment and whose unspecified function was similar to that of household assistant (*jiachen*).[64] And lord (*jun*), an old title that was popular especially in the state of Chu and designated the highest local official, like *fengjun*, was not used for official titles in the Han bureaucracy. Liu Bang (r. 206–195 BCE), the founding emperor of the Han, decided to adopt the Qin system of "twenty ranks of merit," in which the highest ranks were designated as *hou* (marquis) and *wang* (king).[65] All of this suggests that "the gentleman of the interior in charge of burial" and "the lord in charge of burial" were fictitious underworld bureaucrats. The designation of two tiers of bureaucracy, "the gentleman of the interior" and "the lord," was intended to match the two-tier bureaucrats, in the case of Tomb 3 at Mawangdui, the household assistant and the Marquis of Dai.

The "batch of documents listing burial goods" mentioned in the text refers to the inventory list of funerary objects discovered in Tomb 3. The fact that the Mawangdui document addressed to the underworld authorities assumes a format different from that used for commoners reflects differences in the social rank of the tomb occupant. The kings and marquises of the Han dynasty had privileges that distinguished them from commoners and were not required to register their household and personal property with local officials. Like that of the imperial household, their special registration system was under the control of the imperial court. Therefore, while the Mawangdui document did not follow the format designated for commoners, it was nevertheless intended to be an official memorial addressed to the underworld authorities.

The third type of document addressed to the underworld bureaucracy was designed for convicts. As Huang Shengzhang has pointed out, local household and property registrations were intended only for commoners. A criminal, however, had to first clear his name to be able to register.[66] Such exoneration is precisely the purpose of a document excavated from Tomb 6 at Longgang in Yunmeng County, Hubei.[67] Dated to the end of the Qin dynasty, it is the earliest known example of such a document: "This is formally inquired: Bisi [a personal name, literally, "avoiding death"][68] should not have been sentenced to the hard labor of wall building (*chengdan*). The clerks who made the mistake in his sentence have been punished because of this. In the ninth month, on day *bingshen*, the assistant of Shayi [County] A and clerk C acquitted Bisi and he became a commoner again. Order him to register [it (i.e., household registration)] himself."[69] This document is in the format of official Qin and Han legal documents for appealing a legal judgment. In the Qin and Han legal systems, an initial judgment could be repealed and the convict or his family could request that the case be reopened, initiating a new investigation and inquiry (*qiju*). Moreover, in this modest tomb archaeologists discovered a few ceramic and lacquered vessels, a set of *liubo* chess pieces, and many inscribed bamboo strips regarding Qin legal statutes. The tomb occupant was probably a male and was wrapped in bamboo mats, and the lower half of his skeleton was missing. According to the document, he wrongly received the punishment of *chengdan*, which in the Qin legal codes could be a form of corporal punishment.[70] On the basis of this evidence, scholars have suggested that the tomb occupant was perhaps the convict whose name (Bisi) is mentioned in the document. After his death, this document was written and buried with him with the intention of acquitting him of his crime and allowing him to resume his status as a commoner so that he could register in the underworld.[71] Scholars have also pointed out that this document seems abrupt and incomplete relative to other, similar legal documents. Not only does it acquit Bisi, but it also states that those who have wronged him have been brought to justice. Furthermore, the use of the variables such as A (*jia*) and C (*bing*), instead of the real names of the local officials who supposedly wrote this document, suggests that the text was probably a fictitious, rather than an actual, legal document of a magico-religious nature. It is also possible that this document was created and buried with the corpse behind the backs of the local officials who handled the case. Interestingly, according to the definition discussed in chapter 1 of this book, Bisi could also qualify as one of the blameless dead (*bugu*) who had been wrongfully sentenced and died a violent death; thus, this magico-religious document is designed to clear the deceased's name, to pacify him, and to resolve the problem of his becoming an evil ghost.

A similar document dated to the Eastern Han dynasty was excavated from Tomb 5 at Huchang in Yangzhou City, Jiangsu.[72] The text reads (fig. 4.3):[73]

In the forty-seventh year [of King Guangling] (i.e., 71 BCE) in the twelfth month, which begins on day *bingzi*, on day *xinmao*, the head of the Palace Construction Office of the Guangling Kingdom named Qian (?) and his assistant Neng (?) presume to report to the Lord of Earth: a male adult Wang Fengshi of Shi Village had been in prison. His term of imprisonment has ended. He is set to return to his previous residence. And he shall go there by himself. [This document is] transmitted so as to reach the underground (?). In the forty-eighth year, the prison case has been audited. Upon receiving this letter, set to work according to the statutes and ordinances.[74]

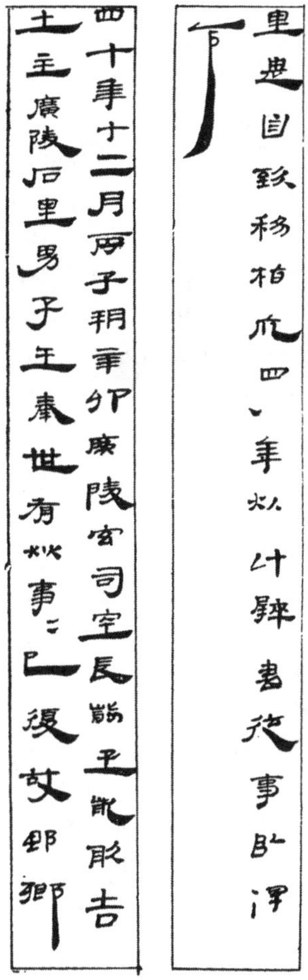

The tomb from which this document was excavated is one of those rare joint burials of a husband and wife in a vertical pit in southeast China. More than two hundred pieces of grave goods were unearthed from this well-preserved tomb. Among the goods, three bronze seals identify the tomb occupant as Wang Fengshi, who was about thirty years old and the same person recorded in the wooden document. The document was discovered in the husband's coffin, within which archaeologists found a skeleton with a deformed skull. Medical examination determined that the deformation resulted from corporeal punishment or long-term heavy pressure on the head, a fact that probably reflects his status as a convict. The occupant died at the end of 71 BCE and was buried the following year. This document is written in the voices of the head of the Palace Construction Office of the Guangling Kingdom and his assistant and addresses "the Lord of Earth." It confirms that the tomb occupant Wang Fengshi had completed his prison term and resumed his status as a commoner in the afterlife. It is possible that both Bisi's and Wang Fengshi's documents were included to clear their names so that they could be registered in the underworld bureaucracy and to resolve the problem of their becoming evil ghosts that haunt the living.

Several other Han documents addressed to the underworld bureaucracy discovered in Wuwei (Gansu) suggest that the practice of burying such documents was not an isolated phenomenon limited to Jiangling in Hubei or to southern China (as some scholars have proposed). Some of the northwest examples provided travel passes for the deceased, featuring phrases such as *guosuo wuliu*, "do not detain [them]." One

Fig. 4.3. Handwritten copy of the wooden boards, with letter addressed to the underworld bureaucracy, excavated from Tomb 5 at Huchang, Yangzhou City, Jiangsu. Middle Western Han period.

document found in Tomb 5 at Wubashan in Wuwei was especially telling: not only was the deceased provided with a travel pass for his journey in the afterlife but a clear statement was also made to divide his estate (in this case, land) among his relatives.[75]

The above discussions of the three types of documents addressed to the underworld strongly suggest that documents addressed to the underworld bureaucracy did not constitute a single genre of document with one format; rather, they represented a range of legal documents that concerned the tomb occupant's legal status, personal belongings, property, and tax and travel privileges. These documents owed much to the establishment of the imperial bureaucratic system and reflected the changing attitude toward the dead, who came to be seen as potentially dangerous beings in need of management in the underworld. Finally, such writings can be traced back to Qin and Han imperial social institutions, which supervised and controlled people in this world and inspired the notion that the dead had to be similarly treated in the next world.

The Formation of the Underworld Bureaucracy

A distinguishing characteristic of Chinese religion is the underworld bureaucracy. While other early civilizations—for instance, ancient Egypt—also developed elaborate and sophisticated religious systems and notions of the afterlife, none were as bureaucratic as the Chinese. Not surprisingly, this concept of a bureaucratized afterlife first emerged during the Qin-Han period of imperial formation. We have seen that in this early stage of development, the underworld bureaucracy had a three-tiered structure consisting of the two tiers of bureaucrats—the lord of the underground and his assistants—and the dead. Its organization did not mirror the full-fledged imperial bureaucratic system but was the equivalent of a largely local administration.

The development of a bureaucratic system to organize and control the dead can be traced back to the Warring States period.[76] Bureaucratized segregation of the dead was conceived not only out of fear of vengeful ghosts and death pollution[77] but also out of the socially constructed "otherness" of the afterworld. In response to the standard classification of the Chinese spirit world, in which gods correspond to bureaucrats, ancestors to living kin, and ghosts to strangers,[78] anthropologist P. Steven Sangren suggests that the conception of the otherworld should not be reduced simply to social categories.[79] Instead of treating the otherworld as a mirror image or imitation of this world, the analysis should place collective cultural conceptions in a dialectical relationship to social structure. This approach emphasizes the social mechanisms through which the imaginary supernatural world is constructed and could be productively applied to the early Chinese case. Integral to the dialectical relationship in Chu religion is the construct of "otherness," which contrasts with the sociopolitical conditions prevalent during the Warring States period.

The dialectical opposition of religious imagination and social structure is revealed in an incantation written on bamboo strips (Strips 43–44) excavated from Tomb 56 at Jiudian in Jiangling County, Hubei, a burial contemporaneous with Tomb 2 at Baoshan (ca. 316 BCE).[80] The incantation, which takes the form of a prayer for men slain with weapons, summoned the men to return home to receive sacrifices:[81]

[*Gû![82] I] dare to declare to Wuyi, the son of XX. You reside at the edge of Mount Fu and in the wilds of Buzhou. The Lord said that you had no occupation and commanded you to direct those who died by weapons. Today, so-and-so (*mou*) will wish to eat. So-and-so dares to take his wife [and offer her] to you. Cut strips of silk and fragrant provisions are offered for the sake of so-and-so at the place of Wuyi. Lord, in the past you received so-and-so's cut strips of silk and fragrant provisions. Will you let so-and-so come back home to eat as usual?[83] (Strip 44)

The incantation was among the bamboo strips discovered in the side niche of the small-scale tomb. The precise organization of the strips is unclear because most were fragments when excavated. The text's formulaic ritual language and its similarity to almanacs, or daybooks (*rishu*), however, suggest that it is a general template rather than a "real" incantation for the tomb occupant.

Here the bureaucratic structure likewise consists of three tiers: the Lord (Di); Wuyi, the director of the war dead; and the war dead. The text of the Jiudian prayer states that Wuyi, probably the son of a prominent figure in the spirit world's pantheon, was assigned as superintendent of the Chinese equivalent of Hades, since he was "the son of XX" and "had no occupation." As scholars have pointed out, the use of the formula "so-and-so, the son of so-and-so" was an old, and probably already obsolete, method of identification used by the aristocracy, as seen in many Spring and Autumn–period bronze inscriptions.[84] Wuyi's appointment as the director of the war dead could stem from his being an important war spirit in early China, but the story told in the strips from Tomb 56 was casual and satirical, which makes one wonder about the meaning of the formula on another level. One's wife could be taken, probably by force, and offered to "you (that is, Wuyi)." The notion of "deities taking mortal women as wives,"[85] often in the form of sacrifices of young females or companions in death, is declared in both received texts and archaeological records.[86] The deities in the afterworld could be bribed with "cut strips of silk and fragrant provisions" in exchange for letting "so-and-so come back home to eat." Here it seems that the principles by which the supernatural world operated were directly opposed to those propagated by the philosophers of the Warring States period. The otherworld is where the ideals of this world were suspended, and its social evils—nepotism, corruption, and even human sacrifice—became natural and normal. Nevertheless, whether the otherworld reflected the reality of Warring States social life or posed it as an alternative, the relationship between actual sociopolitical conditions and these afterlife constructs was anything but merely mechanical.

Furthermore, the creation of an enclave where the war dead could gather was probably one of the earliest instances of an imagined religious community.[87] This bureaucratized segregation of the dead provided a precursor, or model, for the later development of the transcendental paradise by assembling individuals into a community not bound by blood or other type of familial relationship.[88] In the late Warring States period, mass conscription armies were not drawn from kin-based units, and such an imagined community might have created solidarity among the soldiers, dead or alive. The war dead were removed from the predominant model of social organization in early China, as were the transcendents (*xian*) who, by the middle of the third century BCE, were administered by deities such as Wuyi and the Queen Mother of the West, respectively.

The dialectical construction of religious imagination is further illustrated in the transcendence seekers' construction of their ultimate condition and in their attempts to persuade other people to recognize their special religious state.[89] These techniques of persuasion include claims of extraordinary longevity or deathlessness; dietary restrictions; enhanced physical capacities; mastery of space, time, and the elements; peculiar dwelling habits; mastery of nonhuman others; and freedom from social convention and constraint. All the hagiographies of the adepts conveyed a sense of "strangeness" or "otherworldliness" to their contemporaries, and the adepts and their associates consciously exploited the contrast between this world and the otherworld to create a sense of wonder and even magic and to persuade people to "believe in" and to "belong to" such imagined communities. The underworld bureaucracy was the early product of such "cultural repertoires" of dialectical imagination.

Local Officials and Ritual Specialists

Behind all of these lists and documents addressed to the underworld bureaucracy were the people who wrote and read them. They were mainly local officials, scribes, and ritual specialists, all of whom played an important role in the development of early Chinese religion. But modern scholars have not fully recognized their religious function in early China. For example, anthropologist James L. Watson proposes that standardized ritual practice was essential for providing cultural cohesion in China and served as the basis for Chinese cultural identity, and that in this unified ritual structure performance took precedence over belief, and orthopraxy (correct practice) trumped orthodoxy (correct belief).[90] Although his evidence comes mainly from late imperial Chinese sources and anthropological fieldwork conducted in southern China and in Hong Kong, his conclusions are often applied more broadly to Chinese death rituals, as well as to early Chinese religion in general.

This view of Chinese ritual and religion supports two misconceptions. First, it overemphasizes the rigidity of ritual structure; and second, it overlooks the agentic role that ritual participants, local officials, and ritual specialists (who oversaw the ritual performance) played in the formation and transformation of funerary ritual structure in Chinese society. Although many participants in a death ritual might not have been able to articulate the exact (correct) functions and purposes of the rituals performed, this would not necessarily have kept them from speculating about the meaning of the ritual itself. Correct or incorrect, their explanations and speculations were essential parts of ritual action. In essence, performance and belief are inextricably intertwined.

The active agents in the construction of the religious imagination included not only everyday religious practitioners, such as the initiators of the Jiudian incantation, but also, and more importantly, the ritual specialists and local officials such as the occupant of Tomb 56, where the incantation and ritual manuals were discovered. Structurally, this tomb is a typical small-scale, vertical pit-style burial with a single coffin and two niches; we often see all of these features in Warring States tombs.[91] The grave goods and the manner in which they were buried are also quite typical of tombs of this scale. The thirty grave goods were stored in two niches in the walls. A ceramic *ding* tripod and a *hu* vessel (both imitations of bronze ritual vessels), a bronze spoon, two lacquered ear-cups, a lacquered box, and a set of lacquered armor were found in the head niche. The side niche contained a bronze sword in a wooden box, a bamboo quiver with seventeen arrowheads, a bamboo bow, a wooden bow, a coarse-toothed comb and a fine-toothed comb (both made of wood), and a scroll of bamboo strips. Wrapped in the bamboo scroll were an iron book knife and an ink box, which contained a block of black pigment, the earliest ink cake ever discovered in China.[92] By assessing the ritual manuals and other texts in the tomb, archaeologists determined that the occupant was probably a ritual specialist who perhaps worked in the military.

Other official and nonofficial ritual specialists are known from the state of Chu in the Warring States period. There are about seventy diviners and ritual specialists named in Chu divinatory and sacrificial records. Among them, twenty-nine worked for the Lord of Pingye (the occupant of Tomb 1001 at Geling); nineteen for Pan Sheng, a local lord of Diyang (the occupant of Tomb 1 at Tianxingguan); eleven for Shao Tuo, the deputy Chief Minister of the Left (the occupant of Tomb 2 at Baoshan); eight for Dao Gu (the occupant of Tomb 1 at Wangshan); and two or three for the occupants of Tombs 1, 13, and 99 at Qinjiazui in Jiangling County, Hubei. In general, the number of diviners in service corresponded to the social rank of the tomb occupant. That is, those of greater status and means could afford more ritual specialists to serve them.[93]

Ritual specialists were a diverse group of people with special knowledge and skills who hailed from different social and political backgrounds. Some diviners had official titles and must have been incorporated into the imperial or local bureaucratic system, whereas others were freelance experts. Some were commoners, and some were of royal descent. For example, several diviners were surnamed Qu, which was the surname (i.e., lineage name) of an important Chu lineage, and they likely came from this lineage. In the Baoshan divinatory and sacrificial records, two ritualists,

Zang Gan and Shao Ji, were involved in "acting in the position" (*weiwei*) in the sacrifice to Shao Tuo.[94] The Shao branch lineage was descended from King Zhao of Chu.[95] The surname Zang also appears in the inscription on a Chu bronze measuring cup collected in 1984, which documented certain Moxiao (the title of a certain minister in Chu) by the name of Zang Shi.[96] As scholars have pointed out, in the Eastern Zhou period members of powerful lineages generally occupied the important official positions at the Chu court hereditarily.[97] The importance of the Zang lineage in the state of Chu is obvious from this inscription. Therefore, Zang Gan in the Baoshan sacrificial record is likely the descendant of a Chu king, probably King Zhuang of Chu.

These local officials and ritual specialists, who came from diverse social backgrounds, played an important role in forming the Chinese conception of the bureaucratized afterlife, a role that has yet to be fully recognized in the scholarly literature on early Chinese religion. The religious imagination of the afterlife is essentially the social construct of certain members who played leading roles in its formation because of the social, political, and intellectual positions they occupied. In the case of early China, this group encompassed local officials and ritual specialists, whose social and political positions in the emerging bureaucratic empires had a profound impact on the later development of Chinese religion.

The agentic role of religious participants, local officials, scribes, and ritual specialists is reflected in the dynamics of funerary ritual in ancient China. The persistence of ritual structure itself is a vibrant cultural phenomenon, in which diverse explanations and speculations of the meanings of ritual are not a sign of the weakness of the belief system but rather represent the very mechanism of transformation and reinterpretation of ritual in a particular period. As historical circumstances change, the particular functions and meanings of the ritual performance become blurred, and explanations multiply, which in turn facilitates the adaptation of the rituals to new contexts.

The formation of the ritual structure and the standardization of practice occurred as part of a long historical process in which local officials and ritual specialists played a significant role. Whereas Watson's theory emphasizes the predominance of ritual structure and action over belief, my argument is that the dynamics of the death ritual emphasize the agency inherent in ritual practice. Archaeological evidence shows that local officials took a leading role in the practice of funerary ritual in early China and in the imagination (for example, the bureaucratization) of the afterlife. In addition, early Confucian classics such as the *Protocols of Ceremonies* and the *Book of Rites* attempt to explain and discuss the "real" meanings of the funerary rites. This penchant by scholar-officials and ritual specialists to write about and discuss funerary rites continued in later centuries. Classical funerary ritual was simplified, and scholar-officials wrote and rewrote funerary manuals; eventually, in late imperial China, ritual diagrams and funerary manuals were included in daily encyclopedias.

THE TEXTS THAT ACCOMPANIED THE DECEASED into the afterlife shed light on the changing conceptions of the dead in early China. With the development of centralized government and the formation of the empire, writing became an increasingly important means of communication between upper and lower governments, between officials, between individuals, and between this world and the next. Along with increased literacy came the growth of the *literati*, people who could read and write. In local societies in the Warring States period and the early empires, literate local officials and ritual specialists played a vital role in these communications. The inventory lists essentially provided a form of administrative bookkeeping and controlled the flow of both goods and populations. The public reading of the inventory lists in the funerary rites was once part of the mechanism for sumptuary control. During the Warring States period these inventory lists began to be buried in tombs and to function as magico-religious substitutes for the real objects listed therein. The large gap in social status between tomb occupants with inventory lists in the Warring States period and those with lists in the Western Han period also points to the change in the lists' function from sumptuary control of the upper classes to magico-religious and social control of the middle and lower social strata.

Addressed to the underworld bureaucracy and issued by ritual specialists or local officials, these documents had counterparts in the real world. For the dead of different social standings, these documents had different functions and different formats. For local kings and marquises, these documents, along with inventory lists of grave goods, were a means for sumptuary control; but for the commoners, these documents were crucial for the dead's registration in the underworld bureaucracy, much as commoners were controlled and registered in this world. The magico-religious function of the documents manifested most clearly in the case of the convicts, whose punishments were remitted and names restored so that they could register in the afterlife and thus be controlled by the underworld bureaucracy. The formation of this underworld bureaucracy was a dialectical process in which the local officials and ritual specialists played important roles. These letters to the underworld reflect early Chinese concepts of the bureaucratic afterlife.

5

Journey to the Northwest

All cosmologies—or at least all early conceptions of the universe—
have a religious aspect. Chinese cosmology is no exception.
In China the religious aspect of cosmology centered on the
question of abodes of the dead, a subject that also deeply
interested other civilizations.

—JOSEPH A. NEEDHAM AND COLIN A. RONAN

IDEAS ABOUT THE COSMOLOGY and geography of the afterlife altered significantly during the transition from the Warring States period to the unified Qin and Han empires. These changes included an innovative conception of the abode of the deceased, which prompted the notion of an otherworldly journey.[1] Archaeological evidence from the Chu region suggests that a new understanding of the afterlife developed during the Warring States period. According to this understanding, the departed soul took an arduous journey to an imagined cosmic destination in the northwest of the universe. Images, texts, maps, and objects were entombed with the deceased to outfit him or her with travel paraphernalia for the journey; in addition, during the funerary rites, parts of the road ritual that was performed for living travelers were rendered to ward off evil influences for the dead in this liminal stage of transformation. This fresh view of the afterlife revises the conventional wisdom about the tomb as the "happy home" of the dead and provides a new picture of the afterlife before the emergence of transcendental paradises in the mid–Western Han dynasty. This novel vision of the afterlife as an otherworldly journey resulted from the drastic expansion of geographical knowledge of the outside world during the Warring States period and became a source for later literary, poetic, and figural representations in ancient China.[2]

The cult of ancestors in the afterlife has a long history in early China. Bronze inscriptions of the Western Zhou period suggest that the elite dead resided in their lineage cemeteries, in an unspecific "underground" realm, or in "the court of the High God." In a similar vein, one story in the *Zuo Commentary* proposes that deceased family members would meet again in the subterranean Yellow Springs, one of many localities mentioned in classical literature.[3] Kinship ties were as important in the afterlife as they were in this world, and the fact that the family of the deceased willingly invested so much energy and so many resources in the disposal of the corpse reveals the great religious power the dead were believed to possess. As oracle-bone and bronze inscriptions testify, the souls of the ancestors were thought to ascend to and descend from the dwelling of the High God, for the purpose of bringing blessings to their descendants on earth.

Thus there had long existed an idea of a vertical axis between the place of the High God and the human realm (and, by extension, to the Yellow Springs and the "underground"), by means of which the royal ancestors communicated with their descendants. Their passage between Heaven and Earth is technically also a journey, but this trip differs significantly from the otherworldly voyage explored in the following pages. In the Shang and early Zhou periods, the protagonist in the journey is either one of the venerated and almighty ancestors or a religious specialist (like a spirit medium),[4] whereas in the Warring States period, the traveler who undertakes this otherworldly journey is "an *ordinary* guy" who "could be anybody."[5] In emphasizing the breakdown of the Shang and Western Zhou social hierarchy, this ordinariness highlights a defining characteristic of the common religious beliefs and practices during the Warring States period.

There was also a shift in the directional axis for these two types of journeys. Whereas the Shang and early Zhou ancestors ascended to or descended from the place of the High God along a vertical axis, during the Warring States period the traveler's movement shifted to an east-west horizontal orientation, and the idea of a "journey to the west" (or the northwest) in the afterlife became prevalent. With the emergence of these new cosmic destinations came the gradual relocation of postmortem paradises to this world. Mythical places such as Mount Kunlun and the Penglai Isles first mentioned in Warring States texts such as *Zhuangzi* were situated at the margins of the universe.[6] These became part of the construct of the afterlife during the mid-Western Han, along with transcendental paradises such as the realm of the Queen Mother of the West,[7] the gathering place of celestials and immortals, and Mount Tai, to which departed souls were supposed to make an otherworldly journey.[8]

The vision of the afterlife during the Warring States and early Western Han periods is, however, still far from clear, and various theories have been proposed about where the dead resided.[9] The most prevalent are the notions that "before the idea of a transcendent paradise had been fully developed, a happy conclusion to the soul's story might simply be to return to its homeland"[10] and that the tomb was considered the "happy home" or underground "permanent home" of the deceased.[11] As many scholars have pointed out, the models of buildings, servants, domestic animals, rice fields, and even toilets found in later Eastern Han graves give the impression that these tombs were constructed to replicate the domestic landscape. This replication, however, elaborates the concept of a tame space and does not mean that Chinese tombs were conceived as underground domiciles from the outset.

The Jiudian incantation introduced in chapter 4 captures the general concept of the abode of the war dead in the afterlife. Most significant about this incantation is the new information that the dead, in this case the war dead, reside in a place "at the edge of Mount Fu and in the wilds of Buzhou," located in the northwest of the universe. During the Warring States period, a new conception of the afterlife developed in which the departed soul took an arduous journey to an imagined cosmic destination. This argument is partially based on the use of the place-holding pronoun *mou* 某 (so-and-so), a pronoun for an unspecified person, date, or location. In a real incantation, the name of the beneficiary of the ritual would replace this pronoun. This replacement practice is common in early ritual texts (such as the *Protocols of Ceremonies*[12]), in medical texts (such as the "Formulas for Fifty-Two Ailments" and "Formula for Various Cures" in the Mawangdui medical literature[13] and in the medical formula found in Han dynasty Tomb 30 at Zhoujiatai in Jingmen City, Hubei[14]), in exemplary legal documents, and in almanacs.[15] Scholars have debated whether this *mou* refers to a ritual specialist,[16] a person killed by weapons,[17] or the dying patient who was eventually buried in the tomb.[18] These multiple *mou* in the Jiudian incantation do not necessarily represent a single entity. They are rather, as the example from the Mawangdui medical texts shows,[19] the different people involved in this magico-religious performance: of the five *mou* in the Jiudian incantation, the first, third, and fifth refer to the soul of the one who perished in battle, and the second and the fourth denote the person who initiated the incantation. The initiator (a relative of the dead warrior or the ritual specialist) addresses Wuyi, the director of the war dead, to request that the soul of the war dead return to receive sacrificial meals. In short, the Jiudian incantation was not an isolated invocation but a normative prayer that testifies to the common religious beliefs and practices in the Chu area during the Warring States period.

In spite of the different interpretations of *mou*, it is clear that the foot of Mount Fu and the wilds of Buzhou were the "place" of Wuyi (notice the word *suo* 所, or place, in parallel expressions such as the aforementioned *disuo* 帝所, "the place of the High God," of the Shang and Zhou dynasties). It is also worth noting that cut strips of silk (i.e., spirit money) and fragrant provisions were used to entreat Wuyi. Cut strips of silk and food provisions were found among the grave goods buried with the dead in many tombs of this period.[20]

Mount Fu is a double of Buzhou 不周.[21] As a mythological destination, Mount

Buzhou is mentioned in various early Chinese texts, such as "Lisao" in *Songs of the South*, the *Classics of Mountains and Seas*, *Master Lie* (Liezi), and *Master of Huainan* (Huainanzi). Mount Buzhou was considered the nexus of the spirit world, the axis connecting the spirit and human realms, or the Gate to the Dark Capital (*youdu zhi men*)[22] where spirits resided. Buzhou literally means "uncircumscribed" and describes a state of geographic incompleteness and imperfection.[23] This incompleteness is the result of the mythological battle between the two legendary figures of Gonggong and Zhuanxu, an encounter that explains the cosmology and topography of China: "When Gonggong was fighting Zhuanxu for the Empire, he knocked against Mount Buzhou in his rage, breaking one of the pillars of heaven, snapping one of the threads which supported the earth. For this reason heaven leans North West, and the sun, moon and stars move in that direction; the earth does not fill the South East, so the rivers and rain floods find their home there."[24] This story of the battle between Gonggong and Zhuanxu was known in the Chu region during the Warring States period, as recorded in the "Heavenly Questions," or *Tianwen*, a text of Chu origin dated to the same period.[25]

Moreover, the northwest location of Mount Buzhou is not only attested to in the abovementioned received texts but also can be deduced from manuscripts excavated in this region. A passage similar to the one from the *Master Lie* quoted above appears on the bamboo strips recently discovered in a Warring States tomb at Guodian in Jingmen City, Hubei,[26] and again at Tomb 8 at Kongjiapo (early Western Han dynasty) in Suizhou City, Hubei.[27] As their geographical knowledge expanded,[28] people of the Warring States period recognized the topographical features of China—the high altitudes in the northwestern mountain regions and the lowlands in the southeastern plain and coastal regions—and tried out different cosmological theories for why Heaven was tilted to the northwest and the Earth unfilled in the southeast. The Kongjiapo text in particular relates this topographic feature to five phases (*wuxing*) of cosmology. Entitled "Sui," the text is written at the end of a daybook (*rishu*), the beginning of which reads: "The heaven is not filled in the West, therefore the pillar of heaven broke; the earth is not filled in the East, therefore the thread supporting the earth snapped. Thus, name the East and establish it as Wood, and call it Azure. Name the South and establish it as Fire, [and call it Red. Name the West and establish it as] Metal, and call it White. Name the North and establish it as Water, and call it Black. Name the Center and establish it as Earth, and call it Yellow." As in the famous Chu silk manuscript, the subject of this passage concerns the repair of the damaged cosmos using five colored elements to support the heaven. Although Mount Buzhou is not specifically mentioned in these texts, it is implied in references to the imperfection of the northwest (or more generally, the west). Furthermore, a diagram associated with a text titled "Divination on the Placement of Doors" in the bamboo strips from a Qin tomb at Shuihudi in Yunmeng County, Hubei, supports the idea that Mount Buzhou is located in the northwest of the universe.[29] Terms such as *the wind from Buzhou* also appear in *Mas-*

ter of *Huainan*,[30] the "Lüshu" chapter in *Records of the Grand Historian*,[31] *Baihutong*,[32] and in *Explaining Graphs and Understanding Characters*.[33] In these texts, "Buzhou" is almost synonymous with a northwestern direction.

These texts show that the Chinese preoccupation with the northwest did not begin in the middle of the Han dynasty, when the Queen Mother of the West became popular,[34] but has its origins at least three centuries earlier, in the late Warring States period. This fact is the result of the intensive effort to construct a cosmology that accounts for the structure of the cosmos and the geography of the afterlife. As stated in the epigraph to this chapter, "All cosmologies—or at least all early conceptions of the universe—have a religious aspect. . . . In China the religious aspect of cosmology centered on the question of abodes of the dead."[35]

But why should the war dead be treated differently and relocated to Mount Buzhou, the Gate to the Dark Capital, in the northwest? The Jiudian incantation indicates that the place for the war dead is located not in a tomb but "at the edge of Mount Fu and in the wilds of Buzhou." We find no indication here that the site of Wuyi is a site for punishments or rewards. Instead, it is a neutral place, free from moral judgment.[36] One can only speculate that the purpose of gathering the souls of the war dead in a place administered by Wuyi was to control these potent and potentially harmful spirits because, as its name suggests, wars, casualties, and calamities were endemic to the Warring States period, and the vengeful ghosts of war and violence abounded. This approach appears to have been an efficient way to utilize the gods, who naturally occupied a higher position in the religious hierarchy, to control these evil ghosts and demons.

The Jiudian incantation implies that the departed souls of the war dead must make a journey from the tomb to the abode of the dead because of the geographic distance between the two. By the late Warring States period, this journey applied not only to the war dead or other vengeful ghosts but to all dead, including the ancestors. In addition, daybooks, which guided postmortem travel, found in Tomb 56 at Jiudian, and travel paraphernalia became common items for furnishing late Warring States tombs. Moreover, art historical evidence corroborates the notion of spirit travel in the afterlife. One famous example, a painting on silk excavated from a late Warring States–period tomb at Zidanku in Changsha City, Hunan, depicts a male figure riding on a dragon boat (fig. 5.1).[37] Depicted in profile and wearing an elaborate robe, this nobleman, most likely the tomb occupant, stands at the center of the picture in the midst of a high-speed journey, probably from this world to the world beyond. To suggest motion, the tassels of the canopy above him and his chin strap are shown blown to the right. Most scholars have interpreted the renowned Mawangdui silk banner paintings of Lady Dai and her son as illustrations of a staged journey undertaken in the afterlife, the three distinct registers of each painting representing stages of transformation as the deceased morphs from a buried corpse into a benevolent ancestral spirit in the heavenly realm.[38]

Fig. 5.1 "Man and Dragon" silk painting excavated from Tomb 365 at Zidanku, Changsha City, Hunan, the same tomb where the Chu Silk manuscript was discovered. H. 37.5 cm. Warring States period. Hunan Provincial Museum.

The Guidance on Travel in the Daybooks

To understand what the otherworldly journey may have meant in early China, one must first consider the meanings of everyday journeys. The imaginary journey was likely modeled after real travels that people experienced during their lifetimes. Death was conceptually regarded as "a grand journey" (*daxing* 大行),[39] and funerary rites were directly related to travel rituals. Diverse grave goods, connected to the practice and experience of travel found in recently excavated tombs, enable us to understand the principles of travel in early China. These artifacts include calendars, almanacs, cosmographic models, and technical manuals.

Our understanding of travel in everyday life during the Warring States, Qin, and early Han periods has been greatly augmented by late twentieth-century archaeological finds, especially by one type of manuscript that appears often in tombs: daybooks.[40] Timing is an important aspect of the early Chinese notion of a journey; and divination, which in one sense can be understood as the science of timing, plays an important role in determining when one could travel. These daybooks cover many aspects of everyday life, such as coping with illness, offering sacrifices to the ancestors, taking a wife, giving birth to a child, catching thieves, explaining dreams, and so on. Of the subjects covered in daybooks, the timing and rituals associated with travel are the most prominent.[41] Such finds represent the dissemination and popularization of ritual practice via texts. Indeed, because the tomb occupants with whom the daybooks were buried were not necessarily of the highest social rank, we may use the daybooks to generalize about travel in everyday life. In this connection, we will discuss the guidelines for setting off on a journey and returning home and their cosmological significance.

In general, the daybooks detail auspicious and inauspicious dates for travel and return, the directions one should avoid in travel, the magical rites one can perform to ensure a safe journey, and the sacrifices one should deliver to relevant local deities. The earliest daybook discovered so far is from Tomb 56 at Jiudian, the same tomb from which the incantation was excavated. The scroll of bamboo strips, discovered in the side niche of the tomb, consists of 205 pieces of either complete or fragmentary strips.[42] Three strips, numbers 31 to 33, show how the manual worked and belong to one of the hemerological arts called *Congchen* 叢辰 (Collected *Chen*; *chen* referring to the twelve branches). In light of a similar *Congchen* text found in Tomb 11 at Shuihudi in Yunmeng County, Hubei,[43] it is clear that the order of the twelve branches (*shi'er zhi* 十二支 or *shi'er chen* 十二辰) listed on each strip follows that of the twelve months. As a general rule, dates are enumerated by the combination of the denary stems (*gan* 干) and the duodenary branches (*zhi* 支). Thus, the three strips can be translated:

The dates whose branches are [*shen*] [in the first month], *you* [in the second month], *xu* [in the third month], *hai* [in the fourth month], *zi* [in the fifth month], *chou* [in the sixth month], *yin* [in the seventh month], *mao* [in the eighth month], *chen* [in the ninth month], *si* [in the tenth month], *wu* [in the eleventh month], and *wei* [in the twelfth month] are called the "outside sunny days." They are favorable for going out to do business,[44] going out to the four quarters and into the wilds. If going out to hunt, you will get game. If there are people running away, you will not get them, and you will never hear from them again. If you set up a net, you will obtain [game birds]. Greatly auspicious.[45]

The dates whose branches are *you* [in the first month], *xu* [in the second month], *hai* [in the third month], *zi* [in the fourth month], *chou* [in the fifth month], *ying* [in the sixth month], *mao* [in the seventh month], *chen* [in the eighth month], *si* [in the ninth month], *wu* [in the tenth month], *wei* [in the eleventh month], and *shen* [in the twelfth month] are called the "outside harmful days." They are not favorable for going out to do business, going out to the four quarters or into the wilds. [If you do], you will certainly encounter rebels and thieves, and you will encounter wars. Thus it is not favorable for making trips and doing work in the wilds. Inauspicious.[46]

The dates whose branches are *xu* [in the first month], *hai* [in the second month], *zi* [in the third month], *chou* [in the fourth month], *ying* [in the fifth month], *mao* [in the sixth month], *chen* [in the seventh month], *si* [in the eighth month], *wu* [in the ninth month], *wei* [in the tenth month], *shen* [in the eleventh month], and *you* [in the twelfth month] are called the "outside cloudy days." They are favorable for offering sacrifices. It is auspicious to receive goods, but inauspicious to trade. If you go on a long-distance trip, it will be a prolonged journey. Thus it is not favorable to go out to do business.[47]

The dates of a year are classified into one of twelve categories: *jie, yang, jia, hai, yin, da, waiyang, waihai, waiyin, jue, jueguang,* and *xiu* (the exact meanings of these terms remain unclear). The dates pertaining to the same categories share the same luck. For example, in Strip 31, those dates associated with *shen*,[48] having their earthly branch in the first month, are called the date of *waiyang*, or "outside sunny day." Those dates with *you* as their earthly branch in the second month are called the "outside sunny day," and so on.

The method of divination, as seen in the Jiudian daybook, significantly departs from techniques employed in the Shang and Western Zhou periods. Divinations concerning the auspicious and inauspicious dates for hunting, sacrifices, military expeditions, and other activities often appear in late-Shang oracle bones. But in that case the diviners consulted the "will" of the supreme god or the ancestors. Through the cracks on bones of sacrificial animals or on shells of divine turtles, the supreme god or the ancestors directly revealed their intentions.

In the daybooks, however, the elements that determined what was auspicious and what was not belonged to the allocation of cosmic time (*shi'er chen*). Certainly timing was also important in Shang religion. As one scholar suggests, "To the Shang diviner, time was as portentous as place and direction; observed, shaped, and regulated, time was, like space, an indispensable dimension of religious cosmology, an integral part of all religious observance and divinatory prognostication."[49] Warring States divination, however, was more structured and mechanically regulated than that of the Shang and Western Zhou periods. The auspiciousness of a date did not depend on the whimsical "will" of the gods or the ancestors, or on the diviner's interpretations, but on the mechanical allocation of the twelve branches, which were thought to form an essential part of the cosmic system according to which the universe operates.

The cosmic order was in turn associated with the cultural memory of archaic and mythological events. Although gods and spirits were still part of the cultural construction of taboos in everyday life, their role was limited to that of a cultural model for people to emulate. The lower parts of Strips 37 to 40 from Jiudian explain why some dates are inauspicious for certain activities:

> On the five dates that contain *zi* [as their branch in a sixty-day cycle], one should not carry out a great affair. It will not be successful. It will destroy one's body, and one will incur great disasters to oneself, and the disaster will extend to one's eldest son. In the five dates that contain *mao*, one should not carry out great affairs; God ordered Yi to deliver fire to the Great Yu. [On the five dates that contain] *wu*, one should not plant trees. On the five dates that contain *hai*, one should not nurture the six kinds of animals, because this is the day when God ordered the slaughter of the six kinds of animals.[50]

The first taboo on the *zi* dates plays with the multiple meanings of the character *zi*, which can refer to both the first of the twelve branches and to "son." The most interesting taboos are the second and third on the *mao* and *hai* dates, which are based on two legends hinted at in the transmitted classics. In *Mencius*, the mythological sage-emperor Shun ordered his official Yi to help the Great Yu to pacify the flooded realm by burning the forest and killing the animals.[51] No duodenary branches were mentioned in the *Mencius* text, but, in the Jiudian strips, the branches of the dates of these mythological events became the rationale for taboos in daily life. Similarly, cultural memory plays out in the diagram of *genshan* (*Genshan tu* 艮山圖), a hemerological diagram excavated from the Shuihudi Qin tomb. Certain dates are not auspicious for travel because "this was the day when the Great Yu departed": "If you go on a journey, you will never be able to return."[52]

Many other methods were used in the selection of an auspicious date for travel.[53] Special dates determined by the calendrical combinations of the ten stems and twelve branches determined potential success. For example, in the five agents (*wuxing*) cosmology, water, wood, earth, fire, and metal each manifested through the five cosmic elements, on their designated dates or periods of potency.[54] The branch *wu* in Strip 39 quoted above belongs to the element of "fire." That is why one should not plant trees, because trees belong to the "wood" element, which is overcome by "fire." On "earth" dates, the same logic follows. It would be bad to travel because dust (an "earth" element) will be in its most violent condition, making death likely.

Another date designated as bad for travel (including for the "grand journey") is "the day on which the Red God is in charge" (*Chidi lin ri*) and will punish people with catastrophe and misfortune; almost all activities are advised against on this day.[55] Auspices for travel could change according to the time of day, which was divided into four periods (dawn, noon, dusk, and midnight), and each season and direction, in conjunction with the movement of the calendar, affected fortune as well. This technique for determining auspicious dates for travel is elaborated in later *Xingde* and the so-called *Shifa* texts from Mawangdui, which include a cycle of spirits who formed part of the cosmocalendrical plan of the otherworld and with whom a traveler must deal.[56]

As important as divining the timing for setting off on a journey was divining the timing for the homecoming (*guiji* 歸忌). As Wang Zijin has calculated, if we follow the Qin daybooks from Shuihudi, there are altogether fourteen types of taboos, and 165 days in a year are bad for travel in one way or another.[57] Contradictions and inconsistencies abound in the divination. People of the Warring States period certainly understood the contradictory interplay among the different arts of calculation and may have employed magical performances and rituals in part to resolve these contradictions.[58]

Conceptions of Tame and Wild Space

The expansion of geographic knowledge of the outside world during the Warring States period enhanced the contrast between the tame, domestic sphere and the wild, outside world. Awareness of the distinction between these two realms, a kind of "cosmic consciousness,"[59] reinforced the ethnocentric cosmology of the universe[60] by setting the world of the afterlife in peripheral regions, in the remote, cosmologically marginal territories of otherness beyond the cultural core of early China.[61]

In daybooks, this distinction between tame and wild spaces manifests in several ways. First, travel in general was divided into two types: short-distance trips that fell within the domestic realm of a city or a town, such as brief working trips (*xingzuo* 行作); and trips that included ventures into the wild, such as long-distance travel (*yuanxing* 遠行), long-term travel (*jiuxing* 久行 or *changxing* 長行), and traveling into the wilds of the four quarters (*zhi sifang yewai*).

A second distinction concerned road rituals. Each type of travel had its own road rituals. The rituals associated with everyday movements were much simpler than those associated with extended journeys. For a short business trip, a quick reference, such as the "Instant Guide for the Great Yu" (Yu xuyu), was often consulted. But for long-distance travel, elaborate rituals and sacrifices to the deities in charge of travel (*changxing* 常行 or *da changing* 大常行) were often conducted.

Third, the location of the road rituals often marked the borders of two realms. For example, the daybooks from both Shuihudi and Fangmatan identify the location for performing the "Pace of Yu" as the area immediately outside the state gate (i.e., passes or walls; *bangmen* 邦門) or the city or town gate (*yimen* 邑門). These distinctions and locations for the "Pace of Yu" suggest that city and town gates served as thresholds, liminal points of departure, demarcating the two realms (in fact, the Shuihudi text mentions the word *kun*, "the sill of the gate"): the tame world where daily and familiar activities took place and the wild world, which was strange, dangerous, and uncertain.

The classic description of these two spheres is found in the "Summons of the Soul" from the *Songs of the South*.[62] The departed soul is instructed not to go to the east, the south, the west, or the north, and not to go up to Heaven or down to Earth, the Dark Capital, but to "enter the gate of the city," to come back to the sweet home of the former dwelling. The contrast between the tame, sweet, and peaceful home and the wild, grotesque, and perilous outside world is dramatic and has prompted some scholars to conclude that, beginning in the Warring States period, the "happy home" was the only destination for the departed soul and that the tombs were constructed as replicas of the real home.[63] However, the Warring States practice of constructing tombs as replicas of houses is a continuation of the funerary practice of decorating coffins, which dates to the late Western Zhou period.[64] The features of a tomb that invoke a house are part of the construction of a tame space—an old haunt with familiar objects—where the departed soul might prefer to linger. In addition, the examples of houselike construction at Yinshan or the underground palace of the tomb of the Marquis Yi of Zeng are only isolated cases in the Warring States period; these features suggest directions of development, but the idea of the tomb as a "happy home" was not yet prevalent.

Furthermore, in the Warring States religious pantheon, as indicated in the Baoshan sacrificial records, there exist pairs of deities—one in the tame space and the other in the wild. The offering lists name sets of deities: *Ye dizhu* 野地主 (Strip 207) and *Gong dizhu* 宮地主 (Strips 202, 207); *Houtu* 后土 (Strips 213, 215, 237, 243) and *Gong houtu* 宮后土 (Strips 214, 233); and *Xing* 行 (Strip 208) and *Gong xing* 宮行 (Strip 210). Most scholars consider these to be different names for the same deity.[65] Yet both *Ye dizhu* and *Gong dizhu* appear on Baoshan Strip 207 as two separate spirit entities.[66] The tame (*gong*; also "inside," "palace," "house," or "home") and wild (*ye*) distinction also appears in the sacrificial records excavated from such contemporaneous tombs as Tomb 1 at Wangshan (Strips 28, 109, 115),[67] Tomb 1 at Tianxingguan, and Tomb 99 at Qinjiazui.[68] The distinction between the tame and the wild applies exclusively to the terrestrial realm.[69]

The distinction also informs our understanding of the logic of the early Chinese pantheon. In recent years, with the discovery of the types of sacrificial records discussed in chapter 1, scholars have attempted to reconstruct the early Chinese pantheon using a tripartite framework of celestial gods (*tianshen*), terrestrial spirits (*diqi*), and ancestors and ghosts (*rengui*) derived from transmitted texts.[70] This tripartite classification, however, does not fit with the wild and tame (i.e., the inner and the outer) division of spirits outlined above. In the middle Warring States–period tomb discovered at Geling in Xincai (Henan), one strip refers to the spirit world collectively as "the ghosts and spirits of the above and the below, the inner and the outer" ([*shang*] *xia neiwai guishen* [上]下内外鬼神).[71] Thus, the terms "ghosts and spirits of . . . the inner and the outer" referred to the deities of the tame and the wild worlds.

The spheres of the tame and the wild and the boundaries between them are relative, fluid, and socially constructed. They are certainly not fixed on a specific place, such as a house, and they include many other tokens of familiarity and comfort. The relationship between these two realms might be conceived as a concentric structure with the person or home at the center and rings of increasing wildness, from town to city, state, and ultimately the universe, moving outward from there; any one layer is relatively safer than the one outside it.

The early development of cosmic diagrams, maps, and mapping in early China is relevant here.[72] Spatial relationships and a sense of control are at the heart of the distinction between tame and wild spaces. Previous studies of early Chinese cartography and diagrams have been narrowly focused on scientific achievements, especially their mathematical significance,[73] but the social and religious aspects of early maps and diagrams have been largely overlooked. The fact that the earliest extant "architectural diagram" excavated from the tomb of King Cuo (d. ca. 310 BCE) of Zhongshan and his consorts at Sanji in Pingshan County, Hebei, is a plan of a royal mausoleum should alert us to the possible significance of the role of maps and diagrams in the afterlife.[74]

A number of maps have been found among grave goods: a set of seven maps drawn on four wooden boards was excavated from Qin Tomb 1 at Fangmatan (ca. 239 BCE) in Tianshui City, Gansu,[75] and silk maps were excavated from Han Tomb 3 at Mawangdui (ca. 168 BCE) (fig. 5.2).[76] The maps illuminate how space was conceived while testifying to the importance of maps as burial objects. Moreover, the maps display sophisticated mapping skills and are organized around important geographical features such as mountain ranges, river flows, populous settlements and economic centers, and even roads. The maps also cover fairly extensive territories.[77] Calculations for a two-part map from Fangmatan suggest that it depicted an area of 47,520 square (modern) *li*.[78] Interestingly enough, two copies of daybooks were found in the same tomb, along with a written story of a man named Dan returning to life after being released by underworld officials in 297 BCE.[79] The mention of the underworld bureaucracy, which testifies to the wide circulation of common religious ideas during the Warring States period, implies that this account is compatible with the Jiudian incantation.

Similarly, maps were discovered in Tomb 3 at Mawangdui, along with hemerological texts concerning travel.[80] The Mawangdui silk map covers a large area, includ-

Fig. 5.2. Topographic map excavated from Tomb 3 at Mawangdui, Changsha City, Hunan. Second century BCE. Early Western Han period. Hunan Provincial Museum.

ing parts of present-day Hunan, Guangdong, and Guangxi. The maps are defined by their depictions of river flows and emphasize riverine transport and military mobilization. The occupant of Tomb 3 at Mawangdui, a young male, was said to be a military official and had probably frequented the places noted on the map. Given the relatively high degree of detail, these maps suggest a population traversing a tame landscape. At the same time, the seven maps from Fangmatan can be understood more abstractly as projecting a landscape based on three different perspectives: geographic terrain, administrative zones, and economic or military affairs.[81] Thus, in another way the maps represent a conceptual ordering of space, a utilitarian cosmology that is reinforced, in the case of Fangmatan, by the inclusion of a wooden board painted with the cosmological TLV motif, representing another, more remote layer of spatial ordering.[82] Cosmological constructions during the Warring States period went along with a concern for the abodes of the dead,[83] and the emblematic placement of cosmographic motifs on coffins, mortuary furniture, and grave goods can be viewed as an attempt to deal with perceived anxiety in the space of the unknown.[84] Another example of a map serving as a postmortem guide is the fragmentary yellow "paper" (2.6 x 5.6 cm) discovered inside a coffin on the chest of the dead body in Tomb 5 at Fangmatan (dated to between 179–141 BCE).[85]

These cosmographic motifs and cartographic maps suggest a way of dealing with the unknown and of creating a vision that extends beyond the local. Thus, temporal progress can be mapped in terms of orbits and cycles, and physical surroundings can be arranged around registers of social organization that impact how the terrain takes shape. Maps may be understood as subjective representations of some reality: "All advantages and limitations of maps derive from the degree to which maps reduce and generalize reality, compress or expand shapes and distances, and portray selected phenomena with signs that communicate, without necessarily resembling, visible or invisible characteristics of the landscape."[86] On this basis, it perhaps follows logically that conceptual orderings of space provide "an insulated vision" of reality. The map user is able to deal with space that is already tamed, even if only mentally.[87]

Travel, however, upsets this insulation: it tests and challenges the validity of the mapped vision. For a Warring States traveler, road rituals were important, providing, in a sense, an additional level of mapping and map projection. But before discussing road rituals in the afterlife, we must first consider the instruments of these rituals, that is, travel paraphernalia from Warring States tombs.

Travel Paraphernalia

The great challenge posed by recent archaeological discoveries lies in understanding the motivation for burying artifacts and texts in late Warring States and early Han tombs. Some artifacts and texts were probably placed in tombs to note personal preferences (either of the deceased or the bereaved), to mark social prestige,[88] and to serve as tokens of immortality in the afterlife shared by the community at large. Because of the diversity of the materials excavated from tombs, scholars have yet to propose a uniform theory. However, it is conceivable that *The Travel of Mu the Son of Heaven* (Mu tianzi zhuan), for example, was buried for "the purpose of providing the deceased ruler of Wei with a guide to the Nether world, or to paradise, like the dead in ancient Egypt were provided with a copy of the Book of the Dead."[89] Similarly, the materials related to travel—daybooks, cosmographic diagrams and motifs, cartographic maps, and travel paraphernalia—were put in the tomb to direct departed souls on their postmortem journeys. In what follows, we use the inventory list discovered in Tomb 2 at Baoshan to explore possible motivations for burying certain artifacts.

The Baoshan tomb contained a set of twenty-seven bamboo strips (Strips 251–77) that list and classify the objects deposited in the tomb either in fact or only in name (fig. 5.3).[90] Among them, seventeen strips are complete and range from 68 to 72.6 centimeters in length; the other strips are fragments, some of which can be pieced together according to their contents and writing styles. The strips list elaborately decorated chariots, ritual vessels and utensils, prepared food, and other funerary offerings. Those recording chariots and sacrificial instruments (Strips 265–77) constituted one group because they all have three notches through which to fix strings—the function of which is to weave the strips together to form a book—and, as an additional link, they were written in a similar style. The remaining strips, with the exception of Strip 255, which has two notches, are either fragmentary or have no clear sign of carving but have a similar writing style.[91] Therefore, it is possible that two books of inventories were interred in the Baoshan tomb. These strips are buried with corresponding artifacts in the eastern, western, and southern compartments. The inventories divide the grave goods into at least four categories: chariots used in the funeral; bronze and wooden objects used in grand ancestral sacrifices;[92] bronze objects for use in the sacrificial hall[93] and food in the sacrificial hall, including the bamboo food containers there; and finally, paraphernalia gathered for use in travel.[94]

The grave furnishings in the Baoshan tomb are typical of those in a late Warring States high-elite tomb. The tomb contains sets of ritual bronze vessels used in ancestral sacrifices as well as other symbols of social status, such as chariots, continuing the earlier Shang and Western Zhou aristocratic traditions. In addition, the tomb has new categories of grave goods and artistic innovations. The medium-size tombs excavated at Zhaojiahu in Dangyang and at Jiudian and Yutaishan in Jiangling (all of which are in Hubei) show that the new categories, in particular personal belongings, household articles, and food provisions, gradually came to be associated with the traditional sets of ritual vessels.[95] The new artifacts comprised weapons, utensils for dress (combs, mirrors, and belt hooks[96]), musical instruments for personal entertainment (*se*-zithers), utensils for eating and drinking (including earcups and boxes), bamboo cases, mats, pillows, and fans. It is not coincidental that in the Baoshan inventories almost all of these new categories were listed in the section on paraphernalia for travel.

These four categories of objects have unique religious implications: the chariots are symbols of the tomb occupant's social status, and the ritual vessels and food buried in tombs may have been intended for the dead to use in offering sacrifices to their own ancestors in the otherworld. The last section of the Baoshan inventory, "paraphernalia used for travel," suggests that the objects in this group—including caps, shoes, combs, mirrors, pillows, mats, hairpins, lamps, a folding bed, a *se*-zither, and fans—while often labeled as mundane "personal belongings" or "everyday utensils" in archaeological reports and scholarly literature, may actually have religious meanings and serve as the paraphernalia to be used in a journey in the afterlife.[97] Because the bamboo strips are fragmentary, and because many philological issues,

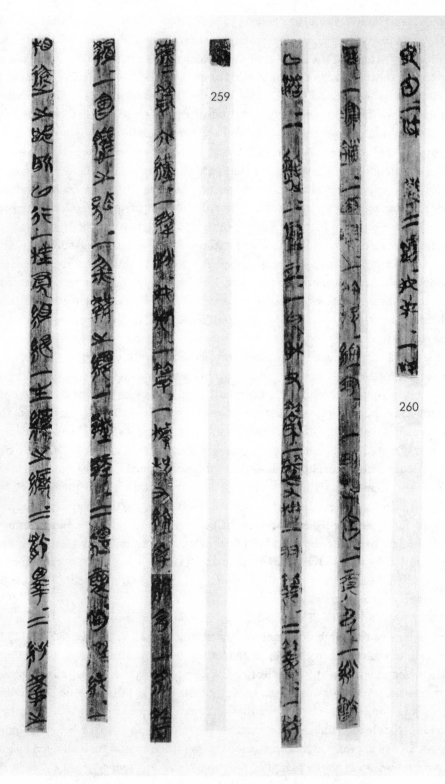

Fig. 5.3. Grave goods inventory recording the travel paraphernalia, excavated from Tomb 2 at Baoshan, Jingmen City, Hubei. Ca. 316 BCE. Warring States period.

especially the detailed descriptions of the grave goods, have yet to be resolved, our understanding of this group of objects is limited. Based on comparative evidence from other contemporaneous tomb inventories in the Chu region, however, we can say that these objects primarily provided basic travel gear and accessories for the dead. By giving the deceased a proper interment, the living descendants played a vital role in determining the deceased's postmortem fate. Furthermore, tomb furnishings, including objects for warding off evil influences, provided the possibility of intercession on behalf of the deceased in the event his or her fate hung in the balance during the postmortem journey.

Although objects classified in the inventory as "paraphernalia used for travel" were originally everyday household utensils, in the religious context of the otherworldly journey they acquired religious meanings, such as the apotropaic function of aiding and protecting the departed soul on the road.[98] Ritual and magic were facets of everyday life.[99] Both ancient and contemporary universal rituals include a class of sacrifices called rites of aversion. In ancient Greek religion, the apotropaic ritual is especially old and basic:[100] "I give in order that you go away," *do ut abeas*, a Latin formula coined by modern scholars to describe the basic dynamics of apotropaic sacrifice. In ancient China, as the Baoshan divinatory and sacrificial records indicate, apotropaic rituals were essential to religious developments during the Warring States period.

Of the various paraphernalia for travel, the item that most obviously has an apotropaic function is the lamp.[101] Bronze and ceramic lamps, such as the bronze lamps excavated from the Jiuliandun and Baoshan tombs, became indispensable tomb furnishings in the Warring States period (fig. 5.4). In particular, the one discovered in Tomb 2 at Wangshan in Jiangling County, Hubei, in which a human lamp-bearer rides upon a camel[102] (fig. 5.5), reflects the popular concern that on their postmortem journey the dead would travel to the northwest in darkness. Early literary sources such as the "Summons of the Soul" in the *Songs of the South* make clear that the Chu people imagined the west (and northwest) to be a barren, dark, and harsh place:

> O soul, come back! For the west holds many perils.
> The Moving Sands stretch on for a hundred leagues.
> You will be swept into the Thunder's Chasm, and dashed in pieces, unable to help
>   yourself;
> And even should you chance to escape from that, beyond is the empty desert,
> And red ants as huge as elephants and wasps as big as gourds.
> The five grains do not grow there; dry stalks are the only food;
> And the earth there scorches men up; there is nowhere to look for water;
> And you will drift there forever, with nowhere to go in that vastness.
> O soul, come back! You cannot long stay there.[103]

Fig. 5.4. Bronze lamp excavated from Tomb 2 at Baoshan, Jingmen City, Hubei. H. 16.3 cm. Ca. 316 BCE. Warring States period. Hubei Provincial Museum.

People in the Chu region must have heard stories, real or fanciful, about desert hardships and the camel's survival skills. Mythical animals, such as the winged beast (fig. 5.6) and the bird-snake (fig. 5.7a and fig. 5.7b), that came from the west often appeared on lamps and other grave objects.[104] These animals' imagined apotropaic function could help the deceased to avoid evil influence on its journey to the northwest.

Another example of the apotropaic function of travel paraphernalia is the *xie* cap (*xieguan* 觟冠). The *xie* cap is a hat with a horn on top. The inventories (Strip 62) from both Tomb 2 at Wangshan and Tomb 2 at Baoshan list two *xie* caps as grave goods. In the Baoshan tomb, a horn carved with three dragons was discovered along with a wig, four jade and bone ornaments, and a miniature sculpture of mythical animals (fig. 5.8).

In addition, such personal belongings as clothing, headdresses, and jewelry enjoy

Fig. 5.5. Bronze lamp excavated from Tomb 2 at Wangshan, Jiangling County, Hubei. H. 19.2 cm. Warring States period. Hubei Provincial Museum.

an intimate relationship with the human body and thus can become part of one's identity. In the ritual of aversion, such personal belongings often serve as substitutes for the human body and were offered to deities to whom the individual was devoted. According to the Baoshan divinatory and sacrificial records, four types of objects were used as offerings: jade ornaments such as rings (*huan*), small rings (*xiaohuan*), slit rings (*jue*), discs (*bi*), and pendants (*hu*); clothing and decoration, including caps and cap strings; wine and food; and animals. The use of jade pendants as sacrificial offerings was also mentioned in other paleographical materials.

These quotidian objects could have had deep apotropaic meanings.[105] Clothing, caps, rings, jade pendants, and so forth were used as material tokens that could substitute for, or at least relate to, the deceased. The personal belongings in the Baoshan and other Chu tombs may have an analogous role in preparing the deceased for potential emergency situations on the road in the afterlife.

Fig. 5.6. Winged beast discovered in King Cuo's tomb at Sanji in Pingshan County, Hebei. H. 24 cm, L. 40 cm; weight 11.45 kg. Middle Warring States period. Hebei Provincial Museum.

In the early literature on the spirit journey, several scenes related to the use of travel paraphernalia are worth noting. In the poem "The Goddess of Xiang" (Xiangjun) the poet seeks the goddess but cannot reach her:

> I throw my thumb-ring (*jue*) into the river.
> I leave my girdle-gem (*pei*) in the bay of the Li.
> Sweet pollia I've plucked in the little islet.
> To send to my far-away Beloved.[106]

The thumb ring and girdle gem are here cast into the river as offerings to the goddess below. In the *Zuo Commentary*, we read a related story: the Chu nobleman Cheng Dechen (aka Zi Yu, d. 632), when travelling outside the Chu territory, dreamed that the local god, the spirit of the Yellow River, demanded sacrificial offerings. The objects of this illicit request were his cap and cap strings.[107] Moreover, a set of clothing was used in the ritual of calling back the departed soul before the start of funerary rites.[108]

Other objects frequently excavated from Warring States tombs and long regarded as personal, quotidian items (e.g., shoes, garment hooks, lamps, mats, beds, fans,

Fig. 5.7a. Bronze lamp excavated from King Cuo's tomb at Sanji in Pingshan County, Hebei. H. 47.5 cm, D. 57 cm. Middle Warring States period. Hebei Provincial Museum.

Fig. 5.7b *(below)*. Detail of the bird-snake on the back of the turtle at the bottom of the bronze lamp.

Fig. 5.8. Horn carved with intertwining snakes, excavated from Tomb 2 at Baoshan, Jingmen City, Hubei (M2: 431). Ca. 316 BCE. Warring States period. Hubei Provincial Museum.

daggers, bags, boxes, and so forth) are listed in the travel paraphernalia section of the Baoshan inventory. These everyday objects, through the casting of spells or particular ritual ceremonies, may have taken on a religious function—as amulets or talismans that could ward off evil influences and protect the deceased person's soul—in the construction of a domesticated space in the wilderness.

In sum, by the mid-Warring States period, travel paraphernalia had become part of burial furnishings. We do not know whether the occupants of all tombs that contain such travel gear suffered violent deaths. More detailed analyses are needed to clarify the connection, if any, between tomb furnishings and the treatment of the dead. But based on cases from Baoshan, Wangshan, and elsewhere, it seems that travel paraphernalia appeared in tombs to facilitate the postmortem journey of the deceased to their new abode.

Road Rituals

If ritual is a transformative process,[109] then we must acknowledge its function as a prescriptive model of a preordained path of action; in this way, ritual can serve as a sort of map for social behavior. Indeed, ritual is praised as such in numerous early Chinese texts. Owing to problems of archeological preservation and the role of chance in archaeological discovery, comparatively few maps and almanacs have been discovered. But based on the pattern of these discoveries—they appear in both rich and middle-class tombs—it seems that from the fourth century through the second century BCE the practice of including maps, almanacs, and other travel gear among the burial goods was fairly common. The texts and objects deposited in tombs can accordingly be understood as contributions to a postmortem ritual journey. The Shuihudi daybook advises that when setting out on a journey, the traveler, after leaving the city gates, should stop and perform a magico-religious rite known as the Pace of Yu: "When traveling, on reaching the threshold-bar of the capital gate, perform the Pace of Yu thrice. Advance on pace. Call out, '*Gû! I dare make a declaration. Let so-and-so [to be filled in with the name of the traveler] travel and not suffer odium; he first acts as Yu to clear the road.' Immediately draw five lines on the ground. Dig up the soil from the center of the lines and put it in your bosom."[110] The Pace of Yu was also a magical strategy for exorcising demons and curing warts, as indicated in medical texts excavated in Tomb 3 at Mawangdui. The ritual involves invoking the name of Yu, a mythological hero with supernatural powers, to rid the road ahead of all demons and calamities while either marking the earth with five-stroke diagrams or throwing a talisman of Yu (Yufu) onto the ground while performing the three steps of Yu and calling out an invocation.[111] This process both divines the road and exorcises it; certainly, the idea is that the coming road will be without disaster. At the beginning of a journey, this road ritual is referred to as *zu* 祖 or *zudao* 祖道 ("the sacrifice to the spirits of the road") in received pre-Qin literature, such as *Book of Poetry* and the *Zuo Commentary*.[112]

One example of a sacrifice preceding a journey is noted in the *Zuo Commentary* as occurring in the seventh year (535 BCE) of Lord Zhao of the state of Lu, before the lord went on a diplomatic trip on the invitation of the rising power, King Ling of Chu (r. 540–529). Lord Zhao anticipated a difficult and dangerous journey. After he dreamed of his deceased father Lord Xiang performing the sacrifice to the spirits of the road, he hesitated, uncertain about his departure. One of his officials persuaded him to embark on the journey by saying, "Go! Our former Lord (i.e., Lord Xiang) never went to Chu. That is why he had once dreamed of the Duke of Zhou performing the sacrifice to the spirits of the road and leading him. Then Lord Xiang went to Chu, and he performed the sacrifice to lead you."[113] In both cases the Duke of Zhou and Lord Xiang, as the divine protectors of the state of Lu, intervened for the sake of the reigning lord on the eve of his dangerous journey.[114] Thus, the sacrifice to the spirits of the road is both an offering to the departed and an exorcism to ask for the ancestral spirits' protection.

It is significant that, in the "Shi sangli" chapter of the *Protocols of Ceremonies*, from the preparation of the grave goods to the last meal served to the deceased (*daqiandian* 大遣奠), death is conceived as the beginning of a long imaginary journey, which is the central image employed in mortuary rituals. The medieval scholar Shen Yue (411–513 CE) noted that the sacrifice to the spirits of the road was performed not only for real journeys but also before the funeral procession from the ancestral temple to the grave. In the *Protocols of Ceremonies*, too, before the funeral procession sets out to the burial site, an assistant "asks the time of the sacrifice to the spirits of the road," and then "for the sacrifice to the spirits of the road, the hearse is turned [and oriented facing outward]" in preparation to set off for travel.[115] The sacrifice to the spirits of the road in the funerary rites, which is performed in the courtyard of the ancestral temple when the deceased is about to be buried, resembles the sacrifice to the spirits of the road performed when the living set out for a journey.[116]

Although the "Shi sangli" chapter does not spell out other details of the ceremony, the "Pinli" chapter details how the road sacrifice was carried out before an official mission. When leaving the city gate, at the beginning of the journey, "the traveler laid down a sacrifice to the spirit of the road, offering wine and dried meat, and then drinking the wine beside the offerings."[117] This action marked the beginning of a journey. Soil was heaped to make an image of a mountain, and the sacrificial animal (usually a dog or a goat) was laid on top of it; after drinking the wine, the traveler would mount the chariot and run over the mound. This ritual is rooted in the five agents (*wuxing*) cosmology: Earth, which is adverse to travel, is overcome.

The Mawangdui medical texts record another magical performance related to the "Pace of Yu," which also alludes to a road ritual. The text reads: "When stopping for the night on the road, one should call out: 'South of Mount Tai . . . city walls, do not collapse, [close] with a golden bolt.' Immediately, [one should] perform the Pace of Yu thrice, and use a two-inch-long thorn [*chanjing*] to draw a circle." Although the text has been severely damaged, both Harper and Liu Zenggui have argued that this road ritual can be reconstructed if read alongside a passage from *The Master Embracing Simplicity* (Baopuzi).[118] In the chapter that details the travel paraphernalia employed when passing through mountains, the traveler in the wilds is advised to use a sword to mark out a square in the earth and then to call out: "The Yin side of Mount Heng, the Yang side of Mount Tai, thieves and bandits, do not arise; tigers and wolves, do not approach; walls and ramparts that are not intact, seal [yourself] with a metal bolt."[119] This ritual can be explained as symbolically recreating the protective walls of a city by transforming through invocation the marked earth into a tame space.

In the *Protocols of Ceremonies*, the road ritual for the departed is presented as a normal procedure in the funerary rites, suggesting that the deceased must journey to reach their abode. As the Jiudian incantation implies, the war dead would reside "at the edge of Fu Mountain and in the wilds of Buzhou." We do not know whether this indicates a change in belief, or if, when the *Protocols of Ceremonies* was written down, the abode of the war dead had already become the land of the dead in general. From these road rituals, however, we can glimpse how people manipulated magical powers to create a tame space. Each road ritual contributes to a larger concept of travel within specific physical and temporal boundaries. In a sense, both rituals and maps, or ritualized maps, delimit travel; that is, they ensure that, while traveling, one can remain oriented through the proper spatial associations. Through such rituals as the Mawangdui text quoted above describes, one can always be stationed within the tamed city walls; departure is always mitigated by arrival and by additional levels of insulation.

THE NOTION OF THE OTHERWORLDLY JOURNEY probably dates to the formative stage of Chinese civilization. We certainly find it reflected in oracle-bone and bronze inscriptions. In those early times, the dead, usually the royal ancestors who traveled to "the place of the High God," were assumed to return frequently to visit the living. The transformation of religious ideas in the Warring States period had several dimensions. The Jiudian incantation shows that the abode of the war dead was relocated to the northwest part of the universe; reaching it involved an otherworldly journey. Daybooks such as those excavated from tombs at Jiudian, Shuihudi, and Fangmatan provide us with a better understanding of how travel, time, and space were conceived in the Warring States period and the early empires. It seems that, despite sophisticated maps and cosmographic diagrams, travel was conceived as movement into the unknown. Given the potential dangers of the road, an overriding concern expressed in the calendrical auspices is the fear of becoming lost or dying (*wang*). Another source of concern is departure without return. This overlap, both metaphoric and actual, between travel and death could shed new light on the much-debated phrase in *Daode jing*, "*si er bu wang zhe shou*" 死而不亡者壽, which probably should be translated as "Those who die but are not lost have longevity (i.e., immortality)."[120] In the case of the Jiudian incantation discussed in chapter 4, the hope was that the director of the war dead, Wuyi, would let the deceased return to receive sacrifices. Thus, feeding the ghosts, although they were already under the jurisdiction of Wuyi, would domesticate them and thereby make them less likely to harm the living.

The late Warring States and early Han conceptions of the afterlife incorporate ideas of the existence of the soul after death, some type of land of the dead, and a postmortem journey of the soul beyond its state of entombment. Our data force us, however, to reconsider the conventional wisdom about the tomb as the "happy home" of the dead. Instead, the tomb in part defines the nature of the otherworldly journey: whether conceived of as a way station or as a starting point, its accumulated chariots and other travel paraphernalia orient the soul in time and space as it undertakes its journey; and the tomb texts are provided as travel documents to orient the deceased within a social, political, and cosmic order. As a temporary resting place or median point, the elaborately furnished tomb conforms to the staged journeys and was likely a ritually created or transformed holding zone for a traveler in the midst of a vague and uncertain wilderness.

The various practices and objects associated with road rituals and travel paraphernalia suggest a process by which the unfamiliar or the unknown is conceptualized and then integrated into an existing familiar framework. Geographic maps can provide a sense of insulation. Most important, perhaps, is the belief that ritual has the power to transform the journey itself, to create a road in the image of its conception, or to create a patch of earth in the image of a walled city. The "Pace of Yu" ritual transforms the performer (momentarily at least) into an embodiment of Yu himself. At the same time, ritual transformation is undertaken with the expectation that a definite outcome will be achieved: the traveler will reach his intended destination; the soul will reach the underworld. Ritual, in this sense, assumes movement between two distinct points, two states of being. One might understand stepping outside a gate or moving beyond a boundary as itself a transformation. Ritual, thus, serves as a map for transformation.

The examples studied here must be treated cautiously in view of the wide range of practices and beliefs that co-existed; sometimes discrepancies surface even within the same burial. Tombs are multidimensional entities, and no one line of reasoning is likely to do full justice to every feature. The data from the Chu tombs, however, do suggest either that the concept of the tomb as the deceased person's everlasting home is not quite right or that a crucial shift in belief systems moved the location of the afterlife away from the tomb and toward a new site—the cosmic destination of the northwest. Moreover, we must expand our understanding of what constituted travel objects to include not only the most obvious items, such as chariots and geographic maps, but also divining boards and calendrical texts such as the daybooks; the latter were crucial for determining when travel might occur and predicting how it would go, for supporting administrative communication between this world and the next.

Scholars have questioned the connection between the otherworldly cult of the dead and the visions of immortal paradises that developed in the middle of the Western Han dynasty.[121] Is there a link between the transcendental paradises where immortals reside and the imagined afterlife? I have discussed conceptions of the afterlife before the middle of the Western Han, that is, before the rise of transcendental paradises or the idea of local destinations for the dead, such as Mount Tai and Liangfu, and have drawn connections between these two phenomena. During the late Warring States period there arose a new conception of the afterlife that shares features with that of the transcendental paradise: both journeys have a cosmic destination in the northwest, either Mount Buzhou or Mount Kunlun; both have similar road rituals and travel processions; both use tokens of immortality as travel paraphernalia. In this new conception of the world beyond, the soul of a person who died from unnatural causes, whether slain in battle or felled by mishap, would take an imaginary journey through a dangerous underworld, a journey that began at the tomb—a liminal point of departure—and eventually reached a final cosmic destination in the northwest of the universe. This conception likely provided a model or template for later notions of otherworldly journeys and transcendental paradises.[122]

Conclusion

OUR FASCINATION WITH ARCHAEOLOGY, as we hold ancient objects in our hands and behold ancient handwritings, comes from the sense that the remote past is close to us, vivid once more. When archaeologists open a tomb and investigate its contents layer by layer, they are reversing the process by which the deceased was buried and the objects interred more than two thousand years ago. But a challenge remains: How do we see these objects and read these texts as the ancients would have seen and read them? There is an inevitable loss of color and feeling. When the wooden covers of a waterlogged Chu tomb are lifted, lacquered wares, floating on the water, shine as if new; once exposed to air, however, their gleaming surfaces begin to tarnish and crack. They must either be moistened or submerged immediately and taken to conservation laboratories for preservation. The discussion of the Jiulian-dun materials at the beginning of this book included several photos of the excavation that give a sense of the excitement as well as the messiness of the archaeological site. The conditions under which modern archaeologists work are complex: the mass media searches for entertainment, and the amateur demands stories and meanings. Such popular understandings exist against a backdrop of stereotypes and biases accumulated over centuries in transmitted texts and later commentaries. This book attempts to locate these bronze ritual vessels, lacquerware, and silk paintings in both their archaeological and mortuary-religious contexts and to glimpse the emic perspective on the religious beliefs and funerary rites practiced in the Chu region during the Warring States period and the early empires.

My interpretative strategy has been to prioritize archaeological, art historical, and epigraphic materials over transmitted texts. The most profound insights come from exploring the religious texts excavated from Chu tombs in the last forty years. I have taken advantage of the latest developments in the paleographical studies of Chu bamboo and silk manuscripts. My analysis of the divinatory and sacrificial records recovered from tombs at Baoshan, Wangshan, Tianxingguan, Qinjiazui, and Geling has disclosed curious, and long overlooked, changes in the religious pantheon and early Chinese conceptions of the dead.

I began by reflecting on the changing attitudes toward death and the dead in the Warring States period, a time of protracted warfare and increasing violence. In the earlier Shang and Western Zhou periods, the dead were mainly conceived of collectively as benevolent but anonymous ancestors. In the Spring and Autumn period, however, the religious importance of the ancestors began to decline. At the same time, the dead came to be considered primarily as individuals and as threatening, and a previously undocumented group of individuals who died violently or without posterity appeared in the Warring States religious pantheon. The notion of violent death as bad death, new theories of the body and soul, and the rise of the afterlife all emerged in the historical context of the political struggles of the Spring and Autumn period. The circumstances surrounding the deaths of these individuals prevented them from being transformed into venerable ancestors. Instead, they were thought to haunt and menace the realm of the living. This fearful attitude toward the dead eventually manifested as an ambivalence about the ancestors, as reflected in the tie-breaking ritual of burying numinous artifacts in tombs.

Based on the view of religion as a social system of communication, this book explores the spatial implications of these new attitudes about the dead. The shift in burial style from the vertical pits of the Shang and Zhou periods to the horizontal chambers of the Qin and Han periods reflects increasing efforts to pacify the dead by creating accessible and hospitable spaces for the cult of the dead in tombs. The emergence of a "personalized death" affected not only how the early Chinese treated and buried the dead but also how they communicated with and managed the dead.

Visually, this new attitude manifested as anthropomorphic representations of the dead in the liminal stage. Human figures were generally not prominent subjects of early Chinese art, and the influence of image magic—images as tools for magical social control—discouraged anthropomorphic depictions of persons of high social status. In earlier periods, ancestral spirits were represented not through images but through an impersonator, that is, a junior member of the lineage. By the Warring States period, however, impersonators and communal ancestor cults had been replaced by household-based ancestral sacrifices, along with personalized representations of the dead in mortuary art. The hybrid representation of the fecundity god and the Grand One in the Chu region during the Warring States period and the early empires captured the fearful attitude toward both the dead and the gods.

The entombment of texts is characteristic of burials from the Warring States, Qin, and Han periods. Yet the texts found in Chu tombs of the Warring States elite—particularly the grave inventories and the official memorials addressed to the underground bureaucracy—were new genres of writing for the dead. The important role that writing played in communicating with the spiritual world manifested in the public reading of such inventories and in the interment of other philosophical, technical, and medical texts, as well as personal materials from the deceased's library, that might be useful in the afterlife. These works included a register of the names of individuals who attended the funeral and the gifts they presented to the deceased, a sign that death did not sever the personal relationship between the deceased and his or her immediate circle. Finally, Warring States tombs contained documents that the deceased was to use in his or her journey through the afterworld. These texts helped articulate early Chinese notions of the afterlife.

Archaeological evidence excavated from tombs in southern China suggests that a new model of the afterlife developed during the late Warring States period. According to this model, the deceased undertook an arduous otherworldly journey from the burial site to an imagined, cosmic destination called Mount Buzhou in the northwest, where dead individuals gathered to form bureaucratized communities. Images, texts, maps, and objects were entombed as travel paraphernalia outfitting the deceased for the journey. Furthermore, the funerary rites consisted, in part, of road rituals intended to ward off evil influences during the postmortem voyage. This vision of the world after death revises the conventional wisdom about the tomb as the "happy home" of the deceased and provides a new picture of the afterlife, as conceived before the emergence of transcendental paradises during the middle of the Western Han dynasty.

This book presents a synthetic account of early Chinese mortuary religion from an archaeological perspective. Combining historical, archaeological, art historical, and paleographic analysis, it explores a critical moment in the development of Chinese mortuary religion during the transition from the Warring States period to the early empires. The changes in religious and ritual practices were connected with tomb culture, particularly burial structure, grave goods, ritual representations, and mortuary ideology. Such changes had a great impact on the development of Chinese mortuary religion.

Chu in the south often arouses people's romantic imagination. As the last state to vehemently compete with Qin and to lose tragically to unification, Chu was considered "the road not taken" in the course of Chinese history, an unrealized alternative to the social, political, and artistic reality of imperial China. However, there is irony in the fact that careful scrutiny of the material and literary evidence points more to the roads' similarities than to their differences. Chu and its adjacent areas in southern China have contributed tremendously to the formation of early Chinese civilization.

Notes

Introduction

Epigraph: Schopen, "Burial *Ad Sanctos*," 114.

1   For different scholarly views on the starting date of the Warring States period, see Zhao Shouyan, "'Zhanguo' yingdang cong na yinian kaishi," 192–96; Lawton, *Chinese Art of the Warring States Period*, 9–10; Yang Kuan, *Zhanguo shi*, 2–5; Miao Wenyuan, *Zhanguo zhidu tongkao*, 1. For archaeological purposes, the most suitable date is ca. 450 BCE; see Falkenhausen, *Chinese Society*, 6–8. Here I take the tripartite division of the state of Jin in 453 BCE as the formal beginning of the Warring States period. This event marked the decline of the ancient polities and lineages that had dominated events during the previous Spring and Autumn period and heralded the social, political, economic, and religious changes that would culminate in the unification of China by the state of Qin in 221 BCE.

2   Hubei sheng wenwu kaogu yanjiusuo, "Hubei Zaoyang," 12.

3   Some scholars suggest that all elite Chu tombs had square, pyramid-like mounds, but because of natural erosion and manmade destruction, it is often difficult to tell whether they were square. Their current forms are often hemispheric. See Huang Xiaofen, *Han mu*, 177–78.

4   Hubei sheng wenwu kaogu yanjiusuo, "Hubei Zaoyang," 11.

5   There are several versions of the legend. In the village near the nine mounds live 225 households of about 900 villagers, most of them surnamed Zhao. They are the guardians of this historic cemetery. In 2000, tomb robbers attempted to loot Tumulus 3. The villagers discovered the theft and reported it to the authorities. In 2005, another group of tomb robbers conspired to raid at Tumulus 2, but the plan was soon discovered; eight tomb robbers were captured and prosecuted. See Liang Jun, "Jiuliandun gumu," 50–51.

6   Hu Yali, "Jiuliandun Chu mu," 16.

7   Hu Yali, "Jiuliandun Chu mu," 16–22.

8   Falkenhausen, *Chinese Society*, 371–72. The archaeologist Guo Dewei gave a number of 9,500 excavated Chu tombs in 1995 (*Chu xi muzang yanjiu*, 5); *Zhongguo Kaoguxue Liang Zhou juan* gave a different number of 6,000 excavated Chu tombs (348). Yang Quanxi gave a number of more than 8,000 excavated Chu tombs (*Chu wenhua*, 65). Certainly, an even larger number of Chu tombs has been identified, mainly in Hubei and Hunan.

9   The use of the greenish-white clay, a type of montmorillonite clay, as sealant was critical for the archaeological preservation of the tomb contents. A study of spore and pollen in

clay samples from Tomb 3 at Mawangdui indicates that the clay was not local to the site but was brought from other areas near Changsha where there were rich deposits of this type of clay; see Hu Jimin, "Changsha Mawangdui Han mu tiantu," 75–79.

10   For example, *Jiangling Mashan yihao Chu mu*; *Jiangling Yutaishan Chu mu*.

11   Xu Yongqing and He Huiqin, *Zhongguo gushi*, 18–23; Tang Weibin, Jian Min, and Wang Guan, "Zhenjing shijie," 20–23. Local tomb robbers dug up the female corpse from Tomb 1 at Guojiagang of the Warring States period in spring 1994; they were searching for treasures in this well-preserved Chu tomb and discarded the corpse in another opened tomb nearby. When this case was reported to the local police, the tomb robbers, most of them local peasants, were captured. Of these, three main culprits were sentenced to execution.

12   In 1980, Yu Weichao first presented the evolution of the "vertical pit-style" tombs (what he called "Zhouzhi," or "Zhou system") toward the "horizontal chamber-style" tombs ("Hanzhi," or "Han system"); see Yu Weichao, "Handai zhuhouwang." Since then many studies have focused on the development of various regional styles. See Wang, *Han Civilization*, 175; Pu Muzhou, *Muzang yu shengsi*, 55–84; Xu Jijun, *Zhongguo sangzang shi*, 25; Li Rusen, *Handai sangzang lisu*, 232–440; *Zhongguo kaoguxue Qin Han juan*, 307–551. Following the Japanese scholarly tradition, Huang Xiaofen classified these tombs into the vertical and the horizontal and pointed out that the defining feature of horizontal chamber-style tombs was the establishment of a separate sacrificial space within the tomb. This was a breakthrough in the discussion on the origin of the horizontal chamber-style tomb, which I will take up in chapter 2. See Kō Gyōfun, "Kanbo no henyō," 1–39; "Sobo kara Kanbo e," 51–57; Huang Xiaofen, *Han mu de kaoguxue yanjiu*. In his recent book, Wu Hung reconceptualized this evolution as moving from "casket grave" to "chamber grave," from an "object-oriented" design to a "space-oriented" design, and from temple to tomb. These formulations, as fresh as they are, do not provide a significant analytic advantage over Huang. For more recent studies, see Pirazzoli-t'Serstevens, "Death and the Dead," 949–1206; Campbell, "The Form and Function," 227; Erickson, "Han Dynasty Tomb Structures and Contents," 13–30.

13   *Xuzhou Beidongshan Xi Han Chu wang mu*; Li, "The 'Underground Palace' of a Chu Prince at Beidongshan," 57–61.

14   *Xuzhou Beidongshan Xi Han Chu wang mu*, 20–29; Liu Rui and Liu Tao, *Xi Han zhuhouwang lingmu zhidu yanjiu*, 106–16; Erickson, "Han Dynasty Tomb Structures and Contents," 19–20.

15   The excavators argued that it was the tomb of the fifth king of the Chu kingdom, Liu Dao (r. 150–129 BCE), but Liu Rui has more convincingly argued that it is probably the tomb of the first king of the Chu kingdom; see Liu Rui and Liu Tao, *Xi Han zhuhouwang lingmu zhidu yanjiu*, 537–50.

16   For the local kingdoms of Chu and Changsha and the related archaeological data in the Western Han period, see Liu Rui and Liu Tao, *Xi Han zhuhouwang lingmu zhidu yanjiu*, 70–96, 102–46. For an excellent study of Changsha during the early Han dynasty, see Emmerich, "Chu und Changsha," 85–137; for the images of Chu in the Warring States period and the Han dynasty, see Blakeley, "Chu Society and State," 9–20; Sukhu, "Monkeys, Shamans, Emperors and Poets," 145–66.

17   The number twenty thousand is quoted in Huang Xiaofen, *Han mu de kaoguxue yanjiu*, 2.

18   Yang Aiguo, "Lingmu fangdao sheshi," 436–44.

19   The term *warring states* (*zhanguo*) was already in use during that epoch, but only in the late Western Han dynasty, when Liu Xiang edited and compiled *Zhanguo ce* (Intrigues of the Warring States), did the term come to be used to refer to the historical period following the Spring and Autumn period. See Yang Kuan, *Zhanguo shi*, 2–4; Lawton, *Chinese Art of the Warring States Period*, 9.

Notes to Introduction

20 He Hao, *Chu mieguo yanjiu*; Sage, *Ancient Sichuan and the Unification of China*.

21 Pines, "Intellectual Change in the Chunqiu Period"; *Foundations of Confucian Thought*.

22 Blakeley, "King, Clan, and Courtier in Ch'u Court Politics," 1–39; see also discussions in Thatcher, "Kinship and Government in Chu"; and Tian Changwu and Zang Zhifei, *Zhou Qin shehui jiegou yanjiu*, 256–76.

23 Nishijima Sadao, *Chūgoku kokai teikoku no keisei to kōzō*.

24 Tian Changwu and Zang Zhifei, *Zhou Qin shehui jiegou yanjiu*, 276–88.

25 Hsu, *Ancient China in Transition*; Pines, *Envisioning Eternal Empire*, 115–35.

26 For discussions of cultural commonalities and differences during the Warring States period, especially between Chu and Qin, see Liang Yun, *Zhanguo shidai de dongxi chabie*.

27 Loewe, "The Heritage Left to the Empires," 967. Michael Loewe has enumerated those institutions—the legacy of the Warring States to the unified empire—in the final chapter of the *Cambridge History of Ancient China*; see Loewe, "The Heritage Left to the Empires," 967–1032.

28 Schopen, "Burial *Ad Sanctos*," 114. For studies on the archaeology of early Chinese religion, see Loewe, *Ways to Paradise*; Kleeman, "Land Contracts and Related Documents," 1–34; Harper, "A Chinese Demonography," 459–98; "Resurrection," 13–28; *Early Chinese Medical Literature*; "Contracts with the Spirit World," 227–67; Seidel, "Traces of Han Religion in Funerary Texts Found in Tombs," 21–57; Wu, "From Temple to Tomb," 78–115; Li Ling, *Zhongguo fangshu kao*; *Zhongguo fangshu xukao*; Poo, "Popular Religion in Pre-Imperial China," 225–48; Pu Muzhou, *Muzang yu shengsi*; Lewis, "Ritual Origins of the Warring States," 73–98; Falkenhausen, "Sources of Taoism," 1–12; *Chinese Society*, 293–325; and the chapters in Lagerwey, ed., *Religion and Chinese Society*, vol. 1, and Lagerwey and Kalinowski eds., *Early Chinese Religion, Part One*, especially those chapters by Keightley, Thote, Eno, and Pirazzoli-t'Serstevens.

29 Schopen, "Burial *Ad Sanctos*," 114.

30 Granet, *The Religion of the Chinese People*.

31 Maspero, *Taoism and Chinese Religion*, 17–25.

32 The only exceptions are the treatises on state religion in *Records of the Grand Historian*, "Fengshan shu," and *Official History of the Western Han Dynasty*, "Jiaosi zhi." See Bilsky, *The State Religion of Ancient China*; Bujard, *Le sacrifice au ciel dans la Chine ancienne*; Bujard, "State and Local Cults in Han Religion," 777–811.

33 Lewis, *Sanctioned Violence*, 43–50; Weld, "Covenant in Jin's Walled Cities"; Schaberg, *A Patterned Past*, 126–30.

34 Harper, "Chinese Religions: The State of the Field," 152.

35 For example, Csikszentmihalyi and Ivanhoe, eds., *Religious and Philosophical Aspects of the Laozi*.

36 For Confucian attitudes toward Heaven and the spirits, see Graham, *Disputers of the Tao*, 15–18. For the date of the *Analects*, see Cheng, "Lun yü," 314; Brooks and Brooks, *The Original Analects*.

37 Girardot, "Very Small Books," 9–10; Paper, *The Spirits Are Drunk*, 4–12.

38 For the modern construction of early Chinese philosophy on the Western model, see Chen Qiyun, *Zhongguo gudai sixiang wenhua de lishi lunxi*, 6–18.

39 This text-centered approach in the study of Chinese religion can be traced back to nineteenth-century Western missionary studies, such as de Groot, *The Religious System of China*. For a critique of de Groot's approach in studying Chinese religions, see Freedman, "On the Sociological Study of Chinese Religion," 24–31.

40 Girardot, "Very Small Books," 11; Kirkland, "Person and Culture in the Taoist Tradition," 79, 83n16.

41 Yang Kuan, *Zhanguo shi*.

42 Shen Changyun and Yang Shanqun, *Zhanguo shi yu Zhanguo wenming*, 247–62.

43 Sullivan, "Seeking an End to the Primary Text," 41–59; Renfrew and Zubrow, eds., *The Ancient Mind*; Schopen, "Archaeology and Protestant Presuppositions in the Study of Indian Buddhism," 1–22.

44 Frend, *The Archaeology of Early Christianity*; Insoll, *The Archaeology of Islam*; *The Archaeology of Islam in Sub-Saharan Africa*; *Archaeology, Ritual, Religion*; Insoll, ed., *Case Studies in Archaeology and World Religion*; *Archaeology and World Religion*; *Belief in the Past*; Pearson, *Shamanism and the Ancient Mind*.

45 Sullivan, "Seeking an End to the Primary Text," 51. Sullivan reevaluates the text-centered approach to religious studies in the context of Derrida's critical theories on Western logocentrism. See Derrida, *Of Grammatology; Writing and Difference*; Jeanrond, *Text and Interpretation as Categories of Theological Thinking; Theological Hermeneutics*.

46 Sullivan, "Seeking an End to the Primary Text," 47–50.

47 Schopen, "Burial *Ad Sanctos*," 114.

48 Schopen, "Burial *Ad Sanctos*."

49 Geary, "The Uses of Archaeological Sources for Religious and Cultural History," 30–45.

50 Dever, *Did God Have a Wife?*

51 See, for example, Yu Weichao, "Xian Qin liang Han meishu kaogu," 111–20; Wu Hong, *Liyi zhong de meishu*; Rawson, "Chinese Burial Patterns," 107–33.

52 Adams and Apostolos-Cappadona, eds., *Art as Religious Studies*, 4.

53 Bagley, "Meaning and Explanation," 48.

54 See Mackenzie, "Meaning and Style in the Art of Chu," 119–49; Thote, "Aspects of the Serpent on Eastern Zhou Bronze and Lacquerware," 150–60.

55 Maquet, "Objects as Instruments," 30–40.

56 Maquet, "Objects as Instruments," 39.

57 Bagley, "Meaning and Explanation," 49–50.

58 Besides Warring States and Qin-Han tomb texts, which will be discussed below, another category of religious texts, Eastern Han and later land contracts, are the focus of Anna Seidel's and Terry Kleeman's studies of later Han religion. See Seidel, "Tokens of Immortality in Han Graves," 79–114; "Traces of Han Religion in Funerary Texts Found in Tombs," 21–57; Kleeman, "Land Contracts and Related Documents," 1–34.

59 Cort, "Art, Religion, and Material Culture," 613–32.

60 Wang Zijin, *Zhongguo daomu shi*, 52–55. For different accounts of Wu Zixu's story and other instances of opening tombs for political revenge, see *Zuozhuan*, Lord Wen 18th year and Lord Ai 26th year.

61 *Shiji*, 389, 3263, 3271, 3284. Wang Zijin, *Zhongguo daomu shi*, 77–80.

62 Yang Quanxi, *Chu wenhua*, 4.

63 Shang Chengzuo, *Changsha guwu wenjian ji; Changsha chutu Chu qiqi tulu*.

64 Barnard, "Ch'u Silk Manuscript"; Rao Zongyi and Zeng Xiantong, *Chu boshu*; Hunan sheng bowuguan, "Changsha Zidanku," 36–43; *Changsha Chu mu*, vol. 1, 43.

65 Guo Dewei, *Chu xi muzang yanjiu*, 1–2; Yang Quanxi, *Chu wenhua*, 5.

66 *Changsha fajue baogao*; Chang, "Major Aspects of Ch'u Archaeology," 5–52; Guo Dewei, *Chu xi muzang yanjiu*; Yang Quanxi, *Chu wenhua*.

67 See Xia Nai, "Chu wenhua yanjiu zhong de jige wenti"; Li, "Chu Bronzes and Chu Culture," 1. There are basically four definitions of "Chu": the region of Chu, a geographical region in southern China; the state of Chu and the kingdom of Chu, as two political entities in Eastern Zhou and Western Han, respectively; Chu people, an ethnic classification, based on cultural and linguistic affiliation; and Chu archaeological culture defined by diagnostic

artifacts. Both Xia Nai and Li Xueqin only refer to the state of Chu in the Eastern Zhou period. Here I add the Chu kingdom of the Western Han dynasty to the broader scope of the Chu. For the Qin and Western Han periods, burials from the Chu and other regions will be included in the discussion. In both Chinese and English literature "the region of Chu," or "Chu di," is increasingly used. For example, the recently published collections of Warring States manuscripts from southern China is called *Chu di chutu Zhanguo jiance (shisizhong)*, instead of "Chu culture" (Chu wenhua), "Chu civilization" (Chu wenming), or "the state of Chu" (Chu guo). The emphasis here is on the geographic region. The so-called Chu culture/civilization defined archaeologically by idiosyncratic cultural features or diagnostic artifacts (such as the "Chu type *li*-tripod") is methodologically problematic, as scholars have pointed out (Li Ling, *Rushan yu chusai*, 274–77; Falkenhausen, *Chinese Society*, 264–71; Shelach and Pines, "Secondary State Formation," 221–22), although these terms are still used loosely and widely in both Chinese and Western literature. Certainly, the Chu had local cultural features and different political identities, but by the late Spring and Autumn and early Warring States periods, the Chu has adopted the Zhou political, social, and religious institutions. It was a part of the Zhou cultural sphere, although politically the Chu had begun to claim a distinct identity. Thus in this book "Chu religion" is largely synonymous with "early Chinese religion," but certainly with local characteristics. Because of the uneven distribution of archaeological data, this book offers a distinctly regional perspective of early Chinese mortuary religion.

For historical geography of the state of Chu, see Blakeley, "In Search of Dangyang," 116–52; "On the Location of the Chu Capital," 49–70; "The Geography of Chu," 9–20.

68 The so-called Qin tombs in this region are identified mainly based on diagnostic artifacts (such as the garlic headed *hu*-vessel, particular Qin bronze coins, or particular Qin bronze mirrors); thus these tombs were either of the Qin period, or culturally influenced by the Qin, or ethnically belong to the Qin people. For Qin tombs in this region, see *Zhongguo kaoguxue Qin Han juan*, 12–136; Guo Dewei, "Shilun Jiangling diqu Chu mu, Qin mu he Xi Han qianqi mu," 81–88; Chen Zhenyu, "Luelun Hubei Qin mu," 209–19; "Shilun Hubei diqu Qin mu de niandai fenqi," 220–35; "Cong Hubei faxian de Qin mu tan Qin Chu guanxi," 236–45; Gao Zhixi, "Lun Hunan Qin mu," 297–306; for discussions on the dating of Qin tombs, see *Zhongguo kaoguxue Qin Han juan*, 143–46; Chen Ping, "Qiantan Jiang Han diqu Zhanguo Qin Han mu," 51–62. For a general survey of Eastern Zhou and Qin archaeological materials, see Li, *Eastern Zhou and Qin Civilizations*.

69 Guo Dewei, *Chu xi muzang yanjiu*, 26–30; Falkenhausen, "Social Ranking in Chu Tombs," 439–526; *Zhongguo kaoguxue liang Zhou juan*, 357–59.

70 *Zhongguo kaoguxue Qin Han juan*, 307–551.

71 There were systematic imperial regulations on mortuary practices during the Han dynasty, as shown in the recently discovered legal codes on burial (*zanglü*) in the early Western Han. See Peng Hao, "Du Yunmeng Shuihudi M77 Han jian zanglü," 130–34.

72 Guo Dewei, "Jiangling Chu mu lunshu,"155–82; *Chu xi muzang yanjiu*; Peng Hao, "Chu mu zangzhi chulun," 33–40; Chen Zhenyu, "Hubei Chu mu zongshu," 54–68; "Luelun jiu zuo Chu mu de niandai," 69–84; Gao Zhixi, "Chu yong yanjiu"; Ding Lan, *Hubei diqu Chu mu fenqu yanjiu*. On the social ranking in Chu tombs, see Falkenhausen, "Social Ranking in Chu Tombs," 439–526; *Chinese Society*, 370–99.

73 James, "An Iconographic Study"; Wu, *The Wu Liang Shrine*; "Art in Its Ritual Context," 111–45; Thompson, "The Yi'nan Tomb"; Lai, "The Baoshan Tomb"; Huang, "From Chu to Western Han"; Beckman, "Layers of Being"; Cook, *Death in Ancient China*.

74 Wu, *The Art of the Yellow Springs*, 14.

75 Wu, *The Art of the Yellow Springs*, 16, 219.

Notes to Introduction

76　There is a vast body of scholarship on the society and culture of the Chu in Chinese; it is not possible to provide detailed bibliographical information here. For studies in English, see chapters in Lawton, ed., *New Perspectives on Chu Culture*; Cook and Major, eds., *Defining Chu*.

77　Thote, "Continuities and Discontinuities," 189–204; Falkenhausen, "Social Ranking in Chu Tombs," 439–526.

78　Falkenhausen, *Chinese Society*, 326–99.

79　For an early discussion of this question, see Major, "Research Priorities in the Studies of Ch'u Religion," 226–43.

80　For mortuary practices in the state of Qin, see Falkenhausen, "Mortuary Behavior in Pre-Imperial Qin," 109–72; Shelach and Pines, "Secondary State Formation," 220–30; Chen Ping, *Guanlong wenhua yu Ying Qin wenming*.

81　This eastern vs. western distinction is a product of the late Warring States political discourses. Based on material remains, modern archaeologists divide archaeological culture in China into either five "cultural spheres"—the Central Plains (including the royal Zhou house, and Zhao, Wei, and Han), Qi, Yan, Chu, and Qin—or seven, adding Wu and Yue in southeast China and Ba, Shu, and Dian in southwest China. See discussions in Liang Yun, *Zhanguo shidai de dongxi chabie*, 1–7. However, the question remains as to whether these differences in material culture can be translated into differences of cultural or religious traditions. Although many scholars assume there is a direct correspondence between these two, I contend that we have to examine the connection case by case.

82　Liang Yun, *Zhanguo shidai de dongxi chabie*.

83　Huang Zhanyue, *Zhongguo gudai de rensheng renxun*; *Gudai rensheng renxun tonglun*.

84　Regardless of whether the elite and/or the dominant inhabitants of Chu were indigenous to the region or came from the Central Plains, the northern steppe and northeast Asia (as Major suggested), or elsewhere, the earlier characterization of Chu religion and culture as particularly "shamanistic," "superstitious," or "barbarous" is misleading. These were the images the Chu self-constructed or other people attributed to them or to the southern culture in general during the Han and later periods. For a summary of early discussions, see Major, "Research Priorities in the Studies of Ch'u Religion," 226–43. For discussions on the images and realities of the Chu, based on archaeological materials, see Lawton, ed., *New Perspectives on Chu Culture*; Cook and Major, eds., *Defining Chu*; and Lai Guolong, "Diguo yu zongjiao."

85　Falkenhausen, *Chinese Society*, 367 and passim; Liang Yun, *Zhanguo shidai de dongxi chabie*.

86　Falkenhausen, *Chinese Society*, 401–4.

87　Liu Lexian, "Chu Qin xuanzeshu de yitong," 19–31.

88　Falkenhausen, "Chu Ritual Music," 47–106; Falkenhausen, *Suspended Music*, 314–18.

89　Li Yunfu, "Zhanguo wenzi 'diyu tedian' zhiyi," 170–82; Zhang Qiyun, "Lun Zhanguo wenzi qiyi zhi shizhi," 271–82.

90　Old Chinese is the language that "was spoken during the Zhou dynasty (eleventh century–221 BCE), in northern China, in an area centered around the middle course of the Huang He river"; see Sagart, *The Roots of Old Chinese*, 4–7; and also Baxter, *A Handbook of Old Chinese Phonology*. For the linguistic differences between the Chu people and their Sinitic northern neighbors, see Sagart, *The Roots of Old Chinese*, 9; Starosta, "Proto-East Asian and the Origin and Dispersal of the Languages of East and Southeast Asia and the Pacific," 190–91; Ōnishi Katsuya, "So no gengo ni tsuite," 121–29. The ongoing study on the excavated bamboo and silk manuscripts from the Chu region continues to illuminate the cultural integration and distinction among Chu and other regions.

91　Shelach and Pines, "Secondary State Formation," 202–22.

92　See the methodological essays by Clifford Geertz, "Religion as a Cultural System," and

Melford E. Spiro, "Religion: Problems of Definition and Explanation," in Banton, ed., *Anthropological Approaches to the Study of Religion*, 1–46, 85–126. See also Renfrew, "The Archaeology of Religion," 47–48.

93 Berger, *The Sacred Canopy*, 25. See also his discussion of the sociological definitions of religion, 175–77.

94 Levi, *Les fonctionnaires divins*.

95 Paper, *The Spirits Are Drunk*, 36–37.

96 Berger, *The Sacred Canopy*, 25.

97 For example, Stein, "Architecture et pensée religieuse en Extrême-Orient," 163–86.

98 Tambiah, *Culture, Thought, and Social Action*, 3.

99 Wang, *Cosmology and Political Culture in Early China*.

100 Needham and Ronan, "Chinese Cosmology," 68.

101 Mote, *Intellectual Foundations of China*. A Chinese translation was published by Peking University Press in 2008. In a recent survey book, *Chinese Religions: Beliefs and Practices*, Jeaneane and Merv Fowler still use "the age of the philosophers" and the theories of *yin* and *yang* and five agents (*wuxing*) to characterize the religious beliefs and practices of the Eastern Zhou period.

102 Needham and Lu, *Science and Civilisation in China*, 98nC.

103 Mote, *Intellectual Foundations of China*, 17.

104 Mote, *Intellectual Foundations of China*, 17.

105 Yü, "Life and Immortality in the Mind of Han China," 80–122; "O Soul, Come Back!" 363–95; Loewe, *Ways to Paradise; Chinese Ideas of Life and Death*; Seidel, "Tokens of Immortality in Han Graves," 79–121; "Traces of Han Religion in Funerary Texts Found in Tombs," 21–57; Dien, "Chinese Beliefs in the Afterworld," 1–15; Wu, "The Earliest Pictorial Representations of Ape Tales," 86–112; "Art in Its Ritual Context," 111–45; Li Ling, *Zhongguo fangshu kao; Zhongguo fangshu xukao*; Li Xueqin, "Fangmatan jian zhong de zhiguai gushi," 181–90; Ikeda Suetoshi, *Chūgoku kodai shūkyōshi kenkyū: Seido to shisō*; Pu Muzhou, *Muzang yu shengsi*; Poo, *In Search of Personal Welfare*. For the voluminous Chinese and Japanese scholarship on the early Chinese conception of the afterlife, see works quoted by these authors and the chapters that follow.

106 Kleeman, "Land Contracts and Related Documents," 1–34; Seidel, "Traces of Han Religion in Funerary Texts Found in Tombs," 21–57.

107 Loewe, *Ways to Paradise*, 17–59; Wu, "Art in Its Ritual Context," 111–45.

108 Pu Muzhou, *Muzang yu shengsi*.

1. The Dead Who Would Not Be Ancestors

Epigraph: Qu Yuan, *The Songs of the South*, 116–17.

1 Schopen, "Burial *Ad Sanctos*," 114.

2 Here I use the term *pantheon* to refer, as Robert Eno does for the Shang, to "those spirit entities that appear in the oracle texts as objects of sacrifice or as forces whose future intentional actions were topics of divination." See Eno, "Shang State Religion and the Pantheon of the Oracle Texts," 54. For a brief overview of the religious pantheon in ancient China, see Lagerwey, *China: A Religious State*, 19–55.

3 On early efforts to distill the religious and mythological layers in transmitted texts, see Maspero, "Légendes mythologiques dans le Chou King," 1–100; Karlgren, "Legends and Cults in Ancient China," 199–365; Bodde, "Myths of Ancient China," 45–84; Boltz, "Kung Kung and the Flood," 141–53; Riegel, "Kou-Mang and Ju-Shou," 55–83.

4 Li Xueqin, *Zhouyi suyuan*, 263–72; Yan Changgui, *Wugui yu yinsi*, 28–34.

5   Mattos, "Eastern Zhou Bronze Inscriptions," 85–124.

6   The concept of ancestor worship or ancestor cults in early China has been examined re-
      cently in several chapters in Lagerwey and Kalinowski, eds., *Early Chinese Religion, Part One*.
      In their conclusion, Lagerwey and Kalinowski describe ancestor worship in early China
      as "an expression of political power and legitimacy that was by definition sumptuary and
      therefore emphatically not an integral part of some kind of universal, unchanging Chinese
      religion." See Lagerwey and Kalinowski, eds., *Early Chinese Religion, Part One*, vol. 1, 34. Dis-
      cussing the Han imperial rites, Stephen Bokenkamp also questions the usage of the phrase
      "ancestor worship" in Western literature and posits that "what Western sources mistakenly
      called 'ancestor worship' actually involved not 'worship' of ancestors but the maintenance
      of family ties through ritual means in the hope that one's forebears might continue to aid
      their descendants." See Bokenkamp, "Record of the Feng and Shan Sacrifice," 253. What
      Bokenkamp defined is a weaker form of the Shang and Zhou ancestor cults in Qin and Han
      state and common religion. The topics of ancestor cults and ancestor worship were exten-
      sively discussed in African anthropology throughout the twentieth century. Some of the
      classic texts include Gluckman, "Mortuary Customs and the Belief in Survival after Death
      among the South-Eastern Bantu," 117–36; Fortes, "Pietas and Ancestor Worship," 166–91;
      "Some Reflections on Ancestor Worship in Africa"; Goody, *Death, Property and the Ancestors*;
      Kopytoff, "Ancestors as Elders," 129–42; Calhoun, "The Authority of Ancestors," 304–19;
      Glazier, "Mbeere Ancestors and the Domestication of Death," 133–47, and many correspon-
      dences in the *Journal of the Royal Anthropological Institute* (formerly *Man*). These discussions
      provide useful analytic frameworks to compare with the changing status of ancestors in
      early China. In this book, I use the term *ancestor cults* to describe this religious phenome-
      non and, following Max Glukman, distinguish the ancestor cults of the Shang and Western
      Zhou periods from the "cults of the dead (including the deceased relatives)" of the Warring
      States period and that of the early empires.

7   Keightley, "The Making of the Ancestors," 26–29.

8   Lai Guolong, "Jiyi de momie."

9   Lewis, *Sanctioned Violence*; "Warring States Political History," 620–29.

10   For a summary of anthropological studies on death, see Palgi and Abramovitch, "Death:
      A Cross-Cultural Perspective," 385–417. See also Robben, ed., *Death, Mourning, and Burial*.

11   Ariès, *Western Attitudes toward Death*; "The Reversal of Death," 536–65; *The Hour of Our
      Death*; Vovelle, "Les attitudes devant la mort," 120–32; *La mort et l'Occident de 1300 à nos
      jours*. For a comparison and evaluation of the different approaches taken by Ariès and
      Vovelle, see Kselman, "Death in Historical Perspective," 591–97; Darnton, *The Kiss of Lam-
      ourette*, 268–90. For reactions to Ariès's work, see Mitchell, "Philippe Ariès and the French
      Way of Death," 684–95; Stone, *The Past and the Present Revisited*, 22–32.

12   The literature on this topic is vast. On modern French attitudes toward death, see Ksel-
      man, *Death and Afterlife in Modern France*; on American attitudes, see Laderman, *The
      Sacred Remains*; on attitudes in ancient Rome, see Kyle, *Spectacles of Death in Ancient Rome*;
      Edwards, *Death in Ancient Rome*; on Greek attitudes, see Garland, *The Greek Way of Death*; on
      attitudes in biblical times, see Hallote, *Death, Burial, and Afterlife in the Biblical World*; and
      on attitudes toward the death of children, see Golden, "Did the Ancients Care when Their
      Children Died?" 152–63.

13   The methodological debates surrounding the study of ancient Greek attitudes toward death
      are of great interest for students of early Chinese religion. Using Homeric epics and other
      literary as well as archaeological evidence, the classical scholar Christiane Sourvinou-
      Inwood (1945–2007) argued for a significant change in attitudes toward death in the
      eighth century BCE in ancient Greece, before and after Homer (Sourvinou-Inwood, "To Die

and Enter the House of Hades," 15–39; "A Trauma in Flux," 33–49; *"Reading" Greek Death*). Sourvinou-Inwood's approach, however, was heavily criticized by another Greek specialist, Ian Morris, who disputed the change based on the assumption that burial data could be used to study only the social structure of a given society but not its religious beliefs (Morris, *Burial and Ancient Society*, 29; *Death Ritual and Social Structure in Classical Antiquity*). Morris strictly followed Ariès's general five modes of evolution in attitudes toward death and argued that in archaic Greece, as in other early civilizations, the main attitude toward death could be described as "tame death," wherein death is considered familiar and inevitable (Morris, "Attitudes toward Death in Archaic Greece," 296–320). Sourvinou-Inwood and Morris differed not only in their interpretation of the Greek materials but also in their methodology. Even though Morris agreed that attitudes toward death in a given society were not static over time and that different social groups could have different views, he emphasized that literary and archaeological evidence is insufficient for this inquiry. But Sourvinou-Inwood argued, in agreement with the Annales school of historians, that it is possible to distill a collective, dominant attitude in specific social circumstances based on literary and archaeological data.

From their discussions, several ideas become clear: (1) attitudes toward death and the dead change over time, at both the individual and collective levels; (2) literary and archaeological data can be used to study ancient religious beliefs and attitudes; (3) a change can be measured only relative to a local society, and its significance can be defined by how the change affects the local society. I leave the Greece specialists to debate the interpretation of the Greek materials and here apply some of their methods to the study of early Chinese attitudes toward death and the dead.

14 Few materials are available for reconstructing the religious pantheon of the Western Zhou period. As Robert Eno has remarked, the Shang oracle-bone inscriptions and the Western Zhou bronze commemorative inscriptions have different natures. See Eno, "Shang State Religion and the Pantheon of the Oracle Texts"; Lagerwey and Kalinowski, eds., *Early Chinese Religion, Part One*, vols. 1, 2.

15 For the changing attitudes toward death and the dead in the Chinese medieval period, see Bokenkamp, *Ancestors and Anxiety*.

16 For the studies on Tomb 2 at Baoshan, see Chen Wei, *Baoshan Chu jian chutan*; Lai, "The Baoshan Tomb"; Beckman, "Layers of Being"; Cook, *Death in Ancient China*; Guo, "Reconstructing Fourth Century B.C.E. Chu Religious Practices." Cook's recent book has a good description of the Baoshan archaeological materials, but her interpretation and translation of the archaeological and textual data are problematic, as the reviewers of Cook's book have pointed out. See Kalinowski, "Review of *Death in Ancient China*," 251–63; Lewis, Review of *Death in Ancient China*, 360–64; Mackenzie, Review of *Death in Ancient China*, 683–85. For an excellent contextualized study and translation of the Baoshan divination texts, see Kalinowski, "Diviners and Astrologers under the Eastern Zhou," 373–85.

17 Kalinowski, "Diviners and Astrologers under the Eastern Zhou," 375–85.

18 Yan Changgui, *Wugui yu yinsi*, 34–36. I translate the term *shui* 說 (verb) as "pray" (verb) on the basis that *shui* here designates verbal communication between men and spirits in the form of petition, confession, praise, or thanksgiving.

19 Exorcism involves using coercive measures such as curses, spells, and other verbal formula, objects (animal feces, shoes, etc.), gestures (e.g., spitting), and actions thought to possess particular powers to expel invasive, often evil, spirits from a person or place. Sacrifice involves offering food, drink, and other forms of gifts (such as personal belongings), and often the slaughter of animals, to feed and please gods and spirits. In the state of Chu, sacrifice often took place during the night. See Yan Changgui, *Wugui yu yinsi*, 236–99. For

a discussion on the religious ritual of verbal attack, see Arbuckle, "An Unnoticed Religious Metaphor in the *Analects*?" 1–12; on the promise of sacrificial offerings as an act of negotiation with gods and spirits, see the discussion below and Lai Guolong, "Chu bushi jidao jian zhong de 'yudao.'"

20   There are exceptions, such as those found in the Tianxingguan and Geling divination records, where the *yidao* is directed to nature deities such as Taiyi and to directional deities. See Yan Changgui, *Wugui yu yinsi*, 262.

21   Lai Guolong, "Chu bushi jidao jian zhong de 'yudao,'" 359–78.

22   The Lord of Pingye also appears in the Zeng Hou Yi and Geling manuscripts; in the *Zuozhuan*, Lord Ai, 17th year, he is described as the son of King Zhao, the younger brother of King Hui, and the first Lord of Pingye. See *Xincai Geling Chu mu*, 183.

23   The three royal ancestors of the state of Chu—Laotong, Zhurong, and Yuxiong—were the three mythic ancestors. For further discussion, see Yan Changgui, *Wugui yu yinsi*, 153–58.

24   The meaning of "Shi" here is not clear. It is possibly an honorific prefix, placed in front of the name Taiyi. Alternatively, Taiyi is referred to as Futai, "Father Tai." See Yan Changgui, *Wugui yu yinsi*, 92–94.

25   The identity of the two terrestrial deities called "Ertianzi" is not clear. Some scholars suggest they are the daughters of the mythic emperor Yao. For further discussion, see Yan Changgui, *Wugui yu yinsi*, 150–51.

26   The cult of sacred mountains is a common religious feature of early China, although in these divinatory texts the specific details of the Five Mountains are unknown. See Yan Changgui, *Wugui yu yinsi*, 138–39.

27   Mount Wei is the mythic mountain in the sacred geography of Chu, which was developed and historicized in the Han dynasty and became a real geographic name. Various theories concern the location of Mount Wei, but most situate the mountain in the northwest or southwest of China. See Yan Changgui, *Wugui yu yinsi*, 139–42.

28   Liu Xinfang points out that, according to the sequence in the list of the recipients of sacrificial offerings, Dongling Lianxiao (Zifa) was probably Shao Tuo's uncle; see Liu Xinfang, *Baoshan Chu jian jiegu*, 238. A certain Zifa was mentioned in the *Xunzi* (in the "Qiangguo" chapter) and again in the *Huainanzi* (in the "Daoying" and "Renjian" chapters). But it is very difficult to say whether or not, as Liu Xinfang suggests, these refer to the same person.

29   The identity of the last two spirits is uncertain. Li Jiahao suggests that Zhu is located near present-day Fuliji in Su County, Anhui. See Li Jiahao, "E jun Qi jie mingwen zhongde gaoqiu," 138–40.

30   See discussion in chapter 3.

31   This probably refers to those who drown but are found floating on the water, their nature, baleful or beneficent, is uncertain. Reference to these spirits also appears in the Xuning prayer and sacrificial documents of 79 CE; see Harper, "Contracts with the Spirit World," 240n37.

32   The blameless dead also appear in other divination and sacrifice records and later in the Qin daybook, where it refers to a category of the dead who were wrongfully killed. There are stories in transmitted texts in which the ghosts of "blameless" men exact vengeance against their perpetrators; see Yan Changgui, *Wugui yu yinsi*, 169–70.

33   For a summary of some related hypotheses, see Li Jiahao, "Baoshan bushi jian 218–219 hao yanjiu," 198–99, and Chen Wei et al., *Chu di chutu Zhanguo jiance (shi si zhong)*, 118. Here my interpretation of *jian mu wei* as fecundity god is based on the observation that the graph *jian* (OCM *tsam) was the result of the phonetic assimilation of *zu* (OCM *tsaʔ) by the initial (*m-) in the following word *mu* (OCM *môk). Thus *jian mu wei* is really *zu mu wei* 祖木位 (the wooden stand of the *zu* god; *zu* was a phallic symbol that represented the fecundity

god in early China). On the linguistic phenomenon of phonetic assimilation (called *sandhi*) in Old Chinese texts and inscriptions, see Lai Guolong, "Shuo sha, san." Both the fecundity god (*zu*) and those who died without posterity were the targets of exorcism and pledge sacrifice. Therefore, this interpretation is consistent with the internal structure and evidence from the divinatory and sacrificial records. For further discussions on the term *jian mu wei* and the interpretation of *zu* as fecundity god, see chapter 3. All Old Chinese reconstructions, including the ones above, marked by OCM ("Minimal Old Chinese") are based on Schuessler, *Minimal Old Chinese and Later Han Chinese*.

34 Chen Wei, "Churen daoci jilu," 383–86.

35 Huang Shengzhang suggests that the occupant of Tomb 1 at Tianxingguan was descended from the polity of Pan of the Spring and Autumn period; see Huang Shengzhang, "Dangyang liang ge mingwen kao," 42–45.

36 Chen Mengjia and many other scholars classify the Shang pantheon according to the categorization in the *Zhouli*, which includes celestial deities, terrestrial deities, and human ghosts. Keightley and Eno, however, classify these figures according to the different sacrificial treatments they received. Chen Mengjia, *Yinxu buci zongshu*, 333–400, 561–603.

37 The Chinese term *di* or *shangdi* in the oracle-bone inscriptions of the Shang dynasty is translated variously as "god," "lord," "power," or "thearch." Here I use the familiar "god," but this certainly does not imply that it carried the same meaning in early China as it does in the Judeo-Christian tradition. For further discussion on the nature of the supreme god, see Eno, "Was There a High God Ti in Shang Religion?" 1–26, and chapter 3 in this study.

38 Keightley, "The Making of the Ancestors," 5–6; Eno, "Shang State Religion and the Pantheon of the Oracle Texts," 54–77.

39 Shaughnessy, "Extra-Lineage Cult in the Shang Dynasty," 182–90; Zhang Yongshan, "Cong buci zhong de Yi yin kan 'min busi feizu,'" 1–5.

40 *Zuozhuan*, Lord Xi, 10th year; Yang Bojun, *Chunqiu Zuozhuan zhu*, 334; Legge, *The Ch'un Ts'ew with the Tso Chuen*, 157. A similar saying occurs a little later in the same text; see *Zuozhuan*, Lord Xi, 31st year; Yang Bojun, *Chunqiu Zuozhuan zhu*, 483. The date of the *Zuo Commentary*, compiled as short narratives and attached to the chronicle of the state of Lu, called *Spring and Autumn* (Chunqiu, meaning "annals"), has been hotly debated among modern scholars. The scholarly consensus is that it was compiled in the Warring States period based on earlier materials. In this chapter I use the *Zuo Commentary* materials, with due caution, to discuss the political struggles among the lineages that characterize the Spring and Autumn period. On the dates and the historical veracity of the *Zuo Commentary*, see Karlgren, *On the Authenticity and Nature of the Tso chuan*; Cheng, "Ch'un ch'iu, Kung yang, Ku liang and Tso chuan"; Pines, "Intellectual Change in the Chunqiu Period"; *Foundations of Confucian Thought*; Schaberg, *A Patterned Past*.

41 *Lunyu zhengyi*, 41; Lau, *The Analects*, 66.

42 Kleeman, "Licentious Cults and Bloody Victuals," 185–211.

43 Cai Zhemao, "Yin buci Yi Yin jiushi kao," 755–808.

44 Subordinate groups, however, could sacrifice to the royal ancestors to show their allegiance and respect. This paradox of the ancestor cults and the shifting boundaries of religious propriety became the focus of political debates in the Warring States period and the early empires, when the rulers broke off from the old feudal system and began to claim universal authority. See Lai Guolong, "Diguo yu zongjiao"; "Jiandawang bohan."

45 In the imperial era, the situation was different. The ruling imperial house made everybody sacrifice to its ancestors. See discussions in Peng Hao, "Shuihudi Qinjian 'wangshici,'" 239–48; Lai Guolong, "Diguo yu zongjiao," 206–7.

46 Some scholars have stoutly rejected this idea, suggesting that these were generic terms

referring to deities, either collectively or individually; see Eno, "Was There a High God Ti in Shang Religion?" 1–26.

47 Li Ling, "An Archaeological Study of Taiyi (Grand One) Worship," 1–39; Liu Yi, *Jingtian yu chongdao*, 130–99.

48 Yan Changgui, *Wugui yu yinsi*, 95–99.

49 Harper, "The Nature of Taiyi in the Guodian Manuscript," 1–23.

50 Lai Guolong, "Chu bushi jidao jian zhong de 'yudao,'" 359–78.

51 Wolf, "God, Ghosts, and Ancestors," 162.

52 In Keightley's words, "The Shang conceived of the Nature and the Ancestral Powers as occupying a hierarchy of negotiability, with the close ancestors and ancestresses of the pantheon being most open to this kind of pledging, and the higher Powers, both ancestral and natural, being less approachable in this way." See Keightley, "The Making of the Ancestors," 9–11.

53 Mattos, "Eastern Zhou Bronze Inscriptions," 85–124.

54 In the Geling manuscripts, Strip B4-109. See Chen Wei, "Churen daoci jilu," 380–81.

55 Wolf, "God, Ghosts, and Ancestors," 131–82.

56 *Zuozhuan*, Lord Wen, 1st year.

57 *Zuozhuan*, Lord Xi, 28th year.

58 *Zuozhuan*, Lord Wen, 10th year.

59 Yin Zhenhuan, "Cong wangwei jicheng," 17–24.

60 There are two possible etymologies for the word *gui* (ghost, Old Chinese: Baxter-Sagart *k-ʔujʔ, OCM *kwəiʔ): either it derives from the word *wei* (fear, Baxter-Sagart *ʔuj-s, OCM *ʔuih) as suggested here, or it is related to the word *gui* 歸 (return, Baxter-Sagart *kʷəj, OCM *kwəi), a hypothesis supported by *Shuowen jiezi*. Although both work well within the contexts I describe (see below), the former has better textual support in the Shang oracle-bone inscriptions. See also Schuessler, *ABC Etymological Dictionary of Old Chinese*, 267; Baxter and Sagart, "Word Formation in Old Chinese," 47–48.

61 Poo, "The Concept of Ghost," 176; Pu Muzhou, "Zhongguo gudai gui lunshu," 26–27; "Zhongguo gudai de xinyang," 30–33.

62 Ogata Nobuo, "Shunjū jidai ni okeru kōshi no shoso," 25–37.

63 *Yinxu jiagu keci leizuan*, 125–26; Shen Jianshi, "'Gui' zi yuanshi yiyi zhi shitan," 186–202.

64 *Zuozhuan*, Lord Cheng, 10th year; Yang Bojun, *Chunqiu Zuozhuan zhu*, 849–50.

65 Schuessler, *A Dictionary of Early Zhou Chinese*, 374; *ABC Etymological Dictionary of Old Chinese*, 352.

66 The *Zuo Commentary* story is complex but well structured, moving among multiple narratives of dreams and the real world of the Lord of Jin. As a third-person omniscient narrator, the author of the text gives us a panoramic view of these different spheres. In the dream world, the fear of the vengeful ghost is vividly described in spatial terms: the approach of the ghost from the outer regions of the palace to the lord's inner chamber, and later, the progression of the illness into the inner recesses of the lord's body. In the real world, the lord, who is described as a timid but cruel ruler, was unable to escape the death predicted by the shaman. Although the narrator detached himself from these worlds, the narrative shift between reality and the imagination gives readers a convincing vision of the ghost's power and the terror it elicited. For a discussion of the same story, see Li, *The Readability of the Past in Early Chinese Historiography*, 240–42.

67 *Zuozhuan*, Lord Cheng, 8th year.

68 *Zuozhuan*, Lord Xi, 10th year; Yang Bojun, *Chunqiu Zuozhuan zhu*, 334–35.

69 *Zuozhuan*, Lord Cheng, 18th year; Yang Bojun, *Chunqiu Zuozhuan zhu*, 906.

70 Legge, *The Ch'un Ts'ew with the Tso Chuen*, 515.

71 *Shanghai bowuguan cang Zhanguo Chu zhushu (7)*, plates 38–49, 171–88.

72 Kotera Atsushi, "Shangbo Chu jian 'Zhengzijiasang' yakuchō," 1–35; "Shangbo Chu jian 'Zhengzijiasang' no shiryoteki seikaku," 17–43.

73 *Zuozhuan*, Lord Ai, 2nd year; Yang Bojun, *Chunqiu Zuozhuan zhu*, 1615.

74 Sun Yirang, *Zhouli zhengyi*, 1696–97.

75 Lü Simian, *Lü Simian dushi zhaji*, 277–78; Yang Kuan, *Xizhou shi*, 435; Lu Defu, "Shuo 'bingsi zhe.'"

76 Suetsugu Nobuyuki, "Senshin no sensō giseisha," 29–52; "Inkyo ni okeru 'yūkōsha' no ba"; "Inkyo seihokukō ōryōku no 1174 gō shyōba o megutte," 34–64.

77 *Xichuan Xiasi Chunqiu Xiasi Chu mu*, 52–93.

78 *Xichuan Xiasi Chunqiu Xiasi Chu mu*, 104–89.

79 *Xichuan Xiasi Chunqiu Xiasi Chu mu*, 212–30.

80 On the excavators' incorrect identification of Prince Wu as the occupant of Tomb 2, see *Xichuan Xiasi Chunqiu Chu mu*, 320–324; Li Ling, "'Chu Shuzhisun Peng' jiujing shi shei?" 36–37; "Zailun Xichuan Xiasi Chu mu," 47–60. Other factors include the size and position of the tombs in the cemetery, the presence of weapons or chariot fittings among the burial goods (which tend to be absent from female tombs), and the presence of dowry vessels. See also Falkenhausen, "The Bronzes from Xiasi," 755–86.

81 Li Ling, "'Chu Shuzhisun Peng' jiujing shi shei?" 36–37; "Zailun Xichuan Xiasi Chu mu," 47–60.

82 *Zuozhuan*, Lord Xiang, 15th year; Yang Bojun, *Chunqiu Zuozhuan zhu*, 1021.

83 Chen Wei, "Xichuan Xiasi er hao muzhu," 32–33; Falkenhausen, "The Bronzes from Xiasi," 755–86.

84 Lai Guolong, "Jiyi de momie."

85 On the practice of *damnatio memoriae* in the classical world, see Hedrick, *History and Silence*, xii; Varner, *Mutilation and Transformation*.

86 Cohen, "The Avenging Ghost"; "Avenging Ghosts and Moral Judgment in Ancient Chinese Historiography," 97–108; *Tales of Vengeful Souls*; Pines, "History as a Guide to the Netherworld," 101–26.

87 The silk manuscript that Yuri Pines studied—*Chunqiu shiyu*, "The Affairs and Narratives of the Spring and Autumn," excavated from Tomb 3 at Mawangdui—comprises sixteen brief anecdotes of injustice and violent deaths that took place in the Spring and Autumn period. See Pines, "History as a Guide to the Netherworld," 101–26.

88 Feuchtwang, *The Anthropology of Religion, Charisma and Ghosts*, 126–30.

89 Feuchtwang, "An Unsafe Distance," 85.

90 The concept of evil in Chinese culture and religion is a contentious topic; see Schwartz, *The World of Thought in Ancient China*, 268–98; Eberhard, *Guilt and Sin in Traditional China*; Strickmann, "History, Anthropology, and Chinese Religion," 225, 236.

91 *Zuozhuan*, Lord Xiang, 30th year, Yang Bojun, *Chunqiu Zuozhuan zhu*, 1175–77.

92 *Zuozhuan*, Lord Xiang, 30th year, Yang Bojun, *Chunqiu Zuozhuan zhu*, 1175–77.

93 Legge, *The Ch'un Ts'ew with the Tso Chuen*, 618.

94 *Zuozhuan*, Lord Zhao, 7th year; Yang Bojun, *Chunqiu Zuozhuan zhu*, 1292. Translation with modifications follows Legge, *The Ch'un Ts'ew with the Tso Chuen*, 618. See also the discussion of this paragraph in Brashier, "Han Thanatology and the Division of 'Souls,'" 132, 148–49; Poo, *In Search of Personal Welfare*, 62–63.

95 Harper, *Early Chinese Medical Literature*, 378–79.

96 Schafer, *Pacing the Void*, 178; see also Pankenier, "The Metempsychosis of the Moon," 149–59.

97 Yang Bojun, *Chunqiu Zuozhuan zhu*, 1292.

98 Yü, "O Soul, Come Back!" 371. Yü assumed this association without presenting convincing evidence. The terms *jishengba* and *jisiba* in oracle-bone and bronze inscriptions have no obvious connection to the idea of human transformation. Only in transmitted literature is *ba* also written as *po*, although they were homophonous in Old Chinese.

99 The *hun* and *po* theories are essentially based on the theory of *qi* (breath, vapor, or vital energy) as the basic substance of the universe, which was current in the Eastern Zhou period. Its basic tenet is that *qi* constitutes not only the human body but also the physical world. The function of *qi* in the physical and human worlds has been extensively explained in the *Zuozhuan*, but its role in the formation of human beings is not explicitly clarified. See Unschuld, *Medicine in China*, chapter 3; Lewis, *Sanctioned Violence*, 213. Both Unschuld and Lewis date the emergence of the theory of *qi* to the last three centuries BCE. The concept of *qi* was laid out in the *Zuozhuan* and *Guoyu*; see Yang Rubin's introduction in Yang Rubin, ed., *Zhongguo gudai sixiang zhong de qilun ji shentiguan*, 3–59.

100 Legge, *The Ch'un Ts'ew with the Tso Chuen*, 618.

101 Similar stories of vengeful ghosts appear in *Zuozhuan*, Lord Xiang, 18th year; Lord Xi, 10th year; Lord Ai, 17th year; Lord Zhuang, 8th year.

102 von Glahn, *The Sinister Way*, 45–77.

103 On the Queen Mother of the West in the Han and later, see Cahill, *Transcendence and Divine Passion*.

104 See chapter 5.

105 Puyang Xishuipo yizhi kaogudui, "1988 nian Henan Puyang Xishuipo," 1063–65.

106 *Zuozhuan*, Lord Ai, 2nd year.

107 Hsu, *Ancient China in Transition*, 62–68; Lewis, "Warring States Political History," 620–32.

108 *Shiji*, "Bai Qi Wang Jian liezhuan," 73.2335.

109 Zhang Han, "Gu Changping zhanchang ziliao yanjiu," 95–104.

110 Shanxi sheng kaogu yanjiusuo, Jincheng shi wenhuaju, Gaoping shi bowuguan, "Changping zhi zhan yizhi," 33–40.

111 Hawkes, *The Songs of the South*, 117.

112 Hawkes, *The Songs of the South*, 117.

113 The "Jifa" chapter of the *Book of Rites* (Liji) stipulates three levels of public sacrifice to evil ghosts: the grand sacrifice to evil ghosts (*tali*), the public sacrifice to evil ghosts (*gongli*), and the lineage sacrifice to evil ghosts (*zuli*); see *Liji zhengyi* 46.801–2. Both historical records and excavated texts indicate that it was the state's responsibility to bury the military personnel who died in war and to properly take care of their families. See Wang Wentao, "Hanjian suojian Xi Han youfu cuoshi," 233–41.

114 Lewis, "Warring States Political History," 620–32.

115 The earliest reliable estimate of the Chinese population came from the first Han census in the year 2 CE, which records a total population of 59.6 million persons for the Han empire (Chao, *Man and Land in Chinese History*, 33; Bielenstein, "The Census of China during the Period 2–742 AD"; "Chinese Historical Demography"). Different scholars offer various demographic figures for the Chinese population before 2 CE; these include 32 million for 320 BCE in the Warring States period and 18 million for 205 BCE in the early Han dynasty (Zhang Shanyu, *Zhongguo renkou dili*, 14). For the middle Warring States period, Liang Qichao suggests 30 million, Guo Moruo more than 20 million, Guan Donggui 25 million, Lu Yu and Teng Zezhi 26 million, and Ge Jianxiong 40 to 45 million. For the early Han dynasty, Ge Jianxiong estimates the demographic figure at between 15 and 18 million, a range that many scholars have accepted. Although scholars have somewhat different numbers, they all agree that there was a dramatic decline in the population (at least 50 percent) between

the unification of Qin and the early Han dynasty. See Liang Qichao, "Zhongguo shi shang renkou zhi tongji," 902; Guo Moruo, *Zhongguo shigao*, 46; Guan Donggui, "Zhanguo zhi Hanchu de renkou bianqian," 645–56; Lu Yu and Teng Zezhi, *Zhongguo renkou tongshi*, vol. 1, 37–57; Ge Jianxiong, *Zhongguo renkou shi*, 300–4.

116 Watson, "Of Flesh and Bones," 155–86; Li, "Contagion and Its Consequences: The Problem of Death Pollution in Ancient China," 201–22. For a more general discussion see Yates, "Purity and Pollution in Early China," 479–536.

117 Ariès, *Western Attitudes toward Death*.

118 Metcalf and Huntington, *Celebrations of Death*; Morris, *Death Ritual and Social Structure in Classical Antiquity*.

119 Saxe, "Social Dimensions of Mortuary Practices," 4; Peebles, "Moundville and Surrounding Sites," 69.

120 In addition to the goat buried in the "waist pit," other traces of funerary rites discovered in Tomb 2 at Baoshan include a complete turtle shell discovered in the southwest corner of the pit, but its meaning is not clear.

121 Falkenhausen, *Chinese Society*, 192–94.

122 Seidel, "Afterlife: Chinese Concepts," 124.

123 Falkenhausen, *Chinese Society*, 192–94, 269–70.

124 Rosenblatt et al., *Grief and Mourning in Cross-cultural Perspective*, 49–98.

125 Van Gennep, *The Rites of Passage*, 146–65.

126 For ceremonial "killing" of objects, see Grinsell, "The Breaking of Objects as a Funerary Rite," 475–91; "The Breaking of Objects as a Funerary Rite: Supplementary Notes," 111–14. In the Chinese context, tie-breaking rituals certainly did not begin only in the Warring States period but are extensions of much earlier burial rituals, such as intentionally breaking bronze or jade weapons and burying them in tombs. Such was the case with jade and bronze daggers, pottery, and other artifacts, broken and buried underneath coffins; see *Xingan Shang dai damu*, 146; *Zhongguo kaoguxue liang Zhou juan*, 80; Zhongguo shehui kexueyuan Kaogu yanjiusuo Fengxi kaogudui, "1992 nian Fengxi fajue jianbao," 974–85, 964. Another form of the tie-breaking ritual in ancient China was the taboo on the deceased's personal names; see Lai Guolong, "Bihuizi," 127.

127 Thote, "Continuities and Discontinuities," 189–204.

128 On changes in tomb furnishings in the Spring and Autumn period, see Falkenhausen, "The Waning of the Bronze Age," 450–544. For discussions on spirit artifacts, see Falkenhausen, *Chinese Society*, 302–6; Wu, *The Art of the Yellow Springs*, 87–99.

129 Maspero, "Le mot *ming*," 249–96; Bodde, "The Term Ming-ch'i," 283. Both Maspero and Bodde correctly pointed out that *ming* here is the word for *numen* or "spirit." For an all-inclusive study of *mingqi*, see Wu Hong, "'Mingqi' de lilun he shijian," 72–81. But Wu Hung uses this term to cover all funerary objects in all periods (since the Neolithic); see also Wu, *The Art of the Yellow Springs*, 87–99. In my view, such a definition is too broad to have historical analytical value for the study of early Chinese art. Here I use it to refer only to the mortuary phenomena of the Warring States period and early empires.

130 Luo Zhenyu's *Gu mingqi tulu* (Illustrated Catalogue of Ancient Spirit Artifacts, published in 1916) was the first catalogue on *mingqi* in Chinese. But earlier, Édouard Chavannes and Berthold Laufer had recognized the scholarly value of ceramic funerary sculptures. See Chavannes, *Mission archéologique dans la Chine septentrionale*; Laufer, *Chinese Pottery of the Han Dynasty; Chinese Clay Figurines*. Laufer did not use the term *mingqi* specifically but the more general term *mortuary pottery* and did not relate it to the Chinese classical literature on *mingqi*.

131 Wu, "The Art and Architecture of the Warring States Period," 733.

132 *Xunzi*, "Lilun" (*Xunzi jijie*, 368–69; Knoblock, trans. *Xunzi*, vol. 3, 67–68). Two similar passages appear in the *Book of Rites*; see *Liji*, "Tan Gong" (*Liji zhengyi*, 8.144, 9.172–73).

133 Berkson, "Death and the Self in Ancient Chinese Thought," 137.

134 Childe, "Directional Changes in Funerary Practices," 13–19.

135 Burkert, *Creation of the Sacred*, 143.

136 In the *Zuo Commentary*, in the third year of Lord Yin (720 BCE), the "gentleman (*junzi*) comments" stratum of the text includes the discussion of proper sacrificial offerings to the spirits (*Zuozhuan*, Lord Yin, 3rd year; Yang Bojun, *Chunqiu Zuozhuan zhu*, 27–28; Legge, *The Ch'un Ts'ew with the Tso Chuen*, 13). Other similar passages, such as "the spirits have no fixed affiliation to an individual, but it is virtue (*de*) to which they cleave," emphasize sincerity, virtue, and other Confucian values (*Zuozhuan*, Lord Xi, 5th year; Yang Bojun, *Chunqiu Zuozhuan zhu*, 309; Legge, *The Ch'un Ts'ew with the Tso Chuen*, 146; Schaberg, *A Patterned Past*, 154–60). These statements testify to the basic intellectual and religious context within which the practice of burying spirit artifacts developed; see Falkenhausen, *Chinese Society*, 148–49.

137 Falkenhausen, *Chinese Society*, 302–6.

138 Graham, *Disputers of the Tao*, 16–18.

139 Poo, "Ideas concerning Death and Burial." The debate on postmortem intelligence also appears in a recently published Chu manuscript in the Shanghai Museum collection, entitled "All Things Flow into Form" (*Fanwu liuxing*), datable to the fourth century BCE (*Shanghai bowuguan cang Zhanguo Chu zhushu* [7], 75–132, 219–300. For a preliminary study and English translation, see Lai Guolong, "Fanwu liuxing xinyan [gao]"). "All Things Flow into Form" takes the form of a series of rhetorical questions, parts of which interrogate such contemporary cultural notions as life and death, ghosts and sacrifices, and burial practice. Some of the questions include: "Ghosts derive from human beings; why do [they] become divinely numinous? After the flesh and bone disintegrate, why does intelligence become brighter? Where do the departed go? Who knows their borders?" The author of this text assumes that dead people possess greater intelligence and are brighter than the living.

140 Falkenhausen, *Chinese Society*, 302–6.

141 Rosenblatt et al., *Grief and Mourning in Cross-cultural Perspective*, 49–98.

142 *Changsha Chu mu*, vol. 1, 422, 426; vol. 2, plate 162; Zhu Dexi and Qiu Xigui, "Zhanguo wenzi yanjiu (liuzhong)," 36–39. Zhu and Qiu translate the passage as "a pair of new shoes and a pair of old shoes." But based on the inventory from Tomb 2 at Changtaiguan, the lack of the measure word *liang* probably indicates that it is one shoe. The coupling of an old shoe and a new shoe for the dead may have additional magical meaning.

143 *Changsha Chu mu*, vol. 1, 422.

144 Writing just a few years ago, Mark Lewis expressed the perplexity as to why the early Chinese came to perceive the dead primarily as a threat. This chapter attempts to answer this question. See Lewis, *The Construction of Space in Early China*, 124.

2. The Transformation of Burial Space

Epigraph: Tschumi, "Violence of Architecture," 44.

1 The present chapter reprises the discussions first published in Lai, "The Transformation of Space in Early Chinese Burials."

2 Wang, *Han Civilization*, 175; Pu Muzhou, *Muzang yu shengsi*, 55–84; Xu Jijun, *Zhongguo sangzang shi*, 25; Li Rusen, *Han dai sangzang lisu*, 232–440; Huang Xiaofen, *Han mu de kaoguxue*

yanjiu, 90–93; Xing Yitian, "Han dai bihua de fazhan he bihua mu," 33–34; Wu, *The Art of the Yellow Springs*, 29–30.

3 Wu, "From Temple to Tomb," 78–115; *The Art of the Yellow Springs*, 30–33; Thote, "Chinese Coffins from the First Millennium B.C.," 22–37.

4 Wu Hung categorically attributes the shift to major changes in ancestral worship, conceptions of the soul, the idea of the afterlife, and the formation of an underworld bureaucracy. See Wu, *The Art of the Yellow Springs*, 30–31.

5 Lewis, *The Construction of Space in Early China*, 77–133.

6 Huang Wei, "Lun Han dai fuqi hezangmu de leixing yu yanbian," 264–85; "Shilun Zhou Qin liang Han fuqi hezang lisu de jige wenti," 322–35; Liu Rui and Liu Tao, *Xi Han zhuhouwang lingmu zhidu yanjiu*, 289–90.

7 Huang Xiaofen, *Han mu de kaoguxue yanjiu*, 92–93; Thote, "Chinese Coffins from the First Millennium B.C.," 37.

8 Dubs, "The Custom of Mourning to the Third Year," 40–42; Lai, "The Diagram of the Mourning System from Mawangdui."

9 Literature on this subject is vast; see, e.g., Hall, *The Hidden Dimension*; Rapoport, *House Form and Culture*; *The Meaning of the Built Environment*; Tambiah, "Animals Are Good to Think and Good to Prohibit," 423–59; Bourdieu, "The Berber House or the World Reversed," 151–70; Douglas, "Symbolic Orders in the Use of Domestic Space," 513–21; Humphrey, "Inside a Mongolian Tent," 273–75; Fletcher, "Settlement Studies," 47–162; Hugh-Jones, *From the Milk River*; Pader, *Symbolism, Social Relations and the Interpretation of Mortuary Remains*.

10 Schneider, *The Explicit Body in Performance*; Inomata and Coben, eds., *Archaeology of Performance*; Pearson and Shanks, eds., *Theater/Archaeology*; Turnbull, "Performance and Narrative, Bodies and Movement," 125–43; Mitchell, "Performance."

11 Tschumi, *Architecture and Disjunction*.

12 Graham, *Disputers of the Tao*, 39–40, 174–75, 258–60; Fung, *A History of Chinese Philosophy*, 78–79, 89–91, 104, 127–28, 134, 344–50; Gernet, "Être enterré nu," 3–16; Poo, "Ideas Concerning Death and Burial," 25–62.

13 Many of these discussions were recorded in the *Analects*, in *Mozi, Mengzi, Xunzi, Zhuangzi, Han Feizi, Lüshi chunqiu*, and in the Confucian classics such as *Protocols of Ceremonies* and *Book of Rites*.

14 *Qinghai Liuwan*.

15 Thote, "Burial Practices as Seen in Rulers' Tombs of the Eastern Zhou Period," 65–107; "Pratiques funéraires dans le royaume de Chu," 359–69.

16 The Old Chinese reconstruction for *zang* is Baxter-Sagart *tsˤaŋ-s, and for *cang* is *m-tsʰˤaŋ.

17 *Liji*, "Tan Gong shang" (*Liji zhengyi* 8.149); a similar passage appears in *Lüshi chunqiu*, "Ansi" (Zhang Shuangdi et al., *Lüshi chunqiu yizhu*, 271–72); Riegel, "Do Not Serve the Dead as You Serve the Living," 306n19. The translation is slightly modified.

18 Riegel, "Do Not Serve the Dead as You Serve the Living," 306.

19 In *Shuowen jiezi* the word for "coffin," *guan* 棺, was glossed as "to shut, to close," *guan* 關, which Xu Shen also interpreted as "to hide the corpse." But the Old Chinese reconstruction for "coffin," *guan* is *kʷˤan (> Later Han *kuan), and for "to shut, to close," *guan*, is *kˤron (> Later Han *kuan). Therefore it is clear that Xu Shen's interpretation was based on Han dynasty pronunciations, not the pre-Qin pronunciation. See *Shouwen jiezi*, 27b and 125b.

20 *Yili zhushu*, 35.408–432. For the date of the *Protocols of Ceremonies*, see Chen Gongrou, "Shi sangli, jixili zhong suo jizai de sangzang zhidu," 67–84; Wang Hui, "Cong kaogu yu guwenzi de jiaodu kan *Yili* de chengshu niandai," 54–60; Hayashi Minao, "Girei to taite," 1–25.

21 *Zuozhuan*, Lord Xiang, 29th year.

22 Xu Yongqing and He Huiqin, *Zhongguo gushi*; Brown, "Did the Early Chinese Preserve Corpses?" 201–23.

23 Li Jianmin, "Zhongguo gudai 'yanci' lisu kao," 319–43. Also, for reasons of public health and sanitation, public graveyards were set up to bury the bodies of prisoners, the poor, and the homeless. Chinese archaeologists have excavated cemeteries of prison-laborers of the Eastern Han dynasty in the suburb of Luoyang in Henan; see Zhongguo kexueyuan kaogu yanjiu suo Luoyang gongzuodui, "Dong Han Luoyang cheng nanjiao de Xingtu mudi," 2–17. For later Song dynasty public graveyards, see *Bei Song Shanzhou Louzeyuan*. See also de Groot, *The Religious System of China*, vol. 3, 914–21; Eschenbach, "Public Graveyards of the Song Dynasty," 215–52.

24 Johnson, "Epic and History in Early China," 255–71.

25 *Hanshu* 53.2428-2432; Li Jianmin, "Shiti, kulou, hunpo," 3–24.

26 Weiner, *Inalienable Possessions*.

27 For examples of bronze inscriptions, see below; *Zuozhuan*, Lord Yin 1st year; Yang Bojun, *Chunqiu Zuozhuan zhu*, 14.

28 In another article, Hayashi expanded his interpretation to cover whole periods of the Shang and Zhou dynasties, and he posited that during these periods the religious purpose of burying ritual implements was to enable the dead to continue their ancestral sacrifices in the otherworld. See Hayashi Minao, "In Shū jidai ni okeru shisha no saishi," 1–26. In the title "In Shū jidai ni okeru shisha no saishi" (The Sacrifice to/by the Deceased in the Shang and Zhou Dynasties), Hayashi played with the subtle vagueness of the Japanese particle "no," which could mean both "by" and "to" in English in this context. In fact, the author implies both meanings in this article.

29 Chang Yuzhi, *Shang dai zhouji zhidu*; Keightley, *The Ancestral Landscape*, 37–53.

30 Yu Weichao and Gao Ming, "Zhou dai yongding zhidu yanjiu"; Li Ling, "Chu ding tushuo," 31–36; Falkenhausen, "Archaeological Perspectives on the Philosophicization of Royal Zhou Ritual."

31 Chang, *Art, Myth, and Ritual*; Liu and Chen, *State Formation in Early China*.

32 Creel, *The Birth of China*, 176–77.

33 The term *diting* appears on the inscriptions on *Yin Zhou jingwen jicheng*, 8.4317; the term *disuo*, in *Yin Zhou jingwen jicheng*, 1.272–8, 1.285; the term *dizhipi*, in *Yin Zhou jingwen jicheng*, 8.4315.

34 Luoyang bowuguan, "Luoyang Ai Cheng shu mu qingli jianbao," 65–67; Zhao Zhenhua, "Ai cheng shu ding de mingwen yu niandai," 68–69; Zhang Zhenglang, *Zhang Zhenglang wenshi lunji*, 581–86.

35 Xiangfan shi bowuguan, "Hubei Xiangyang Tuanshan Dong Zhou mu," 783; Huang Xiquan and Li Zucai, "Zheng Zanggong zhi sun ding mingwen kaoshi," 855–58.

36 Wang, *Cosmology and Political Culture in Early China*.

37 Scholars have interpreted *yan* and *yi* in the abovementioned phrases as words describing the souls of ancestors. See Ikeda Suetoshi, *Chūgoku kodai shūkyōshi kenkyū: Seido to shisō*, 199–15; Poo, *In Search of Personal Welfare*, 62. But several authors have pointed out that this may not be correct. Recently, one scholar has suggested that the *yan* 嚴 here should be read as *han* 譀 (both words use *gan* 敢, Old Chinese *kˤamʔ, as the phonetic; thus they were cognates in Old Chinese), which means "to boast, to brag." As has been noted, this notion of ancestors who are able to ascend to Heaven and brag about the deeds of their offspring is the precursor of the later Chinese popular religious belief that certain deities (like the stove god) could report the deeds of people on earth to Heaven. See Wang Guanying, "Shuo 'yanzaishang, yizaixia,'" 114–16; "Zaishuo jinwen taoyu 'yanzaishang, yizaixia,'" 56–59;

Wang Rencong, "Xi Zhou jinwen 'yan zai shang' jie," 72–74, 81; Pan Yukun, "Jinwen 'yan zai shang,' 'yi zai xia' yu 'jing nai suye' shijie," 70–75. However, this interpretation is still controversial. Here I read *yan* as cognate with *jian* 監 (Old Chinese *kˤamʔ, "to oversee from above"). I thank Robert Eno for his suggestion.

38 Keightley, "The Religious Commitment," 211–24.

39 One important example is the political ideology of the "Heaven's mandate" (*tianming*): bronze inscriptions show that Qin, Chu, and Qi rulers all adopted this Zhou political ideology and claimed that they received "Heaven's mandate" to rule the realm, but they only made this declaration to their domestic audience, as in the case of the rulers of the non-Ji clan, such as the Qi, Chu, Qin, and Yue, who all used the title "king" (*wang*) in domestic settings in the Spring and Autumn period. See Zhang Zhenglang, *Zhang Zhenglang wenshi lunji*, 706–13. On the "Heaven's mandate," see Pankenier, "The Cosmo-political Background," 121–76.

40 For the use of *shi* meaning both "to sacrifice to" and "to receive from" in classical Chinese, see Qiu Xigui, *Gudai wenshi yanjiu xintan*, 143–45.

41 For more discussion, see chapter 5.

42 Xin Lixiang, *Han dai huaxiangshi zonghe yanjiu*, 67, 71–73.

43 Wu, *The Art of the Yellow Springs*, 32.

44 For the typology and nomenclature of Chu bronzes and their ceramic imitations, see Li, "On the Typology of Chu Bronzes," 57–113. On the evolution of Chu bronzes, see Mackenzie, "Chu Bronze Work," 107–57; "The Evolution of Southern Bronze Styles," 31–48; So, *Eastern Zhou Ritual Bronzes*.

45 Thorp, "The Qin and Han Imperial Tombs and the Development of Mortuary Architecture," 17–37; Rawson, "The Eternal Palaces of the Western Han," 5–58.

46 Thorp, "The Qin and Han Imperial Tombs and the Development of Mortuary Architecture," 18.

47 Wu, "From Temple to Tomb," 78–115; *Monumentality*, 79–121; *The Art of the Yellow Springs*, 31–32.

48 Falkenhausen, Review of *Monumentality*, 193; Lewis, *The Construction of Space in Early China*, 122–23; Zhang Lizhi, "Cong miao dao mu de beihou," 46–52. In his recent book, Wu Hung recapitulates his early arguments without considering these criticisms. It is important in this discussion to distinguish the ancestor cults of the Shang and Western Zhou dynasties from the cult of the dead (including vengeful ghosts and potentially harmful ancestral spirits) developed in the Eastern Zhou, Qin, and early Han periods. Ancestor cults continued after the Warring States period, albeit occupying a comparatively less significant position. The structural correlation between *hun/po* and temple/tomb did not really capture the essence of the temple/tomb dualism. The idea and practice of "postmortem immortality" in the afterlife, as Robert Ford Campany has recently shown, were rhetorical strategies for religious persuasion (Campany, *Making Transcendents*), and we have no evidence that it attracted "millions of people of different classes." See Wu, *The Art of the Yellow Springs*, 32.

49 *Jishi* in Jiudian Strip 49; see *Jiudian Chu jian*, 15–16, 51, 116. *Cishi* in Shuihudi rishu A, Strip 18 back 5; see *Shuihudi Qin Mu zhujian*, 104, 211.

50 Peng Hao, "Shuihudi Qinjian 'wangshici' yu jilü kaobian," 239–43.

51 *Hanshu*, "Wei Xian zhuan," 43.3115–3116; Zhang Lizhi, "Cong miao dao mu de beihou," 46.

52 *Hou Hanshu*, 3195–99.

53 Zhang Lizhi, "Cong miao dao mu de beihou," 46–52.

54 Lewis, *The Construction of Space in Early China*, 122–28. Although the imperial burial practice had a tremendous impact on that of the other levels of society, in this particular case, it did not accord with the general trend. For example, in the middle Western Han period, most

elite and middling landowners, and even commoners, adopted the joint burial of husband and wife in the same horizontal chamber-style tombs. Most Western Han imperial and princely couples, however, were buried separately in different horizontal chamber-style tombs.

55 Machida Akira, *Kahaku chihō ni okeru Kanhaka no kōzō*, 1–66; Takahama Yūko, "Zhongguo gudai dongshi mu," 17–23; Rawson, "The Eternal Palaces of the Western Han," 5–58.

56 Takahama Yūko, "Zhongguo gudai dongshi mu," 17–23; for an analysis of the catacomb tombs at the Zhangjiapo cemetery and in later Qin territory, see Falkenhausen, *Chinese Society*, 205–13, 308–9.

57 Huang Xiaofen, *Han mu de kaoguxue yanjiu*, 41–42.

58 The earliest known tomb with multiple compartments connected by doors is Tomb 1 at Nanzhihui in Fengxiang (Shaanxi), belonging to a ruler of the state of Qin (mid-sixth century BCE), which also features possibly the earliest stave walls (*ticou*) in tomb construction. See Han Wei, "Fengxiang Qin gong lingyuan," 30–37; Han Wei and Jiao Nanfeng, "Qin du Yong cheng kaogu," 111–27; Wenwu bianji weiyuanhui, *Wenwu kaogu gongzuo shinian*, 300–301; Falkenhausen, *Chinese Society*, 306; Campbell, "The Form and Function," 227–58.

59 *Lüshi chunqiu*, "Ansi" (Zhang Shuangdi et al., *Lüshi chunqiu yizhu*, 271–72); Knoblock and Riegel, trans., *The Annals of Lü Buwei*, 230.

60 *Liji*, "Tan Gong shang" (*Liji zhengyi*, 6.112); Wang Zhongshu, "Zhongguo gudai muzang gaishuo," 451; Wang Shimin, "Zhongguo Chunqiu Zhanguo shidai de zhongmu," 459–66; Yang Kuan, *Zhongguo gudai lingqin zhidushi yanjiu*.

61 Gao Quxun, "Yindai muzang yiyou muzhong shuo," 1–13.

62 *Tengzhou Qianzhangda mudi*.

63 Henan Xinyang diqu wenguanhui and Guangshan xian wenguanhui, "Chunqiu zaoqi Huang jun Meng fufu mu fajue baogao," 302.

64 Xinyang diqu wenguanhui and Guangshan xian wenguanhui, "Henan Guangshan Chunqiu Huang Ji Tuofu mu fajue jianbao," 26.

65 Li Xueqin, "Lun Han Huai jian de Chunqiu qingtongqi," 151; Chen Pan, *Chunqiu Dashibiao lieguo juexing ji cunmiebiao zhuanyi*, 216a–218a.

66 Li Xueqin, "Lun Han Huai jian de Chunqiu qingtongqi," 156–59.

67 Xinyang diqu wenguanhui and Xinyang shi wenguanhui, "Henan Xinyang shi Pingxi 5 hao mu fajue jianbao," 20.

68 Anhui sheng wenwu kaogu yanjiusuo and Shucheng xian wenwu guanlisuo, "Anhui Shucheng xian Hekou Chunqiu mu," 58.

69 Hu Fangping, "Zhongguo fengtumu de chansheng he liuxing," 557; "Luelun Chu mu fenqiu chansheng de beijing yu niandai," 79; Han Guohe, "Lun Zhongguo gudai fenqiu mu de chansheng yu fazhan," 35; Huang Xiaofen, *Han mu de kaoguxue yanjiu*, 173–74.

70 *Gushi Hougudui yihao mu*, 5–6.

71 Ou Tansheng, "Gushi Hougudui Wu taizi Fuchai furen mu de Wu wenhua Yinsu," 33–38.

72 Yang Nan, *Jiangnan tudun yicun yanjiu*.

73 Suzhou bowuguan, *Zhenshan Dongzhou mudi*.

74 Guo Dewei, "Jiangling Chu mu lunshu"; Jiangling xian wenwu gongzuozu, "Hubei Jiangling Chu zhong diaocha"; Huang Xiaofen, *Han mu de kaoguxue yanjiu*, 176–77.

75 Huang Xiaofen, *Han mu de kaoguxue yanjiu*, 176–77.

76 Shanxi sheng kaogu yanjiusuo Houma gongzuozhan, *Jin du Xintian*, 24–26. Lothar von Falkenhausen dates them to the late Spring and Autumn period; see Falkenhausen, *Chinese Society*, 336–37.

77 Hebei sheng wenguanchu, Handan diqu wenbaosuo, and Handan shi wenbaosuo, "Hebei Handan Zhao wangling"; Hao Liangzhen, "Zhao guo wangling," 5–12.

78 *Huixian fajue baogao*, 69–109.

79 *Yan Xiadu*, 646–731.

80 Cai Quanfa, "Zheng Han gucheng Han wenhua," 122.

81 Zhang Xuehai, "Tian Qi liuling kao," 20–22.

82 Hebei sheng wenwu guanlichu, "Hebei sheng Pingshan xian Zhangguo shiqi Zhongshanguo muzang fajue jianbao," 1–31; *Cuo Mu*; *Zhangguo Zhongshan guo Lingshou cheng*.

83 Zhang Shuangdi et al., *Lüshi chunqiu yizhu*, 271–72; Riegel, "Do Not Serve the Dead as You Serve the Living," 310.

84 Powers, "Artistic Taste, the Economy and the Social Order in Former Han China," 285–305; "Unit Style and System Style," 743–91; "Classical Chinese Ornament and the Origins of 'Taste' in China," 287–95; *Pattern and Person*.

85 Poo, "Ideas Concerning Death and Burial," 25–62; Pu Muzhou, *Muzang yu shengsi*, 238–53.

86 Guo Dewei, *Chuxi muzang yanjiu*, 17–18.

87 Guo Dewei, *Chuxi muzang yanjiu*, 17.

88 Lewis, *The Construction of Space in Early China*, 77–133.

89 This line is from *Shijng* (The Book of Odes), LXIII, "Daju."

90 For the persistence of the lineage structure in early Chinese society, see Xing Yitian, "Cong Zhanguo zhi Xihan de zuju, zuzang, shiye," 396–435.

91 *Baoji Yuguo mudi*; Falkenhausen, *Chinese Society*, 78–80.

92 See Han Guohe, *Qin Han Wei Jin sangzang zhidu yanjiu*, 222–24. Because the two encasements at Baoxiangsi are not at the same level and a layer of yellow clay, 1.5 meters wide between the fine sticky clay (*qinggaoni*), is used to seal each encasement, it is possible that these encasements were interred in two different pits that partially overlapped. Because the northern encasement and the pit were damaged by the local farmers when they took the bronze vessels out, archaeologists were not able to determine whether there were two pits or one. As Lothar von Falkenhausen observes, however, the published section drawing (303, plate 2) strongly suggests that the southern encasement was completed before the northern one. See Henan Xinyang diqu wenguanhui and Guangshan xian wenguanhui, "Chunqiu zaoqi Huang jun Meng fufu mu fajue baogao," 330; Falkenhausen, "The Waning of the Bronze Age," 505.

93 Li Rusen, *Han dai sangzang lisu*, 217–19.

94 Wang Zhongshu, "Zhongguo gudai muzang gaishuo," 449–58; Huang Wei "Lun Han dai fuqi hezangmu de leixing yu yanbian," 264–85; "Shilun Zhou Qin liang Han fuqi hezang lisu de jige wenti," 322–35.

95 Allan, *The Shape of the Turtle*.

96 Zhang Changshou, "Qiangliu yu huangwei," 49–52.

97 Sun Hua, "Xuanyu yu zhenrong," 90–96. A detailed study of the double coffin found in Marquis Yi's tomb also shows that there is a close connection between the coffin and the domicile. See Thote, "The Double Coffin of Leigudun Tomb No. 1," 23–46, especially 34–36.

98 *Dangyang Zhaojiahu Chu mu*, 145–47.

99 Yu Weichao, "Han dai zhuhouwang," 117–18; Pu Muzhou, *Muzang yu shengsi*, 198; Poo, *In Search of Personal Welfare*, 165–67; Wang, *Han Civilization*, 175.

100 *Yinshan Yue wang ling*.

101 The access ramp is near the surface, almost at the same level as the burial surface, which means one can walk along the access ramp into the burial chamber. The reduction of the distance between the end of the ramp and the burial surface is an important step in the development from vertical pit-style tombs to horizontal chamber-style tombs in the early Han dynasty.

102 On Marquis Yi's tomb, see *Zeng Hou Yi mu*. Judging from the middle and late Spring and Autumn period burials, such as the Xiasi tombs, the Chu elite wholeheartedly embraced the

Shang-Zhou vertical pit-style tradition until the early Warring States period. See *Xichuan Xiasi Chunqiu Chu mu*. No Chu royal burials of the early Warring States period have been excavated.

103 Falkenhausen, *Chinese Society*, 306–8.

104 Wu, "The Art and Architecture of the Warring States Period," 721–23; Huang Xiaofen, *Han mu de kaoguxue yanjiu*, 65–69.

105 Wang Lihua, "Shilun Chu mu muguo zhong de menchuang jiegou," 306–17.

106 Wu, "The Art and Architecture of the Warring States Period," 723.

107 Yantai shi wenwu guanli weiyuanhui, "Shandong Changdao Wanggou Dong Zhou muqun," 57–87.

108 *Xunzi jijie*, 369–71.

109 Stein, "Architecture et pensée religieuse en Extrême-Orient," 163–86.

110 Granet, *La pensée chinoise*, 349–56; Stein, *The World in Miniature*, 121–74.

111 Thote, "Chinese Coffins from the First Millennium B.C.," 22–37.

112 Wu, "Art in Its Ritual Context," 116–18; Falkenhausen, "Sources of Taoism," 5–8.

113 The concepts of the tame and the wild are popular in anthropological literature on spatial conception. Here I borrow theoretical insights from the humanist geographer Yi-Fu Tuan, especially his work on human attitudes and conceptions of space and place (Tuan, *Topophilia*; *Landscapes of Fear*), although he did not use these two terms specifically. See discussion in chapter 5, this volume.

114 Granet, *La pensée chinoise*, 349–56; Stein, "Architecture et pensée religieuse en Extrême-Orient," 163–86; Stein, *The World in Miniature*, 121–74.

115 Falkenhausen, "Mortuary Behavior in Pre-Imperial Qin," 138–41.

116 Anhui sheng wenwu yanjiusuo and Bangbu shi bowuguan, "Anhui Bangbu shi Shuangdun yi hao Chunqiu muzang," 39–45; Anhui sheng wenwu kaogu yanjiusuo and Bangbu shi bowuguan, "Bangbu Shuangdun yi hao Chunqiu mu fajue jianbao," 4–18; Anhui sheng wenwu kaogu yanjiusuo and Fengyang xian wenwu guanlisuo, "Anhui Fengyang Bianzhuang yi hao Chunqiu mu fajue jianbao," 21–29; *Fengyang Dadongguan yu Bianzhuang*.

117 Feng Shi, "Shanggu yuzhouguan de kaoguxue yanjiu," 399–491.

118 Dong Chuping, "Diwen: Tianyuan difang kao," 188–206.

119 *Shiji*, "Qin shihuang benji," 6.265. The emphasis is mine.

120 Duan Qingbo, *Qin Shi Huangdi lingyuan kaogu yanjiu*.

121 Chang Yong and Li Tong, "Qin Shihuang ling zhong maicang gong de chubu yanjiu," 659–63, 671; Wang Xueli, *Qin Shihuang ling yanjiu*, 42–43; Duan Qingbo, *Qin Shi Huangdi lingyuan kaogu yanjiu*.

122 Falkenhausen, *Chinese Society*.

123 On lamps in Warring States tombs, see Lai, "Lighting the Way in the Afterlife," 20–28; in tombs of other ancient civilizations, see De Geus, "*Signum Ignis Signum Vitae*," 65–75; Goebs, "Expressing Luminosity in Iconography," 57–71.

124 Huang Xiaofen, *Han mu de kaoguxue yanjiu*, 70–95.

125 For the translation of *ticou* as "stave wall," see Campbell, "The Form and Function," 227–58.

126 Riegel, "Do Not Serve the Dead as You Serve the Living," 308–9; Campbell, "The Form and Function," 227–58.

127 *Cuo mu*, vol. 1, 104–10, vol. 2, color plate 2.

128 Yang Hongxun, "Zhanguo Zhongshan wangling zhaoyutu yanjiu," 119–38.

129 For textual evidence and Han dynasty examples, see Loewe, "State Funerals of the Han Empire," 5–72, esp. 28–42; Campbell, "The Form and Function," 227–58.

130 Tian Wei, "Jishi jitan mu," 59–67; Yang Aiguo, "Lingmu fangdao sheshi," 436–38.

131 *Hui Xian fajue baogao*, 89.

132 Shijiazhuang shi tushuguan kaogu xiaozu, "Hebei Shijiazhuang beijiao Xi Han mu," 52–55. The date and the identity of the tomb occupant are still debated; see Sun and Zhao, "You chutu yinzhang kan liangchu muzang de muzhu," 333–38.

133 *Changsha Mawangdui yihao Han mu.*

134 The western compartment was not mentioned on the inventory list, but, according to the logic of the names, it must have been called "the right of the encasement" (*guoyou*).

135 Watson, "The Structure of Chinese Funerary Rites," 12.

136 *Yili zhushu,* 39.462–63.

137 *Changsha Mawangdui er san hao Han mu,* 7–9, 28. Interestingly, unlike the two tomb guardian figures in the Wangchengpo tomb, whose extended arms block the passage (see fig. 2.20), the extended arms of the figurines in Tombs 2 and 3 at Mawangdui are parallel to the earth walls of the passage.

138 Wu, "A Deity without Form," 38–45; Wu, *The Art of the Yellow Springs,* 64–68.

139 Hunan sheng bowuguan, "Changsha Xiangbizui yi hao Xi Han mu," 111–30.

140 Song Shaohua, "Changsha Xi Han Yuyang mu," 59–63. Belonging to a queen of the local Kingdom of Changsha, the tomb is called the "Yuyang" queen's tomb because many items of the lacquerware and the timbers used to construct the stave walls were inscribed with the name "Yuyang."

141 Local archaeologists have discovered five such stave-walled tombs in Changsha, but only four were reported and briefly studied. For the other two tombs, see Changsha wenhuaju wenwuzu, "Changsha Xianjiahu Xi Han Cao Zhuan mu," 1–16; Changsha shi wenwu kaogu yanjiusuo, "Changsha Fengpengling yi hao Han mu," 21–41.

142 Tian Lizhen, "Shilun Han dai de huilang zangzhi," 64–70.

143 Huang Xiaofen, *Han mu de kaoguxue yanjiu,* 90–93.

144 Campbell, "The Form and Function," 237.

145 Huang Xiaofen, *Han mu de kaoguxue yanjiu,* 70–95; Liu Rui and Liu Tao, *Xi Han zhuhouwang lingmu zhidu yanjiu,* 459–60; Campbell, "The Form and Function," 237.

146 *Beijing Dabaotai Han mu,* 308–9.

147 *Hanshu,* 68.2948.

148 See the discussion on the meanings of *pianfang* in Gao Chongwen, "Shi 'pianguo,' 'pianfang,' yu 'piandian,'" 46–52; Liu Rui and Liu Tao, *Xi Han zhuhouwang lingmu zhidu yanjiu,* 351–69; Campbell, "The Form and Function," 233–34.

149 *Qinghua daxue cang Zhanguo zhujian (yi).*

150 Chen Wei, "Qinghua jian Chuju 'pianshi' gushi xiaokao."

151 Gao Chongwen, "Shi 'pianguo,' 'pianfang,' yu 'piandian,'" 46–52; Xiao Kangda, "'Pianfang' xinjie," 53–57.

152 Huang Xiaofen, *Han mu de kaoguxue yanjiu.*

153 An inventory discovered in an early Western Han tomb (dated 184 BCE) at Xiejiaqiao in Jiangling (Hubei) lists "an encasement of peace with chambers" (*pianguojushi*). The dimensions are listed, and they match those of the wooden encasement. See Gao Chongwen, "Shi 'pianguo,' 'pianfang,' yu 'piandian,'" 46–47.

154 Huang Xiaofen, *Han mu de kaoguxue yanjiu,* 92.

155 Liu Rui and Liu Tao, *Xi Han zhuhouwang lingmu zhidu yanjiu,* 360–69.

156 Thorp, "Mountain Tombs and Jade Burial Suits," 26–39.

157 Lai, "The Transformation of Space in Early Chinese Burials," 34; Wang, "The Forms and Functions of Mat Weights."

158 Wu, *The Art of the Yellow Springs,* 67.

159 *Mancheng Han mu,* 337.

160 *Hou Hanshu,* 2159–60; Yang Shuda, *Han dai hunsang lisu kao,* 176–78.

Notes to Chapter Two

161 Loewe, *Divination, Mythology and Monarchy in Han China*, 282–83.

162 *Liji* in *Shisanjing zhushu*, vol. 5, 134; Legge, *Li Chi*, vol. 1, 141–42.

163 Loewe, *Divination, Mythology and Monarchy in Han China*, 282–83.

164 In southern China during the Han dynasty, the tombs of the middle and lower levels of society were slow in adopting the horizontal chamber style. The dominant form remained the vertical pit-style, but grave goods certainly changed significantly.

165 *Luoyang Shaogou Han mu*, 45–47.

166 *Luoyang Shaogou Han mu*, 241.

167 Shaanxi sheng kaogu yanjiusuo, "Shaanxi Xunyi faxian Dong Han bihuamu," 76; Greiff and Yin, *Das Grab des Bin Wang*; Zheng Yan, "Guanyu Han dai sangzang huaxiang guanzhe wenti de sikao," 39–55; Zheng, "Concerning the Viewers of Han Mortuary Art," 103–4.

168 Zheng, "Concerning the Viewers of Han Mortuary Art," 103–4.

169 Xin Lixiang, *Han dai huaxiangshi zonghe yanjiu*, 67, 71–73. See also Wu, "From Temple to Tomb."

170 Xin Lixiang, *Han dai huaxiangshi zonghe yanjiu*, 322–24.

171 Wu, "From Temple to Tomb"; Xin Lixiang, *Han dai huaxiangshi zonghe yanjiu*, 66–83.

172 Fairbank, "A Structural Key to Han Mural Art," 52–88. The so-called Zhu Wei's tomb was discovered in the 1930s but not scientifically excavated. While there are hundreds of excavated Eastern Han dynasty cemeteries, in very few have both the tomb and the shrine survived. The two burials excavated in the Wu family cemetery at Jiaxiang, Shandong, include several shrines whose owners have not yet been identified. See Jiang Yingju and Wu Wenqi, *Han dai Wu shi muqun shike yanjiu*, 119–27. There are only two other excavated examples: one is the tomb and shrine at Baiji near Xuzhou City, and the other is Tombs 1 and 2, dating to 171 CE by inscription, at Chulan, Su County, Anhui. See Nanjing bowuyuan, "Xuzhou Qingshanquan Baiji Dong Han huaxiangshi mu," 137–50; Wang Buyi, "Anhui Suxian Chulan Han huaxiangshi mu," 515–49; "Chulan Han huaxiangshi mu ji youguan wuxiang de renshi," 60–67.

3. The Presence of the Invisible

Epigraphs: Gombrich, "Meditations on a Hobby Horse," 9; Freedberg, *The Power of Images*, 201.

1 Armstrong, *The Powers of Presence*; *The Affecting Presence*; Freedberg, *The Power of Images*. In his book, Freedberg makes no mention of Armstrong's pioneering works on this topic. Freedberg sees the living presence that people identified in certain images (exactly Armstrong's point) as a visual recognition of formal likeness. Although he claims to have considered images in the broader sense and from a variety of cultural and artistic traditions, his cases are based primarily on human figures in the Western tradition. Freedberg's conclusion is presented almost exclusively in terms of European standards of representation, which have historically privileged verisimilitude. Despite his effort to universalize the theory, images from traditions that do not privilege formal likeness remain peripheral to his argument. Although Freedberg's work has generated a lively dialogue about images and presence in art history and anthropology (for example, Shepherd and Maniura, eds., *Presence*), many of the earlier discussions in anthropology and in the historiography of non-Western art, especially African art, have been neglected. This chapter presents a more nuanced discussion of the religious context within which the anthropomorphic representation of the dead and gods first appeared in early Chinese art.

2 Freedberg, *The Power of Images*, 201.

3 On the lack of representations of kings in early Chinese art, see Zhao Huacheng and Yu Liqi, "Zunzhe wuxing," 344–53; Trigger, *Time and Traditions*, 165; *Understanding Early*

Civilizations, 556. For previous scholarship on the rise of the human figure in early Chinese art, see Fong, "The Origin of Chinese Pictorial Representation of the Human Figure"; Kesner, "Portrait Aspects and Social Function," 33–42; Seckel, "The Rise of Portraiture in Chinese Art"; Thote, "Intercultural Relations as Seen from Chinese Pictorial Bronzes of the Fifth Century BCE," 10–41; Falkenhausen, "From Action to Image in Early Chinese Art."

4   See Liu Li, "Early Figuration in China: Ideological, Social and Ecological Implications," 271–86.

5   Chengde diqu wenwu baoguansuo and Luanping xian bowuguan, "Hebei Luanping xian Houtaizi yizhi fajue jianbao," 53–71.

6   Wang Yucheng, "Lun Houtaizi yuanshi nüxing fenmian xilie shidiao," 57–61.

7   Tang Chi, "Shilun Luanping Houtaizi chutu de shidiao nüshen xiang," 46–51.

8   For the definition of image magic, see Freedberg, *The Power of Images*, 263.

9   Chen Xingcan, "Fengchan wushu yu zuxian chongbai," 92–98.

10 Hai Yan, "Chifeng diqu faxian de xinshiqi shidai nüxing diaosuxiang," 39–48.

11 See more discussion in Wang Yucheng, "Zhongguo gudai de renxing fangshu jiqi dui Riben de yingxiang," 32–56.

12 Chang, "The Animal in Shang and Chou Bronze Art," 176; Chang, "Changing Relationships of Man and Animals," 174–96.

13 Huang Mingchong, "'Taotiewen' de zai sikao," 1–102.

14 Chen Mengjia, "Shang dai de shenhua yu wushu"; Chang, *Art, Myth, and Ritual*; Rao Zongyi, "Lishijia dui saman zhuyi ying chongxin zuo fansi yu jiantao," 396–412; Falkenhausen, "Reflections on the Political Role of Spirit Mediums"; Keightley, "Shamanism, Death and the Ancestors"; Li Ling, *Zhongguo fangshu xukao*, 41–82.

15 Or in light of later discussions of the phallic symbol in early China, these tablets could be considered representations of the phallus.

16 Keightley, "The Making of the Ancestors," 3–63.

17 Lai, "Uses of the Human Figure in Early Chinese Art," 49–55.

18 Schnapp, "Are Images Animated," 40–44.

19 Kern, *Shi Jing* Songs as Performance Texts," 49–111.

20 Liu Zhao, "Anyang Hougang Yin mu suochu 'bingxingqi' yongtu kao," 623–25, 605.

21 Falkenhausen thinks there was an "image taboo" in early Chinese art. See Luo Tai, "Lüetan Zhongguo qingtongshidai de renwu biaoxian jiqi lishi yiyi," 265–67.

22 Trigger, *Understanding Early Civilizations*, 556.

23 Poo, *Enemies of Civilization*.

24 Barasch, *Icon*.

25 Belting, *Likeness and Presence*.

26 Li and Su, "Jieshao yijian youming de Jin hou tongren," 411–20.

27 Shanxi sheng kaogu yanjiusuo Dahekou mudi lianhe kaogudui, "Shanxi Yicheng xian Dahekou Xi Zhou mudi," 9–18.

28 Xu Lianggao, "Cong Shang Zhou renxiang yishu kan Zhongguo gudai wu ouxiang chongbai chuantong," 334–52.

29 For the image and the role of the other in Han art, see Pirazzoli-t'Serstevens, "Imperial Aura and the Image of the Other in Han Art," 299–317.

30 *Mengzi*, "Liang Huiwang shang" (*Mengzi zhushu*, 1a.14) and also *Liji*, "Tang Gong xia" (*Liji zhengyi*, 9.172–73). Certainly Confucius, if these were indeed his comments, was misinformed about the origins of human sacrifice as well as the origins of the tomb figurine. Judging from archaeological records, we know that human sacrifice occurred long before the use of the tomb figurine. The latter, in fact, represented progress for humanity insofar as figurines were used as substitutes for human sacrifice, a concept that fit well with

Confucius's definition of "benevolence" or "humanity" (*ren*). In fact, in a recent study of the passages discussed here, Tu Baikui suggests that what Confucius criticized was not the use of tomb figurines but human sacrifice itself. He reads "*yong*" 俑 as its homophone "*yong*" 用 in Shang oracle-bone inscriptions; the latter means "to use, to use in sacrifice" (verb) or "the victims used in sacrifice" (noun). Thus the meaning of "*yong*" 俑 (tomb figurine) came from its original meaning of "sacrificial victims." See Tu Baikui, "'Shi zuo yong' xinjie," 25–31.

31 *Han Feizi*, "Wai chushuo zuoshang" (*Han Feizi jijie*, 32.270-271).

32 Wu Hung in his recent book posits that "[m]ore than any other art form in traditional China, the tomb figurine was intimately linked with the notion of verisimilitude" (Wu, *The Art of the Yellow Springs*, 117). He discusses two different modes of mimetic representation in early Chinese art: one emphasizes the outward appearance of a figure, and the other focuses on movable limbs and removable clothing, that is, the operating mechanism of the object. As an example of the first mode he cites the terra-cotta army of the First Emperor of Qin; for the second, he includes the wooden figurines with movable arms from Tomb 2 at Baoshan and the "naked" clay figurines from Yangling, the mausoleum of Emperor Jing of the Han dynasty. As Wu himself acknowledges, these are somewhat unique examples. On the limited role of verisimilitude in the making of the terra-cotta army, see Kesner, "Likeness of No One," 115–32.

33 In his "On Tomb Figurines: The Beginning of a Visual Tradition," Wu Hung posits that the tomb figurine differs from the earlier human figurine and that they belong to "separate traditions" (13). Certainly the functions of the tomb figurine—to substitute for human sacrifice and to take up the roles of servants, guards, and entertainers—are somewhat different from those of the earlier human figurine, but in the beginning both examples belonged to the same tradition of image magic.

34 Gombrich, "Meditations on a Hobby Horse," 4.

35 Huang Zhanyue, *Gudai rensheng renxun tonglun*, 204–7.

36 Shanxi sheng kaogu yanjiusuo Dahekou mudi lianhe kaogudui, "Shanxi Yicheng xian Dahekou Xi Zhou mudi," 10.

37 *Liangdaicun Rui guo mudi*, 47–49, 52–54.

38 Shanxi sheng kaogu yanjiusuo, "Shanxi Changzi xian Dongzhou mu," 503–29.

39 Huang Zhanyue, *Zhongguo gudai de rensheng renxun*, 160.

40 Gao Yingqin, "Dong Zhou Chu mu renxun zongshu," 1121–24.

41 Thote, "Continuities and Discontinuities," 196.

42 Scholars are still debating the earliest appearance of the so-called slim wooden figurine (*mupian yong*) in Tomb 5 at Caojiagang, dated to the late Spring and Autumn period, because examples are often made of a single slim piece of wood and tend to be smaller (the highest is about 17.5 centimeters) and simpler in design than tomb figurines. See Gao Zhixi, "Chu yong yanjiu," 188; Qiu Donglian, "Chu mu zhong renxun yu yongzang jiqi guanxi chutan," 74–79.

43 Qiu Donglian, "Chu mu zhong renxun yu yongzang jiqi guanxi chutan," 74–79.

44 Huang Zhanyue, *Zhongguo gudai de rensheng renxun*, 133–53.

45 Huang Zhanyue, *Zhongguo gudai de rensheng renxun*, 155.

46 Wu, *The Art of the Yellow Springs*, 102–6.

47 *Zeng Hou Yi mu*, vol. 1, 500, 530, vol. 2, plate 231.

48 Here *wang* 亡 (OCM*maŋ) is a homophone for *ming* 明 (OCM*mraŋ).

49 *Wangshan Chu jian*, 62, Strip 49, 112, 127–28.

50 *Jiangling Wangshan Shazhong Chu mu*, 150, plate 80.

51 *Xinyang Chu mu*, 114–16, 130, color plate 14, plates 106–8, 128. Similar records are also found in the inventory from Tomb 3 at Mawangdui.

52 *Xinyang Chu mu*, 59.

53 *Changsha Mawangdui yihao Han mu*, vol. 1, 100–101; vol. 2, plate 200.

54 *Changsha Mawangdui yihao Han mu*, vol. 1, 101.

55 Lai, "The Diagram of the Mourning System from Mawangdui."

56 Gao Zhixi, "Chu yong yanjiu," 188, 206. Gao Zhixi thinks these figurines have an apotropaic function.

57 Wu, *The Art of the Yellow Springs*, 114.

58 For the later magic use of human figures, see Wu, *The Art of the Yellow Springs*, 122–26.

59 Jacobson, "Beyond the Frontier," 201–40; Thote, "Au-delà du monde connu."

60 So, "Chu Art: Link between the Old and New," 33–50.

61 Ashton, *An Introduction to the Study of Chinese Sculpture*, 14; Hawkes, *The Songs of the South*, 226. Hawkes translates the last sentence as "Hear while I describe for you your quiet and reposeful home." The emphasis is mine.

62 The Song dynasty philosopher Zhu Xi (1130–1200) considered the practice of using images of the dead in ancestor cults to be a regional custom from the ancient state of Chu; see *Chuci jizhu* 9.137. This reading was probably informed by the contemporary Song-dynasty use of ancestral images in ancestor cults. For the use of ancestral images in the Song dynasty, see Ebrey, "Portrait Sculptures," 42–92.

63 Gu Yanwu et al., *Rizhilu jishi*, 659–62.

64 Carr, "Personation of the Dead in Ancient China," 1–47, esp. 44, table 2.

65 Laufer, "The Development of Ancestral Images in China," 120. In this article, Laufer placed the ancestral images in the context of ancestor cults and discussed the relationships among impersonators (*shi*), ancestral images, and spirit-tablets. He posited that the ancestral tablets were derived from real anthropomorphic representations of deceased ancestors in early China, and that later in imperial times, when the Chinese needed to distinguish ancestors from gods, such images were reserved for supernatural deities while ancestors came to be represented by tablets. Although not explicitly stated, Laufer's argument seems to respond to Édouard Chavannes, who posited based on later textual materials that the ancestral tablet was originally in the shape of a living human being. See Chavannes, *Le T'aï-Chan*, 476; see also discussions in Lai, "The Baoshan Tomb," chapter 5.

66 Carr, "Personation of the Dead in Ancient China," 56.

67 He Nu and Zhang Wangao, "Jingzhou Guanping wu hao Zhanguo mu," 190–91.

68 Hunan sheng bowuguan, "Changsha Zidanku," 36–43; *Changsha Chu mu*, vol. 1, 428, and fig. 340, 433, vol. 2, color plate 48.

69 Guo Moruo, "Guanyu wan Zhou bohua de kaocha," 113–18.

70 Guo Moruo, "Guanyu wan Zhou bohua de kaocha," 113–18; but Xiong Chuanxin reported that it may have been found on top of the box. See Xiong Chuanxin, "Duizhao xinjiu moben tan Chuguo renwu longfeng bohua," 90.

71 Hunan sheng bowuguan, "Changsha Zidanku Zhanguo muguo mu," 41, fig. 9.

72 Huang Hongxin, "Chu bohua suokao," 45–49; Wu, "The Art and Architecture of the Warring States Period," 742–44.

73 The only difference is that the Mawangdui banner painting was located on top of the innermost coffin. See Wu, "Art in Its Ritual Context," 111–44.

74 Liu Fude, "Mingjing de tuxiang yu wenzi," 12–25.

75 Wu, "Art in Its Ritual Context," 122.

76 Spiro, *Contemplating the Ancients*, 18–19; Keightley, "Ancient Chinese Art," 2–6.

77 Sun Zuoyun, "Changsha Mawangdui yihao Han mu chutu huafan kaoshi," 54–61; Ma Yong, "Lun Changsha Mawangdui yihao Han mu chutu bohua de mingcheng he zuoyong," 118–25; Sofukawa Hiroshi, "Konronzan to shōsenzu," 83–185; *Konronzan e no shōsen*; "Kan dai gazōseki ni okeru shōsenzu no keifu," 23–222.

78 Freedberg, *The Power of Images*, 263–71.

Notes to Chapter Three

79 Wu, "Art in Its Ritual Context," 117. For the Eastern Han scholar Zheng Xuan's commentary, see *Yili zhushu*, 35.412.

80 *Liji zhengyi*, 9.168.

81 This is similar to what Wu Hung correctly argued at the beginning of his article, namely, that the ritual of soul-recalling and the garment used were not part of the funerary service (or the "death related matters"). Likewise, the name banner and the soul stand used in the funerary service (the "cult of the dead") were not part of the next stage—the worship of the ancestors. Both the name banner and the soul stand were buried after the funerary service. See Wu, "Art in Its Ritual Context," 112–14.

82 Thompson, "Death, Food and Fertility," 84.

83 Lai, "Lighting the Way in the Afterlife," 20–28.

84 Thompson, "Death, Food and Fertility," 84.

85 *Zuozhuan*, Lord Xiang, 13th year; Yang Bojun, *Chunqiu Zuozhuan zhu*, 1001.

86 *Chuci*, "Zhao Hun" (*Chuci jizhu* 136). For a detailed correlation between darkness and afterlife in early Greece, see Vermeule, *Aspects of Death in Early Greek Art and Poetry*, 23–32. For the conception of death as pervasive darkness in Han literature and stele inscriptions, see Brashier, "Evoking the Ancestor," 7–10, 27–29.

87 Artificial light is of vital importance to human life. Since ancient times people have attached social value and religious significance to artificial light and the light-producer: the lamp. Light has been thought to possess divine qualities and has been associated with notions of god, holiness, or supernatural existence. See Bleeker, "Some Remarks on the Religious Significance of Light," 193–207; for a general history of light, see Park, *The Fire within the Eye*.

88 Thompson, "Death, Food and Fertility," 85.

89 You Qiumei, "Han dai muzhu huaixang."

90 Zheng Yan, "Muzhu huaxiang yanjiu," 450–68.

91 *Huixian fajue baogao*, 120, plate 94, nos. 23–25.

92 Li Ling, *Rushan yu chusai*, 148–64.

93 Salmony, *Antler and Tongue*; Demattè, "Antler and Tongue," 353–404; for more references, see Cook, *Death in Ancient China*, 136–42.

94 Zhang Jun, *Chu guo shenhua yuanxing yanjiu*, 62–126; Cook, *Death in Ancient China*, 136–42.

95 Li Xueqin, *Eastern Zhou and Qin Civilizations*, 350.

96 *Xichuan Heshangling yu Xujialing*, 24–119.

97 *Xichuan Heshangling yu Xujialing*, 26, fig. 23; 109, fig. 104.

98 Li Ling, *Rushan yu chusai*, 151.

99 Guolong Lai, "Zhenmushou yu jianmuwei."

100 Qiu Xigui, "Zaitan guwenxian yi 'shi' biao 'she,'" 1–13.

101 Zhao Ping'an, "Henan Xichuan Heshangling," 37–44.

102 Gao Chongwen, "Chu 'zhenmushou' wei 'zuchong' jie," 54–60, 46.

103 Cook, *Death in Ancient China*, 136–42.

104 The reconstructed form for *shi* 埶 in Old Chinese is **ŋet-s*, which is the nominal form of *she* 設 (**ŋet*, "to establish," "to set up"). See Bai Yiping, "'Shi' 'shi' 'she'deng zi de gouni he zhonggu sy- (shumu = shensan) de laiyuan," 161–77. For the function of adding the **-s* suffix to adjectives or verbs to form a derived noun, see Baxter and Sagart, "Word Formation in Old Chinese," 54–59.

105 *Guxun huizuan*, 429.

106 Yan Changgui, *Wugui yu yinsi*, 364–65.

107 In Chu manuscripts, the graph *zu* 襠 (OCM **tsā?*) is written consistently with a tiger radical 虍 (hu, OCM **hlā?*), which marks an additional phonetic for this special graph denoting the fecundity god. Yan Changgui, *Wugui yu yinsi*, 118–20.

108 Guo Moruo, "Shi 'zubi,'" 1–60.

109 Karlgren, "Some Fecundity Symbols in Ancient China," 1–54.

110 Zhang Guangzhi, *Kaoguxue liujiang*, 62–73.

111 Major, "Characteristics of Late Chu Religion," 132.

112 Ding Lan, "Chu shi 'zhenmushou' tezheng zonglun," 98–106.

113 Ding Lan, "Chu shi 'zhenmushou' tezheng zonglun," 98–106.

114 Thote, "Chinese Coffins from the First Millennium B.C.," 36–37.

115 Huang Ying, "Chu shi zhenmushou lujiao yanjiu," 71–76; Xie Chengxia, "Zailun Zhongguo xiyou lu lei," 63–64; You Xiuling, "Milu he yuanshi daozuo ji Zhongguo wenhua," 1–7.

116 Zhang Changping, *Zeng guo qingtongqi yanjiu*, 316.

117 Henan Xinyang diqu wenguanhui and Guangshan xian wenguanhui, "Chunqiu zaoqi Huang jun Meng fufu mu fajue baogao," 302–32, 348.

118 Zhang Changping, *Zeng guo qingtongqi yanjiu*, 43–47.

119 Yichang diqu bowuguan, "Hubei Dangyang Zhaoxiang 4 hao Chunqiu mu fajue jianbao," 25–32.

120 Bloch and Parry, *Death and the Regeneration of Life*, back cover.

121 Bloch and Parry, *Death and the Regeneration of Life*, 1–2.

122 Bloch and Parry, *Death and the Regeneration of Life*.

123 Chen Songchang, *Xianggang Zhongwen daxue wenwuguan cang jiandu*, 97–108; Harper, "Contracts with the Spirit World," 227–67.

124 Harper, "Contracts with the Spirit World," 242.

125 Lai Guolong, "Lun Chu bushi jidao jian zhong de 'yudao,'" 359–78, esp. 368, 371.

126 Yan Changgui suggests that a deity named *gongwu* cited in the Tianxingguan manuscripts may be the founding ancestress (*gongmei*) who was ultimately dubbed the fecundity god and presided over fertility and longevity in early Chinese texts. But the evidence is too fragmentary to draw a firmer conclusion. See Yan Changgui, *Wugui yu yinsi*, 167–68.

127 Jin Kaicheng et al., *Qu Yuan ji jiaozhu*, 245–46; Sun Zuoyun, "Han dai siming shenxiang de faxian," 471–73.

128 Chang, "Changing Relationships of Man and Animal in Shang and Chou Myths and Art," 174–96; "The Animal in Shang and Chou Bronze Art," 527–54; *Art, Myth, and Ritual*; Keightley, "Shamanism, Death, and the Ancestors," 763–831.

129 Loewe, "Man and Beast: The Hybrid in Early Chinese Art and Literature," 38–54.

130 Thote, "Au-delà du monde connu," 57–74.

131 Poo, *In Search of Personal Welfare*, 95.

132 Puett, *To Become a God*.

133 Lai Guolong, "Mawangdui Taiyi zhu tu kao."

134 Lai Guolong, "Mawangdui Taiyi zhu tu kao."

135 For more details, see Lai Guolong, "Mawangdui Taiyi zhu tu kao."

136 For discussions on the "Pace of Yu," see Rao Zongyi, *Yunmeng Qinjian rishu yanjiu*, 20–23; Fujino Iwatomo, "Uho kō," 302–16; Liu Zhaorui, "Lun 'Yubu' de qiyuan ji Yu yu wu, dao de guanxi," 264–79.

137 *Zuozhuan*, Lord Zhao, 8th year.

138 Puett, *To Become a God*.

139 *Huainan honglie jijie*, 9.303

140 Hayashi Minao, "Kan dai danshi no kaburimono," 80–126; Sun Ji, *Han dai wuzhi wenhua ziliao tushuo*, 236.

141 Bulling, "Notes on Two Unicorns," 109–13.

142 See the images in Juliano and Lerner, *Monks and Merchants*, 44–46.

143 Mitchell, *Picture Theory*, 78–80.

144 Gombrich, *The Sense of Order*, 272–81.

145 Joseph LeDoux and others have discussed the neurophysiologic process of fear response in the human brain. Scientists discovered that central to all fear reaction is the amygdala, the almond-shaped group of nuclei located deep within the medial temporal lobes. Visual information is transmitted via two passages: the cortical and subcortical pathways. Visual stimuli first go to the thalamus, which then passes rough, archetypal information directly to the amygdala. The second route passes visual information by a slower path to the visual cortex, which creates an accurate representation and determines whether the image we saw is a real snake or only a stick or a rope. The first path, what LeDoux calls the "quick and dirty reaction mechanism," allows the brain to start to respond to the possible danger. The information is relayed to the amygdala, causing heart rate and blood pressure to increase and muscles to contract, which is the classical "fight-or-flight response." This "quick-and-dirty reaction," which is what we often call the "instinct" reaction, is not limited to snakes or things that look like snakes but extends to frightening faces, threatening animals, and dangerous representations. Therefore, in early China the gods and spirits were represented in hybrid form because these attributes of dangerous animals can trigger the feeling of fear or produce a sense of awe. See LeDoux, "Emotion, Memory and the Brain," 32–39.

146 For the case of the First Emperor's terra-cotta army, see Kesner, "Likeness of No One," 115–32.

4. Letters to the Underworld

Epigraph: Lewis, *Writing and Authority*, 363.

1 Postgate et al., "The Evidence for Early Writing," 459–80; Keightley, "The Origins of Writing in China," 171–202; Bagley, "Anyang Writing and the Origin of the Chinese Writing System," 190–249; Lai Guolong, "Wenzi qiyuan yanjiu"; Boltz, "Literacy and the Emergence of Writing in China," 51–84.

2 Lai Guolong, "Chu bushi jidao jian zhong de 'yudao.'"

3 *Jiaguwen heji*, no. 1027 recto.

4 Harper, "Contracts with the Spirit World," 227–67.

5 Seidel, "Traces of Han Religion in Funerary Texts Found in Tombs," 24.

6 An interesting case in point is the last chapter, "Qifu" (Objects and Clothes), of the extant *Yi Zhoushu* (Remaining Zhou Documents). This chapter was in all likelihood originally the inventory list from the Warring States-era tomb of a nobleman from the state of Wei. Note that the *Yi Zhoushu*, or part of it, was alleged to have been excavated in Ji County (present-day Henan) in 281 CE. The scholars who were responsible for reestablishing the order of these scattered bamboo strips mistook the inventory list for a chapter of the *Yi Zhoushu*. The constituent elements of the "Qifu" chapter are truncated and fragmentary. Beyond listing objects with brief descriptions, they seem to have no overarching theories or themes. The fragmentary state of the texts and the paucity of historical information surrounding the excavation and editing of the excavated manuscripts in the Jin dynasty prevent us from proving or disproving the hypothesis ably set out by Luo Jiaxiang; yet given the common association of inventory lists with other manuscripts in the Warring States era, that conclusion is very likely. Scholars have different opinions about the relationship between the extant *Yi Zhoushu* and the manuscripts excavated at Ji County. See Luo Jiaxiang, "'Yi Zhoushu Qifujie' shi yifen qiance," 4–10. On the "Qifu" chapter, see *Yi Zhoushu huijiao jizhu*, 1177–94; Huang Huaixin, *Yi Zhoushu yuanliu kaobian*, 35–51.

7 See Ye Gongchuo's preface in Shi Shuqing, *Changsha Yangtianhu chutu Chu jian yanjiu*, 3; Li Xueqin, "Tan jinnian lai xin faxian de jizhong Zhanguo wenzi ziliao," 48–49.

8   Chen Zhi, "Changsha Mawangdui yihao Han mu de ruogan wenti kaoshu," 30–35.

9   Chen Wei, *Baoshan Chu jian chutan*, 187–92.

10 For example, Li Jiahao, "Baoshan 266 hao jian suoji muqi yanjiu"; Liu Guosheng, "Chu sang-zang jiandu jishi"; Tian He, "Chutu Zhanguo qiance suoji mingwu fenlei huishi."

11 Pian Yuqian and Duan Shuan, *Ben shiji yilai chutu jianbo gaishu*.

12 *Wangshan Chu jian*, 51, 107, and 114.

13 For the reading of the surname *dao* 悼, see *Wangshan Chu jian*, 87n6, and 90–91n24. Schol-ars still debate whether the date refers to the year in which that event took place or the year following. See Wang Hongxing, "Baoshan jiandu suo fanying de Chu guo lifa wenti," 521–32; Liu Binhui, "Cong Baoshan Chu jian jishi cailiao lun ji Chu guo jinian yu Chu li," 533–47; Chen Wei, *Baoshan Chu jian chutan*, 9–20; Weld, "Chu Law in Action," 83. Based on comparative evidence from ancient Babylonia, where the name of the year was derived from an event that happened in the preceding year, I here hypothesize that "event nota-tion" refers to the following year. See the evidence from ancient Babylonia in Oppenheim, *Ancient Mesopotamia*, 145–46.

14 Chen Wei, *Baoshan Chu jian chutan*, 181–82.

15 Goody, *The Domestication of the Savage Mind*, 80.

16 *Changsha Mawangdui er san hao Han mu*, 54.

17 The story of Yuan She is in the *Official History of the Western Han Dynasty*; see *Hanshu*, 92.3716.

18 Oppenheim, *Ancient Mesopotamia*, 244–49; Krispijn, "The Early Mesopotamian Lexical Lists," 12–22; Gelb, "Two Assyrian King Lists," 209–30; Jacobsen, *The Sumerian King List*; Kitchen, "The King List of Ugarit," 131–42; Goody, *The Domestication of the Savage Mind*, 77–111; Michalowski, "History as Charter," 237–48; Beaulieu, *The Pantheon of Uruk during the Neo-Babylonian Period*, 41–102; Barta, *Die altägyptische Opferliste*; Barta, *Aufbau und Bedeu-tung der altägyptischen Opferformel*; Gordon, "What's in a List?" 239–77.

19 Nissen, Damerow, and Englund, *Archaic Bookkeeping*.

20 Bagley, "Anyang Writing and the Origin of the Chinese Writing System," 190–249; Wang, *Writing and the State*. See also Barbieri-Low, "Artisan Literacy in Early China"; on the appearance of artisan's names on objects as a mechanism of quality control, see Thote, "Artists and Craftsmen in the Late Bronze Age of China," 201–41.

21 Bagley hypothesizes that lexical lists as well as administrative documents may have existed in Shang China but vanished because of the poor preservation conditions; see Bagley, "Any-ang Writing and the Origin of the Chinese Writing System," 190–249. For the use of lists in the Han dynasty, see Yates, "Soldiers, Scribes, and Women," 360–61.

22 Hu Houxuan thought that the bone was genuine but that the inscriptions were faked. See Hu Houxuan, "Jiaguwen 'jiapu keci' zhenwei wenti zai shangque," 115–38; Yu Xingwu, "Ji-aguwen 'jiapu keci' zhenwei bian," 139–46. Chen Mengjia and Li Xueqin have made the case for authenticity. See Chen Mengjia, *Yinxu buci zongshu*, 652; Li Xueqin, "Lun Yindai de qinzu zhidu."

23 For the Shi Qiang *pan* and a discussion of Wei family genealogy, see Yin Shengping, ed., *Xi Zhou weishi jiazu qingtongqiqun yanjiu*, 58–79.

24 Huang Ranwei, *Yin Zhou qingtongqi shangci mingwen yanjiu*, 162–207.

25 Zhang Zhenglang pointed out that *liujia* inscribed on oracle bones were most likely model texts or student exercises. Zhang Zhenglang, *Zhang Zhenglang wenshi lunji*, 215–37.

26 Guo Daoyang, *Zhongguo kuaiji shigao*, 115–19, 150–62, 191–221; *Kuaiji fazhan shigang*, 204–14; Lu Xixing, "Shi 'yi,'" 1112–15.

27 For an example of Chu official control of the flow of strategic goods, see Falkenhausen, "The E Jun Qi Metal Tallies."

28 For the importance of lists in later Chinese art and society, see Hou, "Trésors du monastère Long-hing à Touen-houang," 149–68.

29 *Yili zhushu* 39.466; cf. Steele, *The I-li or Book of Etiquette and Ceremonial*, 89.

30 Quoted in Yang Tianyu, *Yili yizhu*, 627.

31 Lagerwey, "The Oral and the Written," 301–22.

32 Hunan sheng wenwu guanli weiyuanhui, "Changsha Yangtianhu di 25 hao muguo mu," 85–94; Guo Ruoyu, "Changsha Yangtianhu Zhanguo zhujian wenzi de moxie he kaoshi," 21–34; *Zhanguo Chu jian wenzi bian*, 105–6.

33 Falkenhausen, "Social Ranking in Chu Tombs," 485.

34 Yang Hua, "Sui, feng, qian," 54–55; Liu Guosheng, "Chu qiance zhidu shulüe," 236.

35 Because the areas surrounding the tomb of Marquis Yi were damaged and we do not have a complete overview of the tomb and its associated burials, we do not know the exact extent of this discrepancy.

36 Yang Hua, "Sui, feng, qian," 54–55.

37 *Liji*, "Tan Gong" (*Liji zhengyi* 9.149; Legge, *Li Chi*, vol. 1, 154).

38 Legge, *Li Chi*, vol. 1, 154.

39 Bourdieu, *Outline of a Theory of Practice*, 14.

40 Bell, *Ritual: Perspectives and Dimensions*, 78–79.

41 Vandermeersch, *Wang Dao ou La voie royale*, 473–77.

42 Keightley, "Report from the Shang," 20–54.

43 See Takashima's comments on Keightley's paper, in Keightley, "Report from the Shang," 44–46.

44 See the discussion of communication between humans and spirits in *Zhouli* in Falkenhausen, "Reflections on the Political Role of Spirit Mediums," 294–95.

45 Austin, *How to Do Things with Words*; Searle, *Speech Acts*. For an introduction to and discussion of Austin's and Searle's theories, see Petrey, *Speech Acts and Literary Theory*; Holdcroft, *Words and Deeds*.

46 Giele, "Using Early Chinese Manuscripts as Historical Source Materials," 420–22.

47 *Sanjian jiandu heji*, 66–67; Wang Guihai, *Qin Han jiandu tanyan*, 271–72.

48 四年後九月辛亥，平里五大夫[敢告]地下主：偃衣器物所以□□。令□以律令從事。

49 Chen Zhi, "Guanyu 'Jiangling cheng' gao 'dixia cheng,'" 76.

50 Feuchtwang, *Popular Religion in China*.

51 Qiu Xigui, "Hubei Jiangling Fenghuangshan shihao Han mu," 49–63; *Guwenzi lunji*, 540–63.

52 *Suizhou Kongjiapo Han mu jiandu*.

53 *Jingzhou Gaotai Qin Han mu*, 222–29; Liu Guosheng, "Gaotai Han du 'Andu' biejie," 444–48.

54 Jingzhou bowuguan, "Hubei Jingzhou Xiejiaqiao yihao Han mu fajue baogao," 26–42; Liu Guosheng, "Xiejiaqiao yihao Han mu gaodishu du de chubu kaocha," 120–22.

55 五年十一月癸卯朔庚午，西鄉辰敢言之：郎中[五]大夫昌自言，母大女子聿死，以衣器、葬具及從者婦、偏下妻、奴婢、馬牛，物、人一牒，牒百九十七枚。昌家復無有所與，有詔令。謁告地下丞以從事。敢言之。

56 十一月庚午，江陵丞虒移地下丞，可令吏以從事。／臧手。

57 郎中五大夫昌母家屬當復毋有所與。

58 Chen Songchang, "Gaodice de xingwen geshi yu xiangguan wenti," 21–25; Friedrich, "The 'Announcement to the World Below' of Ma-wang-tui 3," 7–15.

59 十二年二月乙巳朔戊辰，家丞奮移主葬郎中，移葬物一編，書到先質，具奏主葬君。

60 Here my translation follows Friedrich, "The 'Announcement to the World Below' of Ma-wang-tui 3," 7–15, but I disagree with his interpretation. See further discussion below.

61 Chen Songchang, "Mawangdui sanhao Han mu mudu sanlun," 64–70; "Mawangdui sanhao Han mu jinian mudu xingzhi de zai renshi," 62–64, 61.

62 The ordinance of 148 BCE, recorded in the *Official History of the Western Han Dynasty*, gives detailed regulations for the funerals of kings and the lower nobility.

63 Friedrich, "The 'Announcement to the World Below' of Ma-wang-tui 3," 9.

64 Yan Gengwang, "Qin Han langli zhidu kao," 21–84.

65 Nishijima Sadao, *Chūgoku kokai teikoku no keisei to kōzō*.

66 Huang Shengzhang, "Dixiashu yu gaodice, qiance," 155–62; "Fawang dixia de wenshu: Gaodi ce," 19–22.

67 *Yunmeng Longang Qin jian*; *Longgang Qin jian*.

68 Liu Guosheng, "Yunmeng Longgang jiandu," 64–71; *Yunmeng Longgang Qin jian*, 45; Liu Zhaorui, *Kaogu faxian yu zaoqi daojiao yanjiu*, 382.

69 鞫之：辟死論不當為城旦。吏論失者已坐以論。九月丙申，沙羨丞甲、史丙免辟死為庶人，令自尚也。

70 Liu Zhaorui, *Kaogu faxian yu zaoqi daojiao yanjiu*, 383–84.

71 Huang Shengzhang, "Jiangling Gaotai Han mu xinchu 'gaodi ce,'" 41–44, 26; "Dixiashu yu gaodice, qiance xinlun," 155–62.

72 Yangzhou bowuguan, Hanjiang xian tushuguan, "Jiangsu Hanjiang Huchang 5 hao mu," 18, fig. 17.

73 [廣陵王]四十七年十二月丙子朔，辛卯，廣陵宮司空長前（？）、丞能（？）敢告土主：廣陵石里男子王奉世有獄事，事已復，故郡鄉里遣自致移詣地。四八年獄計。承書。從事，如律令。

74 *Sanjian jiandu heji*, 102, Strips 1060–61; Wang Guihai, *Qin Han jiandu tanyan*, 274–75; Liu Zhaorui, *Kaogu faxian yu zaoqi daojiao yanjiu*, 380–85.

75 Wang Guihai, *Qin Han jiandu tanyan*, 273–74.

76 Riegel, "Kou-Mang and Ju-Shou," 55–83; Harper, "Resurrection," 13–28.

77 Nickerson, "Taoism, Death, and Bureaucracy in Early Medieval China," 83–174.

78 Wolf, "God, Ghosts, and Ancestors," 131–82.

79 Sangren, *History and Magical Power*, 127–65.

80 *Jiangling Jiudian Dong Zhou mu*, 49–51, 53; see also *Jiudian Chu jian*, 149–55, 161–70.

81 *Jiangling Jiudian Dong Zhou mu*, plate 113; see also *Jiudian Chu jian*, 13, 50. Translation (with revision) follows Harper, "A Warring States Prayer for Men Who Die by Weapons," unpublished manuscript.

82 Schuessler, *Minimal Old Chinese and Later Han Chinese*, 171.

83 ［皋！］敢告□□之子武（夷）：“尔（爾）居（復）山之𡺍，不周之埜（野）。帝胃（謂）尔（爾）無事，命尔（爾）司兵死者。今日某將欲飲（食），某敢以其妻□妻女（汝），[畾幣]、芳糧，以量贖某于武夷之所。君向受某之畾幣、芳糧，凶（思）某迓（來）歸飤（食）[如]故。"

84 Zhou Fengwu, "Jiudian Chu jian Gao Wuyi chongtan," 943n7.

85 *Shuihudi Qinjian*, 215; Li Jiahao, "Jiudian Chu jian Gao Wuyi yanjiu," 322–23.

86 Huang Zhanyue, *Zhongguo gudai de rensheng renxun*, 154–225.

87 Other instances are the ideal communities in *Daodejing* and *Zhuangzi*; see Bauer, *China and the Search for Happiness*, 32–43. The Daoist modes of rejecting the structure of the mundane world—abstaining from grains, the most vital food source for the Chinese over the centuries; escaping from society into the mountains, beyond the usual inhabitable realm; and inward meditation—are all actively imagined and deliberately constructed against the life of this world. See Schipper, *The Taoist Body*.

88 Wolfgang Bauer wrote, "For love forms an inextricable part of the network of familial and social ties which usually are its direct result. . . . The Taoist tendency [is] toward a detachment of the self from all ties of love in order to attain the great freedom of the hermit, who can completely shake off such worldly burdens and ascend to heaven." Bauer, *China and the Search for Happiness*, 185.

89 Campany, *Making Transcendents*.

Notes to Chapter Four

90 Watson, "The Structure of Chinese Funerary Rites," 3–19; "Rites or Beliefs?" 80–103.

91 *Jiangling Jiudian Dongzhou mu*, 49–51.

92 *Jiudian Chu jian*, 150–53.

93 Yan Changgui, *Wugui yu yinsi*, 306.

94 Li Ling, "'Sanlü dafu' kao," 15, 22n14.

95 As for Zang Gan, scholars have proposed that his surname belongs to the Ji clan and derives from the state of Lu, a reading based on certain Zang individuals mentioned in received texts (He Linyi, *Zhanguo guwen zidian*, 703). But in the Baoshan bamboo strips, twelve people bear the surname Zang; see *Baoshan Chu jian*, Strips 23, 38, 60, 121, 122, 160, 163, 166, 167, 172, 173, 186, 224, and 225. Compared to the number of people surnamed Shao (10), Qu (11), and Jing (11), the number of Zang is noteworthy for the importance of the Zang lineage in the life of Shao Tuo. Among the twelve, three occupied important official positions and served as local legal officers *Sibai* (Strips 38, 60) and *Shaosibai* (Strip 23) and a state minister *Moxiao* (Strip 121), and two came from the district where the tomb of King Wei of Chu was located (Strips 166, 172). It is possible that this was a different lineage from the one in the state of Lu and that it derived its surname from King Zhuang of Chu. "Zang" and "Zhuang" are phonologically closely related in Old Chinese. For the surname Shao, see Li Ling, "'Sanlü dafu' kao," 15, 17–19.

96 *Yin Zhou jinwen jicheng* 16.10373; Zhou Shirong, "Chu Yinke tongliang mingwen shishi," 87–88; He Linyi, "Changsha tongliang mingwen bushi," 97–101; Li Ling, "Chu Yanke tongliang mingwen buzheng," 102–3.

97 Li Ling, *Zhongguo fangshu xukao*.

5. Journey to the Northwest

Epigraph: Needham and Ronan, "Chinese Cosmology," 68.

1 The notion of otherworldly journeys has been the subject of several scholarly treatises and academic conferences: e.g., Zaleski, *Otherworld Journey*; Couliano, *Out of the World*; Collins and Fishbane, eds., *Death, Ecstasy and Other Worldly Journeys*.

2 Scholars in the fields of Chinese studies have also examined related phenomena in early and medieval Chinese literature; see Campany, "Return-from-Death Narratives in Early Medieval China," 91–125; "To Hell and Back," 343–60. David Hawkes and David Knechtges have discussed the literary convention of the spirit journeys in the *Chuci* and in the rhapsodies of the Han; see Hawkes, "The Quest of the Goddess," 42–68; Knechtges, "A Journey to Morality," 162–82. This chapter reprises that discussion within the context of what archaeology has taught us about Chu mortuary religion. I first presented my research in a panel discussion entitled "New Insights from Old Tombs" at the Fifty-sixth Annual Meeting of the Association for Asian Studies, San Diego, California, March 4–7, 2004, and later published in Lai, "Death, Travel, and Otherworldly Journey in Early China."

3 Other destinations of the dead mentioned in early texts include the "nine plains" (*jiuyuan*), the "nine hills" (*jiujing*), *haoli*, *xiali*, the Dark Capital (Youdu), the netherland (*xiatu*), Mount Tai, and so on. For the story of Lord Zhuang of Zheng meeting his estranged mother in an underground tunnel, at the beginning of *Zuozhuan*, see Yang Bojun, *Chunqiu Zuozhuan zhu*, 14–15. For the discussion of the multiple abodes of the dead in early China, see Xiao Dengfu, *Xian Qin Liang Han mingjie ji shenxian sixiang tanyuan*, 16–23; Poo, *In Search of Personal Welfare*, 62–68; Thompson, "On the Prehistory of Hell in China," 27–41. The idea of Yellow Springs referring to the final destination of the dead became popular only after the Eastern Han dynasty, as appears on stone steles, bronze

mirror inscriptions, and land contracts. On the Yellow Springs, see also Egashira Hiroshi, "Yomi ni tsuite," 109–26.

4   Chang, "The Animal in Shang and Chou Bronze Art," 527–54; Chang, *Art, Myth, and Ritual*, 44–55.

5   Campany, "To Hell and Back," 343.

6   Gu Jiegang, "*Zhuangzi* he *Chuci* zhong Kunlun he Penglai liangge shenhua xitong de ronghe," 41–80.

7   Loewe, *Ways to Paradise*; Wu, "Where Are They Going?" 22–31.

8   This does not mean that the east-west horizontal axis completely replaced the vertical axis; rather, the dimensions of the spirit journey expanded in multiple directions. The vertical axis was still important, even in later Han tomb texts and land contracts. For example, the Xuning wooden strips state that the deceased Xuning "below enters the Yellow Spring, [and] above enters Blue Heaven"; see Harper, "Contracts with the Spirit World," 227–67.

9   For a recent survey, see Poo, "Afterlife: Chinese Concepts," 169–72.

10 Wu, "The Earliest Pictorial Representations of Ape Tales," 99.

11 Wu, "Art in Its Ritual Context," 111–45.

12 There are many examples in the *Protocols of Ceremonies*. The most instructive one is in "Shi sangli": after a person's death, a banner is made on which is written "the coffin of so-and-so with the surname such-and-such." And indeed, archaeologists found three banners in the Han tombs (tombs 22, 23, and 2) at Mozuizi in Wuwei, Gansu, bearing inscriptions of the names of the deceased. See *Yili zhushu* 35.412; *Wuwei Han jian*, 148–49, *moben* 25, plate 23.

13 *Mawangdui Han mu boshu*, vol. 4, 38, 45, 49, 50, 67, 69, 128–29; in these cases, *mou* appears in medical incantations. See also Harper, *Early Chinese Medical Literature*, 243, 253, 260, 262–64, 291, 294, 370–71; in these cases, Harper translates *mou* as "so-and-so."

14 *Guanju Qin Han mu jiandu*, 129–32, 136.

15 *Shuihudi Qin mu zhujian*, 58, 149–64, 210, 247, to give just a few examples. In the legal texts, the ten heavenly stems are also used as placeholders.

16 Li Ling, "Du Jiudian Chu Jian," 145.

17 Zhou Fengwu, "Jiudian Chu jian Gao Wuyi chongtan," 953–54.

18 Li Jiahao, "Jiudian Chu jian Gao Wuyi yanjiu," 318–38; Zhou Fengwu, "Jiudian Chu jian Gao Wuyi chongtan," 941–59. Li Jiahao's argument about the nature of the Jiudian incantation was based explicitly on the parallel he tried to construct between Tomb 56 at Jiudian and Tomb 2 at Baoshan. But these two sets of manuscripts are very different in character. The Baoshan manuscripts are "real" legal cases, divination and sacrificial records for the tomb occupant, while the Jiudian incantation is a normative manual that is closer in nature to manuscripts such as the daybooks and legal texts from Tomb 11 at Shuihudi.

19 The text runs as follows: "If by misfortune you are shot by the *yu*, venomous snake, and bees, chant an incantation and spit at it thrice. Name the creature that did the shooting with its name, saying 'So-and-so. Your five brothers, so-and-so knows all your names. . . . So-and-so is a murderer. If you do not cause so-and-so's ailment to desist, once again . . .'" See *Mawangdui Han mu boshu*, vol. 4, 128–29. Harper correctly points out that in these two sets of *mou* the first "so-and-so" represents the name of the creature, the second the name of the person. See Harper, *Early Chinese Medical Literature*, 370–71.

20 Zhou Shirong, "Mawangdui Han mu 'niebi' yu Jiangling Mashan yi hao Chu mu 'bobi' kao," 330–48; Zhao Dexin, *Chu guo de huobi*, 123–49.

21 Harper, "A Warring States Prayer for Men Who Die by Weapons." Li Jiahao dismisses Harper's interpretation as "unfounded" and "unbelievable" but provides no substantial

counterevidence. His hypothesis is, like Harper's thesis, that Buzhou and Fushan refer to two mountain peaks in the *Classics of Mountains and Seas* is, like Harper's thesis, also based only on phonological connections. Moreover, he suggests that "later people called this mountain with two uncircumscribed peaks Buzhou, and thus the name of Fushu was gradually forgotten." Thus, Li Jiahao and Harper come to the same conclusion. See Li Jiahao, "Jiudian Chu jian Gao Wuyi yanjiu," 321. Other scholars have attempted to locate the mythological Mount Buzhou and Fushan in specific localities in China, which I think is taking the mythology at face value. See Rao Zongyi, "Shuo Jiudian Chu jian zhi Wuyi (jun) yu Fushan," 36–38; Liu Zhaorui, "Andu jun yu Wuyi jun," 55.

22 Major, *Heaven and Earth in Early Han Thought*, 162–63.

23 Major, *Heaven and Earth in Early Han Thought*, 78–79.

24 Yang Bojun, *Liezi jishi*, 150–51; Graham, *The Book of Lieh-tzu*, 96. For the date of the *Liezi*, see Barrett, "Lieh tzu," 299–301. For a similar passage in *Master of Huainan*, see Liu Wendian, *Huainan honglie jijie*, 80. For an English translation, see Major, *Heaven and Earth in Early Han Thought*, 62–64.

25 Qu Yuan, *The Songs of the South*, 127, 135–36.

26 *Guodian Chu mu zhujian*, 14, Strip 14.

27 Liu Guosheng, "Chu di chutu shushu wenxian yu yuzhou jiegou lilun," 238–52.

28 Tong Shuye and Gu Jiegang, "Han dai yiqian Zhongguo ren de shijie."

29 *Shuihudi Qin mu zhujian*, Strips 114–26; Liu Lexian, *Shuihudi Qinjian rishu yanjiu*, 148–52.

30 Liu Wendian, *Huainan honglie jijie*, 92, 133. See also Major, *Heaven and Earth in Early Han Thought*, 77–79.

31 *Shiji*, 25.1243.

32 Chen Li, *Baihutong shuzheng*, 346.

33 *Shuowen jiezi*, 284.

34 Seidel, "Afterlife: Chinese Concepts," 126.

35 Needham and Ronan, "Chinese Cosmology," 68.

36 As Laurence G. Thompson's study of the prehistory of hell in China indicates, in ancient China before the introduction of Buddhism, the afterlife was not thought to be the place of punishment for evil or reward for good. See Thompson, "On the Prehistory of Hell in China," 27–41.

37 Hunan sheng bowuguan, "Xin faxian de Changsha Zhanguo Chu mu bohua," 3–4, plate 1.

38 Loewe, *Ways to Paradise*, 17–59; Birrell, "Return to a Cosmic Eternal," 3–30; for different interpretations, see Wu, "Art in Its Ritual Context."

39 Tosaki Tetsuhiko has pointed out that at least by the Qin dynasty *daxing* already meant "a grand journey" and was used to refer to the imperial otherworldly journey to Heaven during the liminal stage immediately after death; Tosaki Tetsuhiko, "Chūgoku kodai no daisō ni okeru daikō shu ni tsuite," 40–62, esp. 44–50. *Daxing* is also attested in hemerological texts, such as in the two versions of daybooks excavated from Shuihudi; see *Shuihudi Qin mu zhujian*, 200, 242.

40 Liu Lexian, *Shuihudi Qinjian rishu yanjiu*; Poo, "Popular Religion in Pre-Imperial China," 225–48; *In Search of Personal Welfare*, 69–102; Wang Zijin, *Shuihudi Qin jian rishu jiazhong shuzheng*.

41 Of the 425 bamboo strips of the daybook discovered at Shuihudi, the content of 151 strips (more than 35 percent) is directly related to travel. See Wang Zijin, "Shuihudi Qin jian rishu suojian xing gui yiji," 45.

42 Strips 1–12 offer a text probably concerning a formula calculating the size of the field and the yield of the grains (see Chao Fulin, "Jiudian Chu jian bushi," 51–54); Strips 43–44 are the

incantation text discussed above, and Strips 45–59 are on geomancy; Strips 13–24, 25–36 (two texts written separately in the upper and lower parts of the strips), 37–40 (the upper part), and 41–42, 37–40 (the lower part), 60–99 are hemerological texts. Some have counterparts in the daybook excavated at the Qin Tomb 11 at Shuihudi in Yunmeng (Hubei). The strips after Strip 100 are all fragments that cannot be read coherently. For studies on the Jiudian strips, see Chen Wei et al., *Chu di chutu Zhanguo jiance (shi si zhong)*, 301–33; Takamura Takeyuki, "Kyūten Sokan hisho no seikaku ni tsuite," 1–23; Kudō Motoo, "Kenjyo yori mida hisho no seiritsu katei shirun," 224–40.

43 *Shuihudi Qin mu zhujian*, 231–32; see also *Jiudian Chu jian*, 187–88.

44 For the interpretation of *xingzuo* as "a trip to do labor or business," see Liu Zenggui, "Qin jian 'rishu' zhong de chuxing lisu yu xinyang," 506; Li Jiahao's note may be seen in *Jiudian Chu jian*, 88–89n105.

45 [申], 酉, 戌, 亥, 子, 丑, 寅, 卯, 辰, 巳, 午, 未, 是胃(謂)外易(陽)日, 利以行作, 蹠四方埜(野)外, 吉. 以田獵, 隻(獲). 逃人不得, 無聞. 執(設)网(網), 得, 大吉 (Strip 31). See Chen Wei et al., *Chu di chutu Zhanguo jiance (shi si zhong)*, 309.

46 [酉], 戌, 亥, 子, 丑, 寅, 卯, 辰, 巳, 午, 未, 申, 是胃(謂)外害日, 不利以行作, 蹠四方埜(野)外, 必{無}遇寇逃(盜), 必兵. 是古(故)胃(謂)不利於行作埜(野)事, 不吉 (Strip 32). See Chen Wei et al., *Chu di chutu Zhanguo jiance (shi si zhong)*, 309. The sign "{}" indicates a scribe's mistake.

47 戌, 亥, 子, 丑, 寅, 卯, 辰, 巳, 午, 未, 申, 酉, 是胃(謂)[外]陰日, 利以祭, 內(入)貨, 吉. 以作卯(貿)事, 不吉. 以遠行, 舊(久). 是古(故)胃(謂)不利於行[作] (Strip 33). See Chen Wei et al., *Chu di chutu Zhanguo jiance (shi si zhong)*, 309.

48 Usually two or three dates in a month share the same branch.

49 Keightley, *The Ancestral Landscape*, 17.

50 凡五子, 不可以作大事, 不成, 必毀, 其身又(有)大咎, 非 (Strip 37) 其身, 伥(長)子受其咎. 凡五卯, 不可以作大事; 帝以命 (Strip 38). 益淒禹之火; 午, 不可以樹木. 凡五亥, 不可以畜六牲 (Strip 39) 擾; 帝之所以戮六擾之日 (Strip 40). See Chen Wei et al., *Chu di chutu Zhanguo jiance (shi si zhong)*, 315.

51 *Mengzi*, "Teng wen Gong" (*Mengzi zhushu*, 5b.98).

52 *Shuihudi Qin mu zhujian*, 189–90; Liu Zenggui, "Qin jian 'rishu' zhong de chuxing lisu yu xinyang," 507–8.

53 Liu Zenggui, "Qin jian 'rishu' zhong de chuxing lisu yu xinyang," 503–21.

54 Liu Zenggui, "Qin jian 'rishu' zhong de chuxing lisu yu xinyang," 531–33.

55 Liu Zenggui, "Qin jian 'rishu' zhong de chuxing lisu yu xinyang," 509–11.

56 For the *Xingde* texts, see Fu Juyou and Chen Songchang, *Mawangdui Han mu wenwu*, 132–43, including only *Xingde* B. For a detailed study of these texts, see Kalinowski, "The Xingde Texts from Mawangdui," 125–202; Chen Songchang reproduced all three (A, B, C) copies of the *Xingde* texts in Chen Songchang, *Mawangdui boshu Xingde yanjiu lungao*. Another two diagrams (not yet fully published) from Mawangdui, the so-called *Yinyang wuxing*, contain texts related to travel. Two fragments were published in Chen Songchang, ed., *Mawangdui boshu yishu*, 130–37. One of the diagrams has been renamed *Shifa*; see Mawangdui Han mu boshu zhengli xiaozu, "Mawangdui boshu Shifa shiwen zhaiyao," 85–94. See also a group of articles on *Shifa* in Ai Lan and Xing Wen, eds., *Xinchu jianbo yanjiu*, 168–96. And some fragments were identified as a separate diagram, titled *Chuxing zhan* (Divination on Travel); see Liu Lexian, *Jianbo shushu wenxian tanlun*, 115–30.

57 Wang Zijin, *Qin Han Jiaotong shigao*, 556.

58 Poo, "How to Steer through Life," 107–25.

59 Through the travel writing of the eighteenth century, the literary scholar Mary L. Pratt explores the relationship between the expansion of geographic knowledge and the production

of a Eurocentric "planetary consciousness." See Pratt, *Imperial Eyes*, esp. chapter 2. See also Schaberg, "Travel, Geography, and Imperial Imagination," 152–91.

60 Aihe Wang in her recent study posits that between the Shang dynasty and the Han dynasty, there was a shift from *sifang* cosmology to *wuxing* cosmology. But the latter was built on the former and contained almost all the features of the earlier cosmology. Centrality in the *wuxing* cosmology is manifested in the middle's various forms of superiority over the peripheral. See Wang, *Cosmology and Political Culture in Early China*.

61 Tong Shuye and Gu Jiegang, "Han dai yiqian Zhongguo ren de shijie," 1–42.

62 Qu Yuan, *The Songs of the South*, 219–31.

63 Yu Weichao, "Han dai zhuhouwang," 117–18; Guo Dewei, *Chu xi muzang yanjiu*, 59; Wu, "From Temple to Tomb," 78–115; "Art in Its Ritual Context."

64 Lai, "The Baoshan Tomb," 43–47.

65 Chen Wei, *Baoshan Chu jian chutan*, 162–67; Chen Wei et al., *Chu di chutu Zhanguo jiance (shi si zhong)*, 106.

66 Liu Xinfang, *Baoshan Chu jian jiegu*, 233.

67 *Wangshan Chu jian*, 25, 38, 39.

68 Teng Rensheng, *Chu xi jianbo wenzibian*, 618–20.

69 In discussing the deities of travel in different classical texts, the Qing scholar Sun Xidan (1736–84) had already noticed this distinction between the tame and the wild; see Sun Xidan, *Liji jijie*, 486. The Tang commentator Jia Gongyan (active middle seventh century) also pointed out the difference between these two types of sacrifices; see *Yili zhushu*, 24.283–84.

70 Li Ling, "Kaogu faxian yu shenhua chuanshuo," 61–64; Chen Wei, *Baoshan Chu jian chutan*, 159–74; Chen Wei, "Geling Chu jian suojian de bushi yu daoci," 39–40.

71 *Xincai Geling Chu mu*, plate 76, Strip A2: 40. In the original transcript (188), the graphs *guisheng* were misidentified; and the graph *shang* is reconstructed; see Xu Zaiguo, "Xincai Geling Chu jian zhaji."

72 For discussion of the cosmic cord-hook diagram on tomb texts, which is also used as a decorative motif on objects excavated from Qin and Han tombs, see Kalinowski, "The Xingde Texts from Mawangdui," 138–45.

73 See, for example, Harley and Woodward, eds., *Cartography in the Traditional East and Southeast Asian Societies*.

74 *Cuo mu: Zhanguo Zhongshan guo guowang zhi mu*, vol. 1, 104–10; vol. 2, color plate 2.

75 He Shuangquan, "Tianshui Fangmatan Qin mu chutu ditu chutan," 12–22. For better color plates of these maps, see Cao Wanru et al., eds., *Zhongguo gudai ditu ji: Zhanguo–Yuan*, plates 4–16.

76 Fu Juyou and Chen Songchang, *Mawangdui Han mu wenwu*, 151; Hsu, "The Han Maps and Early Chinese Cartography," 45–60.

77 Hsu, "The Qin Maps," 90–100.

78 He Shuangquan, "Tianshui Fangmatan Qin mu chutu ditu chutan," 16.

79 Li Xueqin, "Fangmatan jian zhong de zhiguai gushi"; Harper, "Resurrection," 13–28.

80 Liu Lexian, *Jianbo shushu wenxian tanlun*, 115–30; Yan Changgui, "Jianbo rishu sui pian hezheng," 73–78.

81 He Shuangquan, "Tianshui Fangmatan Qin mu chutu ditu chutan," 18.

82 For ways of ordering space in early China, see Lewis, *The Construction of Space in Early China*.

83 Needham and Ronan, "Chinese Cosmology," 63–70.

84 Kalinowski, "The Xingde Texts from Mawangdui," 138–45; Liu Guosheng, "Chu di chutu shushu wenxian yu yuzhou jiegou lilun," 241–48.

85 Gansu sheng wenwu kaogu yanjiusuo and Taishui beidaoqu wenhuaguan, "Gansu Tianshui

Fangmatan Zhanguo Qin Han muqun de fajue," 1–11, esp. 9. The interpretation of this artifact as a paper map has caused debate among scholars because, if it were indeed made of paper, then it would be the earliest paper discovered so far. See Chen et al., "The Unearthed Paperlike Objects," 7–22.

86 Monmonier, *Maps, Distortion, and Meaning*, 1.

87 For psychological and anthropological studies of maps, see Gell, "How to Read a Map," 271–86; Hallpike et al., "Maps and Wayfinding," 342–46.

88 Falkenhausen, "Social Ranking in Chu Tombs," 439–526.

89 Hulsewé, "Texts in Tombs," 78–89, especially 87 and 89.

90 *Baoshan Chu jian*, 37–39, plates 110–20.

91 See *Baoshan Chu mu*, 267, and table 43 in *Baoshan Chu mu*, 271–72.

92 Liu Guosheng recently suggested that it is probably *mao* 卯 (OCM*ru), which was a homophone of *liu* 留 (OCM*ru) and *lao* 牢 (OCM*rû) in Old Chinese; thus *dalao* 大牢 refers to the grand sacrifice in which an ox, a pig, and a goat were offered; see Liu Guosheng, "Chu sangzang jiandu jishi." In the bronze tripods unearthed from Baoshan, ox bones were discovered. Bones of pig, fish, and chicken were found in bamboo cases or ceramic jars in the eastern compartment. See *Baoshan Chu mu*, 98, 445–47. However, Liu Guosheng later changed his mind and instead followed Li Jiahao's interpretation of *dalao* as *dapao* 大庖 (OCM*brû). See Liu Guosheng, "Baoshan erhao Chu mu qiance yanjiu er ze," 67–68.

93 *Shishi*, often translated as "dining room," "dining chamber," or "food chamber" (e.g., Wu, "The Art and Architecture of the Warring States Period," 726), is the place where the deceased offer sacrifices to their ancestors. See the discussion in Hayashi Minao, "Concerning the Inscription 'May Sons and Grandsons Eternally Use This [Vessel],'" 51–52. Here I translate it as "sacrificial hall." For *shi* meaning sacrifice, see Qiu Xigui, *Gudai wenshi yanjiu xintan*, 143–45. Most scholars interpret the eastern compartment as the "dining room" or "food chamber." The size of the eastern compartment is 4.14 meters × 0.92 meters × 3.1 meters, which is too cramped to be considered a room. Here it refers to an imaginative, unspecific space in the afterlife.

94 Most scholars interpret the first two graphs as *xiangwei* or *xiangshao*, referring to the rear compartment (what they meant is the western compartment). The objects listed in this category, however, were found in both the western and northern compartments. To reconcile this contradiction, Chen Wei divides this word into two, *xiang* (side rooms in a house) and *shao* (the end, the rear), thereby referring to the two compartments; see Chen Wei, *Baoshan Chu jian chutan*, 193. Although all of these readings are phonologically possible, here I follow Lin Yun, who has convincingly argued that the expression *xiangxi zhi qi* means "the objects that are brought together," referring to the "movable" (i.e., portable) paraphernalia; see Lin Yun, "Du Baoshan Chu jian zhaji qize," 19–21. The interpretation of the graph *xi* as the verb "to move" is firmly established. See the discussion of this graph in Yu Weichao, *Zhongguo gudai gongshe zuzhi*, 1–15, where he quotes Li Jiahao's interpretation. The same graph appears on Baoshan Strip 250, where it also functions as a verb, "to move." See also the discussion in He Linyi, *Zhanguo guwen zidian*, 883.

95 Thote, "Continuities and Discontinuities," 189–204.

96 Wang Renxiang, "Gudai daigou yongtu kaoshi," 75–81, 94; "Daigou gailun," 267–312; "Daigou lüelun," 65–75.

97 Hayashi Minao stated that "these items, however, do not seem to be for travel as suggested by the category heading. Rather they were for the burial rites: the items buried with the coffin are called *xingqi*, 'items for travel.' Apparently the procession to the cemetery was regarded as 'travel.'" See Hayashi, "Concerning the Inscription 'May Sons and Grandsons

Eternally Use This [Vessel],'" 52. Thus, Hayashi did not see the potential functions of these everyday items and only considered the funeral procession to the tomb as travel. But considering the new abode of the dead, the cosmological constructions, other travel-related objects and texts, and especially the Jiudian incantation, which states that the cosmic location of "the edge of Mt. Fu and the wilds of Buzhou" is the gathering place of the war dead, I am arguing that the funeral procession is only the beginning of the postmortem journey; the tomb is only a way station, the final destination for the spirit journey is at the northwest of the universe.

98 As George Basalla reminds us, ordinary tools, instruments, utensils, and other devices can be, and have always been, throughout human history, refashioned, altered, or transformed into objects of different social and cultural functions and meanings. See Basalla, "Transformed Utilitarian Objects," 183–201.

99 Merrifield, *The Archaeology of Ritual and Magic*.

100 Harrison, *Prolegomena to the Study of Greek Religion*, 8–10.

101 Lai, "Lighting the Way in the Afterlife," 20–28.

102 *Jiangling Wangshan Shazhong Chu mu*, color plate 5.

103 Qu Yuan, *The Songs of the South*, 225.

104 Li Ling, "Lun Zhongguo de youyi shenshou," 62–134.

105 Jiang Shaoyuan, *Fa xu zhua; Zhongguo gudai lüxing zhi yanjiu*. Jiang's research was inspired by James Frazer's *Golden Bough* (1922).

106 Qu Yuan, *The Songs of the South*, 109.

107 *Zuozhuan*, Lord Xi 28th year; Yang Bojun, *Chunqiu Zuozhuan zhu*, 467–68. As Yang Bojun discusses in his commentary, the Han scholars all interpreted the cap and strings as the decorations on a horse. But the Western Jin dynasty (266–316) commentator Du Yu interpreted them as the cap and cap strings worn by Zi Yu.

108 *Yili* "Shi sangli" (*Yili zhushu*, 35.409).

109 Van Gennep, *The Rites of Passage*.

110 行到邦門困(闉), 禹步三, 勉壹步, 謼(呼): "皋, 敢告曰: 某行毋(無)咎, 先為禹除道. 即五畫地, 椒其畫中央土 (Strip 111 back) 而懷之 (Strip 112 back). See *Shuihudi Qin mu zhujian*, 112, 223–24; Donald Harper's translation, in Harper, "Warring States Natural Philosophy and Occult Thought," 873.

111 Liu Zenggui, "Qin jian 'rishu' zhong de chuxing lisu yu xinyang," 521–26.

112 Axel Schuessler thinks that both meanings of *zu*, namely, "deceased grandfather, ancestor" and "sacrifice to the spirits of the road," are derived from the basic notion of "move on"; another related word, *cu*, has the meaning of "to go away, pass away, die." See Schuessler, *ABC Etymological Dictionary of Old Chinese*, 41, 636.

113 Yang Bojun, *Chunqiu Zuozhuan zhu*, 1286–87.

114 Shen Yue recorded two accounts of the origin of the sacrifice to the spirits of the road: one posits that the sacrifice was offered to an ancestor who died on the road, whereas the other theory stated that the sacrifice was made to the spirits of ancestors who had been eliminated from the normal sacrificial list, with the hope that they would do no harm to the traveler. See *Songshu*, 260; see also Lewis, *Sanctioned Violence*, 187–90.

115 *Yili zhushu*, 38.452–55.

116 Hayashi, "Concerning the Inscription 'May Sons and Grandsons Eternally Use This [Vessel],'" 52, 55.

117 *Yili zhushu*, 24.283–84; Steele, *The I-li or Book of Etiquette and Ceremonial*, 233 (translation modified).

118 Harper, *Early Chinese Medical Literature*, 354; Liu Zenggui, "Qin jian 'rishu' zhong de chu-xing lisu yu xinyang," 526.

119 Harper, *Early Chinese Medical Literature*, 354.

120 Erkes, "Si er bu wang," 156–61; for a different interpretation, see Brashier, "Longevity Like Metal and Stone," 215.

121 Seidel, "Tokens of Immortality in Han Graves," 110–11. See also Poo, *In Search of Personal Welfare*, 210–11.

122 Nickerson, "Opening the Way," 58–77.

Glossary of Chinese Characters

an 案
Andu 安都

baigaoni 白膏泥
Baizicun 百子村
Balingshan 八嶺山
bangmen 邦門
Baoshan 包山
Baoxiangsi 寶相寺
Beidongshan 北洞山
bi (consort) 妣
bi (jade disk) 璧
Bibing tu 避兵圖
bin (guest) 賓
bin (to encoffin
    a corpse) 殯
bing 丙
bingsi 兵死
Bisi 辟死
bugu 不辜
Buzhou 不周

Cai gong 蔡公
cang 藏
Caojiagang 曹家港
Changping 長平
changxing (the deities
    in charge of travel) 常行

changxing (long
    distance trip) 長行
che 車
chengdan 城旦
Chengpu 城濮
Chenjiadashan 陳家大山
Cheqiao 車橋
chi 尺
Chidi lin ri 赤帝臨日
Chiyou 蚩尤
chong 重
chu 出
Chu 楚
Chu di 楚地
Chu guo 楚國
Chu wenhua 楚文化
Chu wenming 楚文明
chuhe 出禾
Chunqiu 春秋
chuqian 出錢
cishi 祠室
citang 祠堂
Congchen 叢辰
cu 爼/俎

da changxing 大常行
Da Yi 大乙
Dabaotai 大葆台

235

Dahekou	大河口	Geling	葛陵
dalao zhi jinqi	大[太]牢之金器	*Genshan tu*	艮山圖
dali	大厲	gong	宮
dao (to pray,		Gong dizhu	宮地主
to sacrifice)	禱	Gong houtu	宮后土
Dao (a surname)	悼	Gong xing	宮行
daqiandian	大遣奠	gongchu	攻除
Dashui	大水	gongjie	攻解
daxing	大行	gongli	公厲
de	德	gongmei	宮禖
Di	帝	gongwu	宮襡
didao	地道	Gongyin	攻尹
diqi	地祇	Gongzuo	攻佐
disuo	帝所	gou	勾
diting	帝廷	*Gu mingqi tulu*	古明器圖錄
dixia cheng	地下丞	guan (inner coffin)	棺
dixia zhu	地下主	guan (to shut, to close)	關
dizhipi	帝之坏	guannei hou	關內侯
dizhu	地主	Guanping	官坪
Dongling Lianxiao	東陵連嚻	gui	鬼
		Guifang	鬼方
Ertianzi	二天子	guiji	歸忌
		guimeng	鬼夢
Fangmatan	放馬灘	guiri	鬼日
feili	非禮	guo (cutting	
Fenghuangshan	鳳凰山	off heads)	馘
fengjian	封檢	guo (encasement)	槨
fengjun	封君	Guodian	郭店
fengshu	賵書	Guojiagang	郭家崗
fu	賵	*Guoshang*	國殤
furen	夫人	guoshou	槨首
		guosuo wuliu	過所勿留
gan (dare)	敢	guoyou	槨右
gan (heavenly stem)	干	*Guoyu*	國語
gan gao zhi	敢告之	guozhong	槨中
gan yan zhi	敢言之	guozu	槨足
gao (lard)	膏	guozuo	槨左
gao (to inform,		Guweicun	固圍村
to announce)	告		
gaodishu	告地書	han	諴
Gaomiao	高廟	haoli	蒿里
Gaotai	高臺	Hekou	河口

Heshangling	和尚嶺	juewuhouzhe	絕無後者
hou	侯	jun	君
Hougudui	侯固堆	junzi	君子
Houjiazhuang	侯家莊		
Houtu	后土	King Cheng of Chu	楚成王
hu (door)	戶	(r. 671–626 BCE)	
hu (jade pendant)	琥	King Kang of Chu	楚康王
Hua	邬	(r. 559–545 BCE)	
Huchang	胡場	King Mu of Chu	楚穆王
huajiao	畫角	(r. 625–614 BCE)	
huangchang ticou	黃腸題湊	King Wu	武王
Huang Jun Meng	黃君孟	Kongjiapo	孔家坡
huan	環	kun	困[闉]
huaxia	華夏		
huilang	回廊	langzhong	郎中
hun	魂	lao	牢
		Laotong	老童
Ji	姬	leigong	雷公
ji chu zhi qi	集廚之器	Leigudun	擂鼓墩
jia (first heavenly		li (officer)	吏
stem)	甲	li (to stand)	立
jia fu busuan buyao	家賦不算, 不繇	li (tripod with	
jian	僭	hollow legs)	鬲
Jian mu wei	漸木位	li (vengeful ghost)	厲
Jiangling cheng yin	江陵丞印	Liangdaicun	梁帶村
jimiao	極廟	Lianxiao	連囂
Ji'nancheng	紀南城	lihuai yuebeng	禮坏樂崩
Jinbu lü	金布律	ling	令
Jingwang	荊王	Lingshan	陵山
jingyi	敬移	Lisangudui	李三孤堆
Jinqueshan	金雀山	Lishan	驪山
Jishan	紀山	liu	留
jishengba	既生霸	Liuguo nianbiao	六國年表
jishi	祭室	Longgang	龍崗
jisiba	既死霸	Lu	魯
Jiudian	九店	Lunyu	論語
jiujing	九京		
Jiuliandun	九連墩	maidiquan	買地券
jiuxing	久行	mao	卯
jiuyuan	九原	Mawangdui	馬王堆
Jiyin	集尹	men	門
jue	玦	mengzu	盟祖

miaohao	廟號	qingzi she	請子社
milu	麋鹿	Qu	屈
ming	明		
mingjing	銘旌	rengui	人鬼
mingqi	明器	renxing fangshu	人形方術
mingshu	名數	rishu	日書
mingtong	明童	ru	入
mingzu	明祖	ruhe	入禾
mou	某	ruqian	入錢
Mount Tai	泰山		
Moxiao	莫囂	saidao	賽禱
mupianyong	木片俑	san Chu xian	三楚先
muqi	木器	sangli	喪禮
		sangzhu	喪主
na	納	Sanji	三汲
nanfang	南方	se	瑟
niren	溺人	shang	殤
Niujiapo	牛家坡	Shangdi	上帝
		shangxia	上下
Paimashan	拍馬山	shangxia neiwai	
Pan xian	潘先	guishen	上下内外鬼神
pei	珮	Shanhaijing	山海經
Peng	倗	Shao Cheng	邵乘
pian	楩	Shao Ji	邵吉
piandian	便殿	Shao Liang	邵良
pianguo	便槨	Shao Tuo	邵䤸
pianguojushi	便廓[槨]具室	Shaogongzuo	少攻佐
pianshi	楩室	Shaogou	燒溝
pianzuo	便坐	Shaojiyin	少集尹
Pingxi	平西	Shaosibai	少司敗
Pingye jun	平夜君	she	社
pingyi	憑依	shengxiang	聲像
po	魄	Sheshen tu	社神圖
		shi (chamber)	室
qi	器	shi (foods)	食
qiance	遣冊	shi (impersonator)	尸
qiangsi	強死	shi (officer,	
Qianzhangda	前掌大	gentleman)	士
qiju	乞鞠	shi (stand, setting)	執
qin	寢	Shi Tai	蝕太
qinggaoni	青膏泥	shi'er chen	十二辰

shi'er zhi	十二支	wang	王
Shifa	式法	Wangchengpo	望城坡
Shiji	史記	Wanggou	王溝
shishi	食室	Wangshan	望山
shishi suoyi bao		wangshici	王室祠
gong	食室所以貞箕	Wangsun Gao	王孫誥
shishi zhi jinqi	食室之金器	wangtong	亡童
shishi zhi shi	食室之食	Wangzi Wu	王子午
shitang	食堂	wanqi	宛奇
shiwu	什伍	Wei (a lineage	
Shizumiao	世祖廟	name)	蔿
Shuangdun	雙墩	wei (to fear)	畏
shui	說	Weishan	危山
Shuihudi	睡虎地	weiwei	為位
shuishang	水上	wu	巫
Shun	舜	wu dafu	五大夫
si (to feed)	食	wu dizi	武弟子
si er bu wang zhe		Wu gong	鄐公
shou	死而不亡者壽	Wushan	五山
Sibai	司敗	wusi	五祀
Sifang	四方	Wuyi	武夷
Sihuo	司禍	Wuxing	五行
Sima	司馬		
Sima Ziyin	司馬子音	xi yu xiadu	徙於下都
Siming	司命	xiali	下里
		xian	仙
Taichanshu	胎產書	xiang	鄉
taili	泰厲	xiang	像
Taiyi	太一	xiangxi zhiqi suoyi	
Taiyi jiang xing tu	太一將行圖	xing	相徙之器所以行
Taiyi sheng shui	太一生水	Xianluo gong	縣洛公
tiangong	天公	xiaohuan	小環
Tianma-Qucun	天馬-曲村	Xiaoyancun	小沿村
tianming	天命	Xiasi	下寺
tianshen	天神	xiatu	下土
Tianxingguan	天星觀	xie (a mythical	
ticou	題湊	animal)	獬,
tudumu	土墩墓	also written as	觟, 桂
tulou	土蔞	xieguan	觟[桂]冠
tuzhu	土主	Xiejiaqiao	謝家橋
		xin	信

xing	行	yuanxing	遠行
Xing (the deity of travel)	行	yubu	禹步
		yudao	與禱
Xingde	刑德	yueren zhi qi	樂人之器
xingqi	行器	yufu	禹符
xingzuo	行作	yuji	虞祭
Xiongli	熊麗	yushi	雨師
Xishuipo	西水坡	Yutaishan	雨台山
Xujialing	徐家嶺	Yuxiong	毓熊
Xuning	序寧	yuyi	玉衣
xunren	殉人		
		zai di zuoyou	在帝左右
Yan Xiadu	燕下都	zang	葬
yan zai shang	嚴在上	Zang Gan	臧敢
Yangtianhu	仰天湖	zangqi	葬器
yaokeng	腰坑	zao	竈
yayan	雅言	zeng	贈
Ye dizhu	野地主	Zhangjiapo	張家坡
yi (already, cease)	已	zhanguo	戰國
yi (second heavenly stem)	乙	*Zhanguo ce*	戰國策
		Zhanguo shi	戰國史
yi (to move, to transfer)	移	*Zhanguo shi yu Zhanguo wenming*	戰國史與戰國文明
Yi	益		
yi qi gu shui zhi	以其故說之	Zhao	趙
Yi Yin	伊尹	Zhaoxiang	趙巷
yi zai xia	異在下	*Zheng Zijia sang*	鄭子家喪
Yi Zhoushu	逸周書	zhenmushou	鎮墓獸
yidao	弋禱	Zhenshan	真山
also written as	翌禱	zhi (bug)	豸
yimen	邑門	zhi (earthly branches)	支
yinli	淫厲	zhi (suet, grease)	脂
Yinshan	印山	zhi sifang yewai	蹛四方野外
yong (to use, to sacrifice)	用	zhijiang	陟降
		Zhoujiatai	周家臺
yong (tomb figurine)	俑	*Zhouli*	周禮
Yonglu	永祿	zhu	主
youdu	幽都	zhunxi	窀穸
youxuan	右旋	zhuren	主人
Yu xuyu	禹須臾	Zhurong	祝融
yu yi ren	余一人	Zichan	子產
Yuan	蓮	Zichun	子春

Zifa	子發	zu (curse)	詛
Zigeng	子庚	zu (phallus)	且
zigong	梓宮	also written as	祖, 礻且
Zijia	子家	zudao	祖道
Ziliang	子良	zuli	族厲
ziyan	自言	Zuoyin	左尹
zu (ancestor; sacrifice		*Zuozhuan*	左傳
to the spirits of		zushi	且埶
the road)	祖	zuwei	祖位

Bibliography

Works in Chinese and Japanese

Ai Lan 艾蘭 and Xing Wen 邢文, eds. *Xinchu jianbo yanjiu* 新出簡帛研究. Beijing: Wenwu chubanshe, 2004.

Anhui sheng wenwu kaogu yanjiusuo 安徽省文物考古研究所 and Bangbu shi bowuguan 蚌埠市博物館. "Anhui Bangbu shi Shuangdun yi hao Chunqiu muzang" 安徽蚌埠市雙墩一號春秋墓葬. *Kaogu* 2009.7: 39–45.

———. "Bangbu Shuangdun yi hao Chunqiu mu fajue jianbao" 蚌埠雙墩一號春秋墓發掘簡報. *Wenwu* 2010.3: 4–18.

Anhui sheng wenwu kaogu yanjiusuo and Fengyang xian wenwu guanlisuo 鳳陽縣文物管理所. "Anhui Fengyang Bianzhuang yi hao Chunqiu mu fajue jianbao" 安徽鳳陽卞莊一號春秋墓發掘簡報. *Wenwu* 2009.8: 21–29.

Anhui sheng wenwu kaogu yanjiusuo and Shucheng xian wenwu guanlisuo 舒城縣文物管理所. "Anhui Shucheng xian Hekou Chunqiu mu" 安徽舒城縣河口春秋墓. *Wenwu* 1990.6: 53, 58–66.

Bai Yiping 白一平 (= William H. Baxter). "'Shi' 'shi' 'she'deng zi de gouni he zhonggu sy- (shumu = shensan) de laiyuan" 埶勢設等字的構擬和中古sy- (書母=審三) 的來源. *Jianbo* 5 (2010): 161–77.

Baoji Yuguo mudi 寶雞強國墓地. Comp. Lu Liancheng 盧連成 and Hu Zhisheng 胡智生. Baoji bowuguan 寶雞博物館. Beijing: Wenwu chubanshe, 1988.

Baoshan Chu jian 包山楚簡. Hubei sheng Jingsha tielu kaogudui 湖北省荊沙鐵路考古隊. Beijing: Wenwu chubanshe, 1991.

Baoshan Chu mu 包山楚墓. Comp. Hubei sheng Jingsha tielu kaogudui 湖北省荊沙鐵路考古隊 2 vols. Beijing: Wenwu chubanshe, 1991.

Beijing Dabaotai Han mu 北京大葆台漢墓. Comp. Dabaotai Han mu fajue zu 大葆台漢墓發掘組 and Zhongguo shehui kexueyuan kaogu yanjiusuo 中國社會科學院考古研究所. First published in 1989, in *Beijing kaogu jicheng* 北京考古集成, ed. Su Tianjun, 303–486. Vol. 11. Beijing: Beijing chubanshe, 2005.

Bei Song Shanzhou Louzeyuan 北宋陝州漏澤園. Comp. Sanmenxia shi wenwu gongzuodui 三門峽市文物工作隊. Beijing: Wenwu chubanshe, 1999.

Cai Quanfa 蔡全法. "Zheng Han gucheng Han wenhua kaogu de zhuyao shouhuo" 鄭韓故城韓文化考古的主要收穫. In *Qunxiong zhulu: Liang Zhou zhongyuan lieguo wenwu guibao* 群雄逐鹿:兩周中原列國文物瑰寶, comp. Henan bowuyuan, 117–23. Zhengzhou: Daxiang chubanshe, 2003.

Cai Zhemao 蔡哲茂. "Yin buci Yi Yin jiushi kao: jianlun tashi" 殷卜辭伊尹臺示考: 兼論它示. *Zhongyang yanjiuyuan Lishi yuyan yanjiusuo jikan* 58.4 (1987): 755–808.

Cao Wanru 曹婉如, Zheng Xihuang 鄭錫煌 et al., eds. *Zhongguo gudai ditu ji: Zhanguo-Yuan* 中國古代地圖集: 戰國-元. Beijing: Wenwu chubanshe, 1990.

Chang Yong 常勇 and Li Tong 李同. "Qin Shihuang ling zhong maicang gong de chubu yanjiu" 秦始皇陵中埋藏汞的初步研究. *Kaogu* 1983.7: 659–63.

Chang Yuzhi 常玉芝. *Shang dai zhouji zhidu* 商代周祭制度. Beijing: Zhongguo shehui kexueyuan, 1987.

Changsha Chu mu 長沙楚墓. Comp. Hunan sheng bowuguan 湖南省博物館, Hunan sheng wenwu kaogu yanjiusuo 湖南省文物考古研究所, Changsha shi bowuguan 長沙市博物館, and Changsha shi wenwu kaogu yanjiusuo 長沙市文物考古研究所. 2 vols. Beijing: Wenwu chubanshe, 2000.

Changsha fajue baogao 長沙發掘報告. Comp. Zhongguo kexueyuan kaogu yanjiusuo 中國科學院考古研究所. Beijing: Kexue chubanshe, 1957.

Changsha Mawangdui er san hao Han mu 長沙馬王堆二,三號漢墓. Comp. Hunan sheng bowuguan 湖南省博物館, Hunan sheng wenwu kaogu yanjiusuo 湖南省文物考古研究所. Vol. 1: Tianye kaogu fajue baogao. Beijing: Wenwu chubanshe, 2004.

Changsha Mawangdui yihao Han mu 長沙馬王堆一號漢墓. Comp. Hunan sheng bowuguan 湖南省博物館 and Zhongguo kexueyuan kaogu yanjiusuo 中國科學院考古研究所. 2 vols. Beijing: Wenwu chubanshe, 1973.

Changsha shi wenwu kaogu yanjiusuo 長沙市文物考古研究所. "Changsha Fengpengling yi hao Han mu" 長沙風篷嶺一號漢墓. *Wenwu* 2007.12: 21–41.

Changsha wenhuaju wenwuzu 長沙文化局文物組. "Changsha Xianjiahu Xi Han Cao Zhuan mu" 長沙咸家湖西漢曹嬛墓. *Wenwu* 1979.3: 1–16.

Chao Fulin 晁福林. "Jiudian Chu jian bushi" 九店楚簡補釋. *Zhongyuan wenwu* 2002.5: 51–54.

Chen Gongrou 陳公柔. "Shi sangli, jixili zhong suo jizai de sangzang zhidu" 士喪禮既夕禮中所記載的喪葬制度. *Kaogu xuebao* 1956.4: 67–84.

Chen Li 陳立. *Baihutong shuzheng* 白虎通疏證. Beijing: Zhonghua shuju, 1994.

Chen Mengjia 陳夢家. "Shang dai de shenhua yu wushu" 商代的神話與巫術. *Yanjing xuebao* 燕京學報 20 (1936): 485–576.

———. *Yinxu buci zongshu* 殷虛卜辭綜述. Beijing: Zhonghua shuju, 1988.

Chen Mingfang 陳明芳. *Zhongguo xuanguan zang* 中國懸棺葬. Chongqing: Chongqing chubanshe, 1992.

Chen Pan 陳槃. *Chunqiu Dashibiao lieguo juexing ji cunmiebiao zhuanyi* 春秋大事表列國爵姓及存滅表譔異. Taibei: Zhongyang yanjiuyuan Lishi yuyan yanjiusuo, 1997.

Chen Ping 陳平. "Qiantan Jiang Han diqu Zhanguo Qin Han mu de fenqi he Qin mu de shibie wenti" 淺談江漢地區戰國秦漢墓的分期和秦墓的識別問題. *Jiang Han kaogu* 1983.3: 51–62.

———. *Guanlong wenhua yu Ying Qin wenming* 關隴文化與嬴秦文明. Nanjing: Fenghuang chubanshe, 2004.

Chen Qiyun 陳啟雲. *Zhongguo gudai sixiang wenhua de lishi lunxi* 中國古代思想文化的歷史論析. Beijing: Beijing daxue chubanshe, 2001.

Chen Songchang 陳松長. "Mawangdui sanhao Han mu mudu sanlun" 馬王堆三號漢墓木牘散論. *Wenwu* 1994.6: 64–70.

———. "Mawangdui sanhao Han mu jinian mudu xingzhi de zai renshi" 馬王堆三號漢墓紀年木牘性質的再認識. *Wenwu* 1997.1: 61–64.

———. *Mawangdui boshu Xingde yanjiu lungao* 馬王堆帛書刑德研究論稿. Taibei: Taiwan guji chuban youxian gongsi, 2001.

———. *Xianggang Zhongwen daxue wenwuguan cang jiandu* 香港中文大學文物舘藏簡牘. Xianggang: Xianggang Zhongwen daxue wenwuguan, 2001.

———. "Gaodice de xingwen geshi yu xiangguan wenti" 告地策的行文格式與相關問題. *Hunan daxue xuebao* 湖南大學學報 2008.3: 21–25.

Chen Songchang 陳松長, ed. *Mawangdui boshu yishu* 馬王堆帛書藝術. Shanghai: Shanghai shudian, 1996.

Chen Wei 陳偉. "Xichuan Xiasi er hao muzhu jiqi xiangguan wenti" 淅川下寺二號墓主及其相關問題. *Jiang Han kaogu* 1983.1: 32–33.

———. *Baoshan Chu jian chutan* 包山楚簡初探. Wuhan: Wuhan daxue chubanshe, 1996.

———. "Geling Chu jian suojian de bushi yu daoci." 葛陵楚簡所見卜筮與禱祠 *Chutu wenxian yanjiu* 6 (2004): 34–42.

———. "Churen daoci jilu zhong de rengui xitong yiji xiangguan wenti" 楚人禱祠記錄中的人鬼系統以及相關問題. *Guwenzi yu gudaishi* 古文字與古代史 1 (2007): 363–89. Taibei: Zhongyang yanjiuyuan Lishi yuyanyanjiusuo, 2007.

———. "Qinghua jian Chuju 'pianshi' gushi xiaokao" 清華簡楚居"梗室"故事小考. Jianbowang 簡帛網 (Wuhan University), February 3, 2011.

Chen Wei 陳偉 et al. *Chu di chutu Zhanguo jiance (shi si zhong)* 楚地出土戰國簡冊 (十四種). Beijing: Jingji kexue chubanshe, 2009.

Chen Xingcan 陳星燦. "Fengchan wushu yu zuxian chongbai: Hongshan wenhua chutu nüxing suxiang shitan" 豐產巫術與祖先崇拜: 紅山文化出土女性塑像試探. *Huaxia kaogu* 華夏考古 1990.3: 92–98.

Chen Zhenyu 陳振裕. "Cong Hubei faxian de Qin mu tan Qin Chu guanxi." 從湖北發現的秦墓談秦楚關係. First published in 1981, in his *Chu wenhua yu qiqi yanjiu* 楚文化與漆器研究, 236–45. Beijing: Kexue chubanshe, 2003.

———. "Luelun jiu zuo Chu mu de niandai" 略論九座楚墓的年代. First published in 1981, in his *Chu wenhua yu qiqi yanjiu*, 69–84. Beijing: Kexue chubanshe, 2003.

———. "Hubei Chu mu zongshu" 湖北楚墓綜述. First published in 1987, in his *Chu wenhua yu qiqi yanjiu*, 54–68. Beijing: Kexue chubanshe, 2003.

———. "Luelun Hubei Qin mu" 略論湖北秦墓. First published in 1986, in his *Chu wenhua yu qiqi yanjiu* 楚文化與漆器研究, 209–19. Beijing: Kexue chubanshe, 2003.

———. "Shilun Hubei diqu Qin mu de niandai fenqi" 試論湖北地區秦墓的年代分期. First published in 1991, in his *Chu wenhua yu qiqi yanjiu* 楚文化與漆器研究, 220–35. Beijing: Kexue chubanshe, 2003.

Chen Zhi 陳直. "Changsha Mawangdui yihao Han mu de ruogan wenti kaoshu" 長沙馬王堆一號漢墓的若干問題考述. *Wenwu* 1972.9: 30–35.

———. "Guanyu 'Jiangling cheng' gao 'dixia cheng'" 關於"江陵丞"告"地下丞." *Wenwu* 1977.12: 76.

Chengde diqu wenwu baoguansuo 承德地區文物保管所 and Luanping xian bowuguan 灤平縣博物館. "Hebei Luanping xian Houtaizi yizhi fajue jianbao" 河北灤平縣後臺子遺址發掘簡報. *Wenwu* 1994.3: 53–71.

Chuci jizhu 楚辭集注 (*Collected Commentaries on the Songs of the South*), comp. Zhu Xi 朱熹 (1130–1200), traditionally attributed to Qu Yuan 屈原 (343?–ca. 315 BCE), et al. Shanghai: Shanghai guji chubanshe, 1979.

Cuo mu: Zhanguo Zhongshan guo guowang zhi mu 𰯼墓戰國中山國國王之墓. Comp. Hebei sheng wenwu yanjiusuo 河北省文物研究所. 2 vols. Beijing: Wenwu chubanshe, 1995.

Dangyang Zhaojiahu Chu mu. 當陽趙家湖楚墓. Comp. Hubei sheng Yichang diqu bowuguan 湖北省宜昌地區博物館 and Beijing daxue kaoguxi 北京大學考古系. Beijing: Wenwu chubanshe, 1992.

Ding Lan 丁蘭. *Hubei diqu Chu mu fenqu yanjiu* 湖北地區楚墓分區研究. Beijing: Minzu chubanshe, 2006.

———. "Chu shi 'zhenmushou' tezheng zonglun" 楚式 "鎮墓獸" 特徵綜論. *Jiang Han kaogu* 2010.1: 98–106.

Dong Chuping 董楚平. "Diwen: Tianyuan difang kao" 地問: 天圓地方考. *Huaxue* 4 (2000): 188–206.

Duan Qingbo 段清波. *Qin Shi Huangdi lingyuan kaogu yanjiu* 秦始皇帝陵園考古研究. Beijing: Beijing daxue chubanshe, 2011.

Egashira Hiroshi 江頭廣. "Yomi ni tsuite" 黃泉について. In *Tōyōgaku ronshū: Ikeda Suetoshi hakushi koki kinen* 東洋学論集: 池田末利博士古稀記念, ed. Ikeda Suetoshi hakushi koki kinen jigyōkai, 109–26. Hiroshima: Ikeda Suetoshi hakushi koki kinen jigyōkai, 1980.

Fengyang Dadongguan yu Bianzhuang 鳳陽大東關與卞莊. Comp. Anhui sheng wenwu kaogu yanjiusuo 安徽省文物考古研究所 and Fengyang xian wenwu guanlisuo 鳳陽縣文物管理所. Beijing: Kexue chubanshe, 2010.

Feng Shi 馮時. "Shanggu yuzhouguan de kaoguxue yanjiu: Anhui Bangbu Shuangdun Chunqiu Zhongli jun Bai mu jiedu" 上古宇宙觀的考古學研究: 安徽蚌埠雙墩春秋鍾離君柏墓解讀. *Zhongyang yanjiuyuan Lishi yuyan yanjiusuo jikan* 82.3 (2011): 399–491.

Fu Juyou 傅舉有 and Chen Songchang 陳松長. *Mawangdui Han mu wenwu* 馬王堆漢墓文物. Changsha: Hunan chubanshe, 1992.

Fujino Iwatomo 藤野岩友. "Uho kō" 禹步考. In his *Chūgoku no bungaku to reizoku* 中國の文學と禮俗, 302–16. Tōkyō: Kadokawa shoten, 1976.

Gao Chongwen 高崇文. "Chu 'zhenmushou' wei 'zuchong' jie" 楚"鎮墓獸"為"祖重"解. *Wenwu* 2008.9: 54–60, 46.

———. "Shi 'pianguo,' 'pianfang,' yu 'piandian'" 釋便椁便房與便殿. *Kaogu yu wenwu* 2010.3: 46–52.

Gao Yingqin 高應勤. "Dong Zhou Chu mu renxun zongshu" 東周楚墓人殉綜述. *Kaogu* 1991.12: 1121–24.

Gao Quxun 高去尋. "Yindai muzang yiyou muzhong shuo" 殷代墓葬已有墓塚說. *Guoli Taiwan daxue kaogu renlei xue kan* 國立臺灣大學考古人類學刊 41 (1980): 1–13.

Gao Zhixi 高至喜. *Shang Zhou qingtongqi yu Chu wenhua yanjiu* 商周青銅器與楚文化研究. Changsha: Yuelu shushe, 1999.

———. "Chu yong yanjiu" 楚俑研究. In his *Shang Zhou qingtongqi yu Chu wenhua yanjiu*, 180–270.

———. "Lun Hunan Qin mu" 論湖南秦墓. In his *Shang Zhou qingtongqi yu Chu wenhua yanjiu*, 297–306.

Gansu sheng wenwu kaogu yanjiusuo 甘肅省文物考古研究所 and Tianshui beidaoqu wenhuaguan 天水北道區文化館. "Gansu Tianshui Fangmatan Zhanguo Qin Han muqun de fajue" 甘肅天水放馬灘戰國秦漢墓群的發掘. *Wenwu* 1989.2: 1–11.

Gao Ming 高明, comp. *Boshu Laozi jiaozhu* 帛書老子校注. Beijing: Zhonghua shuju, 1996.

Ge Jianxiong 葛劍雄. *Zhongguo renkou shi* 中國人口史, vol. 1. Shanghai: Fudan daxue chubanshe, 2002.

Gu Jiegang 顧頡剛. "Zhuangzi he Chuci zhong Kunlun he Penglai liangge shenhua xitong de ronghe" 莊子和楚辭中崑崙和蓬萊兩個神話系統的融合. In *Gu Jiegang minsuxue lunji* 顧頡剛民俗學論集, ed. Qian Xiaobo, 41–80. Shanghai: Shanghai wenyi chubanshe, 1998.

Gu Yanwu 顧炎武, Huang Rucheng 黃汝成, Yi Baoqun 奕保群, and Lü Zongli 呂宗力. *Rizhilu jishi* 日知錄集釋. Shijiazhuang: Huashan wenyi chubanshe, 1991.

Guan Donggui 管東貴. "Zhanguo zhi Hanchu de renkou bianqian" 戰國至漢初的人口變遷. *Zhongyang yanjiuyuan Lishi yuyan yanjiusuo jikan* 50.4 (1979): 645–56.

Guangxi Guixian Luobowan Han mu 廣西貴縣羅泊灣漢墓. Comp. Guangxi Zhuangzu zizhiqu bowuguan 廣西壯族自治區博物館. Beijing: Wenwu chubanshe, 1988.

Guanju Qin Han mu jiandu 關沮秦漢墓簡牘. Comp. Hubei sheng Jingzhou shi Zhouliangyuqiao yizhi bowuguan 湖北省荊州市周梁玉橋遺址博物館. Beijing: Zhonghua shuju, 2001.

Guo Daoyang 郭道揚. *Zhongguo kuaiji shigao* 中國會計史稿. Beijing: Zhongguo caizheng jingji chubanshe, 1982.

———. *Kuaiji fazhan shigang* 會計發展史綱. Beijing: Zhongyang guangbo dianshi daxue chubanshe, 1984.

Guo Dewei 郭德維. "Jiangling Chu mu lunshu" 江陵楚墓論述. *Kaogu xuebao* 1982.2: 155–82.

———. "Shilun Jiangling diqu Chu mu, Qin mu he Xi Han qianqi mu de fazhan yu yanbian" 試論江陵地區楚墓, 秦墓 和西漢前期墓的發展與演變. *Kaogu yu wenwu* 1983.2: 81–88.

———. *Chu xi muzang yanjiu* 楚系墓葬研究. Wuhan: Hubei Jiaoyu chubanshe, 1995.

Guo Moruo 郭沫若. "Shi 'zubi'" 釋祖妣. First published in 1929, in his *Jiaguwenzi yanjiu* 甲骨文字研究, 1–60. Beijing: Kexue chubanshe, 1962.

———. "Guanyu wan Zhou bohua de kaocha" 關於晚周帛畫的考察. *Renmin wenxue* 人民文學 1953.11: 113–18.

———. *Zhongguo shigao* 中國史稿. Vol. 2. Beijing: Renmin chubanshe, 1979.

Guo Ruoyu 郭若愚. "Changsha Yangtianhu Zhanguo zhujian wenzi de moxie he kaoshi" 長沙仰天湖戰國竹簡文字的摹寫和考釋. *Shanghai bowuguan jikan* 上海博物館集刊 3 (1986): 21–34.

———. *Zhanguo Chu jian wenzi bian* 戰國楚簡文字編. Shanghai: Shanghai shuhua chubanshe, 1994.

Guodian Chu mu zhujian 郭店楚墓竹簡. Comp. Jingmen shi bowuguan 荊門市博物館. Beijing: Wenwu chubanshe, 1998.

Guoyu 國語 (Narratives of the States), with commentary by Wei Zhao 韋昭 (197–278 CE). Traditionally attributed to Zuoqiu Ming 左丘明 (probaby fourth century BCE). 2 vols. Reprint, Shanghai: Shanghai guji chubanshe, 1988.

Guxun huizuan 詁訓匯纂. Ed. Zong Fubang 宗福邦, Chen Shinao 陳世鐃, and Xiao Haibo 蕭海波. Beijing: Shangwu yinshuguan, 2003.

Hai Yan 海燕. "Chifeng diqu faxian de xinshiqi shidai nüxing diaosuxiang ji xiangguan wenti qianyi" 赤峰地區發現的新石器時代女性雕塑像及相關問題淺議. *Neimenggu wenwu kaogu* 內蒙古文物考古 2002.1: 39–48.

Han Guohe 韓國河. "Lun Zhongguo gudai fenqiu mu de chansheng yu fazhan" 論中國古代墳丘墓的產生與發展. *Wenbo* 1998.2: 32–45.

———. *Qin Han Wei Jin sangzang zhidu yanjiu* 秦漢魏晉喪葬制度研究. Xi'an: Shanxi renmin chubanshe, 1999.

Han Wei 韓偉. "Fengxiang Qin gong lingyuan zuantan yu shijue jianbao" 鳳翔秦公陵園鑽探與試掘簡報. *Wenwu* 1983.7: 30–37.

Han Wei 韓偉 and Jiao Nanfeng 焦南峰. "Qin du Yong cheng kaogu zongshu" 秦都雍城考古綜述. *Kaogu yu wenwu* 1988.5/6: 111–27.

Hanshu 漢書 (Official History of the Western Han Dynasty). Comp. Ban Gu 班固 (32–92 CE), et al. Beijing: Zhonghua shuju, 1962.

Hao Liangzhen 郝良真. "Zhao guo wangling ji qi chutu qingtongma de ruogan wenti tanwei" 趙國王陵及其出土青銅馬的若干問題探微. *Wenwu chunqiu* 2003.3: 5–12.

Hayashi Minao 林巳奈夫. "Kan dai danshi no kaburimono." 漢代男子のかぶりもの. *Shirin* 46.5 (1963): 80–126.

———. *Kan dai no bunbutsu* 漢代の文物. Kyōto: Jimbun Kagaku kenkyūjo, 1976.

———. "Girei to taite" 儀禮と敦. *Shirin* 63.6 (1980): 1–25.

———. "Shunjū Sengoku jidai no kinjin to yokujin" 春秋戰國時代の金人と玉人. In *Sengoku jidai shutsuto bunbutsu no kenkyū* 戰國時代出土文物の研究, ed. Hayashi Minao, 57–145. Kyōto: Kyōto daigaku Jimbun kagaku kenkyūjo, 1985.

———. "In Shū jidai ni okeru shisha no saishi" 殷周時代における死者の祭祀. *Tōyōshi kenkyū* 東洋史研究 55.3 (1996): 1–26.

He Hao 何浩. *Chu mieguo yanjiu* 楚滅國研究. Wuhan: Wuhan chubanshe, 1989.

He Linyi 何琳儀. "Changsha tongliang mingwen bushi" 長沙銅量銘文補釋. *Jiang Han kaogu* 1988.4: 97–101.

———. *Zhanguo guwen zidian* 戰國古文字典. 2 vols. Beijing: Zhonghua shuju, 1998.

He Nu 何駑 and Zhang Wangao 張萬高. "Jingzhou Guanping wu hao Zhanguo mu" 荊州官坪五

號戰國墓. In *Zhongguo kaoguxue nianjian 1997* 中國考古學年鑒, ed. Zhongguo kaogu xuehui 中國考古學會, 190–91. Beijing: Wenwu chubanshe, 1999.

He Shuangquan 何雙全. "Tianshui Fangmatan Qin mu chutu ditu chutan" 天水放馬灘秦墓出土地圖初探. *Wenwu* 1989.2: 12–22.

Hebei sheng wenguanchu 河北省文管處, Handan diqu wenbaosuo 邯鄲地區文保所, and Handan shi wenbaosuo 邯鄲市文保所. "Hebei Handan Zhao wangling" 河北邯鄲趙王陵. *Kaogu* 1982.6: 597–605, 564.

Hebei sheng wenwu guanlichu 河北省文物管理處. "Hebei sheng Pingshan xian Zhanguo shiqi Zhongshanguo muzang fajue jianbao" 河北省平山縣戰國時期中山國墓葬發掘簡報. *Wenwu* 1979.1: 1–31.

Henan Xinyang diqu wenguanhui 河南信陽地區文管會 and Guangshan xian wenguanhui 光山縣文管會. "Chunqiu zaoqi Huang jun Meng fufu mu fajue baogao" 春秋早期黃君孟夫婦墓發掘報告. *Kaogu* 1984.4: 302–32.

Hou Hanshu (History of the Latter Han) 後漢書. Comp. by Fan Ye 范曄 (398–445 CE). Beijing: Zhonghua shuju, 1965.

Hu Fangping 胡方平. "Zhongguo fengtumu de chansheng he liuxing" 中國封土墓的產生和流行. *Kaogu* 1994.6: 556–58.

———. "Luelun Chu mu fenqiu chansheng de beijing yu niandai" 略論楚墓墳丘產生的背景與年代. *Jiang Han kaogu* 1995.4: 78–80, 86.

Hu Houxuan 胡厚宣. "Jiaguwen 'jiapu keci' zhenwei wenti zai shangque" 甲骨文家譜刻辭真偽問題再商榷. *Guwenzi yanjiu* 4 (1980): 115–38.

Hu Jimin 胡濟民. "Changsha Mawangdui Han mu tiantu de baozi huafen yanjiu jiqi kaogu yiyi" 長沙馬王堆漢墓填土的孢子花粉研究及其考古意義. *Hunan dizhi* 湖南地質 1993.2: 75–79.

Hu Peihui 胡培翬 (1782–1849). *Yili zhengyi* 儀禮正義. 3 vols. Nanjing: Jiangsu guji chubanshe, 1993.

Hu Yali 胡雅麗. "Jiuliandun Chu mu fajue yu chubu yanjiu" 九連墩楚墓發掘與初步研究. In *Jian wu Chu tian: Yue wang Goujian ji Chu guo chutu wenwu zhan* 劍舞楚天: 越王勾踐暨楚國出土文物展, ed. Wang Jichao, Zhang Yinwu, and Li Wei, 16–22. Taibei: Guoli Taiwan bowuguan, 2010.

Huang Hongxin 黃宏信. "Chu bohua suokao" 楚帛畫瑣考. *Jiang Han kaogu* 1991.2: 45–49.

Huang Huaixin 黃懷信. *Yi Zhoushu yuanliu kaobian* 逸周書源流考辨. Xi'an: Xibei daxue chubanshe, 1992.

Huang Mingchong 黃銘崇. "'Taotiewen' de zai sikao: Yige fangfa de xingsi" 饕餮紋的再思考: 一個方法的省思. *Meishushi yanjiu jikan* 美術史研究集刊 32 (2012): 1–102.

Huang Wei 黃偉. "Lun Han dai fuqi hezangmu de leixing yu yanbian" 論漢代夫妻合葬墓的類型與演變. In *Sichuan daxue Kaogu zhuanye chuangjian sanshiwu zhounian jinian wenji* 四川大學考古專業創建三十五週年紀念文集, comp. Sichuan daxue Kaogu zhuanye, 264–85. Chengdu: Sichuan daxue chubanshe, 1998.

———. "Shilun Zhou Qin liang Han fuqi hezang lisu de jige wenti" 試論周秦兩漢夫妻合葬禮俗的幾個問題. In *Sichuan daxue Kaogu zhuanye chuangjian sishi zhounian ji Feng Hanji jiaoshou bainian danchen jinian wenji* 四川大學考古專業創建四十週年暨馮漢驥教授百年誕辰紀念文集, comp. Sichuan daxue Lishi wenhua xueyuan Kaoguxue xi, 322–35. Chengdu: Sichuan daxue chubanshe, 2001.

Huang Ranwei (aka Wong Yin-wai) 黃然偉. *Yin Zhou qingtongqi shangci mingwen yanjiu* 殷周青銅器賞賜銘文研究. Xianggang: Longmen shudian, 1978.

Huang Shengzhang 黃盛璋. "Dangyang liang ge mingwen kao" 當陽兩戈銘文考. *Jiang Han kaogu* 1982.1: 42–45.

———. "Fawang dixia de wenshu: Gaodi ce" 發往地下的文書: 告地策. *Wenwu tiandi* 1993.6: 19–22.

———. "Jiangling Gaotai Han mu xinchu 'gaodi ce,' qiance yu xiangguan zhidu fafu" 江陵高台漢墓新出"告地策," 遺策與相關制度發復. *Jiang Han kaogu* 1994.2: 41–44, 26.

———. "Dixiashu yu gaodice, qiance xin lunzheng" 地下書與告地冊·遺策新論證. In *Xu Zhongshu xiansheng bainian danchen jinian lunwenji* 徐仲舒先生百年誕辰紀念論文集, ed. Sichuan lianhe daxue and Lishi xi, 155–62. Chengdu: Ba Shu shushe, 1998.

Huang Xiaofen 黃曉芬 (= Kō Gyōfun). *Han mu de kaoguxue yanjiu* 漢墓的考古學研究. Changsha: Yuelu shushe, 2003.

Huang Xiquan 黃錫全 and Li Zucai 李祖才. "Zheng Zanggong zhi sun ding mingwen kaoshi" 鄭臧公之孫鼎銘文考釋. *Kaogu* 1991.9: 855–58.

Huang Ying 黃瑩. "Chu shi zhenmushou lujiao yanjiu" 楚式鎮墓獸鹿角研究. *Jiang Han luntan* 2009.12: 71–6.

Huang Zhanyue 黃展岳. *Zhongguo gudai de rensheng renxun* 中國古代的人牲人殉. Beijing: Wenwu chubanshe, 1990.

———. *Gudai rensheng renxun tonglun* 古代人牲人殉通論. Beijing: Wenwu chubanshe, 2004.

———. "Xi Han lingmu yanjiu zhong de liangge wenti" 西漢陵墓研究中的兩個問題. *Wenwu* 2005.4: 70–74.

Hubei sheng wenwu kaogu yanjiusuo 湖北省文物考古研究所. "Hubei Zaoyang shi Jiuliandun Chu mu" 湖北棗陽市九連墩楚墓. *Kaogu* 2003.7: 10–14.

Hui xian fajue baogao 輝縣發掘報告. Comp. Zhongguo kexueyuan kaogu yanjiusuo 中國科學院考古研究所. Beijing: Kexue chubanshe, 1956.

Hunan sheng bowuguan 湖南省博物館. "Xin faxian de Changsha Zhanguo Chu mu bohua" 新發現的長沙戰國楚墓帛畫. *Wenwu* 1973.7: 3–4, 83.

———. "Changsha Zidanku Zhanguo muguo mu" 長沙子彈庫戰國木槨墓. *Wenwu* 1974.2: 36–43.

———. "Changsha Xiangbizui yi hao Xi Han mu" 長沙象鼻嘴一號西漢墓. *Kaogu xuebao* 1981.1: 111–30, 161–66.

Hunan sheng wenwu guanli weiyuanhui 湖南省文物管理委員會. "Changsha Yangtianhu di 25 hao muguo mu" 長沙仰天湖第25號木槨墓. *Kaogu xuebao* 考古學報 1957.2: 85–94, 118–23.

Ikeda Suetoshi 池田末利. *Chūgoku kodai shūkyōshi kenkyū: Seido to shisō* 中國古代宗教史研究: 制度と思想. Tōkyō: Tōkyō daigaku, 1981.

Itō Michiharu 伊藤道治. "Bokuji ni mieru sorei kannen ni tsuite" 卜辭に見える祖靈觀念について. *Tōhō gakuhō* 26 (1956): 1–35.

Jiaguwen heji 甲骨文合集, ed. Guo Moruo 郭沫若. Editor-in-chief Hu Houxuan 胡厚宣. 13 vols. Beijing: Zhonghua shuju, 1978–1982.

Jiang Shaoyuan 江紹原. *Fa xu zhua: Guanyu tamen de mixin* 髮鬚爪: 關於它們的迷信. 1928. Reprint, Shanghai: Wenyi chubanshe, 1987.

———. *Zhongguo gudai lüxing zhi yanjiu* 中國古代旅行之研究. Shanghai: Kelly & Walsh, 1937.

Jiang Yingju 蔣英炬 and Wu Wenqi 吳文祺. *Han dai Wu shi muqun shike yanjiu* 漢代武氏墓群刻石研究. Ji'nan: Shandong meishu chubanshe, 1995.

Jiangling Jiudian Dong Zhou mu 江陵九店東周墓. Comp. Hubei sheng wenwu kaogu yanjiusuo 湖北省文物考古研究所. Beijing: Kexue chubanshe, 1995.

Jiangling Mashan yihao Chu mu 江陵馬山一號楚墓. Comp. Hubei sheng Jingzhou diqu bowuguan 湖北省荊州地區博物館. Beijing: Wenwu chubanshe, 1985.

Jiangling Wangshan Shazhong Chu mu 江陵望山沙塚楚墓. Comp. Hubei sheng wenwu kaogu yanjiusuo 湖北省文物考古研究所. Beijing: Wenwu chubanshe, 1996.

Jiangling xian wenwu gongzuozu 江陵縣文物工作組. "Hubei Jiangling Chu zhong diaocha" 湖北江陵楚冢調查. *Kaoguxue jikan* 4 (1984): 196–207.

Jiangling Yutaishan Chu mu 江陵雨臺山楚墓. Comp. Hubei sheng Jingzhou diqu bowuguan 湖北省荊州地區博物館, Beijing: Wenwu chubanshe, 1984.

Jiudian Chu jian 九店楚簡. Comp. Hubei sheng wenwu kaogu yanjiusuo 湖北省文物考古研究所 and Beijing daxue Zhongwen xi 北京大學中文系. Beijing: Zhonghua shuju, 2000.

Jin Kaicheng 金開誠, Dong Hongli 董洪利, and Gao Luming 高路明, eds. *Qu Yuan ji jiaozhu* 屈原集校註. Beijing: Zhonghua shuju, 1996.

Jingzhou bowuguan 荊州博物館. "Hubei Jingzhou Xiejiaqiao yihao Han mu fajue baogao" 湖北荊州謝家橋一號漢墓發掘報告. *Wenwu* 2009.4: 26–42.

Kō Gyōfun (= Huang Xiaofen). "Kanbo no henyō" 漢墓の變容. *Shirin* 77.5 (1994): 1–39.

———. 1995. "Sobo kara Kanbo e" 楚墓から漢墓へ. *Shirin* 78.5 (1995): 51–57.

Kotera Atsushi 小寺敦. "Shanhuku So kan 'Teishi ka sō' yakuchū" 上博楚簡《鄭子家喪》譯注. *Tōyō bunka kenkyūjo kiyō* 東洋文化研究所紀要 157 (2010): 1–35.

———. "Shanhuku So kan 'Teishi ka sō' no shiryoteki seikaku." 上博楚簡鄭子家喪の史料的性格. In *Shutsudoshiryo to kanjibunkaken* 出土史料と漢字文化圏, ed. Yanaka Shin'ichi, 17–43. Tōkyō: Kyūko Shoin, 2011.

Kudō Motoo 工藤元男. "Kenjyo yori mita hisho no seiritsu katei shiron" 建除よりみた日書の成立過程試論. *Chūgoku, shakai to bunka* 中國社會と文化 16 (2001): 224–40.

Lai Guolong 來國龍. "Wenzi qiyuan yanjiu zhong de 'yuyanxue yanguang' yu hanzi qiyuan de kaoguxue yanjiu" 文字起源研究中的"語言學眼光"與漢字起源的考古學研究. *Kaoguxue yanjiu* 6 (2006): 53–78.

———. "Bihuizi yu chutu Qin Han jianbo de yanjiu" 避諱字與出土秦漢簡帛的研究. *Jianbo yanjiu* 2006 (2008): 126–33.

———. "Diguo yu zongjiao: Gudai Zhongguo yu Luoma diguo de bijiao yanjiu" 帝國與宗教: 古代中國與羅馬帝國的比較研究. Rome-Han Comparer L'incomparable. *Sinologie française/Faguo Hanxue* 14 (2009): 196–218.

———. "Shuo sha, san, jiantan guwenzi shidu zhongde tongjiazi wenti" 說"殺""散": 兼談古文字釋讀中的通假字問題. *Jianbo* 4 (2009): 315–31.

———. "Fanwu liuxing xinyan (gao)" 凡物流形新研(稿). Jianbowang 簡帛網 (Wuhan University), June 7, 2010.

———. "Jiyi de momie: Chunqiu shiqi tongqi shang youyi mohui gaike de mingwen" 記憶的磨滅: 春秋時期銅器上有意磨毀, 改刻的銘文. Paper presented at Ancient Chinese Bronzes from the Shouyang Studio and Elsewhere: An International Conference Commemorating Twenty Years of Discoveries, The Art Institute of Chicago and The Creel Center for Chinese Paleography, The University of Chicago, November 5–7, 2010.

———. "Mawangdui Taiyi zhu tu kao" 馬王堆太一祝圖考. Paper presented at the Institute of History and Philology, Academia Sinica, Taiwan, July 9, 2010.

———. "Lun Chu bushi jidao jian zhong de 'yudao'" 論楚卜筮祭禱簡中的"與禱." *Jianbo* 6 (2011): 359–78.

———. "Jiandawang bohan de xushi jiegou yu zongjiao beijing: jianshi 'shaji'" 東大王泊旱的敘事結構與宗教背景: 兼釋"殺祭." *2007 nian Zhongguo jianboxue guoji luntan lunwenji* 2007 年中國簡帛學國際論壇論文集, 433–62. Taibei: Tiawan daxue chubanshe, 2011.

———. "Zhenmushou yu Jianmuwei: Chutu wenben yu kaogu shiwu huzheng yili" 鎮墓獸與漸木位: 出土文本與考古實物互證一例. Paper presented at the Institute of History and Philology, Academia Sinica, Taiwan, November 16, 2011.

Li Jiahao 李家浩. "Baoshan 266 hao jian suoji muqi yanjiu" 包山 266 號簡所記木器研究. *Guoxue yanjiu* 國學研究 2 (1994): 525–54.

———. "E jun Qi jie mingwen zhongde gaoqiu" 鄂君啟節銘文中的高丘. *Guwenzi yanjiu* 22 (2000): 138–40.

———. "Baoshan jidao jian yanjiu" 包山祭禱簡研究. *Jianbo yanjiu* 2001(2001): 25–36.

———. "Jiudian Chu jian Gao Wuyi yanjiu" 九店楚簡告武夷研究. In his *Zhuming zhongqingnian yuyanxuejia zixuanji, Li Jiahao juan* 著名中青年語言學家自選集 李家浩卷, 318–38. Hefei: Anhui jiaoyu chubanshe, 2002.

———. "Baoshan bushi jian 218–219 hao yanjiu" 包山卜筮簡 218–219 號研究. In *Changsha Sanguo Wu jian ji bainian lai jianbo faxian yu yanjiu guoji xueshu yantaohui lunwenji* 長沙三國吳簡及百年來簡帛發現與研究國際學術研討會論文集, comp. Changsha shi wenwu kaogu yanjiusuo 長沙市文物考古研究所, 183–204. Beijing: Zhonghua shuju, 2005.

Li Jianmin 李建民. "Zhongguo gudai 'yanci' lisu kao" 中國古代掩骴禮俗考. *Qinghua xuebao* 24.3 (1994), 319–43.

———. "Shiti, kulou, hunpo: Chuantong linghunguan xinkao" 屍體骷髏魂魄: 傳統靈魂觀新考. In his *Fangshu, yixue, lishi* 方術醫學歷史, 3–24. Taibei: Nantian shuju, 2000.

Li Ling 李零. *Changsha Zidanku Zhanguo Chu boshu yanjiu* 長沙子彈庫戰國楚帛書研究. Beijing: Zhonghua shuju, 1985.

———. "Chu Yanke tongliang mingwen buzheng" 楚燕客銅量銘文補正. *Jiang Han kaogu* 1988.4: 102–3.

———. "Chu ding tushuo" 楚鼎圖說. *Wenwu tiandi* 1995.6: 31–36.

———. "Zailun Xichuan Xiasi Chu mu" 再論淅川下寺楚墓. *Wenwu* 1996.1: 47–60; collected in his *Rushan yu chusai* 入山與出塞, 225–41.

———. "Kaogu faxian yu shenhua chuanshuo" 考古發現與神話傳說. In his *Li Ling zi xuanji* 李零自選集, 58–84. Guilin: Guangxi shifan daxue chubanshe, 1998.

———. "Du Jiudian Chu Jian" 讀九店楚簡. *Kaogu xuebao* 1999.2: 141–52.

———. *Zhongguo fangshu kao* 中國方術考. Rev. ed. Beijing: Dongfang chubanshe, 2000.

———. *Zhongguo fangshu xukao* 中國方術續考. Beijing: Dongfang chubanshe, 2000.

———. "'Sanlü dafu' kao" 三閭大夫考. *Wenshi* 文史 54 (2001): 11–23.

———. "Lun Zhongguo de youyi shenshou" 論中國的有翼神獸. *Zhongguo Xueshu* 中國學術 5 (2001): 62–134.

———. *Rushan yu chusai* 入山與出塞. Beijing: Wenwu chubanshe, 2004.

———. "'Chu Shuzhisun Peng' jiujing shi shei?" 楚叔之孫佣究竟是誰? In his *Rushan yu chusai* 入山與出塞, 223–24. Beijing: Wenwu chubanshe, 2004.

——— and Su Fangshu 蘇芳淑. "Jieshao yijian youming de Jin hou tongren" 介紹一件有銘的晉侯銅人. In *Jinhou mudi chutu qingtongqi guoji xueshu yantaohui lunwenji* 晉侯墓地出土青銅器國際學術研討會論文集, comp. Shanghai bowuguan, 411–20. Shanghai: Shanghai shuhua chubanshe, 2002.

Li Rusen 李如森. *Han dai sangzang lisu* 漢代喪葬禮俗. Shenyang: Shenyang chubanshe, 2003.

Li Xueqin 李學勤. "Tan jinnian lai xin faxian de jizhong Zhanguo wenzi ziliao" 談近年來新發現的幾種戰國文字資料. *Wenwu cankao ziliao* 文物參考資料 1956.1: 48–49.

———. "Lun Han Huai jian de Chunqiu qingtongqi" 論漢淮間的春秋青銅器, in his *Xinchu qingtongqi yanjiu* 新出青銅器研究, 151–59. Beijing: Wenwu chubanshe, 1990.

———. "Fangmatan jian zhong de zhiguai gushi" 放馬灘簡中的志怪故事. In his *Jianbo yiji yu xueshushi*, 181–90.

———. *Jianbo yiji yu xueshushi* 簡帛佚籍與學術史. Taibei: Shibao wenhua, 1994.

———. *Zhouyi suyuan* 周易溯源. Chengdu: Ba Shu shushe, 2005.

———. "Lun Yindai de qinzu zhidu" 論殷代的親族制度. In his *Li Xueqin zaoqi wenji* 李學勤早期文集, 71–85. Shijiazhuang: Hebei jiaoyu chubanshe, 2007.

Li Yunfu 李運富. "Zhanguo wenzi 'diyu tedian' zhiyi" 戰國文字地域特點質疑. *Zhongguo shehui kexue* 中國社會科學 1997.5: 170–82.

Liang Jun 梁軍. "Jiuliandun gumu dadao luowangji" 九連墩古墓大盜落網記. *Jiancha fengyun* 檢察風雲 212 (2005): 50–51.

Liang Qichao 梁啟超. "Zhongguo shi shang renkou zhi tongji" 中國史上人口之統計. In his *Liang Qichao quanji* 梁啟超全集, 900–906. Beijing: Beijing chubanshe, 1999.

Liang Yun 梁雲. *Zhanguo shidai de dongxi chabie: Kaoguxue de shiye* 戰國時代的東西差別:考古學的視野. Beijing: Wenwu chubanshe, 2008.

Liangdaicun Ruiguo mudi: 2007 niandu fajue baogao 梁帶村芮國墓地: 2007 年度發掘報告. Comp.

Shaanxi sheng kaogu yanjiuyuan 陝西省考古研究院, Weinan shi wenwu baohu kaogu yanjiusuo 渭南市文物保護考古研究所, and Hancheng shi jingqu guanli weiyuanhui 韓城市景區管理委員會. Beijing: Wenwu chubanshe, 2010.

Liji zhenyi 禮記正義 by Zheng Xuan 鄭玄 (127–200 CE) and Kong Yingda 孔穎達 (574–648 CE), vol. 5 in the *Shisanjing zhushu*. Reprint, Taibei: Yiwen yinshuguan, 1993.

Lin Yun 林澐. "Du Baoshan Chu jian zhaji qize" 讀包山楚簡劄記七則. In his *Lin Yun xueshu wenji* 林澐學術文集, 19–21. Zhongguo dabaike quanshu chubanshe, 1998.

Liu Binhui 劉彬徽. "Cong Baoshan Chu jian jishi cailiao lun ji Chu guo jinian yu Chu li" 從包山楚簡紀時材料論及楚國紀年與楚曆. In *Baoshan Chu mu* 包山楚墓, comp. Hubei sheng Jingsha tielu kaogudui, Vol. 1, 533–47.

———. "Lun Dong Zhou shiqi yongding zhidu zhong Chu zhi yu Zhou zhi de guanxi" 論東周時期用鼎制度中楚制與周制的關係. *Zhongyuan wenwu* 1991.2: 50–58.

Liu Daochao 劉道超. *Zeji yu Zhongguo wenhua* 擇吉與中國文化. Beijing: Renmin chubanshe, 2004.

Liu Dunyuan 劉敦愿. 1994. "Zhongguo zaoqi de diaoke yishu jiqi tedian" 中國早期的雕刻藝術及其特點. In his *Meishu kaogu yu gudai wenming* 美術考古與古代文明, 261–76. Taibei: Yunchen wenhua, 1994.

Liu Fude 劉夫德. "Mingjing de tuxiang yu wenzi" 銘旌的圖像與文字. *Wenbo* 2008.4: 12–25.

Liu Guosheng 劉國勝. "Yunmeng Longgang jiandu kaoshi buzheng jiqi xiangguan wenti de tantao" 雲夢龍崗簡牘考釋補證及其相關問題的探討. *Jiang Han kaogu* 1997.1: 64–71.

———. "Gaotai Han du 'Andu' biejie" 高臺漢牘安都別解. *Guwenzi yanjiu* 24 (2002): 444–48.

———. "Chu sangzang jiandu jishi" 楚喪葬簡牘集釋. PhD dissertation, Wuhan University, 2003.

———. "Chu qiance zhidu shulüe" 楚遣策制度述略. In *Chu wenhua yanjiu lunji* 楚文化研究論集, ed. Chu wenhua yanjiu hui, 229–40. Vol. 6. Wuhan: Hubei renmin chubanshe, 2004.

———. "Chu di chutu shushu wenxian yu yuzhou jiegou lilun" 楚地出土數術文獻與宇宙結構理論. In *Chu di jianbo sixiang yanjiu* 楚地簡帛思想研究, ed. Ding Sixin, 238–52. Wuhan: Hubei jiaoyu chubanshe, 2005.

———. "Xiejiaqiao yihao Han mu gaodishu du de chubu kaocha" 謝家橋一號漢墓《告地書》牘的初步考察. *Jiang Han kaogu* 2009.3: 120–22.

———. "Baoshan erhao Chu mu qiance yanjiu er ze" 包山二號楚墓遣冊研究二則. *Kaogu* 2010.9: 67–68.

Liu Lexian 劉樂賢. *Shuihudi Qinjian rishu yanjiu* 睡虎地秦簡日書研究. Taibei: Wenjin chubanshe, 1994.

———. "Jiudian Chu jian rishu yanjiu" 九店楚簡日書研究. *Huaxue* 2 (1996): 61–70.

———. *Jianbo shushu wenxian tanlun* 簡帛數術文獻探論. Wuhan: Hubei jiaoyu chubanshe, 2003.

———. "Chu Qin xuanzeshu de yitong yu yingxiang: Yi chutu wenxian wei zhongxin" 楚秦選擇術的異同與影響: 以出土文獻為中心. *Lishi yanjiu* 歷史研究 2006.6: 19–31.

Liu Rui 劉瑞 and Liu Tao 劉濤. *Xi Han zhuhouwang lingmu zhidu yanjiu* 西漢諸侯王陵墓制度研究. Beijing: Zhongguo shehui kexue chubanshe, 2010.

Liu Wendian 劉文典. *Huainan honglie jijie* 淮南鴻烈集解. Reprint, Beijing: Zhonghua shuju, 1989.

Liu Xiaolu 劉曉路. "Lun bohua yong: Mawangdui 3 hao mu dongxi bi bohua de xingzhi he zhuti" 論帛畫俑馬王堆 3 號墓東西壁帛畫的性質和主題. *Kaogu* 1995.10: 937–41.

Liu Xinfang 劉信芳. *Baoshan Chu jian jiegu* 包山楚簡解詁. Taibei: Yiwen yinshuguan, 2003.

Liu Xu 劉緒. "Chunqiu shiqi sangzang zhidu zhong de zangyue yu zangri" 春秋時期喪葬制度中的葬月與葬日. *Kaoguxue yanjiu* 考古學研究 2 (1994): 189–200.

Liu Yi 劉屹. *Jingtian yu chongdao: Zhonggu jingjiaodaojiao xingcheng de sixiangshi beijing* 敬天與崇道: 中古經教道教形成的思想史背景. Beijing: Zhonghua shuju, 2005.

Liu Ying 劉瑛. "Du *Zuozhuan* de zeri liji" 讀左傳的擇日曆忌. *Wenshi* 54 (2001): 53–64.

Liu Zenggui 劉增貴. "Qin jian 'rishu' zhong de chuxing lisu yu xinyang" 秦簡日書中的出行禮俗與信仰. *Zhongyang yanjiuyuan lishi yuyan yanjiusuo jika* 72.3 (2001): 503–41.

Liu Zhao 劉釗. "Anyang Hougang Yin mu suochu 'bingxingqi' yongtu kao" 安陽後岡殷墓所出柄形器用途考. *Kaogu* 1995.7: 623–25, 605.

Liu Zhaorui 劉昭瑞. "Lun 'Yubu' de qiyuan ji Yu yu wu, dao de guanxi" 論禹步的起源及禹與巫道的關係. In *Liang Zhaotao yu renleixue* 梁釗韜與人類學, ed. Zhongshan daxue renleixue xi, 264–79. Guangzhou: Zhongshan daxue chubanshe, 1991.

———. "Andu jun yu Wuyi jun" 安都君與武夷君. *Wenshi* 59 (2002): 51–60.

———. *Kaogu faxian yu zaoqi daojiao yanjiu* 考古發現與早期道教研究. Beijing: Wenwu chubanshe, 2007.

Ling Chunsheng 凌純聲. "Zhongguo gudai shenzhu yu yinyang xingqi chongbai" 中國古代神主與陰陽性器崇拜. *Zhongyang yanjiu yuan Minzuxue yanjiusuo jikan* 8 (1959): 1–46.

Longgang Qin jian 龍崗秦簡. Ed. Zhongguo wenwu yanjiusuo 中國文物研究所 and Hubei sheng wenwu kaogu yanjiusuo 湖北省文物考古研究所. Beijing: Zhonghua shuju, 2001.

Lu Defu 陸德富. "Shuo 'bingsi zhe'" 說兵死者. *Chutu wenxian yanjiu* 11(2012): 74–83.

Lu Xixing 陸錫興. "Shi 'yi'" 釋已. *Kaogu* 1987.12: 1112–15.

Lu Yu 路遇 and Teng Zezhi 滕澤之. *Zhongguo renkou tongshi* 中國人口通史. Vol. 1. Shanghai: Shandong renmin chubanshe, 2000.

Lü Simian 呂思勉. *Lü Simian dushi zhaji* 呂思勉讀史劄記. Shanghai: Shanghai guji chubanshe, 1982.

Lunheng jiaoshi 論衡校釋, by Wang Chong 王充 (27–c. 100 CE), comp. Huang Hui 黃暉 (twentieth century), 4 vols. Beijing: Zhonghua shuju, 1990.

Lunyu zhengyi 論語正義, ed. Liu Baonan 劉寶楠 (1791–1855). Reprint, Shanghai shudian, 1986.

Luo Jiaxiang 羅家湘. "'Yi Zhoushu Qifujie' shi yifen qiance" 逸周書器服解是一份遣策. *Wenxian* 文獻 2001.2: 4–10.

Luo Tai. 羅泰 (=Lothar von Falkenhausen). "Lüetan Zhongguo qingtongshidai de renwu biaoxian jiqi lishi yiyi" 略談中國青銅時代的人物表現及其歷史意義. In *Hua Xia wenming de xingcheng yu fazhan: Henan sheng Wenwu kaogu yanjiusuo wushinian qingzhuhui ji Hua Xia wenming de xingcheng yu fazhan xueshu yantaohui lunwenji*, 265–67. Zhenghzou: Daxiang chubanshe, 2003.

Luo Zhenyu 羅振玉, ed. *Gu mingqi tulu* 古明器圖錄. Shanghai: Shanghai Guangcang xuequn, 1916.

Luoyang bowuguan 洛陽博物館. "Luoyang Ai Cheng shu mu qingli jianbao" 洛陽哀成叔墓清理簡報. *Wenwu* 7 1981.7: 65–67.

Luoyang Shaogou Han mu 洛陽燒溝漢墓. Comp. Zhongguo kexueyuan Kaogu yanjiusuo 中國科學院考古研究所 and Luoyang qu kaogu fajue dui 洛陽區考古發掘隊. Beijing: Kexue chubanshe, 1959.

Ma Yong 馬雍. "Lun Changsha Mawangdui yihao Han mu chutu bohua de mingcheng he zuoyong" 論長沙馬王堆一號漢墓出土帛畫的名稱和作用. *Kaogu* 1973.2: 118–25.

Machida Akira 町田章. *Kahaku chihō ni okeru Kanhaka no kōzō* 華北地方における漢墓の構造. *Tōhō gakuhō* 49 (1977): 1–66.

Mancheng Han mu fajue baogao 滿城漢墓發掘報告. Comp. Zhongguo kexueyuan kaogu yanjiusuo 中國科學院考古研究所 and Hebei sheng wenwu guanli chu 河北省文物管理處. 2 vols. Beijing: Wenwu chubanshe, 1980.

Maoshi zhengyi 毛詩正義, annotated by Mao Heng 毛亨 (second century BCE), Zheng Xuan 鄭玄 (127–200 CE), and Kong Yingda 孔穎達 (574–648), in vol. 2 of the *Shisanjing zhushu*. Reprint, Taibei: Yiwen yinshuguan, 1993.

Mawangdui Han mu boshu 馬王堆漢墓帛書. Comp. Mawangdui Han mu boshu zhengli xiaozu 馬王堆漢墓帛書整理小組. Vols. 1, 2, and 4. Beijing: Wenwu, 1980–1985.

Mawangdui Han mu boshu zhengli xiaozu 馬王堆漢墓帛書整理小組. "Mawangdui boshu Shifa shiwen zhaiyao" 馬王堆帛書式法釋文摘要. *Wenwu* 2000.7: 85–94.

Mengzi zhushu 孟子注疏, annotation by Zhao Qi 趙岐 (d. 201) and commentary by Sun Shi 孫奭 (962–1033), in vol. 8 in the *Shisanjing zhushu*. Reprint, Taibei: Yiwen yinshuguan, 1993.

Miao Wenyuan 繆文遠. *Zhanguo zhidu tongkao* 戰國制度通考. Chengdu: Ba Shu shushe, 1998.

Nanjing bowuyuan 南京博物院. "Xuzhou Qingshanquan Baiji Dong Han huaxiangshi mu" 徐州青山泉白集東漢畫像石墓, *Kaogu* 1981.2: 137–50.

Nishijima Sadao 西嶋定生. *Chūgoku kokai teikoku no keisei to kōzō: Nijittō shakusei no kenkyū* 中国古代帝国の形成と構造: 二十等爵制の研究. Tōkyō: Tōkyō daigaku shuppankai, 1961.

Ogata Nobuo 緒形暢夫. "Shunjū jidai ni okeru kōshi no shoso" 春秋時代における強死の諸相. *Nihon Chūgokugaku kaihō* 日本中國學會報 15 (1963): 25–37.

Ōnishi Katsuya 大西克也. "So no gengo ni tsuite" 楚の言語について. *Nicchu bunka kenkyū* 日中文化研究 10 (1996): 121–29.

Ou Tansheng 歐潭生. "Gushi Hougudui Wu taizi Fuchai furen mu de Wu wenhua yinsu" 固始侯古堆吳太子夫差夫人墓的吳文化因素. *Zhongyuan wenwu* 1991.4: 33–38.

Pan Yukun 潘玉坤. "Jinwen 'yan zai shang,' 'yi zai xia' yu 'jing nai suye' shijie" 金文嚴在上異在下與敬乃夙夜試解. *Gugong bowuyuan yuankan* 故宮博物院院刊 2003.5: 70–75.

Peng Hao 彭浩. "Chu mu zangzhi chulun" 楚墓葬制初論. In *Zhongguo Kaogu xuehui di'erci nianhui (1980) lunwenji* 中國考古學會第二次年會 (1980) 論文集, 33–40. Beijing: Wenwu chubanshe, 1982.

———. "Baoshan erhao Chu mu bushi he jidao zhujian de chubu yanjiu" 包山二號楚墓卜筮和祭禱竹簡的初步研究. In *Baoshan Chu mu* 包山楚墓, comp. Hubei sheng Jingsha tielu kaogudui, vol. 1, 555–63.

———. "Shuihudi Qinjian 'wangshici' yu jilü kaobian" 睡虎地秦簡'王室祠'與齎律考辨. *Jianbo* 1 (2006): 239–48.

———. "Du Yunmeng Shuihudi M77 Han jian zanglü" 讀雲夢睡虎地 M77 漢簡葬律. *Jiang Han kaogu* 2009.4: 130–34.

Pian Yuqian 駢宇騫 and Duan Shuan 段書安. *Ben shiji yilai chutu jianbo gaishu* 本世紀以來出土簡帛概述. Taibei: Wanjuanlou, 1999.

Pu Muzhou 蒲慕州 (= Poo, Mu-chou). *Muzang yu shengsi: Zhongguo gudai zongjiao zhi xingsi* 墓葬與生死: 中國古代宗教之省思. Taibei: Lianjing chuban shiye gongsi, 1993.

———. "Zhongguo gudai gui lunshu de xingcheng" 中國古代鬼論述的形成. In *Guimei shenmo: Zhongguo tongsu wenhua cexie* 鬼魅神魔: 中國通俗文化側寫, ed. Pu Muzhou, 19–40. Taibei: Maitian chubanshe, 2005.

———. "Zhongguo gudai de xinyang yu richang shenghuo" 中國古代的信仰與日常生活. In *Zhongguo shi xinlun, Zongjiao shi fence* 中國史新論, 宗教史分冊, ed. Lin Fushi 林富士, 13–64. Taibei: Zhongyang yanjiu yuan and Lianjing, 2010.

Puyang Xishuipo yizhi kaogudui 濮陽西水坡遺址考古隊. "1988 nian Henan Puyang Xishuipo yizhi fajue jianbao" 1988 年河南濮陽西水坡遺址發掘簡報. *Kaogu* 1989.12: 1057–66, 1153–54.

Qinghai Liuwan: Ledu Liuwan yuanshi shehui mudi 青海柳灣: 樂都柳灣原始社會墓地. Comp. Qinghai sheng wenwu guanlichu kaogudui 青海省文物管理處考古隊 et al. 2 vols. Beijing: Wenwu chubanshe, 1984.

Qinghua daxue cang Zhanguo zhujian (yi) 清華大學藏戰國竹簡(壹). Ed. Li Xueqin 李學勤. 2 vols. Shanghai: Zhongxi shuju, 2010.

Qiu Donglian 邱東聯. "Chu mu zhong renxun yu yongzang jiqi guanxi chutan" 楚墓中人殉與俑葬及其關係初探. *Jiang Han kaogu* 1996.1: 74–79.

Qiu Xigui 裘錫圭. "Zaitan guwenxian yi 'shi' biao 'she'" 再談古文獻以"埶" 表"設." In *Xianqin Liang Han guji guoji xueshu yantaohui lunwenji* 先秦兩漢古籍國際學術研討會論文集, ed. He Zhihua 何志華, Shen Pei 沈培 et al., 1–13. Beijing: Shehui kexue wenxian chubanshe, 2011.

———. *Gudai wenshi yanjiu xintan* 古代文史研究新探. Nanjing: Jiangsu guji, 1992.

———. *Guwenzi lunji* 古文字論集. Beijing: Zhonghua shuju, 1992.

———. "Hubei Jiangling Fenghuangshan shihao Han mu chutu jiandu kaoshi" 湖北江陵鳳凰山十號漢墓出土簡牘考釋. In his *Guwenzi lunji*, 540–63.

Rao Zongyi 饒宗頤. "Lishijia dui saman zhuyi ying chongxin zuo fansi yu jiantao: 'Wu' de xin renshi" 歷史家對薩滿主義應重新作反思與檢討: '巫'的新認識. In *Zhonghua wenhua de guoqu, xianzai he weilai: Zhonghua shuju chengli bashi zhounian jinian lunwenji* 中華文化的過去, 現在和未來: 中華書局成立八十週年紀念論文集, ed. Zhonghua shuju, 396–412. Beijing: Zhonghua shuju, 1992.

———. "Shuo Jiudian Chu jian zhi Wuyi (jun) yu Fushan" 說九店楚簡之武夷（君）與復山. *Wenwu* 1997.6: 36–38.

———. *Yunmeng Qinjian rishu yanjiu* 雲夢秦簡日書研究. Xianggang: Zhongwen daxue chubanshe, 1982.

Rao Zongyi 饒宗頤 and Zeng Xiantong 曾憲通. *Chu boshu* 楚帛書. Xianggang: Zhonghua shuju Xianggang fenju, 1985.

Shaanxi sheng kaogu yanjiusuo 陝西省考古研究所. "Shaanxi Xunyi faxian Dong Han bihuamu" 陝西旬邑發現東漢壁畫墓. *Kaogu yu wenwu* 2002.3, 76.

Shanxi sheng kaogu yanjiusuo 山西省考古研究所. "Shanxi Changzi xian Dong Zhou mu" 山西長子縣東周墓. *Kaogu xuebao* 1984.4: 503–29.

Shanxi sheng kaogu yanjiusuo, Jincheng shi wenhuaju 晉城市文化局, and Gaoping shi bowuguan 高平市博物館. "Changping zhi zhan yizhi Yonglu yihao shigukeng fajue jianbao" 長平之戰遺址永錄一號屍骨坑發掘簡報. *Wenwu* 1996.6: 33–40.

Shanxi sheng kaogu yanjiusuo Dahekou mudi lianhe kaogudui 山西省考古研究所大河口墓地聯合考古隊. "Shanxi Yicheng xian Dahekou Xi Zhou mudi" 山西翼城縣大河口西周墓地. *Kaogu* 2011.7: 9–18.

Shanxi sheng kaogu yanjiusuo Houma gongzuozhan 山西省考古研究所侯馬工作站. *Jin du Xintian* 晉都新田. Taiyuan: Shanxi renmin chubanshe, 1996.

Shang Chengzuo 商承祚. *Changsha guwu wenjian ji* 長沙古物聞見記, Taibei: Wenhai chubanshe youxian gongsi, 1971.

———. *Changsha chutu Chu qiqi tulu* 長沙出土楚漆器圖錄. Beijing: Zhongguo gudian yishu chubanshe, 1957.

———. *Zhanguo Chu zhujian huibian* 戰國楚竹簡匯編. Ji'nan: Qi Lu shushe, 1995.

Shanghai bowuguan cang Zhanguo Chu zhushu (1–9) 上海博物館藏戰國楚竹書 1–9. Ed. Ma Cheng-yuan 馬承源. Shanghai: Shanghai guji chubanshe, 2001–2012.

Shen Changyun 沈長雲 and Yang Shanqun 楊善群. *Zhanguo shi yu Zhanguo wenming* 戰國史與戰國文明. Shanghai: Shanghai kexue jishu wenxian chubanshe, 2007.

Shen Jianshi 沈兼士. 1986. "'Gui' zi yuanshi yiyi zhi shitan" 鬼字原始意義之試探. In his *Shen Jianshi xueshu lunwenji* 沈兼士學術文集, 186–202. Beijing: Zhonghua shuju, 1986.

Shen Wenzhuo 沈文倬. "Dui 'Shi sangli, jixili zhong suo jizai de sangzang zhidu' jidian yijian" 對士喪禮既夕禮中所記載的喪葬制度幾點意見. In his *Zongzhou liyue wenming kaolun* 宗周禮樂文明考論, 55–72. Hangzhou: Hangzhou daxue chubanshe, 1999.

———. "Luelun lidian de shixing he Yili shuben de zhuanzuo" 略論禮典的實行和儀禮書本的撰作" In his *Zongzhou liyue wenming kaolun* 宗周禮樂文明考論, 1–54. Hangzhou: Hangzhou daxue chubanshe, 1999.

Shi Shuqing 史樹青. *Changsha Yangtianhu chutu Chu jian yanjiu* 長沙仰天湖出土楚簡研究. Beijing: Qunlian chubanshe, 1955.

Sichuan lianhe daxue lishixi 四川聯合大學歷史系, comp. *Xu Zhongshu xiansheng bainian danchen jinian wenji* 徐中舒先生百年誕辰紀念文集. Chengdu: Ba Shu shushe, 1998.

Shiji 史記 (Records of the Grand Historian). By Sima Tan 司馬談 (?–110 BCE) and Sima Qian 司馬遷 (145 or 135–c. 90 BCE). 10 vols. Beijing: Zhonghua shuju, 1959.

Shijiazhuang shi tushuguan kaogu xiaozu 石家莊市圖書館考古小組. "Hebei Shijiazhuang beijiao Xi Han mu fajue jianbao" 河北石家莊北郊西漢墓發掘簡報. *Kaogu* 1980.1: 52–55.

Shou Xian Cai Hou mu chutu yiwu 壽縣蔡侯墓出土遺物. Comp. Anhui sheng wenwu guanli weiyuanhui 安徽省文物管理委員會 and Anhui sheng bowuguan 安徽省博物館. Beijing: Kexue chubanshe, 1956.

Shuihudi Qin mu zhujian 睡虎地秦墓竹簡. Comp. Shuihudi Qin mu zhujian zhengli xiaozu 睡虎地秦墓竹簡整理小組. Beijing: Wenwu chubanshe, 1990.

Shuowen jiezi 說文解字 (Explaining the graphs and analyzing the characters), by Xu Shen 許慎 (c. 58–147 CE) with commentary by Xu Xuan 徐鉉 (916–991) et al. Reprint, Beijing: Zhonghua shuju, 1963.

Shuoyuan jiaozheng 說苑校證, ed. Liu Xiang 劉向 (79–8 BCE), comp. Xiang Zonglu 向宗魯. Beijing: Zhonghua shuju, 1987.

Sofukawa Hiroshi 曾布川寬. "Konronzan to shōsenzu" 崑崙山と昇仙圖. *Tōhō gakuhō* 51 (1979): 83–185.

———. *Konronzan e no shōsen: Kodai Chūgokujin ga egaita shigo no sekai* 崑崙山への昇仙: 古代中國人が描いた死後の世界. Tokyo: Chūō kōronsha, 1981.

———. "Kan dai gazōseki ni okeru shōsenzu no keifu" 漢代畫像石における昇仙圖の系譜. *Tōhō gakuhō* 65 (1993): 23–222.

Songshu 宋書. Comp. Shen Yue 沈約 (411–513 CE). Beijing: Zhonghua shuju, 1972.

Suetsugu Nobuyuki 末次信行. "Senshin no sensō giseisha: Bunken o chūshin shite" 先秦の戰爭犧牲者: 文獻を中心して. *Kinran tanki daigaku kenkyūshi* 25 (1994): 29–52.

———. "Inkyo ni okeru 'yūkōsha' no ba" 殷墟における'有功者'"の墓. *Kinran tanki daigaku kenkyūshi* 26 (1995): 23–62; 27 (1996): 37–81; 28 (1997): 81–290.

———. "Inkyo Seihokukō ōryōku no 1174 gō shyōba o megutte" 殷墟西北崗王陵區の一一七四號小墓をめぐって. *Yūsei kōgo kiyō* 郵政考古紀要 27 (1999): 34–64.

Suizhou Kongjiapo Han mu jiandu 隨州孔家坡漢墓簡牘. Comp. Hubei sheng wenwu kaogu yanjiusuo 湖北省文物考古研究所 and Suizhou shi kaogudui 隨州市考古隊. Beijing: Wenwu chubanshe, 2006.

Sun Guanwen 孫貫文 and Zhao Chao 趙超. "You chutu yinzhang kan liangchu muzang de muzhu deng wenti" 由出土印章看兩處墓葬的墓主等問題. *Kaogu* 1981.4: 333–38.

Sun Hua 孫華. "Xuanyu yu zhenrong" 懸魚與振容. *Zhongguo dianji yu wenhua* 2000.1: 90–96.

Sun Ji 孫機. *Han dai wuzhi wenhua ziliao tushuo* 漢代物質文化資料圖說. Beijing: Wenwu chubanshe, 1991.

———. *Zhongguo guyufu luncong* 中國古輿服論叢. Beijing: Wenwu chubanshe, 1993.

———. *Zhongguo shenghuo: Zhongguo guwenwu yu Dongxi wenhua jiaoliu zhong de ruogan wenti* 中國聖火中國古文物與東西文化交流中的若干問題. Shenyang: Liaoning jiaoyu chubanshe, 1996.

Sun Xidan 孫希旦. *Liji jieji* 禮記集解. 3 vols. Beijing: Zhonghua shuju, 1989.

Sun Yirang 孫詒讓. *Zhouli zhengyi* 周禮正義. Ed. Wang Wenjin 王文錦 and Chen Yuxia 陳玉霞. 14 vols. Beijing: Zhonghua shuju, 1987.

Sun Zuoyun 孫作雲. "Han dai siming shenxiang de faxian" 漢代司命神像的發現. First published in *Guangming ribao*, December 4, 1963, in *Sun Zuoyun wenji* 孫作雲文集, vol. 1, xia, 471–73. Kaifeng: Henan daxue chubanshe, 2002.

———. "Changsha Mawangdui yihao Han mu chutu huafan kaoshi" 長沙馬王堆一號漢墓出土畫幡考釋. *Kaogu* 1973.1: 54–61.

Suzhou bowuguan 蘇州博物館. *Zhenshan Dong Zhou mudi: Wu Chu guizu mudi de fajue yu yanjiu* 真山東周墓地: 吳楚貴族墓地的發掘與研究. Beijing: Wenwu chubanshe, 1999.

Takahama Yūko 高濱侑子. "Zhongguo gudai dongshi mu" 中國古代洞室墓. Trans. Han Zhao 韓釗. *Wenbo* 1994.1: 17–23.

Takamura Takeyuki 高村武幸. "Kyūten Sokan hisho no seikaku ni tsuite" 九店楚簡日書の性格
について. *Meidai Ajia shi ronshū* 明大アジア史論集 3 (1998): 1–23.

Tang Chi 湯池. "Shilun Luanping Houtaizi chutu de shidiao nüshen xiang" 試論灤平後臺子出土
的石雕女神像. *Wenwu* 1994.3: 46–51.

Tang Weibin 唐衛彬, Jian Min 劍敏, and Wang Guan 王官. "Zhenjing shijie de 'Zhongguo diyi
gushi an'" 震驚世界的"中國第一古屍案." *Liaowang* 瞭望 1994.44: 20–23.

Teng Rensheng 滕壬生. *Chu xi jianbo wenzibian* 楚系簡帛文字編. Wuhan: Hubei jiaoyu
chubanshe, 1995.

Tengzhou Qianzhangda mudi 滕州前掌大墓地. Comp. Zhongguo shehui kexueyuan kaogu
yanjiusuo 中國社會科學院考古研究所. Beijing: Wenwu chubanshe, 2005.

Tian Changwu 田昌五 and Zang Zhifei 臧知非. *Zhou Qin shehui jiegou yanjiu* 周秦社會結構研究.
Xi'an: Xibei daxue chubanshe, 1996.

Tian He 田河. "Chutu Zhanguo qiance suoji mingwu fenlei huishi" 出土戰國遣冊所記名物分類
匯釋. PhD dissertation, Jinlin University, 2007.

Tian Lizhen 田立振. "Shilun Han dai de huilang zangzhi" 試論漢代的回廊葬制. *Kaogu yu wenwu*
考古與文物 1995.1: 64–70.

Tian Wei 田偉. "Shi lun liang Zhou shiqi de jishi jitan mu" 試論兩周時期的積石積炭墓.
Zhongguo lishi wenwu 2009.2: 59–67.

Tong Shuye 童書業 and Gu Jiegang 顧頡剛. "Han dai yiqian Zhongguo ren de shijie guannian yu
wailai jiaotong de gushi" 漢代以前中國人的世界觀念與外來交通的故事. In his *Zhongguo gudai
dili kaozheng lunwenji* 中國古代地理考證論文集, 1–42. Shanghai: Zhonghua shuju, 1962.

Tosaki Tetsuhiko 戶崎哲彥. "Chūgoku kodai no daisō ni okeru daikō shu ni tsuite" 中國古代の大
喪における大行稱について. *Shigaku zasshi* 100.9 (1991): 40–62.

Tu Baikui 涂白奎. "'Shi zuo yong' xinjie" "始作俑"新解. *Shixue yuekan* 史學月刊 2000.2: 25–31.

Wang Buyi 王步毅. "Anhui Suxian Chulan Han huaxiangshi mu" 安徽宿縣褚蘭漢畫像石墓.
Kaogu xuebao 1993.4: 515–49.

———. "Chulan Han huaxiangshi mu ji youguan wuxiang de renshi" 褚蘭漢畫像石墓及有關物
象的認識. *Zhongyuan wenwu* 1991.3: 60–67.

Wang Guanying 王冠英. "Shuo 'yanzaishang, yizaixia'" 說嚴在上異在下. *Zhongguo lishi
bowuguan guankan* 18/19 (1992): 114–16.

———. "Zaishuo jinwen taoyu 'yanzaishang, yizaixia.'" 再說金文套語嚴在上異在下. *Zhongguo
lishi wenwu* 2003.2: 56–59.

Wang Guihai 汪桂海. *Qin Han jiandu tanyan* 秦漢簡牘探研. Taibei: Wenjin chubanshe, 2009.

Wang Hongxing 王紅星. "Baoshan jiandu suo fanying de Chu guo lifa wenti" 包山簡牘所反映的
楚國曆法問題. In *Baoshan Chu mu*, comp. Hubei sheng Jingsha tielu kaogudui, vol. 1, 521–32.

Wang Hui 王輝. "Cong kaogu yu guwenzi de jiaodu kan *Yili* de chengshu niandai" 從考古與古
文字的角度看儀禮的成書年代. *Chuantong wenhua yu xiandaihua* 傳統文化與現代化 1999.1:
54–60.

Wang Lihua 王立華. "Shilun Chu mu muguo zhong de menchuang jiegou ji fanying de wenti"
試論楚墓木槨中的門窗結構及反映的問題. In *Chu wenhua yanjiu lunji* 楚文化研究論集, ed. Chu
wenhua yanjiu hui, vol. 3, 306–17. Wuhan: Hubei renming chubanshe, 1994.

Wang Rencong 王人聰. "Xi Zhou jinwen 'yan zai shang' jie" 西周金文"嚴在上" 解. *Kaogu* 1998.1:
72–74, 81.

Wang Renxiang 王仁湘. "Gudai daigou yongtu kaoshi" 古代帶鉤用途考實. *Wenwu* 1982.10:
75–81, 94.

———. "Daigou gailun" 帶鉤概論. *Kaogu xuebao* 1985.3: 267–312.

———. "Daigou lüelun" 帶鉤略論. *Kaogu* 1986.1: 65–75.

Wang Shimin 王世民. "Zhongguo Chunqiu Zhanguo shidai de zhongmu" 中國春秋戰國時代
的冢墓. *Kaogu* 1981.5: 459–66.

Wang Wentao 王文濤. "Hanjian suojian Xi Han youfu cuoshi" 漢簡所見西漢優撫措施. *Jianbo yanjiu* 2006 (2008): 233–41.

Wang Xueli 王學理. *Qin Shihuang ling yanjiu* 秦始皇陵研究. Shanghai: Shanghai renmin chubanshe, 1994.

Wang Yucheng 王育成. "Lun Houtaizi yuanshi nüxing fenmian xilie shidiao" 論後臺子原始女性分娩系列石雕. *Wenwu jikan* 文物集刊 1997.1: 57–61.

———. "Zhongguo gudai de renxing fangshu jiqi dui Riben de yingxiang" 中國古代的人形方術及其對日本的影響. *Zhongguo lishi bowuguan guankan* 1997.1: 32–56.

Wang Zijin. *Qin Han Jiaotong shigao* 秦漢交通史稿. Beijing: Zhonggong Zhongyang dangxiao chubanshe, 1994.

———. "Shuihudi Qin jian rishu suojian xing gui yiji" 睡虎地秦簡日書所見行歸宜忌. *Jiang Han kaogu* 1994.2: 45–49.

———. *Shuihudi Qin jian rishu jiazhong shuzheng* 睡虎地秦簡日書甲種疏證. Wuhan: Hubei jiaoyu chubanshe, 2003.

———. *Zhongguo daomu shi* 中國盜墓史. Beijing: Jiuzhou chubanshe, 2007.

Wang Zhongshu 王仲殊. "Zhongguo gudai muzang gaishuo" 中國古代墓葬概説. *Kaogu* 1981.5: 449–58.

Wangshan Chu jian 望山楚簡. Hubei sheng bowuguan 湖北省博物館 and Beijing daxue Zhong-wenxi 北京大學中文系. Beijing: Zhonghua shuju, 1995.

Wenwu bianji weiyuanhui 文物編輯委員會. *Wenwu kaogu gongzuo shinian, 1979–1989.* 文物考古工作十年 1979–1989. Beijing: Wenwu chubanshe, 1990.

Wu Hong 巫鴻 (= Wu Hung). *Liyi zhong de meishu: Wu Hong Zhongguo gudai meishu shi wenbian* 禮儀中的美術: 巫鴻中國古代美術史文編. Beijing: Sanlian shudian, 2005.

———. "'*Mingqi*' de lilun he shijian: Zhanguo shiqi liyi meishu zhong de guannianhua qingxiang" 明器的理論和實踐: 戰國時期禮儀美術中的觀念化傾向. *Wenwu* 2006.6: 72–81.

Wu Rongzeng 吳榮曾. "Zhanguo Han dai de 'caoshe zhi shen' ji youguan shenhua mixin de bianyi" 戰國漢代的操蛇之神及有關神話迷信的變異. *Wenwu* 1989.10: 46–52.

Wuwei Han jian 武威漢簡. Comp. Gansu sheng bowuguan 甘肅省博物館 and Zhongguo kexueyuan 中國科學院. Beijing: Wenwu, 1964.

Xia Dean 夏德安 (= Harper, Donald). "Zhanguo shidai bingsizhe de daoci" 戰國時代兵死者的禱辭. Trans. Chen Songchang. *Jianbo yanjiu yicong* 簡帛研究譯叢 2 (1998): 30–42.

Xia Nai 夏鼐. "Chu wenhua yanjiu zhong de jige wenti" 楚文化研究中的幾個問題. *Jiang Han kaogu* 1982.1: 1–2.

Xiangfan shi bowuguan 襄樊市博物館. "Hubei Xiangyang Tuanshan Dong Zhou mu" 湖北襄陽團山東周墓. *Kaogu* 1991.9: 781–802.

Xiao Dengfu 蕭登福. *Xian Qin Liang Han mingjie ji shenxian sixiang tanyuan* 先秦兩漢冥界及神仙思想探原. Taibei: Wenjin chubanshe youxian gongsi, 1990.

Xiao Fan 蕭璠. "Changsheng sixiang he yu toufa xiangguan de yangsheng fangshu" 長生思想和與頭髮相關的養生方術. *Zhongyang yanjiuyuan Lishi yuyan yanjiusuo jikan* 69.4 (1998): 671–725.

Xiao Kangda 蕭亢達. "'Pianfang' xinjie" 便房新解. *Kaogu yu wenwu* 2010.3: 53–57.

Xichuan Heshangling yu Xujialing 淅川和尚嶺與徐家嶺. Comp. Henan sheng wenwu kaogu yanjiusuo 河南省文物考古研究所, Nanyang shi wenwu kaogu yanjiusuo 南陽市文物考古研究所, and Xichuan xian bowuguan 淅川縣博物館. Zhengzhou: Daxiang chubanshe, 2004.

Xichuan Xiasi Chu mu 淅川下寺春秋楚墓. Comp. Henan sheng wenwu yanjiusuo 河南省文物研究所, Henan sheng Danjiang kuqu kaogu fajuedui 河南省丹江庫區考古發掘隊, and Xichuan xian bowuguan 淅川縣博物館. Beijing: Wenwu chubanshe, 1991.

Xie Chengxia 謝成俠. "Zailun Zhongguo xiyou lu lei—milu, bailu, tuolu de lishi yu xianzhuang." 再論中國稀有鹿類—麋鹿, 白鹿, 駝鹿的歷史與現狀. *Zhongguo nongshi* 1994.4: 63–66.

Xin Lixiang 信立祥. *Han dai huaxiangshi zonghe yanjiu* 漢代畫像石綜合研究. Beijing: Wenwu chubanshe, 2000.

Xincai Geling Chu mu 新蔡葛陵楚墓. Comp. Henan sheng wenwu kaogu yanjiusuo 河南省文物考古研究所. Beijing: Wenwu chubanshe, 2003.

Xing Yitian 邢義田. "Han dai bihua de fazhan he bihua mu" 漢代壁畫的發展和壁畫墓. In his *Hua wei xin sheng: Huaxiangshi, huaxiangzhuan yu bihua* 畫為心聲: 畫像石, 畫像磚與壁畫, 1–46. Beijing: Zhonghua shuju 2011.

———. "Cong Zhanguo zhi Xi Han de zuju, zuzang, shiye: Lun Zhongguo gudai zongzu shehui de yanxu" 從戰國至西漢的族居, 族葬, 世業: 論中國古代宗族社會的延續. In his *Tianxia yi jia: Huangdi, guanliao yu shehui* 天下一家: 皇帝, 官僚與社會, 396–435. Beijing: Zhonghua shuju, 2011.

Xingan Shang dai damu 新淦商代大墓. Comp. Jiangxi sheng bowuguan 江西省博物館, Jiangxi sheng wenwu kaogu yanjiusuo 江西省文物考古研究所, and Xingan xian bowuguan 新淦縣博物館. Beijing: Wenwu chubanshe, 1997.

Xinyang Chu mu 信陽楚墓. Comp. Henan sheng wenwu yanjiusuo 河南省文物研究所. Beijing: Wenwu chubanshe, 1986.

Xinyang diqu wenguanhui 信陽地區文管會 and Guangshan xian wenguanhui 光山縣文管會. "Henan Guangshan Chunqiu Huang Ji Tuofu mu fajue jianbao" 河南光山春秋黃季佗父墓發掘簡報. *Kaogu* 1989.1: 26–32.

Xinyang diqu wenguanhui and Xinyang shi wenguanhui 信陽市文管會. "Henan Xinyang shi Pingxi 5 hao mu fajue jianbao" 河南信陽市平西5號墓發掘簡報. *Kaogu* 1989.1: 20–25, 9.

Xiong Chuanxin 熊傳薪. "Duizhao xinjiu moben tan Chu guo renwu longfeng bohua" 對照新舊摹本談楚國人物龍鳳帛畫. In *Chu yishu yanjiu* 楚藝術研究, ed. Hubei sheng wenlian tushu bianjibu lilun yanjiushi, 129–38. Wuhan: Hubei meishu chubanshe, 1991.

Xu Jijun 徐吉軍. *Zhongguo sangzang shi* 中國喪葬史. Nanchang: Jiangxi gaoxiao chubanshe, 1998.

Xu Lianggao 徐良高. "Cong Shang Zhou renxiang yishu kan Zhongguo gudai wu ouxiang chongbai chuantong" 從商周人像藝術看中國古代無偶像崇拜傳統. In *Kaogu qiuzhi ji* 考古求知集, ed. Zhongguo shehui kexueyuan kaogu yanjiusuo, 334–52. Beijing: Zhongguo shehui kexue chubanshe, 1997.

Xu Yongqing 徐永慶 and He Huiqin 何惠琴. *Zhongguo gushi* 中國古屍. Shanghai: Shanghai keji jiaoyu chubanshe, 1996.

Xu Zaiguo 徐在國. "Xincai Geling Chu jian zhaji" 新蔡葛陵楚簡札記. Jianbowang 簡帛網 (Wuhan University), December 7, 2003.

Xuzhou Beidongshan Xi Han Chu wang mu 徐州北洞山西漢楚王墓. Comp. Xuzhou bowuguan 徐州博物館 and Nanjing daxue lishixi 南京大學歷史系. Beijing: Wenwu chubanshe, 2002.

Xunzi jijie 荀子集解, by Xun Kuang 荀況 (c. 313–238 BCE), comp. Wang Xianqian 王先謙 (1842–1918), 2 vols. Beijing: Zhonghua shuju, 1988.

Yan Changgui 晏昌貴. *Wugui yu yinsi: Chu jian suojian fangshu zongjiao kao* 巫鬼與淫祀: 楚簡所見方術宗教考. Wuchang: Wuhan daxue chubanshe, 2010.

———. "Jianbo rishu sui pian hezheng" 簡帛日書歲篇合證. *Hubei daxue xuebao* 河北大學學報 2003.1: 73–78.

Yan Gengwang 嚴耕望. "Qin Han langli zhidu kao" 秦漢郎吏制度考. In his *Yan Gengwang shixue lunwenji* 嚴耕望史學論文集, 21–84. Shanghai: Shanghai guji chubanshe, 2009.

Yan Xiadu 燕下都. Comp. Hebei sheng wenwu yanjiusuo 河北省文物研究所. 2 vols. Beijing: Wenwu chubanshe, 1996.

Yantai shi wenwu guanli weiyuanhui 煙臺市文物管理委員會. "Shandong Changdao Wanggou Dong Zhou muqun" 山東長島王溝東周墓群. *Kaogu xuebao* 1993.1: 57–87.

Yang Aiguo 楊愛國. "Xian Qin liang Han shiqi lingmu fangdao sheshi lüe lun" 先秦兩漢時期陵
墓防盜設施略論. *Kaogu* 1995.5: 436–44.

Yang Bojun 楊伯峻. *Chunqiu zuozhuan zhu* 春秋左傳注. Beijing: Zhonghua shuju, 1981.

———. *Liezi jishi* 列子集釋. Beijing: Zhonghua shuju, 1979.

Yang Hong 楊泓. "Zhongguo guwenwu zhong suojian renti zaoxing yishu" 中國古文物中所見人
體造型藝術. *Wenwu* 1987.1: 54–65.

Yang Hongxun 楊鴻勛. "Zhanguo Zhongshan wangling zhaoyutu yanjiu" 戰國中山王陵兆域圖
研究. *Kaogu xuebao* 1980.1: 119–38.

Yang Kuan 楊寬. *Zhanguo shi* 戰國史. Shanghai: Shanghai renmin chubanshe, 1980.

———. *Zhongguo gudai lingqin zhidushi yanjiu* 中國古代陵寢制度史研究. Shanghai: Shanghai
renmin chubanshe, 1985.

———. *Xizhou shi* 西周史. Shanghai: Shanghai renmin chubanshe, 1999.

Yang Hua 楊華. "Sui, feng, qian: Jiandu suojian Chu di zhusang yili yanjiu" 襚·賵·遣: 簡牘所見楚
地助喪禮儀研究. *Xueshu yuekan* 學術月刊 2003.9: 49–58.

Yang Nan 楊楠. *Jiangnan tudun yicun yanjiu* 江南土墩遺存研究. Beijing: Minzu chubanshe, 1998.

Yang Quanxi 楊權喜. *Chu wenhua* 楚文化. Beijing: Wenwu chubanshe, 2000.

Yang Rubin 楊儒賓, ed. *Zhongguo gudai sixiang zhong de qilun ji shentiguan* 中國古代思想中的氣論
及身體觀. Taibei: Juliu tushu gongsi, 1993.

Yang Shuda 楊樹達. *Han dai hunsang lisu kao* 漢代婚喪禮俗考. Reprint, Shanghai: Shanghai
wenyi chubanshe, 1988.

Yang Tianyu 楊天宇. *Yili yizhu* 儀禮譯註. Shanghai: Shanghai guji chubanshe, 1994.

Yangzhou bowuguan 揚州博物館 and Hanjiang xian tushuguan 邗江縣圖書館. "Jiangsu
Hanjiang Huchang wuhao Han mu" 江蘇邗江胡場五號漢墓. *Wenwu* 1981.11: 12–23.

Yi Zhoushu huijiao jizhu 逸周書彙校集注. Comp. Huang Huaixin 黃懷信, Zhang Maorong 張懋鎔,
and Tian Xudong 田旭東. 2 vols. Shanghai: Shanghai guji chubanshe, 1995.

Yi Zhoushu jixun jiaoshi 逸周書集訓校注. Comp. Zhu Youzeng 朱右曾 (nineteenth century).
Shanghai: Shangwu yinshuguan, 1937.

Yichang diqu bowuguan 宜昌地區博物館. "Hubei Dangyang Zhaoxiang 4 hao Chunqiu mu fajue
jianbao" 湖北當陽趙巷4號春秋墓發掘簡報. *Wenwu* 1990.10: 25–32.

Yili zhushu 儀禮註疏, annotated by Zheng Xuan 鄭玄 and Jia Gongyan 賈公彥 (*fl.* 650), et al., vol.
4 of the *Shisanjing zhushu*. Reprint, Taibei: Yiwen yinshuguan, 1993.

Yin Shengping 尹盛平, ed. *Xi Zhou weishi jiazu qingtongqiqun yanjiu* 西周微氏家族青銅器群研究.
Beijing: Wenwu chubanshe, 1992.

Yin Zhenhuan 尹振環. "Cong wangwei jicheng he shi jun kan junzhu zhuanzhi lilun de zhubu
xingcheng" 從王位繼承和弒君看君主專制理論的逐步形成. *Zhongguoshi yanjiu* 中國史研究
1987.4: 17–24.

Yin Zhou jinwen jicheng 殷周金文集成. Comp. Zhongguo shehui kexueyuan Kaogu yanjiusuo
中國社會科學院考古研究所. 18 vols. Beijing: Zhonghua shuju, 1986–1994.

Yinshan Yue wang ling 印山越王陵. Comp. Zhejiang sheng wenwu kaogu yanjiusuo 浙江省文物
考古研究所 and Shaoxing wenwu baohu guanlichu 紹興文物保護管理處. Beijing: Wenwu
chubanshe, 2002.

Yinxu jiagu keci leizuan 殷墟甲骨刻辭類纂. Ed. Yao Xiaosui 姚孝遂. 3 vols. Beijing: Zhonghua
shuju, 1989.

Yoshikawa Tadao 吉川忠夫. *Kodai Chūgokujin no fushi gensō* 古代中國人の不死幻想. Tōkyō: Tōhō
shoten, 1995.

You Qiumei 游秋玫. "Han dai muzhu huaxiang de tuxiang moshi, gongneng yu biaoxian tese"
漢代墓主畫像的圖像模式功能與表現特色. MA thesis, National Taiwan University, 2007.

You Xiuling 游修齡. "Milu he yuanshi daozuo ji Zhongguo wenhua" 麋鹿和原始稻作及中國文化.
Zhongguo nongshi 2005.1: 1–7.

Yu Weichao 俞偉超. "Han dai zhuhouwang yu liehou muzang de xingzhi fenxi" 漢代諸侯王與列
侯墓葬的形制分析. First published in 1980, in his *Xian Qin liang Han kaoguxue lunji*, 117–124.

———. *Xian Qin liang Han kaoguxue lunji* 先秦兩漢考古學論集. Beijing: Wenwu chubanshe, 1985.

———. *Zhongguo gudai gongshe zuzhi de kaocha* 中國古代公社組織的考察. Beijing: Wenwu
chubanshe, 1988.

———. "Xian Qin liang Han meishu kaogu cailiao zhong suojian shijieguan de bianhua"
先秦兩漢美術考古材料中所見世界觀的變化. In *Qingzhu Su Bingqi kaogu wushiwu nian
lunwenji* 慶祝蘇秉琦考古五十五年論文集, ed. Lunwenji bianjizu, 111–20. Beijing: Wenwu
chubanshe, 1989.

Yu Weichao 俞偉超 and Gao Ming 高明. "Zhou dai yongding zhidu yanjiu" 周代用鼎制度研究.
Beijing daxue xuebao: Shehui kexue ban 1978.1: 84–98; 1978.2: 84–97; 1979.1: 83–96. Beijing:
Wenwu chubanshe, 1985.

Yu Xingwu 于省吾. "Jiaguwen 'jiapu keci' zhenwei bian" 甲骨文家譜刻辭真偽辨. *Guwenzi yajiu* 4
(1980): 139–46.

Yunmeng Longang Qin jian 雲夢龍崗秦簡. Ed. Liu Xinfang 劉信芳 and Liang Zhu 梁柱. Beijing:
Kexue chubanshe, 1997.

Zang Zhenhua 臧振華, ed. *Zhongguo kaoguxue yu lishixue zhi zhenghe yanjiu* 中國考古學與歷史學
之整合研究. 2 vols. Taibei: Institute of History and Philology, Academia Sinica, 1997.

Zeng Hou Yi mu 曾侯乙墓. Comp. Hubei sheng bowuguan 湖北省博物館 2 vols. Beijing: Wenwu
chubanshe, 1989.

Zhanguo ce jizhu huikao 戰國策集注彙考, ed. Liu Xiang 劉向 (77–6 BCE), comp. Zhu Zugeng 諸祖
耿, Jiangsu guji chubanshe, 1985.

Zhanguo Zhongshan guo Lingshou cheng. 戰國中山國靈壽城. Comp. Hebei sheng wenwu yanjiusuo
河北省文物研究所. Beijing: Wenwu chubanshe, 2005.

Zhang Changping 張昌平. *Zeng guo qingtongqi yanjiu* 曾國青銅器研究. Beijing: Wenwu
chubanshe, 2009.

Zhang Changshou 張長壽. "Qiangliu yu huangwei" 牆柳與荒帷. *Wenwu* 1992.4: 49–52.

Zhang Guangzhi. 1988. *Kaoguxue liujiang* 考古學六講. Beijing: Wenwu chubanshe, 1988.

Zhang Han 張頷. "Gu Changping zhanchang ziliao yanjiu" 古長平戰場資料研究. *Shanxi shifan
xueyuan xuebao* 山西師範學院學報 1959.2: 95–104.

Zhang Jun 張軍. *Chu guo shenhua yuanxing yanjiu* 楚國神話原型研究. Taibei: Wenjin chubanshe,
1994.

Zhang Lizhi 張力智. "Cong miao dao mu de beihou: Zuowei zhengzhi xiangzheng de jisi zhidu"
從廟到墓的背後: 作爲政治象徵的祭祀制度. *Meishu yanjiu* 美術研究 2008.4: 46–52.

Zhang Qiyun 張其昀. "Lun Zhanguo wenzi qiyi zhi shizhi, jianji zhuan, zhou tongti deng wenti"
論戰國文字歧異之實質, 兼及篆籀同體等問題. *Zhongguo yuyan xuebao* 中國語言學報 14 (2010):
271–82.

Zhang Shanyu 張善余. *Zhongguo renkou dili* 中國人口地理. Beijing: Kexue chubanshe, 2003.

Zhang Shuangdi 張雙棣, Zhang Wanbin 張萬彬, Yin Guoguang 殷國光, and Chen Tao 陳濤.
Lüshi chunqiu yizhu 呂氏春秋譯註. Changchun Jilin wenshi chubanshe, 1987.

Zhang Xuehai 張學海. "Tian Qi liuling kao" 田齊六陵考. *Wenwu* 1984.9: 20–22.

Zhang Yongshan 張永山. "Cong buci zhong de Yi yin kan 'min busi feizu'" 從卜辭中的伊尹看民
不祀非族. *Guwenzi yanjiu* 22 (2000): 1–5.

Zhang Zhenglang 張政烺. *Zhang Zhenglang wenshi lunji* 張政烺文史論集. Beijing: Zhonghua
shuju, 2004.

Zhao Dexin 趙德馨. *Chu guo de huobi* 楚國的貨幣. Wuhan: Hubei jiaoyu chubanshe, 1995.

Zhao Huacheng 趙化成. "Hanhua suojian Han dai cheming kaobian" 漢畫所見漢代車名考辨.
Wenwu 1989.3: 76–82.

——— and Yu Liqi 虞麗琦. "Zunzhe wu xing: Qin Han lingmu suizangyong de sikao—

Zhongguo wenming de yige zhongyao tedian" 尊者無形: 秦漢陵墓隨葬俑的思考—中國文明的一個重要特點. In *Yu Weichao xiansheng jinian wenji Xueshu juan* 俞偉超先生紀念文集學術卷, ed. Beijing daxue kaogu wenbo xueyuan and Zhongguo guojia bowuguan, 344–53. Beijing: Wenwu chubanshe, 2009.

Zhao Ping'an 趙平安. "Henan Xichuan Heshangling suochu zhenmushou mingwen he Qin Han jian zhong de wanqi" 河南淅川和尚嶺所出鎮墓獸銘文和秦漢簡中的宛奇. In his *Jinwen shidu yu wenming tansuo*, 37–44. Shanghai: Shanghai guji chubanshe, 2011.

Zhao Shouyan 趙守儼. "'Zhanguo' yingdang cong na yinian kaishi" 戰國應當從哪一年開始. In his *Zhao Shouyan wencun*, 192–96. Beijing: Zhonghua shuju, 1998.

Zhao Zhenhua 趙振華. "Ai cheng shu ding de mingwen yu niandai" 哀成叔鼎的銘文與年代. *Wenwu* 1981.7: 68–69.

Zheng Yan 鄭岩. "Muzhu huaxiang yanjiu" 墓主畫像研究. In *Liu Dunyuan xiansheng jinian wenji* 劉敦愿先生紀念文集, ed. Shandong daxue kaoguxi, 450–68. Ji'nan: Shandong daxue chubanshe, 1998.

———. "Guanyu Han dai sangzang huaxiang guanzhe wenti de sikao" 關於漢代喪葬畫像觀者問題的思考. *Zhongguo Hanhua yanjiu* 中國漢畫研究 2 (2005): 39–55.

Zhongguo kaoguxue liang Zhou juan 中國考古學兩周卷. Comp. Zhongguo shehui kexueyuan Kaogu yanjiusuo 中國社會科學院考古研究所. Beijing: Zhongguo shehui kexue chubanshe, 2004.

Zhongguo kaoguxue Qin Han juan 中國考古學秦漢卷. Comp. Zhongguo shehui kexueyuan Kaogu yanjiusuo 中國社會科學院考古研究所. Beijing: Zhongguo shehui kexue chubanshe, 2010.

Zhongguo kexueyuan kaogu yanjiu suo Luoyang gongzuodui 中國科學院考古研究所洛陽工作隊. "Dong Han Luoyang cheng nanjiao de Xingtu mudi" 東漢洛陽城南郊的刑徒墓地. *Kaogu* 1972.4: 2–17.

Zhongguo shehui kexueyuan Kaogu yanjiusuo Fengxi kaogudui 中國社會科學院考古研究所灃西考古隊. "1992 nian Fengxi fajue jianbao" 1992 年灃西發掘簡報. *Kaogu* 1994.11: 974–85, 964.

Zhou Fengwu 周鳳五. "Jiudian Chu jian Gao Wuyi chongtan" 九店楚簡告武夷重探. *Zhongyang yanjiuyuan Lishi yuyan yanjiusuo jikan* 72.4 (2001): 941–59.

Zhou Shirong 周世榮. "Chu Yinke tongliang mingwen shishi" 楚邘客銅量銘文試釋. *Jiang Han kaogu* 1987.2: 87–88.

———. "Mawangdui Han mu 'niebi' yu Jiangling Mashan yi hao Chu mu 'bobi' kao" 馬王堆漢墓聶幣與江陵馬山一號楚墓帛幣考. *Guwenzi yanjiu* 21 (2001): 330–48.

Zhouli zhushu 周禮注疏, annotated by Zheng Xuan, Jia Gongyan, and Lu Deming 陸德明 (556–627), in vol. 3 of *Shisanjing zhushu*. Reprint, Taibei: Yiwen yinshuguan, 1993.

Zhu Dexi 朱德熙 and Qiu Xigui 裘錫圭. "Zhanguo wenzi yanjiu (liuzhong)" 戰國文字研究六種. In *Zhu Dexi guwenzi lunji*, ed. Qiu Xigui and Li Jiahao, 31–53.

———. "Mawangdui yihao Han mu qiance kaoshi buzheng" 馬王堆一號漢墓遣策考釋補正. In *Zhu Dexi guwenzi lunji*, ed. Qiu Xigui and Li Jiahao, 121–36.

Zhu Dexi. *Zhu Dexi guwenzi lunji* 朱德熙古文字論集. Ed. Qiu Xigui and Li Jiahao. Beijing: Zhonghua shuju, 1995.

Zhuangzi jishi 莊子集釋, attributed to Zhuang Zhou 莊周 (traditionally ca. 369–286 BCE), et al. Comp. Guo Qingfan 郭慶藩 (late nineteenth century). 4 vols. Beijing: Zhonghua shuju, 1961.

Zuozhuan 左傳 (Zuo commentary on the *Chunqiu*), traditionally attributed to Zuoqiu Ming. See Yang Bojun, *Chunqiu Zuozhuan zhu*, 4 vols. Beijing: Zhonghua shuju, 1981.

Chinese and Japanese Journals

Chutu wenxian yanjiu 出土文獻研究
Guwenzi yanjiu 古文字研究
Huaxue 華學
Jianbo 簡帛
Jianbo yanjiu 簡帛研究
Jiang Han kaogu 江漢考古
Kinran tanki daigaku kenkyushi 金蘭短期大學研究誌
Kaogu 考古
Kaogu xuebao 考古學報
Kaogu yu wenwu 考古與文物
Wenbo 文博
Wenshi 文史
Wenwu 文物
Wenwu tiandi 文物天地
Shirin 史林
Tōhō gakuhō 東方學報
Zhongguo dianji yu wenhua 中國典籍與文化
Zhongguo lishi bowuguan guankan 中國歷史博物館館刊
Zhongguo lishi wenwu 中國歷史文物
Zhongguo nongshi 中國農史
Zhongyang yanjiuyuan Lishi yuyan yanjiusuo jikan 中央研究院歷史語言研究所集刊
Zhongyuan wenwu 中原文物

Works in Western Languages

Adams, Doug, and Diane Apostolos-Cappadona, eds. *Art as Religious Studies*. New York: Crossroad, 1987.

Allan, Sarah. *The Shape of the Turtle: Myth, Art, and Cosmos in Early China*. Albany: State University New York Press, 1991.

Arbuckle, Gary. "An Unnoticed Religious Metaphor in the *Analects*?" *Journal of Chinese Religions* 21 (1993): 1–12.

Ariès, Philippe. *Western Attitudes toward Death: From the Middle Ages to the Present*. Trans. Patricia M. Ranum. Baltimore, MD: Johns Hopkins University Press, 1974.

———. "The Reversal of Death: Changes in Attitudes toward Death in Western Societies." *American Quarterly* 26 (1974): 536–65.

———. *The Hour of Our Death*. Trans. Helen Weaver. New York: Knopf, 1981. First published in French in 1977.

Armstrong, Robert Plant. *The Powers of Presence: Consciousness, Myth, and Affecting Presence*. Philadelphia: University of Pennsylvania Press, 1981.

———. *The Affecting Presence: An Essay in Humanistic Anthropology*. Urbana: University of Illinois Press, 1971.

Ashton, Leigh. *An Introduction to the Study of Chinese Sculpture*. London: Ernest Benn, 1924.

Austin, J. L. *How to Do Things with Words*. Cambridge, MA: Harvard University Press, 1962.

Bagley, Robert W. "Anyang Writing and the Origin of the Chinese Writing System." In *The First Writing: Script Invention as History and Process*, ed. Stephen D. Houston, 190–249. Cambridge: Cambridge University Press, 2004.

———. "Meaning and Explanation." In *The Problem of Meaning in Early Chinese Ritual Bronzes*, ed. Roderick Whitfield, 34–55. Colloquies on Art and Archaeology in Asia, no. 15. London: Percival David Foundation, 1993.

Baines, John, and Norman Yoffee. "Order, Legitimacy, and Wealth in Ancient Egypt and Mesopotamia." In *Archaic States: A Comparative Perspective*, ed. Gary Feinman and Joyce Marcus, 199–260. Santa Fe: School of American Research Press, 1998.

———. "Order, Legitimacy, and Wealth: Setting the Terms." In *Order, Legitimacy, and Wealth in Ancient States*, ed. Janet E. Richards and Mary Van Buren, 13–17. Cambridge: Cambridge University Press, 2000.

Banton, Michael, ed. *Anthropological Approaches to the Study of Religion*. London: Tavistock Publications, 1966.

Barasch, Moshe. *Icon: Studies in the History of an Idea*. New York: New York University Press, 1992.

Barbieri-Low, Anthony J. "Artisan Literacy in Early China." In *Writing and Literacy in Early China: Studies from the Columbia Early China Seminar*, ed. Li Feng and David Prager Branner, 51–84. Seattle: University of Washington Press, 2011.

Barnard, Noel. "The Ch'u Silk Manuscript and Other Archaeological Documents of Ancient China." In *Early Chinese Art and Its Possible Influence in the Pacific Basin*, ed. Noel Barnard, 77–102. Vol. 1. New York: Intercultural Arts Press, 1972.

Barrett, T. H. *"Lieh tzu."* In *Early Chinese Texts: A Bibliographical Guide*, ed. Michael Loewe, 298–308.

Barta, Winfried. *Die altägyptische Opferliste, von der Frühzeit bis zur griechisch-römischen Epoche*. Berlin: B. Hessling, 1963.

———. *Aufbau und Bedeutung der altägyptischen Opferformel*. Glückstadt: J. J. Augustin, 1968.

Basalla, George. "Transformed Utilitarian Objects." *Winterthur Portfolio* 17.4 (1982): 183–201.

Bauer, Wolfgang. *China and the Search for Happiness: Recurring Themes in Four Thousand Years of Chinese Cultural History*. New York: Seabury Press, 1976.

Baxter, William H. *A Handbook of Old Chinese Phonology*. Berlin: Mouton de Gruyter, 1992.

———. and Laurent Sagart. "Word Formation in Old Chinese." In *New Approaches to Chinese Word Formation: Morphology, Phonology and the Lexicon in Modern and Ancient Chinese*, ed. Jerome L. Packard, 35–76. Berlin: Mouton de Gruyter, 1998.

Beaulieu, Paul-Alain. *The Pantheon of Uruk during the Neo-Babylonian Period*. Leiden: Brill, Styx, 2003.

Beckman, Joy. "Layers of Being: Bodies, Objects and Spaces in Warring States Burials." PhD dissertation, University of Chicago, 2006.

Bell, Catherine. *Ritual: Perspectives and Dimensions*. New York: Oxford University Press, 1997.

Belting, Hans. *Likeness and Presence: A History of the Image before the Era of Art*. Trans. Edmund Jephcott. Chicago: University of Chicago Press, 1997.

Berger, Peter L. *The Sacred Canopy: Elements of a Sociological Theory of Religion*. Reprint, New York: Anchor Books, 1990.

Berkson, Mark. "Death and the Self in Ancient Chinese Thought: A Comparative Perspective." PhD dissertation, Stanford University, 2000.

Bielenstein, Hans. "The Census of China during the Period 2–742 AD." *Bulletin of the Museum of Far Eastern Antiquities* 19 (1947): 125–63.

———. "Chinese Historical Demography, A.D. 2–1982." *Bulletin of the Museum of Far Eastern Antiquities* 59 (1987): 1–288.

Bilsky, Lester James. *The State Religion of Ancient China*. 2 vols. Taipei: Orient Cultural Service, 1975.

Birrell, Anne. "Return to a Cosmic Eternal: The Representation of a Soul's Journey to Paradise in a Chinese Funerary Painting c. 168 BC." *Cosmos* 13.1 (1997): 3–30.

Blakeley, Barry B. "In Search of Danyang I: Historical Geography and Archaeological Sites." *Early China* 13 (1988): 116–52.

———. "On the Location of the Chu Capital in Early Chunqiu Times in Light of the Handong Incident of 701 B.C." *Early China* 15 (1990): 49–70.

———. "King, Clan, and Courtier in Ch'u Court Politics." *Asia Major*, 3rd ser., 5.2 (1992): 1–39.

———. "The Geography of Chu." In *Defining Chu: Image and Reality in Ancient China*, ed. Constance A. Cook and John S. Major, 9–20.

———. "Chu Society and State: Image versus Reality." In *Defining Chu: Image and Reality in Ancient China*, ed. Constance A. Cook and John S. Major, 51–66.

Bleeker, C. J. "Some Remarks on the Religious Significance of Light." In his *The Rainbow: A Collection of Studies in the Science of Religion*, 193–207. Leiden: Brill, 1975.

Bloch, Maurice, and Jonathan P. Parry, eds. *Death and the Regeneration of Life*. Cambridge: Cambridge University Press, 1982.

Bodde, Derk. "The Term Ming-ch'i." *Ars Orientalis* 5 (1963): 283.

———. "Myths of Ancient China." In his *Essays on Chinese Civilization*, 45–84. Princeton, NJ: Princeton University Press, 1981.

Bokenkamp, Stephen. "Record of the Feng and Shan Sacrifice." In *Religions of China in Practice*, ed. Donald S. Lopez, 251–260. Princeton, NJ: Princeton University Press, 1996.

———. *Ancestors and Anxiety: Daoism and the Birth of Rebirth in China*. Berkeley: University of California Press, 2007.

Boltz, William G. "Kung Kung and the Flood: Reverse Euhemerism in the *Yao Tien*." *T'oung Pao* 67.3-5 (1981): 141–53.

———. "Literacy and the Emergence of Writing in China." In *Writing and Literacy in Early China: Studies from the Columbia Early China Seminar*, ed. Li Feng and David Prager Branner, 51–84. Seattle: University of Washington Press, 2011.

Bourdieu, Pierre. *Outline of a Theory of Practice*. Trans. Richard Nice. Cambridge: Cambridge University Press, 1977.

———. "The Berber House or the World Reversed." *Social Science Information* 9.2 (1970): 151–70.

Brashier, Kenneth Edward. "Longevity Like Metal and Stone: The Role of the Mirror in Han Burials." *T'oung Pao* 81.4 (1995): 201–29.

———. "Han Thanatology and the Division of 'Souls.'" *Early China* 21 (1996): 125–58.

———. "Evoking the Ancestor: The Stele Hymn of the Eastern Han Dynasty (25–220 C.E.)." PhD dissertation, University of Cambridge, 1997.

Brooks, Bruce E., and A. Taeko Brooks. *The Original Analects: Sayings of Confucius and His Successors*. New York: Columbia University Press, 1998.

Brown, Miranda. "Did the Early Chinese Preserve Corpses? A Reconsideration of Elite Conceptions of Death." *Journal of East Asian Archaeology* 4 (2002): 201–23.

Bujard, Marianne. *Le sacrifice au ciel dans la Chine ancienne: Théorie et pratique sous les Han Occidentaux*. Paris, EFEO, 2000.

———. "State and Local Cults in Han Religion." In *Early Chinese Religion, Part One: Shang through Han (1250 BC–220 AD)*, ed. John Lagerwey and Marc Kalinowski, 777–811. Leiden: Brill, 2009.

Bulling, Anneliese. "Notes on Two Unicorns." *Oriental Art* 3 (1966): 109–13.

Burkert, Walter. *Creation of the Sacred: Tracks of Biology in Early Religions*. Cambridge, MA: Harvard University Press, 1996.

Cahill, Suzanne E. *Transcendence and Divine Passion: The Queen Mother of the West in Medieval China*. Stanford: Stanford University Press, 1993.

Calhoun, C. J. "The Authority of Ancestors: A Sociological Reconsideration of Fortes's Tallensi in Response to Fortes's Critics." *Man*, n.s., 15.2 (1980): 304–19.

Campany, Robert Ford. "Return-from-Death Narratives in Early Medieval China." *Journal of Chinese Religions* 18 (1990): 91–125.

———. "To Hell and Back: Death, Near-Death, and Other Worldly Journeys in Early Medieval China." In *Death, Ecstasy and Other Worldly Journeys*, ed. John J. Collins and Michael Fishbane, 343–60. Albany: State University of New York Press, 1995.

———. *Making Transcendents: Ascetics and Social Memory in Early Medieval China.* Honolulu: University of Hawai'i Press, 2009.

Campbell, Aurelia. "The Form and Function of Western Han Dynasty *Ticou* Tombs." *Artibus Asiae* 70.2 (2010): 227–58.

Carr, Michael. "Personation of the Dead in Ancient China." *Computational Analyses of Asian & African Languages* 24 (1985): 1–107.

Chang, Kwang-chih (= Zhang Guangzhi). "Major Aspects of Ch'u Archaeology." In *Early Chinese Art and Its Possible Influence in the Pacific Basin*, ed. Noel Barnard, vol. 1, 5–52. New York: Intercultural Arts Press, 1972.

———. "Changing Relationships of Man and Animal in Shang and Chou Myths and Art." In his *Early Chinese Civilization: Anthropological Perspectives*, 174–96. Cambridge, MA: Harvard University Press, 1976.

———. "The Animal in Shang and Chou Bronze Art." *Harvard Journal of Asiatic Studies* 41.2 (1981): 527–54.

———. *Art, Myth, and Ritual: The Path to Political Authority in Ancient China.* Cambridge, MA: Harvard University Press, 1983.

———. "On the Meaning of *Shang* in the Shang Dynasty." *Early China* 20 (1995): 69–77.

Chao, Kang. *Man and Land in Chinese History: An Economic Analysis.* Stanford: Stanford University Press, 1986.

Chapman, Robert, Ian Kinnes, and Klavs Randsborg, eds. *The Archaeology of Death.* Cambridge: Cambridge University Press, 1981.

Chavannes, Édouard. *Mission archéologique dans la Chine septentrionale.* Paris: Ernest Leroux, 1909.

———. *Le T'aï-Chan: Essai de monographie d'un culte chinois.* (Appendice: "Le Dieu du Sol dans la Chine Antique.") Paris: Ernest Leroux, 1910.

Chen, Qi-xin, and Li Xing Guo. "The Unearthed Paperlike Objects are Not Paper Produced before Tsai-Lun's Invention." *Yearbook of Paper History* 8 (1990): 7–22.

Cheng, Anne. "Ch'un ch'iu, Kung yang, Ku liang and Tso chuan." In *Early Chinese Texts: A Bibliographical Guide*, ed. Michael Loewe, 67–76. Berkeley: Society for the Study of Early China and the Institute of East Asian Studies, University of California, Berkeley, 1993.

———. "Lun yü." In *Early Chinese Texts: A Bibliographical Guide*, ed. Michael Loewe, 313–23. Berkeley: Society for the Study of Early China and the Institute of East Asian Studies, University of California, Berkeley, 1993.

Childe, V. Gordon. "Directional Changes in Funerary Practices during 50,000 Years." *Man* 45 (1945): 13–19.

Cohen, Alvin P. "The Avenging Ghost: Moral Judgement in Chinese Historical Texts." PhD dissertation, University of California, Berkeley, 1971.

———. "Avenging Ghosts and Moral Judgment in Ancient Chinese Historiography: Three Examples from Shih-chi." In *Legend, Lore, and Religion in China: Essays in Honor of Wolfram Eberhard on His Seventieth Birthday*, ed. Alvin P. Cohen and Sarah Allan, 97–108. San Francisco: Chinese Materials Center, 1979.

———. *Tales of Vengeful Souls: A Sixth Century Collection of Chinese Avenging Ghost Stories.* Paris: Institut Ricci, Centre d'Etudes Chinoises, 1982.

Cohen, Alvin P., and Sarah Allan, eds. *Legend, Lore, and Religion in China: Essays in Honor of Wolfram Eberhard on His Seventieth Birthday.* San Francisco: Chinese Materials Center, 1979.

Collins, John J., and Michael Fishbane, eds. *Death, Ecstasy and Other Worldly Journeys*. Albany: State University of New York Press, 1995.

Cook, Constance A. *Death in Ancient China: The Tale of One Man's Journey*. Leiden: Brill, 2006.

Cook, Constance A., and John S. Major, eds. *Defining Chu: Image and Reality in Ancient China*. Honolulu: University of Hawai'i Press, 1999.

Cort, John E. "Art, Religion, and Material Culture: Some Reflections on Method." *Journal of the American Academy of Religion* 64.3 (1996): 613–32.

Couliano, I. P. *Out of the World: Otherworldly Journeys from Gilgamesh to Albert Einstein*. Boston and London: Shambhala, 1991.

Creel, Herrlee Glessner. *The Birth of China: A Survey of the Formative Period of Chinese Civilization*. London: Jonathan Cape, 1936.

Csikszentmihalyi, Mark, and Philip J. Ivanhoe, eds. *Religious and Philosophical Aspects of the Laozi*. Albany: State University of New York Press, 1999.

Darnton, Robert. *The Kiss of Lamourette: Reflections in Cultural History*. New York: Norton, 1990.

De Geus, C. H. J. "*Signum Ignis Signum Vitae*: Lamps in Ancient Israelite Tombs." In *Scripta Signa Vocis: Studies about Scripts, Scriptures, Scribes and Languages in the Near East Present to J.H, Hospers by His Pupils, Colleagues and Friends*, ed. H. L. J. Vanstiphout, K. Jongeling, F. Leembuis, and G. J. Reinink, 65–75. Groningen: Egbert Forsten, 1986.

de Groot, Jan Jakob Maria. *The Religious System of China, Its Ancient Forms, Evolution, History and Present Aspect, Manners, Customs and Social Institutions Connected Therewith*. 6 vols. Leiden: Brill, 1892–1910. Reprint, Taipei: Southern Materials Center, 1964.

Demattè, Paola. "Antler and Tongue: New Archaeological Evidence in the Study of the Chu Tomb Guardian." *East and West* 44 (1994): 353–404.

Derrida, Jacques. *Of Grammatology*. Trans. Gayatri Chakravorty Spivak. Baltimore: Johns Hopkins University Press, 1976.

———. *Writing and Difference*. Trans. Alan Bass. Chicago: University of Chicago Press, 1978.

Dever, William G. *Did God Have a Wife? Archaeology and Folk Religion in Ancient Israel*. Grand Rapids, MI: William B. Eerdmans Publishing Company, 2005.

Dien, Albert E. "Chinese Beliefs in the Afterworld." In *The Quest for Eternity: Chinese Ceramic Sculptures from the People's Republic of China*, ed. George Kuwayama, Los Angeles County Museum of Art, 1–16. San Francisco: Chronicle Books, 1987.

Douglas, Mary. "Symbolic Orders in the Use of Domestic Space." In *Man, Settlement and Urbanism*, ed. Peter J. Ucko, Ruth Tringham, and G. W. Dimbleby, 513–21. London: University of London, Institute of Archaeology, 1972.

Dubs, Homer H. "The Custom of Mourning to the Third Year." In his translation *The History of the Former Han Dynasty*, vol. 3, 40–42. Baltimore, MD: Waverly Press, 1955.

Eberhard, Wolfram. *Guilt and Sin in Traditional China*. Berkeley: University of California Press, 1967.

Ebrey, Patricia. "Portrait Sculptures in Imperial Ancestral Rites in Song China." *T'oung Pao* 83.1–3 (1997): 42–92.

Edwards, Catharine. *Death in Ancient Rome*. New Haven, CT: Yale University Press, 2007.

Emmerich, Reinhard. "Chu und Changsha am Ende der Qin-Zeit und zu Beginn der Han-Zeit." *Oriens Extremus* 34.1-2 (1991): 85–137.

Eno, Robert. "Was There a High God Ti in Shang Religion?" *Early China* 15 (1990): 1–26.

———. "Shang State Religion and the Pantheon of the Oracle Texts." In *Early Chinese Religion, Part One: Shang through Han (1250 BC–220 AD)*, ed. John Lagerwey and Marc Kalinowski, 41–102. Leiden: Brill, 2009.

Erickson, Susan N. "Han Dyansty Tomb Structures and Contents." In *China's Early Empires:*

A Re-appraisal, ed. Michael Nylan and Michael Loewe, 13–82. Cambridge: Cambridge University Press, 2010.

Erkes, Eduard. "Si er bu wang." *Asia Major*, n.s., 3 (1953): 156–61.

Eschenbach, Silvia Freiin Ebner von. "Public Graveyards of the Song Dynasty." In *Burial in Song China*, ed. Dieter Kuhn, 215–52. Heidelberg: Edition Forum, 1994.

Fairbank, Wilma. "A Structural Key to Han Mural Art." *Harvard Journal of Asiatic Studies* 7.1 (1942): 52–88.

Falkenhausen, Lothar von (= Luo Tai). "Chu Ritual Music." In *New Perspectives on Chu Culture during the Eastern Zhou Period*, ed. Thomas Lawton, 47–106. Washington, DC: Arthur M. Sackler Gallery, Smithsonian Institution, 1991.

———. *Suspended Music: Chime-Bells in the Culture of Bronze Age China*. Berkeley: University of California Press, 1993.

———. "Sources of Taoism: Reflections on Archaeological Indicators of Religious Change in Eastern Zhou China." *Taoist Resources* 5.2 (1994): 1–12.

———. "Reflections on the Political Role of Spirit Mediums in Early China: The *wu* Officials in the *Zhou li*." *Early China* 20 (1995): 279–300.

———. Review of *Monumentality in Early Chinese Art and Architecture*, by Wu Hung. *Early China* 21 (1996): 183–99.

———. "The Waning of the Bronze Age: Material Culture and Social Developments, 770–481 BC." In *The Cambridge History of Ancient China*, ed. Michael Loewe and Edward L. Shaughnessy, 450–544.

———. "The Bronzes from Xiasi and Their Owners." *Kaoguxue yanjiu* 5 (2003), vol. 2: 755–86.

———. "Social Ranking in Chu Tombs: The Mortuary Background of the Warring States Manuscript Finds." *Monumenta Serica* 51 (2003): 439–526.

———. "Mortuary Behavior in Pre-Imperial Qin: A Religious Interpretation." In *Religion in Ancient and Medieval China*, ed. John Lagerwey, vol. 1, 109–72. Hong Kong: Chinese University Press, 2004.

———. "The E Jun Qi Metal Tallies: Inscribed Texts and Ritual Contexts." In *Text and Ritual in Early China*, ed. Martin Kern, 79–124. Seattle: University of Washington Press, 2005.

———. *Chinese Society in the Age of Confucius (1000–250 BC): The Archaeological Evidence*. Los Angeles: Cotsen Institute of Archaeology, UCLA, 2006.

———. "Archaeological Perspectives on the Philosophicization of Royal Zhou Ritual." In *Perceptions of Antiquity in China*, ed. Dieter Kuhn and Helga Stahl, 135–75. Würzburger Sinologische Schriften. Heidelberg: Edition Forum, 2008.

———. "From Action to Image in Early Chinese Art." *Cahiers d'Extrême-Asie* 17 (2010): 51–91.

Feuchtwang, Stephan. *Popular Religion in China: The Imperial Metaphor*. 2nd rev. ed. New York: Routledge, 2001.

———. "An Unsafe Distance." In *Living with Separation in China: Anthropological Accounts*, ed. Charles Stafford, 85–112. London: RoutledgeCurzon, 2003.

———. *The Anthropology of Religion, Charisma and Ghosts: Chinese Lessons for Adequate Theory*. New York: De Gruyter, 2010.

Fletcher, Roland. "Settlement Studies." In *Spatial Archaeology*, ed. David L. Clarke, 47–162. London: Academic Press, 1977.

Fong, Mary. "The Origin of Chinese Pictorial Representation of the Human Figure." *Artibus Asiae* 49 (1988): 5–38.

Fortes, Meyer. "Pietas and Ancestor Worship." *Journal of the Royal Anthropological Institute* 91.2 (1961): 166–91.

———. "Some Reflection on Ancestor Worship in Africa." In *African Systems of Thought*, ed.

M. Fortes and G. Dieterlen. London: Oxford University Press for the International African Institute, 1965.

Fowler, Jeaneane, and Merv Fowler. *Chinese Religions: Beliefs and Practices*. Brighton: Sussex Academic Press, 2008.

Freedberg, David. *The Power of Images: Studies in the History and Theory of Response*. Chicago: University of Chicago Press, 1989.

Freedman, Maurice. "On the Sociological Study of Chinese Religion." In *Religion and Ritual in Chinese Society*, ed. Arthur P. Wolf, 19–41. Stanford: Stanford University Press, 1974.

Frend, W. H. C. *The Archaeology of Early Christianity: A History*. London: Geoffrey, 1996.

Friedrich, Michael. "The 'Announcement to the World Below' of Ma-wang-tui 3." *Manuscript Cultures Newsletter* 1 (2008): 7–15.

Fung, Yu-lan (= Feng, Youlan). *A History of Chinese Philosophy*. Trans. Derk Bodde. 2 vols. 2nd ed. Princeton, NJ: Princeton University Press, 1952.

Garland, Robert. *The Greek Way of Death*. 2nd ed. Ithaca: Cornell University Press, 2001.

Geary, Patrick J. "The Uses of Archaeological Sources for Religious and Cultural History." In his *Living with the Dead in the Middle Ages*, 30–45. Ithaca, NY: Cornell University Press, 1994.

Gelb, Ignace J. "Two Assyrian King Lists." *Journal of Near Eastern Studies* 13.4 (1954): 209–230.

Gell, Alfred. "How to Read a Map: Remarks on the Practical Logic of Navigation." *Man*, n.s., 20.2 (1985): 271–286.

Gernet, Jacques. "Être enterré nu." *Le Journal des Savants*, janvier-septembre 1985: 3–16.

Giele, Enno. "Using Early Chinese Manuscripts as Historical Source Materials." *Monumenta Serica* 51 (2003): 409–38.

Girardot, Norman J. "'Very Small Books about Very Large Subjects': A Prefatory Appreciation of the Enduring Legacy of Laurence G. Thompson's Chinese Religion, An Introduction." *Journal of Chinese Religions* 20.1 (1992): 9–15.

Glazier, Jack. "Mbeere Ancestors and the Domestication of Death." *Man*, n.s., 19.1 (1984): 133–47.

Gluckman, Max. "Mortuary Customs and the Belief in Survival after Death among the South-Eastern Bantu." *Bantu Studies* 11 (1937): 117–36.

Goebs, Katja. "Expressing Luminosity in Iconography: Features of the Solar Bark in the Tomb of Ramesses VI." *Göttinger Miszellen* 165 (1998): 57–71.

Golden, Mark. "Did the Ancients Care when Their Children Died?" *Greece & Rome*, n.s., 35 (1988): 152–63.

Gombrich, E. H. *The Sense of Order: A Study in the Psychology of Decorative Art*. London: Phaidon Press Limited, 1984.

———. "Meditations on a Hobby Horse or the Roots of Artistic Form." In his *Meditations on a Hobby Horse and Other Essays on the Theory of Art*. London: Phaidon Press, 1994.

Goody, Jack. *The Domestication of the Savage Mind*. Cambridge: Cambridge University Press, 1977.

———. *Death, Property and the Ancestors: A Study of the Mortuary Customs of the LoDagaa of West Africa*. Stanford: Stanford University Press, 1962.

Gordon, Richard. "'What's in a List?' Listing in Greek and Graeco-Roman Malign Magical Texts." In *The World of Ancient Magic*, ed. David R. Jordan, Hugo Montgomery, and Einar Thomassen, 239–77. Bergen: Norwegian Institute at Athens, 1999.

Graham, A. C. *The Book of Lieh-tzu*. New York: Columbia University Press, 1960.

———. *Disputers of the Tao: Philosophical Argument in Ancient China*. LaSalle, IL: Open Court, 1989.

Granet, Marcel. *La pensée chinoise*. 1934. Reprint, Paris: A. Michel, 1950.

———. *The Religion of the Chinese People*. Trans. Maurice Freedman. New York: Harper & Row, Publishers, 1975. First published in French in 1922.

Greiff, Susanne, and Yin Shenping. *Das Grab des Bin Wang: Wandmalereien der Östlichen Han-Zeit in China*. Mainz: Verlag des Römisch-Germanischen Zentralmuseum in Kommission bei Harrassowitz Verlag, Wiesbaden, Mainz, 2002.

Grinsell, L. V. "The Breaking of Objects as a Funerary Rite." *Folklore* 72.3 (1961): 475–91.

———."The Breaking of Objects as a Funerary Rite: Supplementary Notes." *Folklore* 84.2 (1973): 111–14.

Guo, Jue. "Reconstructing Fourth Century B.C.E. Chu Religious Practices: Divination, Sacrifice, and Healing in the Newly Excavated Baoshan Manuscripts." PhD dissertation, University of Wisconsin-Madison, 2008.

Hall, Edward T. *The Hidden Dimension*. Garden City, NY: Doubleday, 1966.

Hallote, Rachel S. *Death, Burial, and Afterlife in the Biblical World: How the Israelites and Their Neighbors Treated the Dead*. Chicago: Ivan R. Dee, 2001.

Hallpike, C. R., Mark Blades, Christopher Spencer, and Alfred Gell. "Maps and Wayfinding." *Man*, n.s., 21.2 (1986): 342–46.

Harley, J. B., and David Woodward, eds. *Cartography in the Traditional East and Southeast Asian Societies*. Vol. 2, Book 2 of *The History of Cartography*. Chicago: University of Chicago Press, 1987.

Harper, Donald. "A Chinese Demonography of the Third Century B.C." *Harvard Journal of Asiatic Studies* 45.1 (1985): 459–98.

———. "Resurrection in Warring States Popular Religion." *Taoist Resources* 5.2 (1994): 13–28.

———. "Chinese Religions: The State of the Field: Warring States, Ch'in, and Han Periods." *Journal of Asian Studies* 54.1 (1995): 152–60.

———. *Early Chinese Medical Literature: The Mawangdui Medical Manuscripts*. New York: Kegan Paul International, 1998.

———. "Warring States Natural Philosophy and Occult Thought." In *The Cambridge History of Ancient China*, ed. Michael Loewe and Edward L. Shaughnessy, 813–84.

———. "The Nature of Taiyi in the Guodian Manuscript: Taiyi sheng shui – Abstract Cosmic Principle or Supreme Cosmic Deity?" *Chūgoku shutsudo shiryō kenkyū* 5 (2001): 1–23.

———. "Contracts with the Spirit World in Han Common Religion: The Xuning Prayer and Sacrifice Documents of A.D. 79." *Cahiers d'Extrême-Asie* 14 (2004): 227–67.

Harrison, Jane E. *Prolegomena to the Study of Greek Religion*. 3rd. ed. Cambridge: Cambridge University Press, 1922.

Hawkes, David. "The Quest of the Goddess." In *Studies in Chinese Literary Genres*, ed. Cyril Birch, 42–68. Berkeley: University of California Press, 1974.

Hayashi Minao. "Concerning the Inscription 'May Sons and Grandsons Eternally Use This [Vessel].'" Trans. Elizabeth Childs-Johnson. *Artibus Asiae* 53.1/2 (1993): 51–57.

Hedrick, Charles W., Jr. *History and Silence: Purge and Rehabilitation of Memory in Late Antiquity*. Austin: University of Texas Press, 2000.

Holdcroft, David. *Words and Deeds: Problems in the Theory of Speech Acts*. Oxford: Clarendon Press, 1978.

Hou, Ching-lang. "Trésors du monastère Long-hing à Touen-houang." In *Nouvelles contributions aux etudes de Touen-houang*, ed. Michel Soymié, 149–68. Genève: Librairie Droz, 1981.

Hsu, Cho-yun. *Ancient China in Transition: An Analysis of Social Mobility, 722–222 B.C.* Stanford: Stanford University Press, 1965.

Hsu, Mei-Ling. "The Han Maps and Early Chinese Cartography." *Annals of the Association of American Geographers* 68.1 (1978): 45–60.

———. "The Qin Maps: A Clue to Later Chinese Cartographic Development." *Imago Mundi* 45 (1993): 90–100.

Huang, Bingyi. "From Chu to Western Han: Re-reading Mawangdui." PhD dissertation, Yale University, 2005.

Hugh-Jones, Christine. *From the Milk River: Spatial and Temporal Processes in Northwest Amazonia*. Cambridge: Cambridge University Press, 1979.

Hulsewé, A. F. P. "Texts in Tombs." *Études Asiatiques/Asiatische Studien* 18/19 (1965): 78–89.

Humphrey, Caroline. "Inside a Mongolian Tent." *New Society* 30 (1974): 273–75.

Inomata, Takeshi, and Lawrence S. Coben, eds. *Archaeology of Performance: Theaters of Power, Community, and Politics*. Lanham, NY: AltaMira Press, 2006.

Insoll, Timothy. *The Archaeology of Islam*. Oxford: Blackwell, 1999.

———. *The Archaeology of Islam in Sub-Saharan Africa*. Cambridge: Cambridge University Press, 2003.

———. *Archaeology, Ritual, Religion*. London: Routledge, 2004.

———, ed. *Case Studies in Archaeology and World Religion. The Proceedings of the Cambridge Conference*. BAR S755. Oxford: Archaeopress, 1999.

———, ed. *Archaeology and World Religion*. London: Routledge, 2001.

———, ed. *Belief in the Past. The Proceedings of the 2002 Manchester Conference on Archaeology and Religion*. Oxford: Archaeopress, 2004.

Jacobsen, Thorkild. *The Sumerian King List*. Chicago: University of Chicago Press, 1939.

Jacobson, Esther. "Beyond the Frontier: A Reconsideration of Cultural Interchange between China and the Early Nomads." *Early China* 13 (1988): 201–40.

James, Jean M. "An Iconographic Study of Two Late Han Funerary Monuments: The Offering Shrines of the Wu Family and the Multichamber Tomb at Holingor." PhD dissertation, University of Iowa, 1983.

Jeanrond, Werner G. *Text and Interpretation as Categories of Theological Thinking*. Trans. Thomas J. Wilson. Dublin: Gill and Macmillan, 1988.

———. *Theological Hermeneutics: Development and Significance*. Houndmills: Macmillan, 1991.

Johnson, David. "Epic and History in Early China: The Matter of Wu Tzu-hsü." *Journal of Asian Studies* 40.2 (1981): 255–71.

Juliano, Annette L., and Judith A. Lerner. *Monks and Merchants: Silk Road Treasures from Northwest China*. New York: Harry N. Abrams, Inc., with the Asia Society, 2001.

Kalinowski, Marc. "The Xingde Texts from Mawangdui." *Early China* 23-24 (1998-1999): 125–202.

———. "Review of *Death in Ancient China. The Tale of One Man's Journey*." *Études chinoises* 25 (2006): 251–63.

———. "Diviners and Astrologers under the Eastern Zhou: Transmitted Texts and Recent Archaeological Discoveries." In *Early Chinese Religion, Part One: Shang through Han (1250 BC–220 AD)*, ed. John Lagerwey and Marc Kalinowski, 341–96.

Karlgren, Bernhard. *On the Authenticity and Nature of the Tso chuan*. Göteborg: Elanders Boktryckeri Aktiebolag, 1926.

———. "Some Fecundity Symbols in Ancient China." *Bulletin of the Museum of Far Eastern Antiquities* 2 (1930): 1–54.

———. "Legends and Cults in Ancient China." *Bulletin of the Museum of Far Eastern Antiquities* 18 (1946): 199–365.

Keightley, David N. "The Religious Commitment: Shang Theology and the Genesis of Chinese Political Culture." *History of Religions* 17 (1978): 211–24.

———. "Report from the Shang: A Corroboration and Some Speculation." *Early China* 9–10 (1983–1985): 20–54.

———. "The Origins of Writing in China: Scripts and Cultural Contexts." In *The Origins of Writing*, ed. Wayne M. Senner, 171–202. Lincoln: University of Nebraska Press, 1989.

———. "Ancient Chinese Art: Contexts, Constraints, and Pleasure." *Asian Art* 3.3 (1990): 2–6.

———. "Shamanism, Death, and the Ancestors: Religious Mediation in Neolithic and Shang China (ca. 5000–1000 BC)." *Asiatische Studien* 52.3 (1998): 763–831.

———. *The Ancestral Landscape: Time, Space, and Community in Late Shang China (ca. 1200–1045 B.C.).* Berkeley: Institute of Asian Studies, University of California, and Center for Chinese Studies, 2000.

———. "The Making of the Ancestors: Late Shang Religion and Its Legacy." In *Religion and Chinese Society*, Vol. 1: *Ancient and Medieval China*, ed. John Lagerwey, 3–63. Hong Kong: Chinese University Press, 2004.

Kern, Martin. "*Shi Jing* Songs as Performance Texts: A Case Study of 'Chu Ci' (Thorny Caltrop)." *Early China* 25 (2000): 49–111.

Kesner, Ladislav. "Portrait Aspects and Social Functions of Chinese Ceramic Tomb Sculpture." *Orientations* 8 (1991): 33–42.

———. "The Taotie Reconsidered: Meanings and Functions of Shang Theriomorphic Imagery." *Artibus Asiae* 51.1–2 (1991): 29–53.

———. "Likeness of No One: (Re)presenting the First Emperor's Army." *The Art Bulletin* 77.1 (1995): 115–32.

Kirkland, Russell. "Person and Culture in the Taoist Tradition." *Journal of Chinese Religions* 20 (1992): 77–90.

Kitchen, K. A. "The King List of Ugarit." *Ugarit-Forschungen* 9 (1977): 131–42.

Kleeman, Terry F. "Land Contracts and Related Documents." In *Chūgoku no shūkyō shisō to kagaku: Makio Ryōkai hakushi shōju kinen ronshū* 中國の宗教思想と科學: 牧尾良海博士頌壽記念論集, ed. Makio Ryōkai hakushi shōju kinen ronshū kankōkai, 1–34. Tōkyō: Kokusho kankōkai, 1984.

———. "Licentious Cults and Bloody Victuals: Sacrifice, Reciprocity, and Violence in Traditional China." *Asia Major*, 3rd ser., 7.1 (1994): 185–211.

Knechtges, David. "A Journey to Morality: Chang Heng's 'The Rhapsody on Pondering the Mystery.'" In *Essays in Commemoration of the Golden Jubilee of the Fung Ping Shan Library (1932–1982): Studies in Chinese Librarianship, Literature, Language, History and Arts*, ed. Chan Ping-leung et al., 162–82. Hong Kong: Fung Ping Shan Library of the University of Hong Kong, 1982.

Knoblock, John, trans. *Xunzi: A Translation and Study of the Complete Works.* 3 vols. Stanford: Stanford University Press, 1988–1994.

Knoblock, John, and Jeffrey Riegel, trans. *The Annals of Lü Buwei.* Stanford: Stanford University Press, 2000.

Kopytoff, Igor. "Ancestors as Elders." *Africa* 41 (1971): 129–42.

Krispijn, Th. J. H. "The Early Mesopotamian Lexical Lists and the Dawn of Linguistics." *Jaarbericht "Ex Oriente Lux"* 32 (1993): 12–22.

Kselman, Thomas A. "Death in Historical Perspective." *Sociological Forum* 2.3 (1987): 591–97.

———. *Death and Afterlife in Modern France.* Princeton, NJ: Princeton University Press, 1993.

Kuwayama, George, ed. *Ancient Mortuary Traditions of China: Papers on Chinese Ceramic Funerary Sculptures.* Los Angeles: Los Angeles County Museum of Art, 1991.

Kyle, Donald G. *Spectacles of Death in Ancient Rome.* New York: Routledge, 1998.

Laderman, Gary. *The Sacred Remains: American Attitudes toward Death, 1799–1833.* New Haven, CT: Yale University Press, 1996.

Lagerwey, John. "The Oral and the Written in Chinese and Western Religion." In *Religion und Philosophie in Ostasien: Festschrift für Hans Steininger zum 65 Geburtstag*, ed. Gert Naundorf,

Karl-Heinz Pohl, and Hans-Hermann Schmidt, 301–22. Würzburg: Königshausen und Neumann, 1985.

———. *China: A Religious State*. Hong Kong: Hong Kong University Press, 2010.

———, ed. *Religion and Chinese Society*. 2 vols. Hong Kong: The Chinese University Press, 2004.

Lagerwey, John, and Marc Kalinowski, eds. *Early Chinese Religion, Part One: Shang through Han (1250 BC–220 AD)*. 2 vols. Leiden: Brill, 2009.

Lai, Guolong. "Uses of the Human Figure in Early Chinese Art." *Orientations* 6 (1999): 49–55.

———. "The Baoshan Tomb: Religious Transitions in Art, Ritual, and Text during the Warring States Period (480–221 BCE)." PhD dissertation, University of California, Los Angeles, 2002.

———. "Lighting the Way in the Afterlife: Bronze Lamps in Warring States Period Tombs." *Orientations* 4 (2002): 20–28.

———. "The Diagram of the Mourning System from Mawangdui." *Early China* 28 (2003): 43–99.

———. "Death, Travel, and Otherworldly Journey in Early China, as Seen through Tomb Texts, Travel Paraphernalia, and Road Rituals." *Asia Major*, 3rd ser., 18.1 (2005): 1–44.

———. "The Transformation of Space in Early Chinese Burials." In *A Bronze Managerie: Mat Weights of Early China*, ed. Michelle C. Wang, Guolong Lai, Roel Sterckx, Eugene Yuejin Wang, 34–49. Boston: Isabella Stewart Gardner Museum, distributed by University of Pittsburg Press, 2006.

Lau, D. C., trans. *The Analects*. New York: Penguin Books, 1979.

Laufer, Berthold. *Chinese Pottery of the Han Dynasty*. Leiden: Brill, 1909.

———. "The Development of Ancestral Images in China." *Journal of Religious Psychology* 51 (1913): 111–23.

———. *Chinese Clay Figurines*. Chicago: Field Museum of Natural History, 1914.

Lawton, Thomas. *Chinese Art of the Warring States Period: Change and Continuity, 480–222 B.C.* Washington DC: Freer Gallery of Art, Smithsonian Institution, 1982.

———, ed. *New Perspectives on Chu Culture during the Eastern Zhou Period*. Washington, DC: Arthur M. Sackler Gallery, Smithsonian Institution, and Princeton University Press, 1991.

LeDoux, Joseph E. "Emotion, Memory and the Brain." *Scientific American* 270.6 (1994): 32–39.

Legge, James, trans. *The Ch'un Ts'ew with the Tso Chuen (The Chinese Classics*, vol. 5). Taibei: Southern Materials Center, 1985. First published in 1872 by Clarendon Press.

———, trans. *Li Chi: Book of Rites*. Ed. Winberg Chai and Ch'u Chai. 2 vols. New Hyde Park, NY: University Books, 1967. First published in 1885 by Oxford University Press.

Levi, Jean. *Les fonctionnaires divins: Politique, despotisme et mystique en Chine ancienne*. Paris: Seuil, 1989.

Lewis, Mark Edward. *Sanctioned Violence in Early China*. Albany: State University of New York Press, 1990.

———. "Ritual Origins of the Warring States." *Bulletin de l'École Française d'Extrême-Orient* 84 (1997): 73–98.

———. *Writing and Authority in Early China*. Albany: State University of New York Press, 1999.

———. "Warring States Political History." In *The Cambridge History of Ancient China*, ed. Michael Loewe and Edward L. Shaughnessy, 587–650.

———. *The Construction of Space in Early China*. Albany: State University of New York Press, 2006.

———. "Review of *Death in Ancient China. The Tale of One Man's Journey.*" *T'oung Pao* 94 (2008): 360–64.

Li Feng, and David Prager Branner. *Writing and Literacy in Early China: Studies from the Columbia Early China Seminar*. Seattle: University of Washington Press, 2011.

Li, Jianmin. "Contagion and Its Consequences: The Problem of Death Pollution in Ancient

China." In *Medicine and the History of the Body: Proceedings of the 20th, 21st and 22nd International Symposium on the Comparative History of Medicine—East and West*, ed. Yasuo Otsuka, Shizu Sakai, and Shigehisa Kuriyama, 201–22. Tokyo: Ishiyaku EuroAmerica, 1999.

Li, Ling. "On the Typology of Chu Bronzes." Trans. Lothar von Falkenhausen. *Beiträge zur Allgemeinen und Vergleichenden Archäologie* 11 (1991): 57–113.

———. "An Archaeological Study of Taiyi (Grand One) Worship." Trans. Donald Harper. *Early Medieval China* 2 (1995-1996): 1–39.

Li, Wai-yee. *The Readability of the Past in Early Chinese Historiography*. Cambridge, MA: Harvard University Asia Center and Harvard University Press, 2007.

Li, Xueqin. *Eastern Zhou and Qin Civilizations*. Trans. K. C. Chang. New Haven, CT: Yale University Press, 1985.

———. "Chu Bronzes and Chu Culture." In *New Perspectives on Chu Culture during the Eastern Zhou Period*, ed. Thomas Lawton, 1–22.

Li, Yinde. "The 'Underground Palace' of a Chu Prince at Beidongshan." *Orientations* 21.10 (1990): 57–61.

Liu, Li. "Early Figuration in China: Ideological, Social and Ecological Implications." In *Image and Imagination: A Global Prehistory of Figurative Representation*, ed. Colin Renfrew and Iain Morley, 271–86. Cambridge: McDonald Institute for Archaeological Research, University of Cambridge, 2007.

———, and Xingcan Chen. *State Formation in Early China*. London: Duckworth, 2003.

Loewe, Michael. *Ways to Paradise: The Chinese Quest for Immortality*. Taipei: SMC Publishing Inc., 1994. First published in 1979 by Allen and Unwin.

———. *Chinese Ideas of Life and Death: Faith, Myth and Reason in the Han Period (202 BC–AD 220)*. London: George Allen and Unwin, 1982.

———, ed. *Early Chinese Texts: A Bibliographical Guide*. Berkeley: Society for the Study of Early China and the Institute of East Asian Studies, University of California, Berkeley, 1993.

———. *Divination, Mythology and Monarchy in Han China*. Cambridge: Cambridge University Press, 1994.

———. "Man and Beast: The Hybrid in Early Chinese Art and Literature." In his *Divination, Mythology and Monarchy in Han China*, 38–54.

———. "State Funerals of the Han Empire." *Bulletin of the Museum of Far Eastern Antiquities* 71 (1999): 5–72.

———. "The Heritage Left to the Empires." In *The Cambridge History of Ancient China*, ed. Michael Loewe and Edward L. Shaughnessy, 967–1032.

———, and Edward L. Shaughnessy, eds. *The Cambridge History of Ancient China: From the Origins of Civilization to 221 B.C.* Cambridge: Cambridge University Press, 1999.

Mackenzie, Colin. "The Evolution of Southern Bronze Styles in China during the Eastern Zhou Period." *Bulletin of the Oriental Ceramic Society of Hong Kong* 7 (1984-1986): 31–48.

———. "Chu Bronze Work: A Unilinear Tradition or a Synthesis of Diverse Sources?" In *New Perspectives on Chu Culture During the Eastern Zhou Period*, ed. Thomas Lawton, 107–57.

———. "Meaning and Style in the Art of Chu." In *The Problem of Meaning in Early Chinese Ritual Bronzes*, ed. Roderick Whitfield, 119–49. London: School of Oriental and African Studies, University of London, 1993.

———. "Review of *Death in Ancient China: The Tale of One Man's Journey*, by Constance A. Cook." *Journal of Asian Studies* 67.2 (2008): 683–85.

Major, John S. "Research Priorities in the Study of Ch'u Religion." *History of Religion* 17. 3/4 (1978): 226–43.

———. *Heaven and Earth in Early Han Thought: Chapters Three, Four and Five of* Huainanzi. Albany: State University of New York Press, 1993.

———. "Characteristics of Late Chu Religion." In *Defining Chu: Image and Reality in Ancient China*, ed. Constance A. Cook and John S. Major, 121–144. Honolulu: University of Hawai'i Press, 1999.

Maquet, Jacques. "Objects as Instruments, Objects as Signs." In *History from Things: Essays on Material Culture*, ed. Steven Lubar and W. David Kingery, 30–40. Washington, DC: Smithsonian Institution Press, 1993.

Maspero, Henri. "Légendes mythologiques dans le Chou King." *Journal asiatique* 204 (1924): 1–100.

———. "Le mot *ming*." *Journal asiatique* 223 (1933): 249–96.

———. *Taoism and Chinese Religion*. Amherst: University of Massachusetts Press, 1981.

Mattos, Gilbert L. "Eastern Zhou Bronze Inscriptions." In *New Sources of Early Chinese History: An Introduction to the Reading of Inscriptions and Manuscripts*, ed. Edward L. Shaughnessy, 85–124. Berkeley: Society for the Study of Early China and Institute of East Asian Studies, University of California, Berkeley, 1997.

Merrifield, Ralph. *The Archaeology of Ritual and Magic*. New York: New Amsterdam Books, 1987.

Metcalf, Peter, and Richard Huntington. *Celebrations of Death: The Anthropology of Mortuary Ritual*. Cambridge: Cambridge University Press, 1991.

Michalowski, Piotr. "History as Charter: Some Observations on the Sumerian King List." *Journal of the American Oriental Society* 103 (1983): 237–48.

Mitchell, Allan. "Philippe Ariès and the French Way of Death." *French Historical Studies* 10 (1978): 684–95.

Mitchell, Jon P. "Performance." In *Handbook of Material Culture*, ed. Christopher Tilley et al., 384–401. London: Sage Publications, 2006.

Mitchell, W. J. T. *Picture Theory: Essays on Verbal and Visual Representation*. Chicago: University of Chicago Press, 1994.

Monmonier, Mark S. *Maps, Distortion, and Meaning*. Washington, DC: Association of American Geographers, 1977.

Morris, Ian. *Burial and Ancient Society: The Rise of Greek City-States*. Cambridge: Cambridge University Press, 1987.

———. "Attitudes toward Death in Archaic Greece." *Classical Antiquity* 8.2 (1989): 296–320.

———. *Death Ritual and Social Structure in Classical Antiquity*. Cambridge: Cambridge University Press, 1992.

Mote, Frederick W. *Intellectual Foundations of China*. 1971. Reprint, New York: Alfred A. Knopf, 1989.

Needham, Joseph A., and Lu Gwei-djen. *Science and Civilisation in China: Chemistry and Chemical Technology*, Part II. Cambridge: Cambridge University Press, 1974.

Needham, Joseph A., and Colin A. Ronan. "Chinese Cosmology." In *Encyclopedia of Cosmology: Historical, Philosophical, and Scientific Foundations of Modern Cosmology*, ed. Norriss S. Hetherington, 63–70. New York: Garland Publishing, 1993.

Nickerson, Peter. "Taoism, Death, and Bureaucracy in Early Medieval China." PhD dissertation, University of California, Berkeley, 1996.

———. "'Opening the Way': Exorcism, Travel, and Soteriology in Early Daoist Mortuary Practice and Its Antecedents." In *Daoist Identity: History, Lineage, and Ritual*, ed. Livia Kohn and Harold D. Roth, 58–77. Honolulu: University of Hawai'i Press, 2002.

Nissen, Hans J., Peter Damerow, and Robert K. Englund. *Archaic Bookkeeping: Early Writing and Techniques of Economic Administration in the Ancient Near East*. Trans. Paul Larsen. Chicago: University of Chicago Press, 1993.

Nylan, Michael. "On the Politics of Pleasure." *Asia Major*, 3rd ser., 65.1 (2001): 73–124.

———. "Toward an Archaeology of Writing: Text, Ritual, and the Culture of Public Display in the Classical Period (475 BC–AD 220)." In *Text and Ritual in Early China*, ed. Martin Kern, 3–49. Seattle: University of Washington Press, 2005.

———. "Empire in the Classical Era in China (304 BC–AD 316)." *Oriens Extremus* 46 (2007): 1–36.

———. "Beliefs about Seeing: Optics and Moral Technologies in Early China." *Asia Major*, 3rd ser., 21.1 (2008): 89–132.

Oppenheim, A. Leo. *Ancient Mesopotamia: Portrait of a Dead Civilization*. Chicago: University of Chicago Press, 1977.

Pader, Ellen-Jane. *Symbolism, Social Relations and the Interpretation of Mortuary Remains*. Oxford: B.A.R., 1982.

Palgi, Phyllis, and Henry Abramovitch. "Death: A Cross-Cultural Perspective." *Annual Review of Anthropology* 13 (1984): 385–417.

Pankenier, David W. "The Metempsychosis of the Moon." *Bulletin of the Museum of Far Eastern Antiquities* 58 (1986): 149–59.

———. "The Cosmo-political Background of Heaven's Mandate." *Early China* 20 (1995): 121–76.

Paper, Jordan. *The Spirits are Drunk: Comparative Approaches to Chinese Religion*. Albany, NY: State University of New York Press, 1995.

Park, D. A. *The Fire within the Eye: A Historical Essay on the Nature and Meaning of Light*. Princeton, NJ: Princeton University Press, 1997.

Pearson, James L. *Shamanism and the Ancient Mind*. Walnut Creek, CA: Altamira, 2002.

Pearson, Mike, and Michael Shanks, eds. *Theater/Archaeology*. New York: Routledge, 2001.

Peebles, Christopher S. "Moundville and Surrounding Sites: Some Structural Considerations of Mortuary Practices." In *Approaches to the Social Dimensions of Mortuary Practices*, ed. James A. Brown, 68–91. Washington, DC: Society for American Archaeology, 1971.

Petrey, Sandy. *Speech Acts and Literary Theory*. New York: Routledge, 1990.

Pines, Yuri. "Intellectual Change in the Chunqiu Period: The Reliability of the Speeches in the Zuo Zhuan as Sources of Chunqiu Intellectual History." *Early China* 22 (1997): 77–132.

———. *Foundations of Confucian Thought: Intellectual Life in the Chunqiu Period, 722–453 B.C.E.* Honolulu: University of Hawai'i Press, 2002.

———. History as a Guide to the Netherworld: Rethinking the Chunqiu shiyu." *Journal of Chinese Religions* 31 (2003): 101–26.

———. *Envisioning Eternal Empire: Chinese Political Thought of the Warring States Era*. Honolulu: University of Hawai'i Press, 2009.

Pirazzoli-t'Serstevens, Michèle. "Imperial Aura and the Image of the Other in Han Art." In *Conceiving the Empire: China and Rome Compared*, ed. Fritz-Heiner Mutschler and Achim Mittag, 299–317. Oxford: Oxford University Press, 2008.

———. "Death and the Dead: Practices and Images in the Qin and Han." In *Early Chinese Religion, Part One: Shang through Han (1250 BC–220 AD)*, ed. John Lagerwey and Marc Kalinowski, 949–1026. Leiden: Brill, 2009.

Poo, Mu-chou (= Pu Muzhou). "Ideas concerning Death and Burial in Pre-Han and Han China." *Asia Major*, 3rd ser., 3.2 (1990): 25–62.

———. "Popular Religion in Pre-Imperial China: Observations on the Almanacs of Shui-hu-ti." *T'oung Pao* 79 (1993): 225–48.

———. *In Search of Personal Welfare: A View of Ancient Chinese Religion*. Albany: State University of New York Press, 1998.

———. 2004. "The Concept of Ghost in Ancient Chinese Religion." In *Religion and Chinese Society*, Vol. 1: *Ancient and Medieval China*, ed. John Lagerwey, 173–91. Hong Kong: Chinese University Press, 2004.

———. "Afterlife: Chinese Concepts." In *The Encyclopedia of Religion*, new ed., ed. Lindsay Jones, vol. 1, 169–72. New York: Macmillan Co., 2005.

———. *Enemies of Civilization: Attitudes toward Foreigners in Ancient Mesopotamia, Egypt and China*. Albany: State University of New York Press, 2005.

———. "How to Steer through Life: Negotiating Fate in the Daybook." In *Magnitude of Ming: Command, Allotment, and Fate in Chinese Culture*, ed. Christopher Lupke, 107–25. Honolulu: University of Hawai'i Press, 2005.

Postgate, Nicholas, Tao Wang, and Toby Wilkinson. "The Evidence for Early Writing: Utilitarian or Ceremonial." *Antiquity* 69 (1995): 459–80.

Powers, Martin J. "Artistic Taste, the Economy and the Social Order in Former Han China." *Art History* 9.3 (1986): 285–305.

———. "Unit Style and System Style: A Preliminary Exploration." In *Zhongguo kaoguxue yu lishixue zhi zhenghe yanjiu*, ed. Zang Zhenhua, vol. 2, 743–91.

———. "Classical Chinese Ornament and the Origins of 'Taste' in China." In *New Perspectives on China's Past: Chinese Archaeology in the Twentieth Century*, ed. Yang Xiaoneng, 287–95. Vol. 1. New Haven, CT: Yale University Press, 2004.

———. *Pattern and Person: Ornament, Society, and Self in Classical China*. Cambridge, MA: Harvard University Asia Center, 2006.

Pratt, Mary Louise. *Imperial Eyes: Travel Writing and Transculturation*. New York: Routledge, 1992.

Puett, Michael J. *To Become a God: Cosmology, Sacrifice, and Self-Divinization in Early China*. Cambridge, MA: Harvard University Asia Center, 2002.

———. "Combing the Ghosts and Spirits, Centering the Realm: Mortuary Ritual and Political Organization in the Ritual Compendia of Early China." In *Early Chinese Religion, Part One: Shang through Han (1250 BC–220 AD)*, ed. John Lagerwey and Marc Kalinowski, 695–720. Leiden: Brill, 2009.

Qu Yuan, et al. *The Songs of the South: An Ancient Chinese Anthology of Poems by Qu Yuan and Other Poets*. Trans. David Hawkes. Harmondsworth, Middlesex, UK: Penguin Books, 1985.

Rapoport, Amos. *House Form and Culture*. Englewood Cliffs, NJ: Prentice-Hall, 1969.

———. *The Meaning of the Built Environment: A Nonverbal Communication Approach*. Beverly Hills: Sage Publications, 1982.

Rawson, Jessica. "Chinese Burial Patterns: Sources of Information on Thought and Belief." In *Cognition and Material Culture: The Archaeology of Symbolic Storage*, ed. Colin Renfrew and Chris Scarre, 107–33. McDonald Institute for Archaeological Research, 1998.

———. "The Eternal Palaces of the Western Han: A New View of the Universe." *Artibus Asiae* 59.1-2 (1999): 5–58.

Renfrew, Colin. "The Archaeology of Religion." In *The Ancient Mind: Elements of Cognitive Archeology*, ed. Colin Renfrew and Ezra B. Zubrow, 47–54. Cambridge University Press, 1994.

Renfrew, Colin, and Ezra B. Zubrow, eds. *The Ancient Mind: Elements of Cognitive Archeology*. Cambridge: Cambridge University Press, 1994.

Reynolds, Frank E., and Sheryl L. Burkhalter, eds. *Beyond the Classics? Essays in Religious Studies and Liberal Education*. Atlanta, GA: Scholars Press, 1990.

Richards, Janet E., and Mary Van Buren, eds. *Order, Legitimacy, and Wealth in Ancient States*. Cambridge: Cambridge University Press, 2000.

Riegel, Jeffrey K. "Kou-Mang and Ju-Shou." *Cahiers d'Extrême-Asie* 5 (1989–1990), 55–83.

——— "Do Not Serve the Dead as You Serve the Living: The Lüshi chunqiu Treatises on Moderation in Burial." *Early China* 20 (1995): 301–30.

Robben, Antonius C. G. M., ed. *Death, Mourning, and Burial: A Cross-cultural Reader*. Malden, MA: Blackwell Publishers, 2004.

Rosenblatt, Paul C., R. Patricia Walsh, and Douglas A. Jackson. *Grief and Mourning in Cross-cultural Perspective*. New Haven, CT: Human Relations Area Files Press, 1976.

Sagart, Laurent. *The Roots of Old Chinese*. Amsterdam and Philadelphia: John Benjamins Publishing Company, 1999.

Sagart, Laurent, Roger Blench, and Alicia Sanchez-Mazas, eds. *The Peopling of East Asia: Putting together Archaeology, Linguistics and Genetics*. London: RoutledgeCurzon, 2005.

Sage, Steven F. *Ancient Sichuan and the Unification of China*. Albany: State University of New York Press, 1992.

Salmony, Alfred. *Antler and Tongue: An Essay on Ancient Chinese Symbolism and Its Implications. Artibus Asiae, supplementum* 13. Ascona, Switzerland: Artibus Asiae Publishers, 1954.

Sangren, P. Steven. *History and Magical Power in a Chinese Community*. Stanford: Stanford University Press, 1987.

Saxe, Arthur A. "Social Dimensions of Mortuary Practices." PhD dissertation, University of Michigan, 1970.

Schaberg, David. *A Patterned Past: Form and Thought in Early Chinese Historiography*. Cambridge, MA: Harvard University Asia Center, 2001.

———. "Travel, Geography, and the Imperial Imagination in Fifth-Century Athens and Han China." *Comparative Literature* 51.2 (1999): 152–91.

Schafer, Edward H. *Pacing the Void: T'ang Approaches to the Stars*. Berkeley: University of California Press, 1977.

Schipper, Kristofer. *The Taoist Body*. Berkeley: University of California Press, 1993.

Schnapp, Alain. "Are Images Animated: The Psychology of Statues in Ancient Greece." In *The Ancient Mind: Elements of Cognitive Archaeology*, ed. Colin Renfrew and Ezra B. Zubrow, 40–44. Cambridge: Cambridge University Press, 1994.

Schneider, Rebecca. *The Explicit Body in Performance*. London: Routledge, 1997.

Schopen, Gregory. "Archaeology and Protestant Presuppositions in the Study of Indian Buddhism." In his *Bones, Stones, and Buddhist Monks: Collected Papers on the Archaeology, Epigraphy, and Texts of Monastic Buddhism in India*, 1–22. 1991. Reprint, Honolulu: University of Hawai'i Press, 1997.

———. "Burial *Ad Sanctos* and the Physical Presence of the Buddha in Early Indian Buddhism: A Study in the Archaeology of Religions." In his *Bones, Stones, and Buddhist Monks: Collected Papers on the Archaeology, Epigraphy, and Texts of Monastic Buddhism in India*, 114–47. Honolulu: University of Hawai'i Press, 1997.

Schuessler, Axel. *A Dictionary of Early Zhou Chinese*. Honolulu: University of Hawai'i Press, 1987.

———. *ABC Etymological Dictionary of Old Chinese*. Honolulu: University of Hawai'i Press, 2007.

———. *Minimal Old Chinese and Later Han Chinese: A Companion to* Grammata Serica Recensa. Honolulu: University of Hawai'i Press, 2009.

Schwartz, Benjamin. *The World of Thought in Ancient China*. Cambridge, MA: Belknap Press, 1985.

Searle, John R. *Speech Acts: An Essay in the Philosophy of Language*. Cambridge: Cambridge University Press, 1969.

Seckel, Dietrich. "The Rise of Portraiture in Chinese Art." *Artibus Asiae* 53 (1993): 7–26.

Seidel, Anna K. "Tokens of Immortality in Han Graves: A Review of *Ways to Paradise*." *Numen* 29.1 (1982): 79–114.

———. "Afterlife: Chinese Concepts." In *The Encyclopedia of Religion*, Mircea Eliade, editor in chief, vol. 1, 124–26. New York: Macmillan, 1987.

———. "Traces of Han Religion in Funerary Texts Found in Tombs." In *Dōkyō toshūkyō bunka*, ed. Akizuki Kan'ei, 21–57 (page order reversed). Tokyo: Hirakawa shuppansha, 1987.

Shaughnessy, Edward L. "Extra-Lineage Cult in the Shang Dynasty: A Surrejoinder." *Early China* 11–12 (1985–1987): 182–94.

—————, ed. *New Sources of Early Chinese History: An Introduction to the Reading of Inscriptions and Manuscripts.* Berkeley: The Society for the Study of Early China, 1997.

Shelach, Gideon, and Yuri Pines. "Secondary State Formation and the Development of Local Identity: Change and Continuity in the State of Qin (770–221 B.C.)." In *Archaeology of Asia*, ed. M. T. Stark, 202–30. Oxford: Blackwell Publishing Ltd., 2006.

Shepherd, Rupert, and Robert Maniura, eds. *Presence: The Inherence of the Prototype within Images and Other Objects.* Aldershot, England: Ashgate, 2006.

So, Jenny F. *Eastern Zhou Ritual Bronzes from the Arthur M. Sackler Collections.* Cambridge, MA: Harvard University Press, 1995.

—————. "Chu Art: Link between the Old and New." In *Defining Chu: Image and Reality in Ancient China*, ed. Constance A. Cook and John S. Major, 33–50. Honolulu: University of Hawai'i Press, 1999.

Sourvinou-Inwood, Christiane. "To Die and Enter the House of Hades: Homer, Before and After." In *Mirrors of Mortality: Studies in the Social History of Death*, ed. Joachim Whaley, 15–39. London: St. Martin's Press, 1981.

—————. "A Trauma in Flux: Death in the Eighth Century and After." In *The Greek Renaissance of the Eighth Century B.C: Tradition and Innovation, Proceedings of the Second International Symposium, 1–5 June, 1981*, ed. Robin Hägg, 33–49. Stockholm: Svenska institutet i Athen; Lund, Sweden: Distributor, P. Åström, 1983.

—————. *"Reading" Greek Death: To the End of the Classical Period.* New York: Oxford University Press, 1995.

Spiro, Audrey. *Contemplating the Ancients: Aesthetic and Social Issues in Early Chinese Portraiture.* Berkeley: University of California Press, 1990.

Starosta, Stanley. "Proto-East Asian and the Origin and Dispersal of the Languages of East and Southeast Asia and the Pacific." In *The Peopling of East Asia: Putting Together Archaeology, Linguistics and Genetics*, ed. Laurent Sagart, Roger Blench, and Alicia Sanchez-Mazas, 182–97. London: Routledge Curzon, 2005.

Steele, John. *The I-li or Book of Etiquette and Ceremonial.* 2 vols. London: Probsthain & Co., 1971.

Stein, Rolf A. "Architecture et pensée religieuse en Extrême-Orient." *Arts asiatiques* 4 (1957): 163–86.

—————. *The World in Miniature: Container Gardens and Dwelling in Far Eastern Religious Thought.* Trans. Phyllis Brooks. Stanford: Stanford University Press, 1990.

Stone, Lawrence. *The Past and the Present Revisited.* London: Taylor & Francis, Ltd., 1987.

Strickmann, Michel. "History, Anthropology, and Chinese Religion (review article)." *Harvard Journal of Asiatic Studies* 40.1 (1980): 201–48.

Sukhu, Gopal. "Monkeys, Shamans, Emperors and Poets: The Chuci and Images of Chu during the Han Dyansty." In *Defining Chu: Image and Reality in Ancient China*, ed. Constance A. Cook and John S. Major, 145–65.

Sullivan, Lawrence E. "'Seeking an End to the Primary Text' or 'Putting an End to the Text as Primary.'" In *Beyond the Classics?: Essays in Religious Studies and Liberal Education*, ed. Frank E. Reynolds and Sheryl L. Burkhalter, 41–59. Atlanta, Ga.: Scholars Press, 1990.

Tambiah, Stanley J. "Animals Are Good to Think and Good to Prohibit." *Ethnology* 8 (1969): 423–59.

—————. *Culture, Thought, and Social Action: An Anthropological Perspective.* Cambridge, MA: Harvard University Press, 1985.

Thatcher, Melvin P. "Kinship and Government in Chu during the Spring and Autumn Era, 722–453 B.C." PhD dissertation, University of Washington, 2004.

Thompson, Laurence G. "On the Prehistory of Hell in China." *Journal of Chinese Religion* 17 (1989): 27–41.

Thompson, Lydia D. "The Yi'nan Tomb: Narrative and Ritual in Pictorial Art of the Eastern Han (25–220 C.E.)." PhD dissertation, New York University, 1998.

Thompson, Stuart E. "Death, Food and Fertility." In *Death Ritual in Late Imperial and Modern China*, ed. James L. Watson and Evelyn S. Rawshi, 71–108. Berkeley: University of California Press, 1988.

Thorp, Robert L. "The Qin and Han Imperial Tombs and the Development of Mortuary Architecture." In *The Quest for Eternity: Chinese Ceramic Sculptures from the People's Republic of China*, ed. George Kuwayama, Los Angeles County Museum of Art, 17–37. San Francisco: Chronicle Books, 1987.

———. "Mountain Tombs and Jade Burial Suits: Preparations for Eternity in the Western Han." In *Ancient Mortuary Traditions of China: Papers on Chinese Ceramic Funerary Sculptures*, ed. George Kuwayama, 26–39. Los Angeles: Los Angeles County Museum of Art, 1991.

Thote, Alain. "The Double Coffin of Leigudun Tomb No. 1: Iconographic Sources and Related Problems." In *New Perspectives on Chu Culture during the Eastern Zhou Period*, ed. Thomas Lawton, 23–46.

———. "Aspects of the Serpent on Eastern Zhou Bronze and Lacquerware." In *The Problem of Meaning in Early Chinese Ritual Bronzes*, ed. Roderick Whitfield, 150–60. London: School of Oriental and African Studies, 1993.

———. "Continuities and Discontinuities: Chu Burials during the Eastern Zhou Period." In *Exploring China's Past: New Discoveries and Studies in Archaeology and Art*, ed. Roderick Whitfield and Wang Tao, 189–204. London: Saffron, 1999.

———. "Intercultural Relations as Seen from Chinese Pictorial Bronzes of the Fifth Century BCE." *Res* 35 (1999): 10–41.

———. "Burial Practices as Seen in Rulers' Tombs of the Eastern Zhou Period: Patterns and Regional Traditions." In *Religion and Chinese Society*, ed. John Lagerwey, vol. 1, 65–107.

———. "Au-delà du monde connu: Représenter les dieux." *Arts asiatiques* 61 (2006): 57–74.

———. "Pratiques funéraires dans le royaume de Chu (Chine du Centre-Sud, VIᵉ–IIIᵉ siècles avant J.-C.): De la représentation du statut social à l'expression d'un destin individuel." In *Pratiques funéraires et sociétés: Nouvelles approches en archéologie et en anthropologie sociale*, ed. Luc Baray, Patrice Brun, and Alain Testard, 359–67. Dijon: Éditions Universitaires de Dijon, 2007.

———. "Artists and Craftsmen in the Late Bronze Age of China (Eighth to Third Centuries BC): Art in Transition." *Proceedings of the British Academy* 154 (2008): 201–41.

———. "Chinese Coffins from the First Millennium B.C. and Early Images of the Afterworld." *RES* 61/62 (2012): 22–40.

Trigger, Bruce G. *Time and Traditions, Essays in Archaeological Interpretation*. Edinburgh: Edinburgh University Press, 1978.

———. *Understanding Early Civilizations*. Cambridge: Cambridge University Press, 2003.

Tschumi, Bernard. "Violence of Architecture." *Artforum* 20.1 (1981): 44–47.

———. *Architecture and Disjunction*. Cambridge, MA: MIT Press, 1994.

Tuan, Yi-Fu. *Topophilia: A Study of Environmental Perception, Attitudes, and Values*. Englewood Cliffs, NJ: Prentice-Hall, 1974.

———. *Landscapes of Fear*. New York: Pantheon Books, 1979.

Turnbull, David. "Performance and Narrative, Bodies and Movement in the Construction of Places and Objects, Spaces and Knowledges: The Case of the Maltese Megaliths." *Theory, Culture & Society* 19.5/6 (2002): 125–43.

Unschuld, Paul U. *Medicine in China: A History of Ideas*. Berkeley: University of California Press, 1985.

van Gennep, Arnold. *The Rites of Passage*. Trans. Monika B. Vizedom and Gabrielle L. Caffee. Chicago: University of Chicago Press, 1960. First published in French in 1909.

Vandermeersch, Léon. *Wang Dao ou La voie royale: Recherches sur l'esprit des institutions de la Chine archaïque*. 2 vols. Paris: Maisonneuve, 1977 and 1980.

Varner, Eric R. *Mutilation and Transformation:* Damnatio Memoriae *and Roman Imperial Portraiture*. Leiden: Brill, 2004.

Vermeule, Emily. *Aspects of Death in Early Greek Art and Poetry*. Berkeley: University of California Press, 1984.

Von Glahn, Richard. *The Sinister Way: The Divine and the Demonic in Chinese Religious Culture*. Berkeley: University of California Press, 2004.

Vovelle, Michel. "Les attitudes devant la mort: Problèmes différentes de méthode, approches et lectures différentes." *Annales (ESC)* 31 (1976): 120–32.

———. *La mort et l'Occident de 1300 à nos jours*. Paris: Gallimard, 1983.

Wang, Aihe. *Cosmology and Political Culture in Early China*. Cambridge: Cambridge University Press, 2000.

Wang, Haicheng. *Writing and the State in Early China in Comparative Perspective*. Cambridge: Cambridge University Press, forthcoming.

Wang, Michelle. "The Forms and Functions of Mat Weights." In *A Bronze Menagerie: Mat Weights of Early China*, ed. Michelle C. Wang, Guolong Lai, Roel Sterckx, and Eugene Yuejin Wang, 19–33. Boston, MA: Isabella Stewart Gardner Museum, 2006.

Wang, Zhongshu. *Han Civilization*. Trans. K. C. Chang. New Haven, CT: Yale University Press, 1982.

Watson, James L. "Of Flesh and Bones: The Management of Death Pollution in Cantonese Society." In *Death and the Regeneration of Life*, ed. Bloch and Parry, 155–86.

———. "The Structure of Chinese Funerary Rites: Elementary Forms, Ritual Sequence, and the Primacy of Performance." In *Death Ritual in Late Imperial and Modern China*, ed. James L. Watson and Evelyn S. Rawski, 3–19. Berkeley: University of California Press, 1988.

———. "Rites or Beliefs? The Construction of a Unified Culture in Late Imperial China." In *China's Quest for National Identity*, ed. Lowell Dittmer and Samuel S. Kim, 80–103. Ithaca: Cornell University Press, 1993.

Watson, William. "Traditions of Material Culture in the Territory of Ch'u." In *Early Chinese Art and Its Possible Influence in the Pacific Basin*, ed. Noel Barnard, 77–102. Vol. 1. New York: Intercultural Arts Press, 1972.

Weiner, Annette. *Inalienable Possessions: The Paradox of Keeping while Giving*. Berkeley: University of California Press, 1992.

Weld, Susan. "Covenant in Jin's Walled Cities: The Discoveries at Houma and Wenxian." PhD dissertation, Harvard University, 1990.

———. "Chu Law in Action: Legal Documents from Tomb 2 at Baoshan." In *Defining Chu: Image and Reality in Ancient China*, ed. Cook and Major, 77–97.

Whitfield, Roderick, ed. *The Problem of Meaning in Early Chinese Ritual Bronzes*. London: Percival David Foundation, 1993.

Wolf, Arthur P., ed. *Religion and Ritual in Chinese Society*. Stanford: Stanford University Press, 1974.

———. "God, Ghosts, and Ancestors." In *Religion and Ritual in Chinese Society*, ed. Wolf, 131–82.

Wu, Hung. "The Earliest Pictorial Representations of Ape Tales." *T'oung Pao* 73.1 (1987): 86–112.

———. "From Temple to Tomb: Ancient Chinese Art and Religion in Transition." *Early China* 13 (1988): 78–115.

———. *The Wu Liang Shrine: The Ideology of Early Chinese Pictorial Art*. Stanford: Stanford University Press, 1989.

———. "Art in Its Ritual Context: Rethinking Mawangdui." *Early China* 17 (1992): 111–45.

———. *Monumentality in Early Chinese Art and Architecture.* Stanford: Stanford University Press, 1995.

———. "Where Are They Going? Where Did They Come From?: Hearse and 'Soul-carriage' in Han Dynasty Tomb Art." *Orientations* 6 (1998): 22–31.

———. "The Art and Architecture of the Warring States Period." In *The Cambridge History of Ancient China*, ed. Michael Loewe and Edward L. Shaughnessy, 651–744.

———. "A Deity without Form: The Earliest Representation of Laozi and the Concept of Wei in Chinese Ritual Art." *Orientations* 4 (2002): 38–45.

———. *The Art of the Yellow Springs: Understanding Chinese Tombs.* Honolulu: University of Hawai'i Press, 2010.

Yates, Robin D. S. "Soldiers, Scribes, and Women: Literacy among the Lower Orders in Early China." In *Writing and Literacy in Early China: Studies from the Columbia Early China Seminar*, ed. Li Feng and David Prager Branner, 339–69.

———. "Purity and Pollution in Early China." In *Zhongguo kaoguxue yu lishixue zhi zhenghe yanjiu* 中國考古學與歷史學之整合研究, ed. Zang Zhenhua, vol. 2: 479–536.

Yü, Ying-shih. "Life and Immortality in the Mind of Han China." *Harvard Journal of Asiatic Studies* 25 (1964): 80–122.

———. "'O Soul, Come Back!' A Study in the Changing Conceptions of the Soul and Afterlife in Pre-Buddhist China." *Harvard Journal of Asiatic Studies* 47.2 (1987): 363–95.

Zaleski, Carol. *Otherworld Journey: Accounts of Near-Death Experience in Medieval and Modern Times.* New York and Oxford: Oxford University Press, 1987.

Zheng, Yan. "Concerning the Viewers of Han Mortuary Art." In *Rethinking Recarving: Ideals, Practices, and Problems of the "Wu Family Shrines" and Han China*, trans. Eileen Hsiang-ling Hsu, 92–109. New Haven, CT: Yale University Press, 2008.

Index

Note: italic page numbers indicate illustrations

access ramps: distance to burial surface and, 213n101; in early Han period, 213n101; in horizontal chamber-style tombs, 86, 88; in vertical tombs, 2; Warring States tombs and, 67

afterlife, conceptions of: ancestral sacrifice and, 60–63; before Buddhism, 23, 228n36; burial texts and, 190; as cosmic journey, 12, 161, 191; ritual specialists and, 156–59; in Spring and Autumn period, 43–46, 61–62; in Warring States period, 162–66; in Western Han period, 46, 161, 162–63, 164, 187, 191. *See also* ancestor cults; attitudes toward the dead; cosmology; cult of the dead; liminal stage; spirit journeys

almanacs, 20, 64, 144; journeys and, 167, 183; language in, 155, 163. *See also* daybooks

Analects (Lunyu), 13, 34

ancestor cults: burial structure and, 58–60, 80; changes in Warring States pantheon and, 32–36; collective benevolence and, 28, 102, 190; cults of the dead and, 211n48; fecundity god and, 128; "good" and "evil" in, 43; images in, 102–3, 219n62, 219n65; otherworldly journey and, 61–62, 162, 185, 210n37, 228n39; spirit possession and, 130, 132. *See also* cult of the dead

ancestral sacrifice: exclusivity and, 33–34, 203n44; objects used in, 175, 210n28; shift

in emphasis and, 28, 35, 60–63, 80, 97, 190. *See also* sacrificial spaces in tombs

ancestral temple, 60–61, 64, 94, 184. *See also* lineage cemeteries; temple-tomb dualism

ancient Greece, 141, 200n13

aniconism. *See* anthropomorphic images; early Chinese art; "image taboo"; spirit tablet; stone tablets; wooden tablets

anthropomorphic images: attitudes toward the dead and, 190; Neolithic sculptures and, 99–101, *100*; Shang gods and, 102; Warring States use of, 12, 99, 115, 122. *See also* fecundity god; hybrid imagery

Anyang City, Henan, Shang tombs at: divination records from, 102, 137; human imagery and, 102–3, *104*, Plate 9. *See also* Houjiazhuang site, Anyang City, Henan

apotropaic rituals, 177–83

archaeological approaches, 12–16, 19, 23; "cultural spheres" and, 198n81; excavated religious texts in, 25; interpretation in, 16–21, 186; source limitations and, 19–21; spirit artifacts and, 51–53

Ariès, Philippe, 29

Armstrong, Robert Plant, 216n1

Art Institute of Chicago, *126*

artificial light, 220n87. *See also* lamps in tombs

artworks. *See* early Chinese art

At-the-Water (Shuishang), spirit of, 31, 202n31

attitudes toward the dead: funeral rites and, 117–20; "personalized death" and, 190; post-mortem intelligence and, 208n139; spatial implications of, 190; Warring States shifts in, 28–29, 34–35, 46–51, 190; Western studies of, 29, 200n13. *See also* liminal stage; violent death

Bachofen, Johann Jakob, 128

bad death, 36, 53, 190. *See also* ghost narratives; posterity, those who died without; Shao Tuo

Bagley, Robert W., 15, 223n21

Bai Qi (Qin general), 47

Baiji site, Xuzhou City, Jiangsu, 216n172

Baizicun site, Xunyi County, Shaanxi, 96

Balingshan site, Jiangling County, Hubei, 67–68

bamboo manuscripts, religious nature of, 25–28, 26–27. *See also* burial texts; divination records; funerary texts; sacrificial records

banner paintings, 13, 23, 116–17, 118, 119, 121

Baoshan site, Jingmen City, Hubei, 51–52; burial structure in, 69, 76, 77; funerary-object lists from, 139–40, 142, 146, 174–83, 176; human figurines from, 109–10, 115; pantheon and, 53, 171; religious texts from, 25–28, 26–27, 29–32, 50, 157–58, 227n18; tomb figurines in, 109–10, 218n32; travel and, 51–52, 132–33, 174–83, 176, 178, 182; types of ritual objects at, 179; Warring States grave goods and, 50–53, 62–63, 103, 104; wooden tablets from, 103, 104, 135. *See also* Shao Tuo

Baoxiangsi site, Guangshan County, Henan, 66, 70, 128, 213n92

Basalla, George, 232n98

Bauer, Wolfgang, 225n88

Beidongshan site, Xuzhou City, Jiangsu, 7–9, 8, 10, 90

Berger, Peter L., 21

Bianzhuang site, Fengyang County, Anhui, 78, 79

blameless dead (*bugu*), 31, 32, 35, 152, 202n32

Bloch, Maurice, 128

Bokenkamp, Stephen, 200n6

Book of Poetry (Shijing), 62, 102, 109, 183

Book of Rites (Liji): human figures and, 102,

109; levels of sacrifices and, 206n113; liminal stage and, 93–94, 120; meaning of rites and, 158; reading of lists and, 145

Bourdieu, Pierre, 145

Boyou (Liang Xiao, Chu nobleman), 43–44, 46

brick chamber-style tombs. *See* horizontal chamber-style tombs

British Museum, 126

bronze inscriptions: abode of the dead and, 162, 185; good death and, 36; identity of tomb occupants and, 40, 70, 123, 155; potency of ancestors and, 28, 35, 162; social memory of enemies and, 39–40, 42. *See also* ritual bronze vessels

Buddhism, introduction of, 13, 22, 23, 228n36

burial artifacts. *See* grave goods

burial ideology: ritual vessels and, 60–61; stave-walled tombs and, 80–81; vertical pit-style tombs and, 56–60; Warring States transition in, 55, 191

"The Burial of Zijia of Zheng" (Chu manuscript), 38–39

burial rites, denial of, 38–39

burial space, 55–97; Beidongshan rock-cut tomb and, 7, 9; as chariot, 74–75; compartmentalization of, 73, 74, 83–84, 212n58; as cosmological model, 77–80; cross-shaped tomb structure and, 62, 70, 77–80, 79; elite Warring States tombs and, 3, 5–6, 63–80, 89, 90, 193n3, 213n102; in Han period, 84–88, 87, 90–93, 91, 92; hiding of corpse vs. display of wealth and, 55, 58–60, 68–69, 70; horizontal chamber-style tomb structure and, 80–93; as house, 70–73; joint burial practices and, 55–56, 69–70; mound development and, 65–68, 78; as palace, 73–74; Shang-Zhou elite tombs and, 58, 59, 62, 66, 81; shifts in ancestral sacrifice and, 60–63, 80–93; tomb plans and, 2, 7–8, 87, 108; transitional structures and, 81–89; vertical pit-style ideology and, 56–60; Warring States innovations in, 63–80; as way station, 75–77. *See also* horizontal chamber-style tombs; mounded burials; size and shape of tombs; vertical pit-style tombs

burial texts, 2; communication with spirit world and, 12, 190; cosmic cord-hook diagram on, 230n72; from elite Chu burials, 29–32; interpretation of artifacts and,

15–16, 196n58; language in, 21, 198n90; notions of afterlife and, 190; pre-Buddhist religion and, 23; regional differences and, 20–21. *See also* divination records; funerary texts; sacrificial records

Campany, Robert Ford, 211n48

Caojiagan site, Dangyang County, Hubei, 111, 128, 140, 218n42, Plate 11

catacombs, 55, 65

chamber of peace (*pianfang*), 89–90

chamber of rest (*qin*), 64, 94

Chang, K. C., 130

Changsha City, Hunan: Chu objects from tombs near, 16; stave-walled tombs near, 215n141

Changtaiguan site, Xinyang City, Henan, 110, 111, 140, 208n142

chariots: burial of, 2, 51, 107, 146; in inventory lists, 139, 140, 144, 175; social status and, 175; tomb as, 74–75; Warring States warfare and, 48

Chavannes, Édouard, 219n65

Chen Mengjia, 203n36

Chen Songchang, 131, 150, 229n56

Chen Wei, 231n94

Chen Zhongxing, Plate 7

Cheng Dechen (Zi Yu, Chu nobleman), 180

Chengpu, battlefield of, 46, 47. *See also* Xishuipo site, Puyang County, Henan

Chenjiadashan site, Changsga City, Hunan, 116, 117, 120

Cheqiao site, Jingmen City, Hubei, 129–30

"Chinese" (*huaxia*) cultural sphere, 11

Chinese State Administration for Cultural Heritage, 4

Christianity, 14, 104, 203n37

Chu, definitions of, 17, 196n67

Chu, kingdom of (Western Han dynasty), 9–10, 130, 194n15, 194n16, 196n67. *See also* Beidongshan site, Xuzhou City, Jiangsu; Western Han period

Chu, state of (?–223 BCE): bureaucracy in, 151, 157; burial spaces in, 63, 66; imagery in, 116, 120, 219n62; power of lineages in, 158; royal ancestors of, 30, 202n23; social status in, 68; tomb guardians and, 122; violent death and, 36; written materials from, 21; Zeng burials and, 73. *See also* elite burials; Shao Tuo

Chu religion: "otherness" and, 154–56; as "shamanistic," 198n84; as term, 197n67; *zushi, zuwei* in, 125. *See also* early Chinese religion; shamanism

Chu silk manuscript (Warring States period), 16, 129, 164, Plate 6

Chulan site, Su County, Anhui, 216n172

classical written sources. *See* text-centered scholarship

Classics of Mountains and Seas, 130, 164, 228n21

clay layers (*baigaoni, qinggaoni*), 6, 78, 89, 193n9

cliff tombs. *See* horizontal chamber-style tombs

coffin (*guan*): burial outside lineage cemeteries, 38–39; decoration of, 70–71, 76, 121, 129, 171, 174, Plate 7, Plate 8; double, in Marquis Yi's tomb, 213n97; in horizontal chamber-style tombs, 9, 88–89, 90–92, 93–94, 95; of Marquis Yi, 73–74, Plate 7; in mounded burials, 66–67; placement of burial objects and, 107, 111, *112*, *121*, 140, 144; in vertical pit-style tombs, 2, *3*, *4*, 5, 50, 55–56, 57, 58, 64–65, 107; word for, 209n19. *See also* encasements; joint burial practices

commoners: burials of, 17, 19, 58, 68, 97, 212n54; as diviners, 157–58; funerary texts and, 147–50, 159; grave goods and, 109; war dead and, 29, 46, 48; in Warring States period, 12, 19. *See also* war dead

companions in death (*xunren*): burial structure and, 66–67, 74, 78, 79, 107; deities and, 155; identities of, 105, 107; tomb figurines and, 105, 107, 109

compartments in tombs, 83–84, 212n58; artifacts in, 110, 111, 131, 133, 140, 144, 148, 231n92; earliest tomb with, 212n58; horizontal chamber-style tombs and, 65, 86, 88–89; orientation of the corpse and, 83; placement of grave goods and, 140; sacrificial space and, 90–92; structure of lists and, 140; tomb as dwelling and, 70–77; vertical pit-style burials and, *4–5*, 50–51, 62–63, 69, 76, 81–83, *82*, 86; Warring States burials and, 62–63, 73–74, 76

Confucius, 11, 13, 66, 105, 217n30. *See also Analects; Book of Rites; Protocols of Ceremonies*

Congchen text, 167–68

Controller of Lifespan (Siming), 30, 32

convicts, funerary documents for, 147, 152–54, 159

core lineage ancestors, 33–34, 35

corpse: hiding of, 55, 58–60, 69; preservation of, 6, 7, 58, 60. *See also* attitudes toward the dead; coffin; human remains

cosmic consciousness, 170

cosmology: definition of, 21–23; Shang burial structures and, 70; *sifang* and *wuxing* shift and, 230n60; tame and wild spaces and, 170–74; timing of journeys and, 167–70; Warring States tomb innovations and, 12, 22, 75, 78, 79, 162. *See also* afterlife, conceptions of; directional axis; Mount Buzhou; northwest, preoccupation with; spirit journeys

Creel, Herrlee G., 13, 61

cross-shaped tomb structure, 62, 70, 77–80, 79

cult of the dead, 12, 46; development of, 45–46, 56; shift in burial style and, 12, 80, 190. *See also* afterlife, conceptions of

"cultural spheres," 198n81

Dabaotai tombs, near Beijing, 89, 90, 91

dagger axe, from Chequio site, Jingmen City, Hubei, 129–30

Dahekou site, Yicheng County, Shanxi, 105, 107

dao. See sacrifices

Dao Gu (tomb occupant, Chu official), 32–33, 157. *See also* Wangshan site, Jiangling County, Hubei

Daode jing, phrase in, 185–86

Daoism, 13, 132, 225n87

daxing, as term, 228n39

daybooks (*rishu*): cosmology and, 164; divination and, 167–69; Jiudian site and, 144, 155, 165, 167, 227n18; location of Mount Buzhou and, 164; Qin period and, 170, 171, 172, 202, 228n39, 228n42; travel and, 167–70, 171, 183, 185, 186; Warring States period and, 165, 174, 185; *zushi* and, 124, 125. *See also* almanacs

death as journey. *See* spirit journeys; travel paraphernalia

death pollution, 48, 56, 58, 60, 94, 154

depersonalized ancestors, 28, 102. *See also* ancestor cults; stone tablets; wooden tablets

depersonalized figurines, 109

Dever, William G., 14–15

dialectical imagination, 154–56, 159. *See also* underworld bureaucracy

Ding Lan, 127

dining chamber. *See* sacrificial hall

directional axis: shift in, for spirit journeys, 162, 227n8; structure of lists and, 140. *See also* cosmology; northwest, preoccupation with

directional deities, 32, 202n20

disuo, as term, 61, 163

divination records: anthropomorphic representation and, 102; from Baoshan site, 26–27, 29–32, 157–58, 177; fecundity god and, 124–25; intentions of gods and ancestors and, 168; oracle-bone inscriptions and, 25–28, 137–38, 145, 168–69; ritual specialists in, 157–58; sacrificial objects and, 179; Warring States pantheon and, 32–36, 189. *See also* daybooks; sacrificial records

documents addressed to the otherworld authorities (*gaodishu*), 146–54

Dongshanzui site, Kazuo County, Liaoning, 101

Dou Wan (consort), tomb of, 91, 92

drowning victims (*niren*), 31, 32, 35, 202n31

Du Yu (third-century commentator), 37, 120, 232n107

early Chinese art, 10; challenges for interpretation of, 15–16; figure painting in, 115–22; human figures in, 99–105, 103, 130, 190; hybrid imagery in, 129–34; iconography of fecundity god in, 122–29; questions raised by tomb objects and, 10–11; verisimilitude and, 105–15, 218n32. *See also* human imagery; tomb figurines; tomb guardian figure

early Chinese religion, 19–21, 25, 35, 45–46; agents in construction of, 156–59; inclusive approach to study of, 2, 13–16. *See also* afterlife, conceptions of; archaeological approaches; burial texts; Chu religion; pantheon; text-centered scholarship

earthen cave tombs. *See* horizontal chamber-style tombs

Eastern Han period (25–220 CE): Buddhism and, 13; burial texts from, 152–53, 196n58; cult image and, 120, 122; grave goods in, 117, 163; public graveyards and, 210n23; sacrificial space in, 62, 64, 94, 96, 97, 216n172; Yellow Springs idea and, 226n3

Eastern Zhou period (771–249 BCE): ghost narratives of, 28, 29, 53; Jiuliandun site and, 2; lineage power in, 158; new class of spirits in, 28, 46, 53, 211n48; religious beliefs in, 130, 199n101, 206n99; ritual music and, 20–21; temple-tomb dualism and, 64, 211n48; tomb figurines and, 109, 111. *See also* Spring and Autumn period; Warring States period

elite burials, 2, 83; ancestor cult in Shang-Zhou tradition and, 60–62, 162–63; artifacts in tombs of women and, 127–28; burial space in, 3, 5–6, 63–80, 89, 90, 193n3, 213n102; cemetery layout and, 68; figure paintings and, 115–22; funerary-object lists in, 138–46, 190–91; "good death" and, 36; human figures and, 102, 103, 107, 109, 115; letters to underground bureaucracy and, 150–51; preservation and, 19; religious texts from, 25, 26–27, 29–32; spirit artifacts in, 50–51; tomb figurines and, 109, 123, 127–28, 129; tomb furnishings in, 175–183; violent death and, 44, 46, 53; Warring States pantheon and, 32–36. *See also* burial space; social status

Emperor Jing (Han dynasty), tomb of, 218n32

Emperor Wudi (156–87 BCE), 134

encasements (*guo*), 3, 215n153; at Baoxiangsi site, 213n92; coffins in vertical pit-style tombs and, 2, 4, 5, 6, 50, 58, 65, 66, 69; compartments and, 50, 74, 83; grave robbers and, 4, 30, 57; house structure and, 71; Jiuliandun site and, 4; at Mawangdui site, 83, 85; mounded burials and, 66, 67; passage to, 88; as *pianfang* and, 90, 215n153; preservation and, 6, 58, 65; social class and, 74; stave-walled tombs and, 81; tomb as chariot and, 74, 75

Eno, Robert, 201n14, 211n37

excavation sites: map of, 18; number of tombs at, 5–6, 17; public interest in, 4, 69, 76. *See also entries for specific sites*

exorcism (*gongjie, gongchu*): Baoshan Tomb 2 and, 30, 31, 32, 35–36; death pollution and, 58; process of, 201n19; road rituals and, 183, 184; targets of, 32, 35–36, 124–25, 129, 203n33; texts in tombs and, 15, 25. *See also* ritual practices; sacrifices

extralineal sacrifice, 33–34

Falkenhausen, Lothar von, 213n92

Fangmatan site, Tianshui City, Gansu, 171, 172, 173, 174, 185

fear of the dead, 37, 48, 222n145. *See also* attitudes toward the dead; death pollution; ghost narratives

fecundity god (*zu* or *mingzu*), 35, 50, 221n126; base for figure, 123, 127–28; exorcisms and, 31–32, 129; graph *zu* and, 125, 202n33, 220n107; lifespan and, 31–32, 129; origin of cult of, 128; phallic symbolism and, 122, 125, 129, 202n33, Plate 11; representations of, 122–29, 126, 190, Plate 11, Plate 12, Plate 13; typology of, 127. *See also* tomb guardian figure

Feng Youlan, 13

Fenghuangshan site, Jiangling County, Hubei, 6, 7, 147–48

Feuchtwang, Stephan, 43

figure paintings, 115–22, 118, 119, 121

First Emperor of Qin (259–210 BCE), 64, 78, 134; terra-cotta army of, 111, 114, 218n32

five agents/phases (*wuxing*) cosmology, 164, 169, 184, 199n101, 229n56, 230n60

five domestic deities, 103, 104, 135

food provisions, 4, 6; for the dead, 51, 63, 86, 91, 92, 117, 119, 120, 184; documents and, 140, 147, 148, 175; as offerings, 62, 63, 90, 97, 119, 134, 155, 175, 201n19. *See also* sacrificial hall

formal likeness, 134, 216n1. *See also* verisimilitude, and early Chinese art

Frazer, James, 128

Freedberg, David, 134–35, 216n1

Friedrich, Michael, 150

Fu Hao (Fu Zi), tomb of, 56

funerary rites: death pollution and, 48, 58; as public, 84; punishment of enemies and, 38; tomb space and, 56, 86; use of spirit artifacts in, 51 funerary texts, 23; administrative functions of, 141–42, 147–54; categories of grave goods in, 140–41, 175; checkmarks in inventory lists and, *143*; funerary-object lists and, 138–46; letters to underground bureaucracy, 146–54; pledge sacrifice as, 137–38. *See also* burial texts; inventory lists; underworld bureaucracy

Gaoping, Shanxi, battlefield at, 47–48, *49*
Gaotai site, Jiangling County, Hubei, 148–49
Geary, Patrick J., 14
Geling site, Xincai, Henan, 157, 172, 189. *See also* Lord of Pingye
genealogies, writing and, 141
Gennep, Arnold van, 51
gentleman of the interior (*langzhong*), 150–51
geographic knowledge, and cosmology, 161, 170–74
ghost narratives: emergence of the afterlife and, 43–45; *gui* (ghost) as term and, 37, 204n60; social memory and, 42–43; violent death and, 36–43. *See also* vengeful ghost; violent death
gift lists (*fengshu*), 138–39, 142–44
"The Goddess of Xiang" (Xiangjun), 180
Gonggong and Zhuanxu, story of battle between, 164
good death, ideal of, 36–37
Grand One (Taiyi), 30, 35, 131–34, 190
Granet, Marcel, 12, 19
grave goods: Baoshan site and, 51, 52–53, 174–83; at Beidongshan site, 9, *10*; Jiuliandun site and, 2, 4–5, Plates 1–5; list of (*qiance*), 53, 110, 138, 142–44, 190 (*see also* funerary texts; inventory lists); placement of, 74; Warring States changes in, 51–53. *See also* burial texts; inventory lists; ritual bronze vessels; spirit artifacts; tomb figurines; tomb guardian figure; travel paraphernalia
grave robbers. *See* tomb robbery
grave-securing writs, 23
Guanping site, Jingzhou City, Hubei, 116
gui (ghost), as term, 37, 204n60
Guo Dewei, 193n8
Guo Moruo, 13, 125
Guo Zigao (Qi nobleman), 58, 68
Guodian site, Jingmen City, Hubei, 35, 144, 164

Guojiagang site, Jingmen City, Hubei, 6, 194n11
Guweicun site, Hui County, Henan, 68, 81

Han dynasty (206 BCE–220 CE), 17, 64, 197n71, 210n23, 216n164. *See also* Eastern Han period; Western Han period
Handan City, Hebei, Zhao royal mausoleum in, 81
Harper, Donald, 13, 185, 227n19, 227n21
Hawkes, David, 226n2
Hayashi Minao, 60, 210n28, 231n97
"Heavenly Questions" (*Tianwen*), 164
"Heaven's mandate" (*tianming*), 62, 211n39
Hekou site, Shucheng County, Anhui, 66
Heshangling site, Xichuan County, Henan, 70, 123–24, 125, 127–28
hiding of corpse vs. display of wealth, 55, 58–60, 68–69. *See also* luxurious display
History of the Warring States (Zhanguo shi), 13–14
hollow brick tombs. *See* horizontal chamber-style tombs
home, tomb as, 70–77, 163, 171, 186
homecoming (*guiji*), timing of, 170
Hongshan culture, *101*
horizontal chamber-style tombs: origin of, 6–7, 194n12; regional variations in, 7; ritual practices and, 12; sacrificial spaces in, 56, 80, 88, 90–93; structural innovations and, 80–93. *See also* stave-walled tombs
horn, with intertwining dragons, 178, *182*
horse-and-chariot burials, 2
Hougudui site, Gushi County, Henan, 66–67
Houjiazhuang site, Anyang City, Henan, 57–58
house, tomb as, 70–73
Houtaizi site, Luanping County, Hebei, 99–101, *100*
Hu Houxuan, 223n22
Hu Shi, 13
Huai River valley burial mounds, 66, 78
Huang Ji Tuofu (tomb occupant), 66
Huang Jun Meng (tomb occupant), 66, 70
Huang Shengzhang, 152, 203n35
Huang Xiaofen, 194n12
huangchang ticou ("yellow battens aligned together"), 89. *See also* stave-walled tombs
Huchang site, Yangzhou, Jiangsu, 152–53

human imagery, 99–105, 190; in early Chinese art, 99–105, 190; figure painting and, 115–22; social status and, 103, 104–5; "sympathetic magic" and, 99–101, *100*; zoomorphic motifs and, 101–2. *See also* fecundity god; hybrid imagery; image magic; tomb figurines; tomb guardian figure

human remains: in Jiuliandun tombs, 5; mass graves and, 47–48, *49*; preservation of, 6, *7*. *See also* attitudes toward the dead; corpse

human sacrifice, 20, 105–7, 109, 217n30. *See also* companions in death

hun and *po* dualism, 44–45

hybrid imagery, 102, 104, 122, 190, 222n145; power of, 129–34. *See also* anthropomorphic images; tomb guardian figure

"Hymn to the Fallen" (*Guoshang*), 25, 29, 46, 48

image magic, 101, 105, 111–15, 218n33

"image taboo," 103

impersonator (*shi*), 102, 103, 116, 132, 190, 219n65

incantation texts: on Jiudian bamboo strips, 155, 157, 163, 165, 167, 172, 185–86, 227n18, 232n97; Mawangdui silk diagram and, 131–32, 134

initial sacrifice (*yidao*), 30

interlineage conflict: notions of an afterlife and, 43–46; vengeful ghosts and, 36, 38–43

inventory lists: administrative practice and, 141–44, 146; categories of contents in, 139–40; check marks in, *143*; discrepancies between tomb contents and, 144–46; gift lists (*fengshu*) and, 138–39; magico-religious function of, 144–46; public reading of, 142–44; social control and, 139, 141–42, 143–44, 146, 151, 159; textual structure of, 139–40

"items for travel" (*xingqi*), 51, 231n97. *See also* travel paraphernalia

jade ornaments, 10, 107, 133, 178, *179*

jade pendant, 111, *114*, 179

jade suit (*yuyi*), 89, 91

Jia Gongyan (Tang dynasty scholar), 230n69

jian mu wei, interpretation of, 30, 202n32. *See also* fecundity god

Ji'nancheng, Jiangling County, Hubei, 67–68, 116. *See also* Baoshan site, Jingmen City, Hubei

Jinqueshan site, Linyi City, Shandong, 116–17

Jishan site, Jiangling County, Hubei, 67

Jiudian site, Jiangling County, Hubei, 19, 51; daybooks from, 144, 165, 167–69; incantation texts from, 155, 157, 163, 165, 167, 172, 185–86, 227n18, 232n97; objects from, 177

Jiuliandun site, Zaoyang City, Hubei: burial goods found at, 2, 4–5, *6*, 115, 146, 177, Plates 1–5; excavation of, 2–5, *3*, *4*; joint burial practices and, 55, 70; ritual objects at, 5, Plate 5; structure of, 2, 50, 69; tumuli at, 2, 4, 193n5

joint burial practices, 55, 69–70, 211n54; in same pit, 55, 69–70, 153, 212n54; in separate pits, 3, 40, 69–70; separate vertical pits and, 3, 55, 70; transformation of burial space and, 55–56, 69–70

Kalinowski, Marc, 200n6

Karlgren, Bernhard, 125

Keightley, David, 130

King Chen of Chu, 36

King Cuo of Zhonshan, tomb of, 80–81, 172, *180*, *181*

King Ling of Chu, 107

King Zhuang of Chu, 158

kinship ties. *See* ancestor cults; lineage cemeteries; tie-breaking rituals

Knechtges, David, 226n2

Kongjiapo site, Suizhou City, Hubei, 148, 164

lacquerware, at Jiuliandun site, 4–5, Plate 2

Lagerwey, John, 200n6

lamps in tombs, 214n123; figures and, 105, 178, *179*; function of, 120, 142, 177; images of, *6*, *179*, *181*; at Jiuliandun site, 5, *6*; significance of, 220n87

Laufer, Berthold, 219n65

LeDoux, Joseph, 222n145

Legge, James, 145

Leigudun site, Suizhou City, Hubei: coffin at, 76, 129, Plate 7; inventories from, 110, 140, 143, 144; tomb at, 19, 72, *73–74*, 171

Lévi-Strauss, Claude, 14

Lewis, Mark, 208n144

li (vengeful ghost), as term, 37

Index

Index

promissory sacrifice. *See* pledge sacrifice

Protocols of Ceremonies (Yili), 58, 84, 93–94, 102, 117–19, 120, 227n12; funerary rites and, 58, 84, 93–94, 102, 117–19, 120, 158, 227n12; public reading of lists and, 142, 143, 151; road ritual and, 184, 185

provincial historic sites. *See* Jiuliandun site, Zaoyang City, Hubei

public graveyards, 210n23

Puett, Michael, 132

Qi, state of, 20

Qianzhangda site, Tengzhou City, Shandong, 66

Qin, state of (ca. 800–221 BCE): burial traditions in, 58, 62, 77; catacombs and, 65, 77; comparisons with, 20, 198n80; sociopolitical change and, 11, 47; spirit artifacts and, 52. *See also* Fangmatan site, Tianshui City, Gansu; Shuihudi site, Yunmeng County, Hubei

Qin Empire (ca. 221–207 BCE), 1, 20; burial practices in, 63; burial spaces in, 64, 190; burial texts from, 124, 125, 132, 138, 144, 146, 152, 167, 190; Chu region tombs and, 17, 197n68; human figures and, 109; pre-unification Chu tombs and, 17; social institutions in, 147–48, 149, 151, 152, 154; spirit journey and, 164, 167, 169, 170, 172; unification of, 11–12, 21–23, 65, 156, 191. *See also* First Emperor of Qin; Shuihudi site, Yunmeng County, Hubei

Qinghua University, Chu manuscripts at, 89

Qinjiazui site, Jiangling County, Hubei, 157, 171, 189

qinzi she (earth altar from whom one requested sons), 129. *See also* fecundity god

Qu lineage, 157

Queen Mother of the West, 46, 156, 162, 165

Records of the Grand Historian (Shiji), 47, 78, 165

regional cultural influences, 19–21, 67

relief tombs. *See* horizontal chamber-style tombs

religion: archaeological approaches to, 14–16, 19; definition of, 21–22; dialectical imagination and, 154–56, 159; role in political

change and, 11–12; textual approaches to, 12–14

religious texts, 15, 25, 29–32, 94, 189, 196n58. *See also* burial texts; divination records; incantation texts; sacrificial records

requital sacrifice (*saidao*), 30, 35. *See also* thanksgiving sacrifice

ritual bronze vessels: in ancestral temples, 60–61; erasure of names on, 40, 41; humble substitutes for, 52–53, 62; inscriptions on, 28, 39–40, 41, 42, 60; at Jiuliandun site, 5, Plate 3; placement in tombs, 61, 62–63; twentieth-century knowledge of, 16; at Xiasi site, 39–40, 41, 42. *See also* bronze inscriptions

ritual diagrams, 158, 164, 169, 170, 172, 174, 183, 230n72; from Mawangdui site, 131–32, 134, 229n56, Plate 14

ritual music, 20–21

ritual performance: Mawangdui diagram and, 131–33; religious belief and, 156–57; ritual space and, 56, 92, 93–97; road ritual and, 183–85, 186. *See also* "Pace of Yu" ritual; ritual practices; road rituals

ritual practices: changing views of the dead and, 190–91; dissemination of, by texts, 167 (*see also* daybooks); horizontal chamber-style tombs and, 12; role of officials in formation of, 156–59. *See also* divination records; exorcism; pledge sacrifice; road rituals; sacrifices; sacrificial records

ritual specialists, 156–59

road rituals, 170–71, 232n114; "Pace of Yu" and, 132, 135, 171, 183, 184–85, 186

rock-cut cave tombs. *See* horizontal chamber-style tombs

Rosenblatt, Paul, 53

royal ancestors, 30, 31, 32, 33, 34, 162, 185

Sackler Gallery of Art, Washington, DC, 16, Plate 6, Plate 12

"sacrifice of repose" (*yuji*), 94, 119, 120

sacrifices (*dao*), types of, 30. *See also* human sacrifice; pledge sacrifice; sacrificial records

sacrificial hall (*shishi*), 62, 64, 80, 231n93

sacrificial records: apotropaic rituals and, 177–83; from Baoshan site, 26–27, 171,

social status: ancestral sacrifice and, 60–61,
62–63; Chu mortuary practice and, 19, 68,
144; Han mortuary practice and, 17, 97, 144;
image-making and, 103–5, 109; inventory
lists and, 143–44 (*see also* sumptuary
control); ritual specialists and, 157; size of
tombs and, 57–58; "those slain with weapons" and, 39, 46; tomb figurines and, 109.
See also commoners; elite burials
sociocultural anthropology, 14
sociopolitical transformation, and mortuary
religion, 11–12, 20, 22, 28–29, 46, 154–56
Songs of the South (Chuci), 120, 164; "Summons of the Soul," 61, 115–16, 171, 177,
219n61
soul, concepts of, 43–46, 186
soul stand (*chong*), 117, 119, 120, 124, 220n81
Sourvinou-Inwood, Christiane, 200n13
speech act theory, 145
spirit artifacts (*mingqi*), 12, 21, 51–53, 63,
207n129. *See also* grave goods; tomb
figurines
spirit journeys: ancestor cults and, 61–62,
185, 210n37, 228n39; destinations of, 46,
61, 162–65, 226n3; directional axis and,
162, 227n8; maps and, 172–74, 173, 231n85;
tame and wild space and, 170–74; timing of,
167–70; underworld bureaucracy and, 62,
191. *See also* daybooks; liminal stage; northwest, preoccupation with; ritual diagrams;
road rituals; travel paraphernalia
spirit money (cut strips of silk), 155, 163
spirit possession (*pingyi*), 130, 132
spirit tablet (*zhu*), 56, 64, 119, 120, 135,
219n65; Baoshan tablets and, 103, 104, 135
Spring and Autumn period (771–ca. 453 BCE):
attitudes toward the dead in, 28, 35, 36–43,
58–60, 190; bronze ritual vessels from, 28,
39–40, 41, 42; burial structures in, 58, 71,
77; concept of afterlife in, 43–46, 61–62;
fecundity god in, 123, 125, 127, 128; human
figures in tombs and, 104–5, 107, 108, 111,
116, 218n42; human sacrifice and, 20; joint
burial practices in, 69–70; mounded burials
and, 66–68, 77–78, 79; notions of violent
death in, 36–43, 205n87; sociopolitical
turmoil in, 11–12, 36, 47, 60, 203n40; spirit
artifacts and, 52; spirit possession and, 132.
See also Zuo Commentary

stave-walled tombs (*ticou*), 80–81, 86, 87, 89,
91, 212n58, 215n141
Steele, John, 119
stone chamber-style tombs. *See* horizontal
chamber-style tombs
stone tablets, 102–3
Suetsugu Nobuyuki, 39
Sui (celestial deity), 31
sumptuary control, 68–69, 141–44
Sun Xidan, 230n69

Taiyi ("Grand One"). *See* Grand One
Tambiah, Stanley, 22
tame and wild spaces, 163, 170–74, 214n113.
See also Mount Buzhou
temple name (*miaohao*), 102
temple-tomb dualism, 62, 64, 194n12,
211n48, 216n172
text-centered scholarship, 2, 12–13, 22, 52,
169
thanksgiving sacrifice, 137–38. *See also* requital sacrifice
Thompson, Laurence G., 228n36
Thote, Alain, 130
Tianma-Qucun site, Quwo County, Shanxi,
59, 104
Tianxingguan site, Jiangling County, Hubei,
33, 69, 124, 157, 171, 189
ticou (stave-walled tombs). *See* stave-walled
tombs
tie-breaking rituals, 12, 51–56, 207n126
tomb figurines (*yong*): at Beidongshan site,
10; bronze kneeling figures and, 104–5,
Plate 10; human sacrifice and, 20, 105–7,
109, 217n30; image magic and, 99–101,
105, 111–15, 120, 134, 190, 218n33; painted
wooden figurine and, 5, Plate 5; slim
wooden figurine and, 111, 112, 218n42;
stone female sculptures and, 100–101; at
Xiaotun site, Plate 9; *yong* as term and,
218n30. *See also* fecundity god; tomb guardian figure
tomb guardian figure, 5, 129, 215n137; association of death and fecundity and, 128–29;
Chu archeological discoveries and, 122–28;
components of, 122; in Eastern Zhou
tomb, 111; in Han tombs, 10, 84, 86, 87, 88,
215n137. *See also* fecundity god
tomb robbery, 4, 16, 193n4

way station, tomb as, 75–77

weapons, those slain with (*bingsi*): burial of, 38, 39; in pantheon, 28, 31, 35, 43, 46; prayer for, 155; shift in meaning of, 39, 46. *See also* war dead

Western Han period (206 BCE–9 CE): banner paintings of, 13, 23, 116–17, *118*, 119, *121*; burial structure in, 6–7, 9, 70, 80–81, *82*, *83*, *85*, *88*, 89, 90, *91*, 95; burial texts from, 139, 144, *149*, 150–54, *153*, 159; *Chu* as term and, 17, 196n67; figurines in, *10*, *84*, *88*, *112*, *113*; joint burial in, 55–56, 70, 211n54; pantheon of, 35; preservation in, 6, 7, 89, 139; sacrificial space and, 90, *92*, *93*, 95; stave-walled tombs and, *87*; temples and, 64; tombs at Dabaotai and, 89, 90, *91*; underworld bureaucracy and, 150–57, *153*; vision of the afterlife in, 46, 161, 162–63, 164, 187, 191. *See also* Mawangdui site, Changsha City, Hunan; Wangchengpo site, Changsha City, Hunan

Western Zhou period (ca. 1046–771 BCE): bronze vessels in, 60, 104, 105, 141, 162, 201n14; coffin decoration and, 70–71, 171; joint burial in, 69; tomb figurines and, 105, 106, 107, 109, 128. *See also* Shang period

wine vessels, Plate 3, Plate 4. *See also* food provisions

winged beast, *180*

wives, burial of. *See* joint burial practices

Wolf, Arthur P., 35

wooden chambered coffin tombs. *See* horizontal chamber-style tombs

wooden screen, *86*

wooden tablets, 102–3, *104*, 135, 138

writing, 134, 137, 141, 143, 159; role in religious expression, 13, 14, 135, 138, 145, 190–91. *See also* bronze inscriptions; burial texts; funerary texts; inventory lists; oracle-bone inscriptions

Wu, royal cemetery of the state of. *See* Zhenshan site, Suzhou City, Jiangsu

Wu family cemetery, Jiaxiang, Shandong, 216n172

Wu Hung, 17, 119, 194n12, 218n32, 218n33, 220n81

Wu Zixu (Wu general), 16, 60

Wubashan site, Wuwei, Gansu, 153–54

wuxing cosmology. *See* five agents/phases cosmology

Wuyi (deity), 155, 156, 163, 186

xi ("to move"), 231n94

Xia Nai, 196n67

Xiangbizui site, Changsha City, Hunan, 86, 87, 88–89, 90

xiangxi zhi qi (travel paraphernalia), 231n94. *See also* travel paraphernalia

Xiaotun site, Anyang City, Henan, 104, Plate 9

Xiaoyan village, Shijiazhuang City, Hebei, 81

Xiasi site, Xichuan County, Henan, 70, 213n102; ritual bronzes from, 39–40, *41*, *42*; tomb occupants at, 39–40, 128, 205n80

xie cap (*xieguan*), 133, 178

Xiejiaqiao site, Jiangling County, Hubei, 148, 150, 215n153

Xin dynasty (9–23 CE). *See* Han dynasty

xingqi. *See* "items for travel"; travel paraphernalia

Xiong Chuanxin, 219n70

Xishuipo site, Puyang County, Henan, 46, *47*

Xu Shen (Eastern Han scholar), 209n19

Xujialing site, Xichuan County, Henan, 70

Xuning (Han woman), 129, 227n8

Xunzi (Warring States period philosopher), 52, 69

Yan Changgui, 221n126

Yang Bojun, 45, 232n107

Yang Kuan, 13–14

Yang Quanxi, 193n8

Yangling (mausoleum of Han Emperor Jing), 218n32

Yangtianhu site, Changsha City, Hunan, 53, *143*

yellow "paper" map, 174, 231n85

Yellow Springs, 162, 226n3, 227n8

Yi Zhoushu (Remaining Zhou Documents), 222n6

yidao. *See* initial sacrifice

Yinshan site, Shaoxing City, Zhejiang, 71–72, 73, 74, 171

yinyang. *See* five agents/phases cosmology

Yinyang wuxing (Mawangdui texts), 229n56

Yishen (Zixi, Chu official), 36

Index